THE MOST TRUSTED NAME IN TRAVEL: **FROMMER'S**

FROMMER'S EasyGuide to

TORONTO, NIAGARA FALLS AND WINE COUNTRY

1st Edition

By Caroline Aksich

W9-BZV-419

FROMMER'S STAR RATINGS SYSTEM

Every hotel, restaurant, and attraction listed in this guide has been ranked for quality and value. Here's what the stars mean:

★	Recommended
★★	Highly Recommended
★★★	A must! Don't miss!

AN IMPORTANT NOTE

The world is a dynamic place. Hotels change ownership, restaurants hike their prices, museums alter their opening hours, and buses and trains change their routings. And all of this can occur in the several months after our authors have visited, inspected, and written about, these hotels, restaurants, museums, and transportation services. Though we have made valiant efforts to keep all our information fresh and up-to-date, some few changes can inevitably occur in the periods before a revised edition of this guidebook is published. So please bear with us if a tiny number of the details in this book have changed. Please also note that we have no responsibility or liability for any inaccuracy or errors or omissions, or for inconvenience, loss, damage, or expenses suffered by anyone as a result of assertions in this guide.

Niagara Falls

CONTENTS

The Toronto skyline.

A LOOK AT TORONTO, NIAGARA AND THE WINE COUNTRY

Brassy, bustling Toronto has come a long way from its demure puritan roots. This is Canada's shining city on a hill, a global powerhouse building glass and steel castles in the sky while welcoming all with its earthbound parks and heart-felt hospitality. As Ontario's provincial capital, Toronto is the beating heart of Canada's most populous region. With Lake Ontario lapping its shores, it has a big pool to play in, and a waterfront revival is adding beaches, boardwalks, and rolling greenswards. Toronto is a city that blends old and new with brash aplomb. It's also one of North America's most diverse metropolitan areas, home to some 230 different nationalities—a polyglot citizenry that flavors urban life and energizes an already effervescent foodie scene. If food and wine are foremost on your mind, Toronto is just a day trip from the bucolic wineries and orchards of Niagara and Prince Edward County. It's also an easy drive to the Canadian side of thundering Niagara Falls, one of the world's natural wonders. Take a boat close to the cascading falls or ride a zipline over the swirling waters—it's a perfect complement to your sojourn in cosmopolitan Toronto.

Skaters take a twilight twirl on the glittering ice rink in Toronto's Nathan Phillips Square (p. 121).

A mannequin decked out in purple wig and flowers in the Allan Gardens conservatory, where six greenhouses overflow with flowering and tropical plants. See p. 131.

The ever-expanding Toronto cityscape.

At Ripley's Aquarium of Canada (p. 122), visitors take a moving sidewalk through the underwater tunnel tank known as the Dangerous Lagoon, for up-close views of sharks, turtles, and stingrays.

The eye-popping crystalline-shaped addition to the Royal Ontario Museum opened with a street party in 2007. See p. 127.

The distinctive flatiron shape of the Roman-esque Gooderham Building makes it an iconic sight in downtown Toronto. It was completed in 1892, some 10 years before New York's similarly famed Flatiron Building. See p. 194.

A giant panda enjoys a bamboo break in his home in the Toronto Zoo. See p. 128.

A small roller coaster in the old-fashioned Centerville Amusement Park on Centre Island, a leisurely boat ride away from downtown Toronto. See p. 123.

ABOVE: Toronto City Hall (p. 119) and the colorful Toronto sign in downtown at twilight.
BELOW: A production of the musical *Aladdin* in the Ed Mirvish Theatre. See p. 158.

TORONTO LIFE

Celebrating cannabis legalization day in Trinity Bellwoods Park in October 2018. See p. 44.

The "living garden" lobby of Hotel X features a towering wall of green. See p. 61.

Patrons take a break during a performance by the Canadian Opera Company in the multi-tiered glass-and-steel Four Seasons Centre for the Performing Arts. See p. 159.

Selling Tex-Mex tacos and more, Seven Lives (p. 96) is one of the many popular food vendors in Kensington Market.

The Avocado Attitude, a house specialty cocktail from the mixologists at Canoe restaurant. See p. 84.

"Our Game" iron sculpture, the work of Canadian artist Edie Parker, fronts the entrance to the Hockey Hall of Fame. See p. 134.

Toronto-born and -bred rocker Neil Young at a hometown concert in Massey Hall. (p. 163).

This plumed-horse ice sculpture is just one of many finely carved ice figures showcasing the annual Icefest celebration in the Village of Yorkville Park neighborhood.

A 2018 performance by Canadian rapper Tory Lanez at the Rebel Night Club for the "Come Up Show," which showcases the latest in Canadian hip hop and R&B.

NIAGARA FALLS

A tour boat braves the swirling waters at the base of Bridal Veil and Horseshoe Falls.

The frozen falls. See chapter 11.

Tourists wearing protective rain ponchos feel the spray from Horseshoe Falls, which carries nine times more water than its American counterpart.

Viewing Niagara Falls in winter from the Canadian side. See p. 226.

ABOVE: Niagara's 177-foot-high Horseshoe Falls in an aerial view. BELOW: Riding the Whirlpool Aero Car above the Niagara Whirlpool is a real thrill. This pioneering cable car has been in operation since 1916. See p. 227.

WINE COUNTRY: NIAGARA

The elegant stone entrance to the lakeshore Konzelmann Estate Winery. See p. 221.

Wood-fired thin-crust pizzas with wine complements are a specialty at the Norman Hardie Winery. See p. 236.

The white blossoms of fruit orchards in Niagara-on-the-Lake, where the local bounty includes sweet stone fruit and berries. See p. 213.

An outdoor wine tasting at the Trius Winery (p. 225).

The verdant grounds of Rosewood Estates
(p. 221), dedicated to "low-intervention"
winemaking.

Vidal white wine grapes hanging on the
vine.

WINE COUNTY: PRINCE EDWARD COUNTY

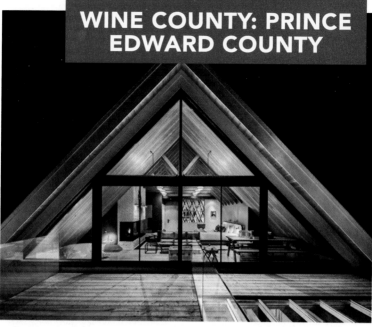

Book a stay in the "Owner's Suite" A-frame room in the Drake Devonshire Hotel (p. 238) and you'll have spectacular Lake Ontario views, a private deck, and a cozy fireplace.

A summertime wine gathering at the June Motel (p. 239), outdoors under twinkling lights.

A smattering of quirky wood objects for sale at the Wellington Farmer's Market.

The Hayloft Dancehall is a throwback summer hang, a rustic barn offering honky-tonk music and the chance to dance the night away. See p. 241.

Waupoos Estates Winery's Maple Ice Wine, infused with maple syrup and an iteration of the region's specialty, ice wine. See p. 220.

The tasting room at Kinsip, a farm-based distillery that handcrafts small-batch, grain-to-glass spirits. See p. 237.

THE BEST OF TORONTO

B link, and you'll miss a new tower joining the Toronto skyline. Once a prim puritan town, Toronto has exploded into a bustling metropolis. It's now Canada's largest city: More than 6.5-million people call this ethnic melting pot home. Here, you can travel the world from Little Portugal to Koreatown with a pit stop at an Indian bazaar. Despite the breakneck speed with which Toronto is changing, it's still an orderly metropolis, with most of the action happening in the heart of the city. That's good news for visitors. It's possible to drop in for a few days and easily do the town without running yourself ragged from one end of the city to the other.

TORONTO'S best AUTHENTIC EXPERIENCES

o **Catch a Game:** Torontonians are big into sports. Here, a sports jersey doesn't mean it's game night; it's a fashion staple. The Rogers Centre is home base for the Toronto Blue Jays baseball team. The Scotiabank Arena is where the Maple Leafs (hockey) and the Raptors (basketball) play, while the Argonauts (football) and TFC (soccer) call BMO Field home. Toronto even has its own rugby team, the Wolfpack, who tackle their British opponents at Lamport Stadium. See p. 134.

o **Comedy Clubs:** Maybe it's something in the water: Toronto has produced more than its share of top-notch comedians, among them Mike Myers, Jim Carrey, Dan Aykroyd, funny lady Samantha Bee, and the late, great John Candy. Checking out local talent or international standup stars at one of the city's many comedy clubs is a favorite pastime for Torontonians. See p. 169.

o **Checking Out Local Theater & Music:** Sure, Toronto mounts its fair share of blockbusters. But the fine, and often more rewarding, theater offerings from Soulpepper, Tarragon, Aluna Theatre, the Canadian Stage Company, and Factory Theatre are innovative and generally excellent. And seeing the Canadian Opera Company onstage at the Four Seasons Centre for the Performing Arts is breathtaking.

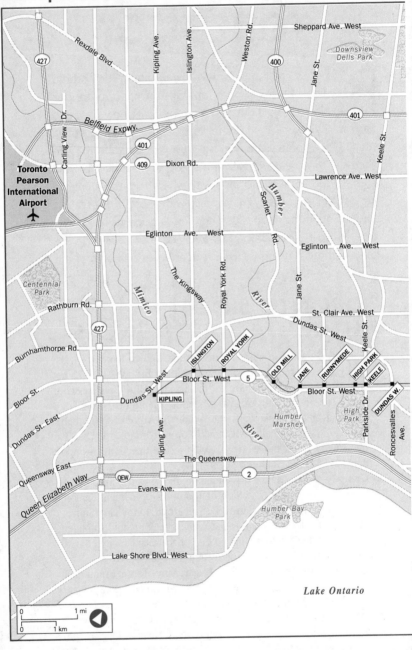

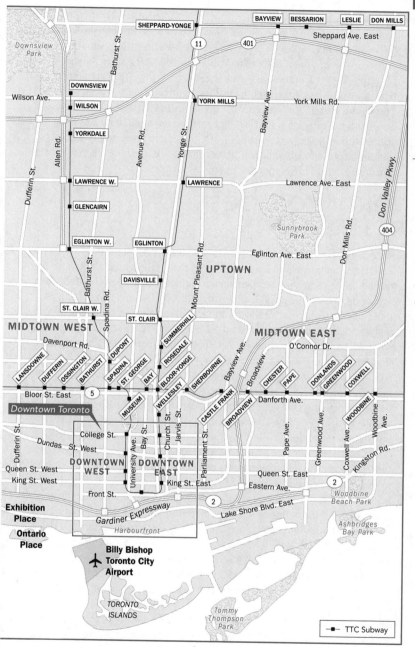

○ **Tour King in a Red Rocket:** Hitch a ride down King Street on one of the new bright red streetcars (they're air-conditioned now!). With a day pass, you can hop on and off starting at the historic Distillery District, making your way west with stops at the St. Lawrence Market, through the towering financial district, and to King West, one of the most animated nightlife strips in town. *Note:* Although locals affectionately refer to the TTC (Toronto Transit Commission) as "The Rocket," the streetcars aren't particularly fast, which makes them ideal for sightseeing, not so ideal in a rush.

○ **The Drake Hotel:** This Queen West staple isn't just a hotel. The Drake is a Toronto-born institution that has become synonymous with the local art scene. At the Drake, you're just as likely to walk in on a literary reading as you are a punk band wreaking havoc onstage. If you hate feeling like a tourist, this place is for you. See p. 66.

TORONTO'S best RESTAURANTS

○ **Actinolite:** Chef Justin Cournoyer is not just a perfectionist. He's also a zealot, and an obsessive. His commitment to representing Ontario's *terroir* on the plate knows no comparison in Toronto. At his jewel-box 30-seat restaurant, located on a residential street a good 10-minute walk from anything trendy, Cournoyer produces an incredible tasting menu created from ingredients foraged, grown, and raised in Ontario. Courses are thoughtful, building on each other, with flavors echoed between plates and garnishes snatched from the garden out back. See p. 101.

○ **Alo:** After *Restaurant* magazine named Alo one of the top 100 restaurants in the world in 2018, a reservation here became a lusted-after commodity. In fact, there are whole online forums dedicated to strategizing how to snag a table at Alo, a French restaurant that singlehandedly rehabilitated the tasting menu's reputation in Toronto. Chef Patrick Kriss turns dinner into high art, where each four-bite plate is pretty enough hang in a gallery. The service is impeccably choreographed down to the napkins, which are chosen to match a guest's outfit. See p. 81.

○ **Boralia:** The menu at this gem delves deep into Canada's culinary history. Chef Wayne Morris draws inspiration from colonial French and English dishes as well as indigenous foods. The L'éclade, a mussel dish that dates back to the French settlers who created the Order of Good Cheer, comes from a circa-1605 recipe. Originally, the mussels were cooked and served atop a smoldering bed of pine needles. Here, the bivalves come in a smoke-filled bell jar—a theatrical delight that sends plumes drifting across the table. See p. 24.

○ **DaiLo:** Second-generation Canadian Nick Liu loved his parents' Chinese home cooking, but as a young chef, he was convinced multi-starred Michelin fare was the pinnacle of culinary excellence. Lucky for us, he's now married haute French technique with Chinese, Thai, and Korean traditions. Best of all, he's executing his menu with seasonal Canadian ingredients. It sounds complicated, but it works. Truffle fried rice (with XO sauce) is spicy and decadent, while Ontario pea dumplings (made with bone marrow and bacon dashi) are addictive. See p. 86.

o **Canoe:** On the 54th floor of a busy Financial District skyscraper, executives with enviable expense accounts woo new clients over multi-course tasting menus at this long-standing fine-dining destination. Long before the farm-to-table movement took over the city, Canoe was elevating local ingredients and showing Toronto that Canadian food wasn't dull, but inspirational. Provincial *terroirs* are evoked with game meats and native plants like balsam fir, reindeer moss, cattails, daylilies, and sumac. In the evenings, with the town twinkling below, Canoe's vibe shifts from corporate to romantic. See p. 84.

o **Mira:** No signs point the way to this Peruvian restaurant tucked in an alley off King Street. A trail of flickering lanterns leads diners down a redbrick pathway and up to the unassuming front door. Inside, an open kitchen greets diners. Trays of ceviche (five varieties on offer) are being sent down to the sunken dining room. There, modern mad men sip refreshing pisco cocktails. Don't skip the finale: The chocolate bomb might be the best dessert in town. See p. 91.

o **Auberge du Pommier:** Tucked among the North York office buildings, these two charming woodcutters' cottages are relics from the 1860s, when this area was still a forest, not even yet farmland. The O&B hospitality group has turned the stone buildings into a fabulous French restaurant. Few places are equally alluring in summer as they are in winter. During the snowy months, Auberge du Pommier is animated by the crackle of a half-dozen woodburning fireplaces scattered among the dining rooms. Come spring, the terrace becomes a slice of St. Tropez in Toronto. Chef Malcolm Campbell's Michelin pedigree shows on the plate: His contemporary Franco fare is some of the best in town. See p. 111.

TORONTO'S BEST HOTELS

o **Four Seasons:** This internationally renowned luxury brand was born in Toronto. In 2012, hotelier Isadore Sharp hit the refresh button when he opened Four Seasons' 90th location in his hometown, replacing the original. Toronto's new Four Seasons caters to old-money tastes (read: subdued opulence) with twice-daily housekeeping visits, Canadian limestone bathrooms featuring freestanding soaker stubs, and floor-to-ceiling windows with sweeping views of the city. See p. 73.

o **Shangri-La Hotel Toronto:** The glittering exterior of this 66-story hotel-condo belies its peaceful interior, a luxe respite from the tumult of the city. The Shangri-La brings Hong Kong panache to Toronto: Cherry blossoms adorn wallpaper and consoles, while Chinese tracery patterns are found on doors, knobs, and carpets. The furniture, too, looks Qing Dynasty regal.

Opulent details include raw silk-upholstered walls and marble from around the world. Sun-drenched marble bathrooms are spectacular, but the best luxuriating happens on the fifth floor in the Turkish-inspired **Miraj Hammam.** Between the lush tropical plants, waterfall feature, and private cabanas, the place feels more Bali beach resort than downtown Toronto. See p. 62.

o **The Anndore House:** Silver Hotel Group has transformed a once-shabby budget hotel into an 11-story boutique experience that bills itself as a "fusion of our quirky past with modern style." The sleek suites designed by Cecconi Simone have been given an industrial-loft feel thanks to exposed brick and midcentury modern furniture. Rooms have such thoughtful touches as C.O. Bigelow toiletries, Crosley turntables (plus a few records), and plush robes. See p. 73.

o **Broadview Hotel:** To say the old Broadview Hotel was rundown after a decades-long stint as strip club would be a gross understatement. Fortunately, this Richardsonian Romanesque beauty of a building was rehabilitated to its turn-of-the-20th-century glory in 2017. The 58 guest rooms, transformed by local firm DesignAgency, could double as Wes Anderson movie backdrops. Bespoke furniture made from dark woods are balanced with pops of color: a bold floral wallpaper here, a magenta curtain there. See p. 69.

o **Hotel X:** Walking distance from Billy Bishop Airport, this 404-room hotel has more amenities than a five-star Cancun resort: two rooftop pools, four tennis courts, nine squash courts, four restaurants, two libraries, a spinning studio, a yoga sanctuary, a spa, and a beer garden. Children and pets are a priority here, with designer dog beds for Fido and a sprawling indoor play area for the kids. See p. 61.

o **St. Regis:** The A-list meets pomp and tradition in this deliciously luxe property, opened in 2018 and the brand's first foray into the Canuck market. Butlers are on hand to shoulder the mundane details of modern life—giving you more time to sip high tea on weekend afternoons, have a cocktail in the 31st-floor restaurant, or simply swaddle yourself in your room in silky Italian linens. See p. 63.

o **The Gladstone Hotel:** This groovy hotel is moderately priced overall, and a locale along West Queen West, the many bars, lounges, and restaurants on-site (and nearby), and friendly service make for a fun stay. Each of the 37 artist-designed rooms is distinct, making every visit special. See p. 66.

TORONTO'S best MUSEUMS

o **Art Gallery of Ontario:** Locals were thrilled with Toronto native Frank Gehry's renovation of the AGO—the design brilliantly revised (and expanded) the space. The fabulous circular, floating staircase is especially impressive. There's a lot to see here beyond the building itself, of course;

the collection numbers 95,000 pieces and growing. Don't miss the Thomson Collection; central to the AGO, it spans 20 rooms and includes an unparalleled collection of great Canadian art. See p. 115.

o **Royal Ontario Museum:** Good for the whole family, especially the massive dinosaur collection and the creepy bat cave, the Royal Ontario boasts many other impressive exhibits, including Chinese temple art, Roman statues, and Middle Eastern mosaics. See p. 127.

o **Aga Khan Museum:** From the outside, Japanese architect Fumihiko Maki's Cubist structure strikes an unapologetically modern pose. Inside, the collection of Islamic and Iranian art and artifacts is the antithesis of its postmodern exterior. Many of the gorgeously preserved centuries-old objects are from the Aga Khan's personal collection. See p. 127.

o **Museum of Contemporary Art Toronto Canada:** On an industrial stretch in west Toronto, down the street from a still-working chocolate factory, is the city's largest collection of contemporary Canadian art. The museum takes up the bottom five floors of a former Depression-era automotive building. See p. 126.

o **Bata Shoe Museum:** Imelda Marcos' name might be synonymous with footwear fetishization, but Sonja Bata's collection of some 13,500 shoes and accessories has the former first lady of the Philippines beat. The largest draw at this foot-focused temple? Celebrity shoes, which include John Lennon's Beatle boot and ballroom slippers worn by Queen Victoria. See p. 119.

TORONTO'S best FREE THINGS TO DO

o **Catch a Movie under the Stars:** Throughout the summer a number of city parks screen films after dusk. Christie Pits, thanks to its natural bowl shape, is one of the best spots to settle in for an alfresco viewing party. Selections vary from classics like *Casablanca* to indie flicks like *Before Sunrise*.

o **Listen to a Concert at the Toronto Music Garden:** Cellist Yo-Yo Ma co-designed this serene space, which is intended to evoke Bach's "First Suite for Unaccompanied Cello." It's easy on the eyes, but the best time to come here is for a summertime concert. Pure bliss. See p. 130.

o **Stroll the Lakeside Boardwalk:** You can choose from a number of starting points, but don't miss the quirky parks, open-air concert venues, and wintertime skating rink near Harbourfront. Or venture east to the long boardwalk in the neighborhood known as the Beach, where you'll share the lake views with locals and their many dogs and youngsters.

o **See Great Museums at a Discount—or for Free:** Admission to the Royal Ontario Museum and the Art Gallery of Ontario has jumped since their massive renovations. However, you can pay less—or nothing—if you know when to go. See "Saving on Admission Costs," p. 118.

o **Visit the Botanical Gardens:** These stunningly planted plots occupy 4 acres within the Don Valley Ravine. Wander about the themed gardens and enjoy the blooms, or join one of the free, volunteer-run tours to learn about the various plants and Toronto's rare Carolinian Forest. See p. 132.

o **Check out Ryerson Image Centre:** Fans of photography shouldn't miss this spot, which is much more than the word "gallery" suggests. Not only is admission free, but the exhibits are thoughtful and detailed, and the permanent collection is fascinating—particularly for its wealth of works by female photographers such as Berenice Abbott, an early-20th-century American known for her portraits and landscapes, and British photographer Jo Spence, who used her work as a tool for social change in the 1970s and '80s.

TORONTO'S best ACTIVE ADVENTURES

o **Paddle Lake Ontario:** Rent a kayak or canoe from the Harbourfront Canoe & Kayak Centre and explore Toronto's waterfront from an aquatic vantage point. The traffic in the channel between Toronto and the Island can get congested, and traversing the waterway is best left to black-belt paddlers. For a mellow day, follow the shoreline east to the Leslie Street Spit. This manmade peninsula is home to heaps of beautiful birds, including a colony of double-crested cormorants. See p. 138.

o **Reel in a Salmon:** Lake Ontario is home to some serious fish (trout, pike, and pickerel, to name a few), but the best trophies swimming the depths are chinook salmon, which can reach up to 50 pounds. Chinook are beasts; they'll take hundreds of feet of line at such an impressive pace that it can cause the reel to smoke from friction. Fishing charters like Epic Sport Fishing have all the equipment and know-how needed to make for a breezy day of casting. See p. 130.

o **Bike the Town:** Grab a bike from one of the hundreds of Bike Share Toronto stands and explore the town on two wheels. The Martin Goodman Trail, which runs from the Beaches neighborhood to the Humber River along the waterfront, is car-free and takes you through park after waterside park.

o **Scale a Frozen Waterfall:** Drive 45 minutes east from Toronto, and you'll reach the waterfall capital of the world: Hamilton. Toronto's neighboring city is surrounded by more than 130 waterfalls. In the summer, cycling routes and hiking trails deliver you past the flowing stunners. In winter, these falls turn into slippery sheets of ice. If you're an intrepid type (or just a Sir Edmund Hillary wannabe), you can attempt to scale the falls via ice axe, crampons, and rope. One Axe Pursuits provides the equipment and the training. See p. 213.

- **Skydiving at the CN Tower:** Okay, it's not really skydiving…but it's close. From the ground, it looks simply mad, but the EdgeWalk is a thrill-seekers' dream. You're locked into a harness attached to a pulley system as you navigate the narrow ledge circling the perimeter of the tower's main pod. Not for vertigo sufferers! See p. 120.
- **Yogic SUP:** Achieve inner peace while balancing atop a stand-up paddleboard: The smallest of waves makes a downward dog at risk of becoming a wet dog. It's hard, but finish the hour-and-half-long class without getting soaked and you'll have balancing bragging rights. Toronto Island Stand Up Paddle Boarding offers biweekly classes throughout the summer. See p. 138.

TORONTO'S most OVERRATED EXPERIENCES

- **Nuit Blanche:** This all-night art bash has lines longer than an amusement park's on a long weekend. The citywide 4am last call has turned the event into more of a bar crawl than an art crawl. Those keen to check out up-and-coming local artists should instead visit the Museum of Contemporary Art Toronto Canada.
- **Toronto Christmas Market:** Early on a weekday morning, before the crowds crush into the Distillery District, checking out this Old World–inspired Christmas market can be downright jolly. The stalls peddling a mix of crafts and craft food are fun to peruse, the towering tree is impressive, and a mug of hot chocolate makes everything better. But when the place becomes packed to bursting, the yuletide spirits become a challenge to muster—even with some (overpriced) mulled wine in hand.
- **Yonge-Dundas Square:** Unless there's a concert taking place on the free outdoor stage, Toronto's Times Square Lite is an area to pass through en route, not a destination in and of itself. It's mostly blaring billboards, middling buskers, pickpockets, and vegan protesters.
- **Waiting for Brunch:** Torontonians are obsessed with brunch. But it's not standard eggs benny with home fries that draws those hour-long Saturday-morning queues. Locals are crazy for zany morning foods like breakfast poutine, chorizo empanadas topped with poached eggs, and runny egg sandwiches that swap out bread for doughnuts. There's no shortage of good brunches in town, however—so, if the wait's more than 20 minutes, it's time to bail and find your bacon elsewhere. See p. 93 for a list of the best brunch bets in town.
- **Dinner at the CN Tower:** The whole point of going up to the top of the tower is to see the city fan out around you. But after sunset, Toronto's skyline highlights are but a shimmer below. Best go for lunch, or an embarrassingly early dinner, so that you can soak in the panorama while tasting the Restaurant 360's take on Canadiana.

TORONTO'S best FESTIVALS

- **Caribana:** Originally based on Trinidad's Carnival, this multi-week, mid-summer celebration now draws on numerous cultures—Jamaican, Guyanese, Brazilian, and Bahamian, to name a few—for its music, food, and events. The 2-week fete starts with a bang—think steel drums—at Nathan Phillips Square with a free concert featuring calypso, salsa, and soca music. In the days that follow, there are boat cruises, dances, and concerts. The highlight is the closing weekend parade: a riot of feathers, dancing, and floats.

- **Pride Toronto:** Celebrating Toronto's gay and lesbian community, Pride features events, performances, symposiums, and parties. The month-long June celebrations culminate in an extravagant Sunday parade, one of the biggest in North America. Expect bared bodies, heaps of rainbow everything (from flags to dye jobs), and endless dancing.

- **Toronto International Film Festival:** The second week of September, it's common to see Bill Murray biking about town, or run into Diane Keaton antiquing in the Junction. Just about every A-lister makes their way to Toronto for TIFF, one of the world's largest film festivals, which screens close to 400 films over a 2-week period against a backdrop of red-carpet premieres and over-the-top parties.

- **North by Northeast:** Known in the music biz as NXNE, this is the sister festival to Austin's vaunted South by Southwest. The mid-June event takes place at over 50 different Toronto venues and features rock and indie bands as well as comedy performers and a film festival. Although the focus is on emerging artists, NXNE has featured some star-powered closers, including free performances by the Flaming Lips, Ludacris, and Iggy and the Stooges.

- **Doors Open Toronto:** This hugely popular May event invites city residents and visitors alike to tour some of Toronto's architectural marvels. For this one weekend, 150 participating buildings that aren't normally open to the public are free of charge to explore. Some of the niftiest spots to check out include the Toronto Reference Library's Conservation Lab, the R.C. Harris Water Treatment Plant, and the Don Jail.

- **Luminato:** Since its launch in 2007, this 10-day June arts festival has presented nearly 10,000 performances. The globe-spanning roster has included musicians, actors, visual artists, speakers, and dancers. Venues are peppered throughout the city. One year, the festival even took over a decommissioned power plant. The best part: Most of the events are free.

TORONTO'S best FOR FAMILIES

- **Ontario Science Centre:** You don't have to be a tyke to appreciate the impressive interactive displays here, which take in the realm of science disciplines, from biology to technology, and make them fun and interactive. See p. 128.

o **Toronto Islands:** Toronto is blessed with a chain of leafy, mostly residential islands just a brief ferry ride away that offer a pretty, quiet, car-free spot for a stroll or a bike ride (you can rent regular tandem bikes, as well as quadra-cycles on Centre Island). The petting zoo and amusement park are geared towards the preschool set. See p. 25.

o **Wandering through Riverdale Farm:** In case you need more proof that Toronto is a very green city, its downtown area holds a 7.5-acre farm. Cows, sheep, pigs, goats, and other critters call it home—but this is no petting zoo; Riverdale is a working farm, where visitors can accompany farmers as they milk goats, collect eggs, and groom horses. Plus, it's free. See p. 199.

o **Toronto Zoo:** Some 5,000 animals call the zoo's seven geographic zones (Africa, Americas, Australasia, Canada, Eurasia, Indo-Malaya and Tundra Trek) home. Canada's largest zoo has everything from nearly invisible stick insects to unmissable rhinos and polar bears. Feel good about the price of admission; a portion of every ticket sale helps the zoo's conservation efforts, which include captive breeding and release programs.

o **Ripley's Aquarium of Canada:** Adults and children alike will be mesmer-ized by the exhibits at this aquarium adjacent to the CN Tower. Of the 10 galleries, the Dangerous Lagoon—an underwater tunnel with a moving sidewalk that invites fish fanatics to stand in awe as snaggle-toothed sharks sail overhead—is the most buzzed-about. Planet Jellies, a giant color-changing tank of aimlessly floating stingers, brings a Zen-like calm to visi-tors, while Ray Bay evokes excited squeals from youngsters as divers hand-feed elegant rays.

TORONTO'S best
NEIGHBORHOODS

o **Kensington Market:** You'll hear a United Nations' worth of languages and dialects as merchants spread out their market wares. Think squid and crabs in pails; local breads; cheese from around the world; Mexican cooking cactuses and chilies; artisan chocolates; and heaps of great cheap eats. Kensington Avenue itself is a treasure trove of vintage clothing stores. You'll see a lot of junk here, but the hunt for gems is half the fun. During Pedestrian Sundays, the entire place becomes one big party: drumming bands hold impromptu marches, patios spill out into the streets, buskers entertain with magic and music, while artists add whimsy with installations peppered about the place.

o **Queen Street West:** This street was once considered the heart of Toronto's avant-garde scene. That would be a stretch today. Sure, it's home to several clubs—such as the Rivoli (p. 169) and the Horseshoe (p. 170)—where major Canadian artists and singers have launched their careers, but it's also where you'll find mainstream shops such as Aritzia, Gap, and Le Chateau. Edgy? Not anymore, although you'll still find a number of antiquarian bookstores, junk shops, nostalgic record emporiums, kitchen supply stores, and discount fabric houses.

- **West Queen West:** The artsy population has relocated farther west along Queen Street. Even *Vogue* magazine has taken notice, naming the stretch of Queen that begins west of Bathurst one of the coolest strips in the world. Here you'll find Trinity Bellwoods Park (popular with both hipsters and the preschool set); chic hotels the Drake (p. 66) and the Gladstone (p. 66); and a bounty of good cafes, small clubs, and restaurants.
- **The Beaches:** This is one of the neighborhoods that makes Toronto a unique city. Here, near the terminus of the Queen Street East streetcar line, you can stroll or cycle along a lakefront boardwalk. The sandy beaches are popular with volleyball players, families, and sunbathers alike.
- **Chinatown:** Crammed with shops and loud restaurants, Chinatown has bilingual street signs and red-painted poles topped by dragons. A walk through Chinatown at night is especially exciting—the sidewalks fill with people, and neon lights shimmer everywhere. You'll pass gleaming noodle houses, windows hung with rows of glossy roasted ducks, trading companies filled with Asian produce, and peddlers selling knock-off Gucci and Dior. Chinatown's eastern front is also where you'll find the AGO.
- **Yorkville:** Since its founding in 1853 as a village outside the city proper, Yorkville has experienced many transformations. It's going through another right now. In the 1960s, it was Toronto's answer to Haight-Ashbury. In the 1980s, it became the hunting ground of the chic, who spent liberally at Hermès, Chanel, and Cartier. Today, the area is still a shopper's paradise, from high-end Holt Renfrew (p. 147) to bargain-basement Winners.
- **Roncesvalles:** Strolling distance from High Park is Roncesvalles Avenue, a charming boulevard that has everything it needs to be its own, self-contained village: quaint cafes, Polish bakeries, a rep cinema, excellent bars pulling craft beers, live-music venues, and great boutiques selling made-in-Toronto wares.

SUGGESTED TORONTO ITINERARIES & NEIGHBORHOODS

Toronto is a patchwork of neighborhoods with a remarkably vibrant downtown core. Once you're in the heart of the city, you can head in just about any direction and end up somewhere with plenty to see, eat, and do. Where most North American urbanites might know the heart of their metropolis as a workplace, more than 300,000 Torontonians eat, play, sleep—yes, and work—in the downtown core. If you're coming in from Pearson International Airport, the city might seem sprawling, but once you're grounded downtown, you'll find that everything is here: shoulder-to-shoulder shops, theaters, parks, galleries, restaurants and cafes, bars and nightclubs, and places of worship.

With upwards of 115,000 new Torontonians funneling into the city every year, Toronto has spent decades expanding outwards. In 1990, a greenbelt was established around the GTA (Greater Toronto Area) to preserve the many rivers, waterfalls, ravines, and forests. The result: The city center has densified, reaching new heights every year, while stunning hiking trails remain accessible by city transit.

For the past 2 decades, Toronto's skyline has been a canopy of cranes. The majority of the building activity is new condo towers, anchored by offices and retail. These mixed-purpose buildings have endowed downtown with its frenetic live-work-play energy. Whether it's suits bustling to work in the morning, revelers filling the dance clubs on weekends, or shoppers browsing window displays, the core is always humming.

Start anywhere in the center, walk in any direction for no more than 15 minutes, and you'll see eclectic contemporary buildings beside neo-Gothic and Brutalist architecture. Just outside downtown, you'll start to notice Toronto's ethnic spectrum. From the residential laneways of Little Italy, lined with garages where wine ferments and tomato sauces simmer in late summer, to West Indian barbecues smoking jerk chicken along Eglinton West, foods reflect the city's diverse cultural makeup. This is one of the best eating cities in North America. Toronto offers something for everyone: cultural centers of every stripe, music to suit any taste, galleries galore, and interesting shops all around.

Toronto is a safe, walkable city and is best explored on foot. The layout and organization of the city means you *will* almost certainly get lost at least once during your stay. Streets have names, not numbers, and have a crazy-making habit of changing their monikers as they go along. Key urban artery University Avenue, for example, turns into Queen's Park Crescent, then into Avenue Road, before becoming Oriole Parkway. To make matters more confusing, Avenue then recommences (a few hundred feet west) at Eglinton. My best advice: Find the CN Tower and use it for orientation (it, typically, marks south). Located almost smack-dab in the city's center, Toronto's tallest tower is unmissable from any vantage.

THE BEST OF TORONTO IN 1 DAY

You'd better put on your walking shoes: Seeing the best of Toronto in a day means covering a lot of territory. This itinerary explores the city's colonial origins before whisking you up to Toronto's highest point (the CN Tower). You'll then follow the waterfront to Old Town. Take comfort: There is plenty of refreshing green space along the way. *Start: Bathurst Station and a street-car south to Fort York Boulevard.*

1 Fort York ★

Today, Toronto is the fourth-largest city in North America, with a skyline growing ever higher. Two hundred years ago it wasn't much more than a muddy outpost. Tucked behind Fort York's defensive walls sits Canada's largest collection of War of 1812 buildings, which now houses interactive, historic exhibits. The lush, 7-acre site is animated by costumed historians keen to talk about everything from the Napoleonic Wars to fur trade routes. Make sure to stop by the mess kitchen, where you can taste the past: Darby Cakes, warm off the hearth, are baked in the working ovens from a recipe that dates to 1831. The place is most lively in summertime when the Fort York Guard marches the premises, firing cannons.

2 Toronto Music Garden ★

Getting to the waterfront may be no joy, but it's entirely worth it when you reach this lovely and tranquil green space flanked by boardwalks, parks, and beaches. The Toronto Music Garden, also reached by a comfortable streetcar ride, was designed by world-renowned cellist Yo-Yo

Ma and landscape architect Julie Moir Messervy to invoke Bach's "First Suite for Unaccompanied Cello." It may sound highfalutin', but when you're wandering the grounds, it's simply serene. See p. 130.

3 Rogers Centre ★

The domed multi-use stadium formerly known as the SkyDome is the home of MLB's Toronto Blue Jays. The formal tour is for sports fans only; otherwise, just idly appreciate Michael Snow's massive statues of cheering (and jeering) spectators on the facade. If you want to see a Blue Jays game, come back later in the day. See p. 135.

4 CN Tower ★★

Taking the glass elevator up to the top of the Tower gives you a bird's-eye perspective on the city's general layout, even if the view from the heights makes it all seem on a model scale. Getting your bearings is made easy by downloading the CN Tower's Viewfinder app, which helps identify landmarks and neighborhoods. If it's a clear day, you might be able to see all the way to Niagara Falls or even across the border to New York. But even if it's overcast, you can check out the stomach-churning glass floor. Lie flat, I dare you, or just jump up and down on it for a vertiginous thrill. Up the adrenaline ante by strapping on an **EdgeWalk** harness and circumnavigating the Tower's perimeter, some 1,136 feet above the ground. Don't bother paying extra to visit the SkyPod, though—it might be an additional 33 stories higher than the LookOut level, but that just makes the landmarks even tinier. *Pro tip:* Skip the admission fees and soak in the view by booking a table at the Tower's rotating **Restaurant 360** (p. 120).

5 Harbourfront Centre ★★★

This is the kind of place where you could easily spend a day, so you may need to tear yourself away to stay on track. Watch glassblowers, potters, jewelry makers, and other artisans at their work in the **Craft Studio.** In winter, you can skate on the lakeside rink; in summer it becomes a charming pond animated by kids bobbing around in mini paddleboats while parents relax at the dockside restaurant **The Slip.** The Centre has excellent theater and concerts, as well the **Power Plant Contemporary Art Museum,** housed in a decommissioned powerhouse.

6 Scotiabank Arena ★

One nice thing about walking back to the downtown core this way is that you can cross through the Scotiabank Arena, a much more pleasant alternative to other busy and often traffic-congested routes. This sports complex is not only home to both the Raptors basketball team and the Maple Leafs hockey team, but it also hosts blockbuster music concerts; check out the photos of some of the famous acts who've played here as you walk through the passageway. See p. 136.

Toronto Itineraries

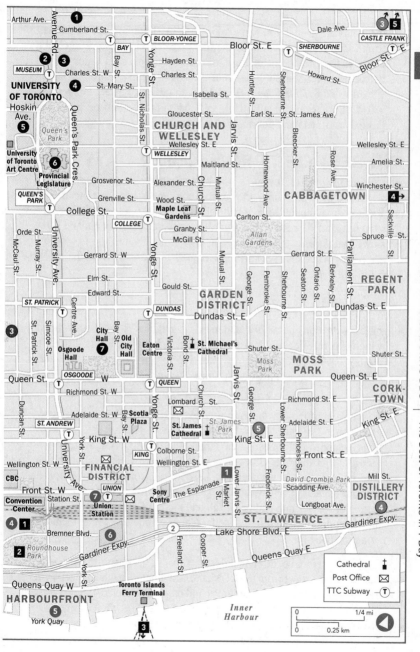

Arthur Ave.
Cumberland St.
Avenue Rd.
BAY
BLOOR-YONGE
Dale Ave.
Bloor St. E
SHERBOURNE
CASTLE FRANK
Bloor St. E

MUSEUM
Charles St. W
Charles St.
Hayden St.
Howard St.
St. Mary St.

UNIVERSITY
OF TORONTO
Hoskin
Ave.
Isabella St.
Huntley St.
Gloucester St.
Earl St.
St. James Ave.

Queen's
Park
University
of Toronto
Art Centre
Provincial
Legislature
CHURCH AND
WELLESLEY
Wellesley St. E
Maitland St.
Wellesley St. E
Amelia St.

QUEEN'S
PARK
Queen's Park Cres.
Grosvenor St.
Alexander St.
Winchester St.
CABBAGETOWN
Rose Ave.

Orde St.
College St.
Grenville St.
Wood St.
Maple Leaf
Gardens
Carlton St.
Spruce St.
Sackville St.

University Ave.
McCaul St.
Murray St.
COLLEGE
Granby St.
McGill St.
Allan
Gardens
Gerrard St. E
Parliament St.
REGENT
PARK

Gerrard St. W
Elm St.
Edward St.
Yonge St.
Gould St.
George St.
Pembroke St.
Seaton St.
Ontario St.
Berkeley St.
Dundas St. E

ST. PATRICK
DUNDAS
GARDEN
DISTRICT
Dundas St. E
Mutual St.

Simcoe St.
St. Patrick St.
Centre Ave.
City
Hall
Old
City
Hall
Eaton
Centre
Victoria St.
Bond St.
St. Michael's
Cathedral
Shuter St.
Moss
Park
MOSS
PARK
Shuter St.

Osgoode
Hall
OSGOODE
Queen St.
Richmond St. W
Bay St.
QUEEN
Lombard St.
Jarvis St.
George St.
Queen St. E
Richmond St. E
CORK-
TOWN

Duncan St.
ST. ANDREW
Adelaide St. W
Scotia
Plaza
St. James
Cathedral
St. James
Park
Adelaide St. E
King St. E
Lower Sherbourne St.
King St. E

King St. W
Colborne St.
KING
Wellington St. E
Church St.
Princess St.
Front St. E

CBC
Wellington St. W
Front St. W
FINANCIAL
DISTRICT
UNION
Sony
Centre
The Esplanade
Lower Jarvis St.
Market St.
Frederick St.
David Crombie Park
Scadding Ave.
Mill St.
DISTILLERY
DISTRICT

Convention
Center
Station St.
Union
Station
Bremner Blvd.
York St.
Gardiner Expy.
Longboat Ave.
ST. LAWRENCE
Gardiner Expy.

Roundhouse
Park
Lake Shore Blvd. E
Freeland St.
Cooper St.
Queens Quay E

Queens Quay W
Toronto Islands
Ferry Terminal
HARBOURFRONT
York Quay
Inner
Harbour

Cathedral
Post Office
TTC Subway

0   1/4 mi
0   0.25 km

7 Union Station ★

This is one of the city's underappreciated wonders. Toronto's temple to trains is a Beaux Arts beauty, and it's worth your while to stroll through the main hall, even if you're not taking a train. Before the age of mass air travel, Union Station was often the first place new immigrants saw upon arrival in their new home of Toronto. You've probably seen Union Station before, too—it's starred in heaps of cameos in big-box flicks, including *Chicago* and *Suicide Squad*. Head down to the Front Street Promenade, below street level, for affordable eats, including handmade pasta and pastries at Amano and gourmet sausages at Wvrst.

THE BEST OF TORONTO IN 2 DAYS

After taking in some of Toronto's best-known landmarks on your first day, you've walked the waterfront and your feet could probably use a break. This tour focuses on a smaller area, albeit with tons to take in, especially at the city's top museum. The Royal Ontario Museum could easily command a day on its own, but it's easy to add Yorkville, U of T, and the Ontario Legislature to the itinerary when they're basically a stone's throw away from the ROM. *Start: Bay Station.*

1 Yorkville ★★

Filled with chic boutiques and elegant galleries, this neighborhood, which is part residential, mostly commercial, has long departed from its groovy 1960s vibe when it was home to the city's hippies; a century before that, it was a cemetery. Progress? See p. 33.

2 Royal Ontario Museum (ROM) ★★★

Toronto's most famous museum was given a Daniel Libeskind–designed extension in 2007, the Michael Lee-Chin Crystal. The dynamic new additions expanded the viewing area, largely through six crystal-shaped galleries that jut out over Bloor Street West. Where you spend your time here will depend on whether you have kids in tow: The collection of dinosaur bones is truly awesome; the Schad Gallery, a breathtaking collection of species rare and beautiful, and the Bat Cave, are musts. Adults may be more interested in the stellar Chinese galleries, which include a Ming tomb. See p. 127.

3 George R. Gardiner Museum of Ceramic Art ★★

Just across the street from the ROM, the **Gardiner** is an understated gem. The singular collection of ceramics and carefully curated exhibits are a rare find. For those who want to get their hands dirty, the Gardiner also offers hands-on workshops, including some geared for kids. See p. 120.

4 Victoria College ★

Next door to the Gardiner is **Victoria College,** a college federated with the **University of Toronto.** Like the other seven colleges that founded U of T, Victoria maintains its own digs. It has a pretty college quad bordered by imposing Romanesque architecture (plus some blocky '60s stuff), and was home to the celebrated scholar Northrop Frye. Excellent coffee can be found inside Old Vic (the red sandstone building) at **Caffiends,** a student-run cafe.

5 Trinity College & Hart House ★

Stroll by **Trinity College** and appreciate the Jacobethan architectural grandeur, or head over to **Hart House,** which is open to the public and often hosts interesting lectures and concerts.

6 Queen's Park & the Ontario Legislature ★

This sweeping, pretty park is also home to the less beautiful provincial legislative building. (A *New Yorker* humor writer once dubbed it "Early Penitentiary.") It's possible to take a tour on most days, or just enjoy the setting and, if you're in luck, one of the many peaceful protests that take place on the lawn. See p. 126.

7 New City Hall ★

It's an iconic piece in Toronto's history, as well as a popular gathering place throughout the year. In warm weather, the reflecting pool and fountains create a piazza, and when the mercury drops, it's fun to visit the skating rink, complete with festive lights and music. Framing the whole scene, quite perfectly, is the Modernist masterpiece of the building itself; walk up toward and around it, and you'll see the Henry Moore sculpture *The Archer.* Most victors, though, are more entranced with snapping a selfie in front of the giant, multicolored Toronto sign. See p. 119.

THE BEST OF TORONTO IN 3 DAYS

This tour for your third day in Toronto focuses on downtown west and includes the city's top art gallery—the AGO. Then you'll hit some of the city's hippest neighborhoods, where you'll find great food, independent shops, and more galleries (as if you hadn't seen enough great art today). *Start: St. Patrick Station and a streetcar west to Beverly Street.*

1 Chinatown ★★

Toronto's first Chinatown hasn't been immune to gentrification. Chinese grocery stores are closing, and dumpling joints are being replaced by snack bars, such as **Peoples Eatery,** serving fancy Chinese remakes. Today, the neighborhood is a fascinating mixture of old and new.

Hole-in-the-wall restaurants share the sidewalks with glitzy shopping centers built with Hong Kong money. In recent year, northern suburbs Markham and Richmond Hill have become the top destinations for Chinese immigrants relocating to Toronto, and some of the best Chinese restaurants in town are found north of Hwy. 401. Still, you can get good dim sum and *xiaolongbao* here, even if it's not the city's very best. See p. 81.

2 Art Gallery of Ontario ★★★

It took Toronto boy Frank Gehry 50 years to finally design a building for his hometown. The famed architect—who grew up around the corner from the AGO—didn't have the luxury of building something from scratch. Instead, he was given the daunting task of redesigning the town's top art museum. From the outside, the glass-clad Gehry facade looks like a futuristic dirigible floating above Chinatown traffic. The light-filled insides make it a delight to explore the 90,000-plus works of art, among them works by Canadian legends, European masters, and modern masterpieces like Andy Warhol's *Campbell's Soup.* See p. 115.

3 Sharp Centre for Design ★

Although Toronto has long suffered an (outdated) reputation for being straitlaced, when wacky things are introduced here, the new additions are quickly absorbed into the cityscape. This brilliant bit of design from Will Alsop is a cube on stilts and requires a first-hand view to really appreciate its beauty. It's home to the **Ontario College of Art and Design** (OCAD) and is closed to the public except on special occasions such as **Doors Open.** See p. 184.

4 Queen Street West ★

Many of the indie shops that long gave this strip its hipster cred have been replaced with names like Zara and Lululemon. You'll still find the odd vintage shop (**Black Market** remains a trove of used treasures from bygone eras) as well as some great shoe stores like **Getoutside.** Despite the influx of big-brand names, the area remains the go-to destination for local designers thanks to the concentration of textile shops. Just south of Queen, between Spadina Avenue and Portland Street, you'll also find **Graffiti Alley,** a concentration of kaleidoscope murals by various street artists.

5 West Queen West ★★★

Vogue calls it one of the hippest districts in the world, second only to Tokyo's Shimokitazawa. West Queen West has some of the city's best window-shopping, from homegrown fashion labels to apothecaries promising eternal youth in the form of $60 serums. There's tons to browse here, including excellent galleries such as **Koffler Gallery, Mulherin Toronto,** and **Paul Petro.** The **Drake** and **Gladstone** hotels are more than just comfy spots for tourists to lay their heads; both function as art hubs with excellent kitchens, great bar scenes, and cool concerts on the regular.

6 Trinity Bellwoods ★

This site used to be the home of the precursor to the **University of Toronto.** The buildings have been torn down, but the impressive stone and wrought-iron gates that face Queen Street West remain. There are benches where you can rest and take in the scene, but it's more fun to wander. As you do, watch out for the legendary albino squirrels who reside in the park. Stop by **Nadège** (at the park's southeast corner) for almost-too-pretty-to-eat French pastries. See p. 131.

7 Dundas West ★★

For years, this was a sleepy part of town, part of Toronto's Little Portugal neighborhood, where many of the houses have religious icons painted near the front door. But now Dundas West and Ossington Avenue have become the epicenter of Toronto nightlife. Drop in at **Painted Lady,** a bar/dance hall with bar-top burlesque shows; eat mainland Chinese delights and knock back sake cocktails at **Soso's** (p. 173, which transforms after dinner into an epic dance floor); or go more low-key at **Sweaty Betty's** (p. 177).

THE BEST OF TORONTO IN 4 DAYS

Top off your 4-day Toronto sojourn with this tour, which takes you to a castle on a hill and then to a couple of the city's most dynamic, reinvented destinations. One combines environmental rehabilitation with great food, superb events, and lush parkland, while the other is a Victorian distillery transformed into a redbrick pedestrian paradise. *Start: Dupont Station, and then walk 2 blocks north.*

1 Casa Loma ★

This kitschy castle on a hill offers an inspiring view of the city. But while you can admire the panorama for free, the castle is worth a visit, too. The elegant rooms and period furniture are appropriately grand, though most interesting is perhaps a tower climb to explore the secret passages (including an 800-ft. underground tunnel that had a cameo in *X-Men*). Admission-averse visitors can opt to peer inside by playing "Escape from the Tower," an escape room that puts riddle-solvers in a WWII scenario where the Casa Loma stables function as an undercover research center for sonar detection technology.

2 Spadina Museum: Historic House & Gardens ★

This mansion and its spectacular seasonal gardens reopened in 2010 after an extensive and expensive renovation. The result is worth a visit year-round: Now a museum run by the City of Toronto, it offers a sense of domestic life in Toronto in the 1920s and '30s. The garden is also themed: It's a Victorian-Edwardian masterpiece. See p. 129.

3 Evergreen Brick Works ★★★

Once the home of the city's founding brick factory, this sprawling 19th-century structure has been reinvented by the dynamic Canadian Evergreen foundation (national in scope, its business is to "green" cities) to include a Saturday-morning farmer's market that runs year-round, a cafe and restaurant featuring local goods under the **Cafe Belong** (p. 97) moniker, marshlands, a beautiful park, and thoughtful exhibits that take advantage of the unique setting, including age-old kilns where Toronto's signature red bricks were once formed. A taste of past and present, the Brick Works is proving to be one of the city's most attractive locales for brilliant events, offering programs for families, parties for grown-ups, and more. See p. 124.

4 Distillery District ★★★

At its peak, Gooderham & Worts was the largest distillery in the British Empire and, for a brief moment, in the world. Today, this multifaceted complex has something for everyone. The redbrick architecture—a signature of Toronto's red-clay brickworks (see above)—is a Victorian wonder, but the art galleries, restaurants, and boutiques are all completely modern. You might want to stay well into the evening: Performing-arts troupe **Soulpepper** is based here, as is the city's annual **Christmas market** (visit on a weekday morning; the crowds suck the yuletide joy out of the experience). Restaurants worth sampling include **Cluny,** for fancy French fare, and **Madrina,** (p. 100), for great chocolate and gelato, too, at **SOMA** (p. 113).

5 Old Town ★★

The city was born from these 10 square blocks. This is still home to some of Toronto's most coveted heritage buildings, including Toronto's first **City Hall,** police station, and post office. Some of the most important structures are now no more than plaques. The original parliament buildings once stood at the corner of Parliament and Front. They were burned down by the Americans in 1813, then rebuilt only to burn down again in 1824 (an accident, not arson, this time). Focus on the area around the **St. Lawrence Market** (p. 141). From there it's an easy stroll to the **Hockey Hall of Fame** (p. 134), the **Gooderham Building** (the town's only flat-iron), and **Berczy Park** (a charming little park where you can relax by the dog-themed fountain while snacking on treats picked up at the nearby St. Lawrence Market). Those on a budget will appreciate the free concerts in **St. James Park,** a stunning Victorian garden (next to an equally stunning cathedral) that's worth a visit, even without a complimentary soundtrack.

THE BEST OF TORONTO FOR FOODIES

This hungry city offers of a mix of authentic eats (thanks to the globe-spanning immigrant population) and contemporary restaurants. Whether you're hankering after Korean tacos, designer chocolate, Persian stews, or pasta better than nonna's, Toronto is sure to deliver. This tour introduces you to some of the city's best markets and restaurant strips and takes you to one of the top gourmet shops in Canada. *Start: King Station, and streetcar west to Jarvis Street.*

1 St. Lawrence Market ★★★

When the late Anthony Bourdain visited Toronto for *The Layover,* his first stop was Toronto's St. Lawrence Market. This is ground zero for food lovers: a two-level historic market with butchers, fishmongers, greengrocers, and more. On Saturdays a farmer's market adds to the cornucopia. The grab-and-go restaurants here make some top-tier bites. Musts include: **Carousel Bakery,** for the "world-famous" peameal (aka Canadian bacon) sandwich, and **Yianni's Kitchen,** where the apple fritters are addictive. A bottle of Canadian maple-mustard from **Kozlik's** makes for a tasty keepsake.

2 Kensington Market ★★★

A bustling neighborhood of fishmongers, vintage retailers, coffee shops, and music stores, Kensington Market pulses to its own beat. This multi-ethnic mélange was once a Jewish neighborhood—the original synagogue still remains—and has been gradually layered with successive waves of immigrants from Portugal, the Caribbean, and the Middle East. The northeast corner of the market has a clutch of excellent Japanese options including sake bar **Koi Koi** (p. 95) and dessert shop **Little Pebbles.** Stop at **CXBO** (p. 186) for designer chocolates. Scandinavian cafe **Fika** has exquisite lattes, including one infused with cardamom. The Tijuana-style tacos from **Seven Lives** (p. 96) are overloaded to the point of busting, and that's a good thing so long as you're not wearing white. The no-name Latin food court at **214 Augusta St.** has well-priced (and delicious!) ceviche, empanadas, tostadas, churros, and more. **El Rey's** mezcal list knows no equal in town. **Grey Gardens** boasts the market's fanciest fare; head there for ingredient-driven dishes like lamb tartare and grilled pork tongue. Finish with a bracing cocktail at **Cold Tea** (p. 175), a secret bar tucked into the back of a nondescript strip mall. The red light marks the spot.

3 707 Market ★

At the corner of Dundas and Bathurst, this quirky market is housed in a dozen (or so) retrofitted shipping containers. Here you'll find fledging restaurants flexing their culinary chops—some will make it and become brick-and-mortar joints; others won't. The food options are always

Cheese Boutique

Ask any Toronto chef what his or her favorite go-to shop is and you'll get one common denominator: the **Cheese Boutique** (45 Ripley Ave.; www.cheeseboutique.com; ✆ **416/762-6292**). It's the only gourmet grocer in Canada with its own cheese vault (where 10-ft.-tall provolones hang from the ceiling and toddler-sized Parm wheels ripen to your specifications). The foodie mecca carries more than just cheese, though. It boasts a huge selection of olive oils, balsamic vinegars, sauces, fancy salts, and cooking implements, including hand-painted Turkish dinner plates and Shun knives.

interesting (from Japanese street food to Filipino pastries), but don't come expecting to try anything in particular; the rent roll changes frequently.

4 Ossington Avenue ★★

Little Portugal's main north-south artery was, until recently, a semi-industrial strip. Today, Ossington maintains its shaggy-cool charm while being home to some of the city's best eats. For snacks, **Bang Bang** is a must for custom ice-cream sandwiches (pick your cookie, pick your ice cream). Housed in an old mechanic's shop, **Bellwoods Brewery** (p. 180) makes phenomenal beers with cheeky names like Cat Lady (a double dry-hopped IPA). The pizza slices at **Superpoint** are as advertised (super). Just about any cafe here will be a winner, be it **Jimmy's, Ideal,** or **Te Aro.** The two most coveted Ossington Street reservations are **La Banane** (exquisite French) and **Boralia** (www.boraliato.com; smart New Canadian that digs deep into the nation's culinary history for dishes like pemmican and pigeon pie).

THE BEST OF TORONTO FOR FAMILIES

Toronto has no shortage of family-friendly fun. There are urban farms, aquariums where you can pet sharks, and interactive museums. This itinerary can be used as child-enchanting supplement to other plans—visiting both Centre Island and the Ontario Science Centre in 1 day is near impossible. (I recommend the island only if the weather's agreeable.) Otherwise, the Science Centre is a great space to let the wee ones unleash some of that rainy-day energy.

1 Ripley's Aquarium of Canada ★★

There are 1.5 million gallons of water at the base of the CN Tower. No, about it's not Lake Ontario I'm referring to, but Ripley's Aquarium. Some 20,000 water-dwelling critters (including mesmerizing jellyfish, giant sawfish, Pacific octopi, blue lobsters, and nine species of shark) call this home. A trip through the Dangerous Lagoon is as close to scuba diving as you can get without getting wet. A moving sidewalk carries the whole family through an underwater tunnel as 400-pound sharks circle above.

2 John Street Roundhouse ★

This preserved roundhouse was where locomotives would be flipped around after arriving in Toronto. The space is now an arcade shared by three different entities—the **Rec Room,** the **Toronto Railway Museum,** and the **Steam Whistle Brewery**—containing both kid- and adult-geared fun, from VR zombie games to leisurely replica locomotive rides. Parents might want to trade off minding duties and pop into Steam Whistle for the 30-minute tour, which brings you across catwalks above the brewhouse and includes a few samples of beer.

3 Centre Island ★★★

Every part of visiting the Toronto Islands is a delight. Even the getting there is fun. The antique ferries take 15 minutes to reach Centre Island, offering postcard-worthy views of the city along the way. Families with kids 12 and under will enjoy the sandy beaches and **Centreville Park,** an amusement park meant to entertain, not terrify. Most of the rides are of the old-school variety: Ferris wheel, pony rides, a carousel, a log ride, bumper boats, and even a petting zoo. For the older set there's plenty to explore in this 600-acre park, whether by land (rent a bike or quadracycle from **Toronto Island Bicycle Rental**) or by water (kayaks and canoes can be rented at the **Boat House**). While older children might be ready to brave the waters around the island, it's recommended that novice paddlers confine their boating to the lagoons. There's tons to see inside these serene spaces, including herons, turtles, and swans.

4 Riverdale Farm ★★

This farm is sacred space to many. Whenever you visit, you'll find kids here, many of them locals, learning about farm life, interacting with chickens and rare-breed piglets, and cuddling bunnies. Sound bucolic? See p. 125.

5 Ontario Science Centre ★★

If the weather's a write-off, skip Centre Island altogether and trek up to the Ontario Science Centre; there's a subway and bus transfer involved, but it's worth the journey. When it opened in 1969, this was one of the world's first science museums, and it remains a top spot to dazzle curious minds. **KidSpark** is a learn-through-play space designed to delight children under 8. Other exhibits are out of this world (there's a **planetarium**), while some delve into natural wonders (the simulated tornado is a crowd-pleaser). Let the kids run wild in the **Science Arcade,** a hands-on area where youngsters can test pulleys, play with magnets, and solve puzzles.

ORIENTATION

Toronto is laid out in a grid . . . with a few interesting exceptions. **Yonge Street** (pronounced *young*) is the main north-south artery, stretching from Lake Ontario in the south well beyond Hwy. 401 in the north. Yonge Street divides western cross streets from eastern cross streets. The main east-west artery is **Bloor Street,** which cuts through the heart of downtown.

"Downtown" usually refers to the area from Eglinton Avenue south to the lake, between Spadina Avenue in the west and Jarvis Street in the east. Because this is such a large area, it's been divided, for the purposes of this book, into five sections. **Downtown West** runs from the lake north to College Street; the eastern boundary is Yonge Street. **Downtown East** goes from the lake north to Carlton Street (once College Street reaches Yonge Street, it becomes Carlton Street); the western boundary is Yonge Street. **Downtown North** extends from College Street north to Davenport Road; the eastern boundary is Jarvis Street. **The East End** runs east until Woodbine, bound by Danforth and the lake. **Downtown North** is the area north Davenport Road to Eglinton Avenue. **Uptown** is anything north of Eglinton.

In Downtown West, you'll find many of the lakeshore attractions: Harbourfront, Ontario Place, Fort York, Exhibition Place, and the Toronto Islands. It also boasts the CN Tower, City Hall, the Four Seasons Centre for the Performing Arts, the Rogers Centre (formerly known as SkyDome), Roy Thomson Hall, Chinatown, Kensington Market, the Art Gallery of Ontario, and the Eaton Centre. Downtown East includes the Distillery District, the St. Lawrence Market, the Sony Centre, the St. Lawrence Centre for the Arts, and St. James's Cathedral. Downtown North contains the Royal Ontario Museum, the Gardiner Museum, the University of Toronto, and chic Yorkville, a prime area for shopping and dining. The East End features Riverdale Farm, the historic Necropolis, Leslieville, Greektown, and The Beaches. Midtown is anchored by the Yonge–Eglinton intersection (colloquially referred to as "Young and Eligible" by locals, as most of the sparkly new high rises cater to the city's young professional population). Uptown has traditionally been a residential area, but it's now a fast-growing entertainment area, too. Its attractions include the Sunnybrook park system, the Ontario Science Centre, and the stunning Aga Khan Museum.

North Toronto is another developing area, with theaters such as the Toronto Centre for the Arts, galleries, and excellent dining. It's not yet a prime tourist destination, but it is on the rise and gets a few mentions throughout this guide.

Note: Some of the primary attractions lie outside the downtown core or even the city limits. The Toronto Zoo, Paramount Canada's Wonderland, and the McMichael Canadian Art Collection are all full- or half-day trips.

THE NEIGHBORHOODS IN BRIEF

Downtown West

THE TORONTO ISLANDS

Best for: Outdoor activities, amusement park

What you won't find: Great dining, museums

Neighborhood parameters: Islands Ward's, Algonquin, and Centre

These three islands in Lake Ontario are a slice of cottage country with a cityscape backdrop. They're home to some 600-odd residents and no cars. During the warmer months, the islands are a top recreation destination, where locals go to bike, swim, boat, and picnic. Centre Island, the most visited of the islands, holds the children's theme park Centreville and a cedar maze confusing enough to trap Dedalus. Catch the ferry at the foot of Bay Street by Queen's Quay. You can rent bicycles, canoes, kayaks, and SUPs on the island.

HARBOURFRONT

Best for: Museums, skating, festivals, concerts, and accessing the Toronto Islands by ferry

What you won't find: Great dining, good bars

Neighborhood parameters: Queens Quay from Bathurst Street to Yonge Street

The landfill where the railroad yards and dock facilities once stood is now a glorious playground opening onto the lake. The waterfront has been enlivened with pristine sand beaches (for sunbathing, not swimming—this is still a working port) and a multi-sport trail that tourists often accidentally stroll into only to meet oncoming bikes. The main draw is the **Harbourfront Centre** (p. 121), one of the most vibrant literary, artistic, and cultural venues in Canada. The Harbourfront Centre is home to the **Power Plant**

underground TORONTO

In cold weather, it's a good idea to quickly familiarize yourself with the labyrinthine walkways beneath the pavement. This miles-long network is an excellent way to get around the downtown core when the weather is grim. You can eat, sleep, dance, shop, and go to the theater without ever needing a coat.

You can walk from the Dundas subway station south through the Eaton Centre until you hit Queen Street; turn west to the Sheraton Centre and then head south. You'll pass through the Richmond-Adelaide Centre, First Canadian Place,

and Toronto Dominion Centre, and go all the way (through the dramatic Royal Bank Plaza) to the recently revamped Union Station. En route, branches lead off to the stock exchange, Sun Life Centre, and Metro Hall. Additional walkways link Simcoe Plaza to 200 Wellington West and to the CBC Broadcast Centre. Other walkways run around Bloor Street and Yonge Street, and elsewhere in the city. Look for the large, clear underground PATH maps throughout the concourse.

Toronto Neighborhoods

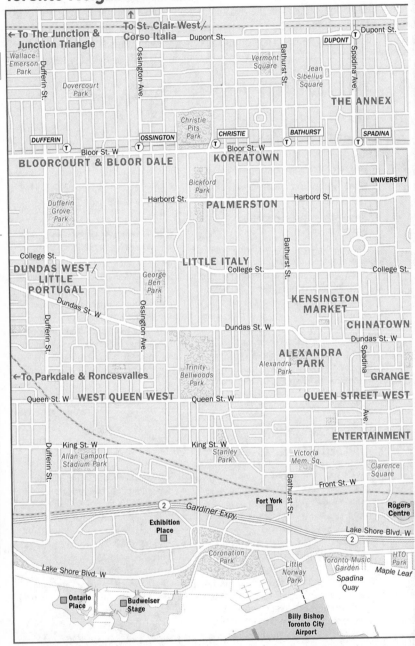

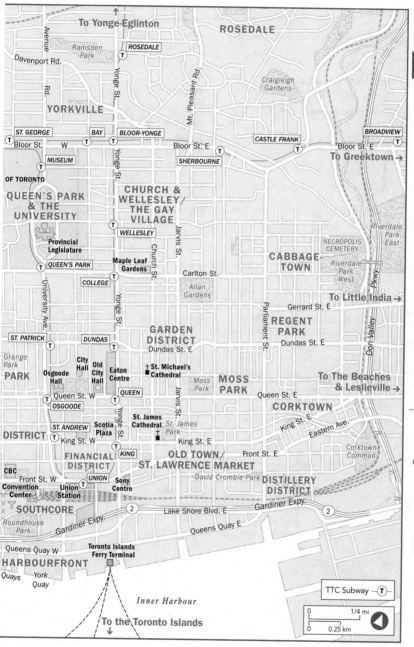

To Yonge-Eglinton

ROSEDALE

Ramsden Park

Avenue Rd.

Davenport Rd.

ROSEDALE Ⓣ

Craigleigh Gardens

Mt. Pleasant Rd.

YORKVILLE

Yonge St.

ST. GEORGE Ⓣ   BAY Ⓣ   BLOOR-YONGE Ⓣ   CASTLE FRANK Ⓣ   BROADVIEW Ⓣ

Bloor St. W   Ⓣ   Bloor St. E Ⓣ   Bloor St. E Ⓣ

MUSEUM Ⓣ   SHERBOURNE   To Greektown →

OF TORONTO

QUEEN'S PARK & THE UNIVERSITY

CHURCH & WELLESLEY / THE GAY VILLAGE

WELLESLEY Ⓣ

Jarvis St.

Riverdale Park East

Provincial Legislature

QUEEN'S PARK Ⓣ

Maple Leaf Gardens

Church St.

NECROPOLIS CEMETERY

CABBAGE-TOWN

Don Valley Pkwy.

COLLEGE Ⓣ

Carlton St.

Riverdale Park West

University Ave.

Allan Gardens

Gerrard St. E

To Little India →

REGENT PARK

Parliament St.

ST. PATRICK Ⓣ   DUNDAS Ⓣ

GARDEN DISTRICT

Dundas St. E

Dundas St. E

Grange Park

City Hall

Old City Hall

Eaton Centre

† St. Michael's Cathedral

Moss Park

MOSS PARK

To The Beaches & Leslieville →

PARK

Osgoode Hall

ST. PATRICK Ⓣ   QUEEN Ⓣ

Queen St. W   Ⓣ

Queen St. E

OSGOODE Ⓣ

Jarvis St.

CORKTOWN

ST. ANDREW Ⓣ

Scotia Plaza

St. James Cathedral

St. James Park

King St. E

King St. E

Eastern Ave.

DISTRICT   Ⓣ King St. W

KING Ⓣ

OLD TOWN / ST. LAWRENCE MARKET

Front St. E

Corktown Common

FINANCIAL DISTRICT

CBC

Front St. W   UNION Ⓣ   Sony Centre

David Crombie Park

DISTILLERY DISTRICT

Convention Center   Union Station

SOUTHCORE

Gardiner Expy.

Lake Shore Blvd. E

Gardiner Expy.   ②

Roundhouse Park

②

Queens Quay E

Queens Quay W

Toronto Islands Ferry Terminal

HARBOURFRONT

Quays   York Quay

Inner Harbour

To the Toronto Islands ↓

TTC Subway — Ⓣ

0   1/4 mi
0   0.25 km

Contemporary Art Gallery (p. 15), seven stages (some outdoors) that feature an eclectic range of programming (from vegetarian food festivals to klezmer bands), and a skating rink that looks out over Lake Ontario.

SOUTHCORE

Best for: Sports games, concerts, the CN Tower, access to Union Station

What you won't find: Good nightlife, shopping, culture

Neighborhood parameters: Front Street to the Gardiner, bookended by Reese and Yonge streets

Toronto's youngest neighborhood was born from underutilized railroad lands that began sprouting condos in the late aughts. The fast-growing hood is expected to reach a population of 130,000 by 2031 with most of the condos populated by locals in their 20s and 30s. Here, you'll also find the **Rogers Centre** (home base for the Toronto Blue Jays) and the **Scotiabank Arena** (home to both the Maple Leafs and Raptors) (p. 136. Other top attractions include the **CN Tower** (p. 120) and **Ripley's Aquarium of Canada** (p. 122).

FINANCIAL DISTRICT

Best for: Fine dining, access to the PATH system (the underground networks connecting buildings and subways)

What you won't find: Nightlife, aboveground shopping

Neighborhood parameters: Front Street north to Queen Street, between Yonge and York streets

The city's first skyscrapers rose here. Today, Toronto's major banks and insurance companies still have their headquarters here. Although the 19th-century office buildings have been dwarfed by glass towers, some of the older structures have been preserved. Ultramodern Brookfield Place incorporated the facade of a historic bank building into its design. The original Toronto Stock Exchange, similarly, is nested into the base of the Ernst & Young Tower. The ex-TSX is now home to the **Design Exchange (DX)** (p. 120), a museum dedicated to Canadian design.

Thanks to generous expense accounts, this area boasts no shortage of luxe restaurants including fine-dining stalwart **Canoe** (p. 84). Below the sidewalk are heaps of stores and restaurants along the subterranean avenues of the PATH system.

ENTERTAINMENT DISTRICT/ SOUTH CORE

Best for: Nightlife, restaurants, shopping, celebrity spotting, live theater

What you won't find: Museums

Neighborhood parameters: Front Street north to Queen Street and from Bay Street west to Bathurst Street

Also known as the Theatre District, this area is dense with big-name venues, including the **Royal Alexandra Theatre** (p. 159), the **Princess of Wales Theatre** (p. 159), **Roy Thomson Hall** (p. 162), and **Four Seasons Centre for the Performing Arts** (p. 159). The stretch of King Street from Spadina to Bathurst has become the city's party mecca. Avoided by locals, swarmed by suburbanites, the strip becomes one big bash come Saturday night. In September, the festive atmosphere is amplified by the Toronto International Film Festival. The **TIFF Bell Lightbox** (p. 167) transforms into red-carpet HQ for 2 weeks of celebrities, premieres, and epic fetes.

CHINATOWN

Best for: Cantonese and Vietnamese food, made-in-China trinkets, bubble tea, the Art Gallery of Ontario

What you won't find: Evening entertainment

Neighborhood parameters: Dundas Street West from University Avenue to Spadina Avenue and north to College Street

Toronto has a large Chinese population dispersed throughout the city, but this was home to the first great wave of Chinese immigrants. It's changed since its early days, particularly because of the infusion of Hong Kong money. The strip's eastern front is marked by the glass-and-blue-titanium-clad **Art Gallery of Ontario** (p. 115).

KENSINGTON MARKET

Best for: Cheap eats, hip bars, gourmet groceries, vintage stores

What you won't find: Cars on the last Sunday of the summer months

Neighborhood parameters: Spadina Avenue to Bathurst Street, Dundas Street West to College Street West

This is one of Toronto's most colorful neighborhoods. Successive waves of immigrants—Eastern European Jews, Latin Americans, Portuguese, West Indians, and more—have left their mark. Filled with tiny but wonderful food shops, restaurants, and vintage clothing stores, it's easy to while away an afternoon here (especially on the car-free summer Sun, when the area becomes a pedestrian-only zone with impromptu parades and buskers on every corner).

QUEEN STREET WEST

Best for: Shopping, casual dining, live music

What you won't find: Museums, parks

Neighborhood parameters: University Avenue to Bathurst Street

This stretch offers an eclectic mix of mainstream shops, funky boutiques, textile stores, and vintage-clothing emporiums. It's also packed with eateries: Bistros, cafes, and gourmet food shops line the street. Despite the intrusion of mega-retailers, many independently owned boutiques still flourish. It's also home to the city's oldest still-operating music venue, the **Horseshoe Tavern** (p. 170), which remains a great place to catch local bands on the upswing.

WEST QUEEN WEST

Best for: Unique shopping, great coffee, park strolls, people-watching

What you won't find: Quiet—this area is populated by colorful characters

Neighborhood parameters: Queen Street from Bathurst to Roncesvalles

West Queen West is full of fine-art galleries, one-of-a-kind boutiques (selling everything from fair-trade spices to locally made jewelry), and some truly great restaurants. Come summer, **Trinity Bellwoods** (p. 131) park is packed with locals chatting under the maple trees.

PARKDALE

Best for: Local designers, Tibetan and vegan food, bar scene

What you won't find: Museums, parks

Neighborhood parameters: Dufferin Street to Roncesvalles Avenue along Queen Street West

Originally a village outside the city limits, Parkdale was a posh burg popular with Toronto's well-to-do, thanks to its proximity to **Sunnyside Beach** and the **Canadian National Exhibition** (p. 54). Then in 1955 the city built the Gardiner Expressway, severing Parkdale from the lake. Property values plummeted, and mansions become rooming houses and fell into disrepair. Today, the neighborhood attracts artists and eccentrics and is home to the city's largest Tibetan population.

RONCESVALLES

Best for: Polish food, shopping, brunch, cafes, parks

What you won't find: Museums

Neighborhood parameters: Roncesvalles Avenue runs from Queen Street to Dundas Street

Once a predominantly Polish enclave, Roncy, as it's called by locals, has become one of Toronto's most coveted neighborhoods. You can still buy great pierogis and pączki here, and Sunday mornings the streets are crowded with Catholic worshipers, but most days the avenue is full of stroller-pushing young families. The retail strip is made up of enchanting independent shops selling everything from eco furniture to fresh-made pasta and locally designed clothes. Thankfully, there's a cafe every few hundred feet to fuel the shopping spree. Flanked by **High Park** (p. 131) to the west and Sorauren Park to the east, this is a great area to while away a low-key afternoon.

DUNDAS WEST/LITTLE PORTUGAL

Best for: Nightlife, indie concerts, snack bars, quirky shops, galleries, local beer

What you won't find: Mainstream retailers

Neighborhood parameters: Extending just north of Dundas West, this area stretches from Ossington Avenue to Lansdowne Avenue, bound on the south by the railroad tracks and Queen Street

This neighborhood became Toronto's hippest dining destination when Ossington Avenue, a once-downtrodden strip of mechanics, became *the* street to eat and drink. Dine at one of the excellent restaurants or people-watch from a patio—**Bellwoods Brewery** (p. 180) has great beer and the best view. The watering holes continue west down Dundas Street, with many of the cooler spots tucked into secret basements, with only a queue announcing their existence.

LITTLE ITALY

Best for: Contemporary dining, Italian trattorias, cafes, upscale bars, live music at the Mod Club

What you won't find: Museums, galleries

Neighborhood parameters: College Street, between Bathurst and Ossington streets

Charming sidewalk cafes and bodegas cater to the longstanding Italian and Portuguese communities that call these winding streets home. The trattorias along College are being slowly replaced by a new generation of restaurants serving upscale Chinese, elegant Spanish, esoteric beers, and fancy tacos. In the evenings, the **Royal Cinema** (http://the royal.to) is a great place to catch an art-house flick. During the day, the Art Deco building operates as a production studio where you can sometimes spy famous Canadian directors like Atom Egoyan and Bruce McDonald.

THE JUNCTION & JUNCTION TRIANGLE

Best for: Antiquing, breweries, brunch, restaurants, galleries, independent shops

What you won't find: Easy transit accessibility, other tourists

Neighborhood parameters: Dundas West to Annette Street between Keele and Runnymede streets

Although this neighborhood is now home to three breweries and dozens of chic-yet-affordable restaurants with interesting wine lists, prohibition was only lifted here in 2000. The Junction was long a rough area, a pocket of abattoirs, foundries, and factories that attracted unsavory characters and drink-fueled debauchery. Booze was banned here

in 1904. With few restaurants and no bars, the retail strip went dormant until the 21st century, when people awoke to its heaps of yesteryear charm. Just east, in the Junction Triangle, is Sterling Road, an industrial street that has become a cultural destination for its new **Museum of Contemporary Art Toronto Canada** (p. 126).

Downtown East

OLD TOWN/ST. LAWRENCE MARKET

Best for: Antiquing, historical buildings (like the old City Hall and the Gooderham and Worts Distillery), galleries, live theater, the St. Lawrence Market

What you won't find: Free parking

Neighborhood parameters: East of Yonge Street, between the Esplanade and Adelaide Street

During the 19th century, this area was the focal point of the community (it's the site of Toronto's first city hall). Today, the St. Lawrence Market is still going strong, and attractions such as the glorious St. James Cathedral, Sony Centre for the Arts, and Hockey Hall of Fame continue to draw visitors. It's also an area on the rise with fine restaurants and stellar furniture shops.

CABBAGETOWN

Best for: Riverdale Farm, Parks, Lunch

What you won't find: Good nightlife, museums,

Neighborhood parameters: Wellesley Street East to Shuter Street, Parliament Street to Sherbourne Street

Once considered a slum, Cabbagetown is now filled with beautifully restored Victorian and Queen Anne–style houses. Even the first housing project in Canada, Spruce Court (at the intersection of Sumach and Spruce streets), looks like a charming collection of cottages.

THE BEACHES

Best for: Outdoor summer fun, the Beaches International Jazz Festival, beaches, parks

What you won't find: Good nightlife, bad ice cream

Neighborhood parameters: Victoria Park Avenue on the east to Kingston Road on the north, to Coxwell Avenue on the west, south to Lake Ontario

Located just 35 minutes from downtown at the end of the Queen Street East streetcar line is a beach community with small-town pride and a bustling main strip animated by independent specialty shops. A popular summer resort in the mid-1800s, the Beaches is a top sunny-weather destination for swimming along the sandy beaches and strolling the boardwalk. Walk the leafy streets to see gorgeous Victorians with wraparound porches, but note that the prettiest building might just be the R. C. Harris Water Treatment Plant. This Art Deco water palace is free to walk around (the grounds boast amazing views), but the building only opens to the public during Doors Open Toronto, an annual springtime event.

LESLIEVILLE

Best for: Sunday brunch, specialty shops, cafes, sundowners atop the Broadview Hotel

What you won't find: Museums, crowds

Neighborhood parameters: Bound by the railway track to the north, Eastern Avenue to the south and bookended by the Don River and Coxwell Avenue

Once a down-on-its-luck nabe, this area has been entirely transformed. The **Broadview Hotel** (p. 69), a breathtaking red-sandstone Romanesque Revival building that spent decades as a flophouse before being remade into a ultra-trendy boutique hotel in 2018, was the last of the grimy old guard to fall. From the hotel's swanky rooftop patio you can see Toronto's silhouette to the west. Leslieville fans out to the east with boutiques, vintage and antique stores, cafes, bars, and excellent bistros.

LITTLE INDIA

Best for: Indian food, textiles

What you won't find: Museums, nightlife

Neighborhood parameters: Gerrard Street East, between Greenwood Avenue and Main Street

This strip is known for its festival-like atmosphere, partly because of the multicolored lights that light up the street at night. But the vibrant street life is visible at any time of day. The blocks are filled with Indian restaurants, grocers, and shops that specialize in saris, beautiful textiles, and treasure chests of trinkets.

Downtown North

QUEEN'S PARK AND THE UNIVERSITY

Best for: Architecture, lectures at U of T, the Ontario Legislature, museums (the Gardiner and Royal Ontario)

What you won't find: Shopping, exciting dining options

Neighborhood parameters: From College Street to Bloor Street, between Spadina Avenue and Bay Street.

This is home to the many of the colleges and buildings that make up the handsome campus of the University of Toronto and the Ontario Legislature. When the lush lawn of Queens Park isn't the scene of a peaceful protest, you can often spy some of the province's top politicians taking strolls between parliamentary sessions. The neighborhood's main artery, Avenue Road, is flanked by two of the best museums in town. On the east is the **Gardiner Museum** (p. 120), holding a trove of globe-spanning ceramics. On the west is the **Royal Ontario Museum** (p. 127), Canada's most-visited museum, which boasts a broad collection ranging from natural history to world culture.

YORKVILLE

Best for: People-watching, upscale shopping, luxe dining

What you won't find: Anything affordable

Neighborhood parameters: Bloor Street to the south, Davenport Road to the north, Yonge Street to the east and Avenue Road to the west

Yorkville was Toronto's Haight-Ashbury in the 1960s (Neil Young and Joni Mitchell got their starts performing at the coffeehouses here). In the '80s, the vibe shifted from hippie to haute. Now, Hermes, Chanel, and Versace all have flagships along a stretch of Bloor nicknamed the Mink Mile for its high-end shops. Tucked north of Bloor are pretty streets with small boutiques and heaps of fancy restaurants, many worth their price tags.

THE ANNEX

Best for: Bookstores, youthful nightlife, lunch specials catering to student budgets, concerts at Koerner Hall

What you won't find: Honest Ed's (the landmark discount store, with its giant marquee lit up with 23,000 light bulbs). It was demolished in 2018.

Neighborhood parameters: Bedford Road to Bathurst Street and from Harbord Street to Dupont Avenue

This largely residential neighborhood is a mix of small parks, handsome homes, and a strip along Bloor Street West that offers some good shopping for books and knick-knacks, plus a few attractive restaurants and pubs and two unique attractions, the **Bata Shoe Museum** (p. 119) and **Koerner Hall** (p. 162). Revered urban-planning guru the late Jane Jacobs called this area home.

KOREATOWN

Best for: Korean restaurants, Korean tchotchkes, movies screened under the stars at Christie Pits park

What you won't find: Museums, galleries

Neighborhood parameters: Bloor Street West, between Bathurst and Christie streets

This bustling stretch of Bloor is filled with Korean restaurants, alternative-medicine practitioners (such as herbalists and acupuncturists), and shops filled with made-in-Korea merchandise.

BLOORCOURT & BLOOR DALE

Best for: Cafes, nightlife, multicultural pockets

What you won't find: Museums, parks

Neighborhood parameters: Bloor Street West from Christie Street to Lansdowne

This unpolished section of Bloor Street is Toronto in a nutshell. Ethiopian convenience stores, vegan bakeries, pho purveyors, Mexican hot tables, Jamaican patty shops, and red-sauce Italian joints do brisk business during the daytime. Come night, the unfussy watering holes attract stylish hipsters. The bars here tread the line between dive-y and cool, but stay firmly in the latter category thanks to excellent beer lists and well-curated soundtracks.

ROSEDALE

Best for: Access to the Evergreen Brick Works and Edwardian, Victorian, and neo-Georgian architecture

What you won't find: Nightlife

Neighborhood parameters: Bloor Street to the train tracks just south of St. Clair Avenue, spanning from Yonge Street to Rosedale Valley Road

Rosedale is named after the residence of Sheriff William Jarvis, who is largely credited with ending the 1837 Upper Canada Rebellion. Meandering these quiet, tree-lined avenues offers a tour of some of Toronto's grandest old homes, many backing onto wildlife-filled ravines. GPS is helpful here; the snaking streets make it easy to get lost. Make sure to use it when braving 30-minute ravine walk to the **Evergreen Brick Works** (p. 124)—the signs aren't particularly helpful. Straight as an arrow, though, is the Yonge retail strip, crowned by the Summerhill LCBO, an expansive liquor store housed in a restored train station (a great spot to pick up Canadian spirits, beers, and wines).

CHURCH AND WELLESLEY/THE GAY VILLAGE

Best for: Gay bars, great nightlife, exhibitions at the Canadian Lesbian and Gay Archives, queer theater, rainbow paraphernalia

What you won't find: Lesbian bars (they're scattered about the west end)

Neighborhood parameters: Between Gerrard Street and Bloor Street East, along Church Street

In the heart of Toronto's LGBT community you'll find the world's oldest queer bookstore (Glad Day Bookshop), excellent nightlife (**Crews & Tangos** [p. 179] is known for epic drag performances that erupt into dance parties), and alternative theatre (**Buddies in Bad Times Theatre** [p. 164] produces edgy, contemporary plays that put queer voices front and center). Come June, the Village, as it's called by locals, is a riot of color and bared bodies—this is the epicenter of Toronto's Gay Pride festivities.

The East End

CABBAGETOWN

Best for: Visiting the animals at Riverdale Farm, concerts at the Phoenix, design shops

What you won't find: Nightlife, museums

Neighborhood parameters: East of Parliament Street to the Don Valley and between Gerrard and Bloor streets

Writer Hugh Garner described this as the largest Anglo-Saxon slum in North America, long before it became a gentrified neighborhood of restored, often pretty and pricey, Victorian and Edwardian homes. The name is an historical reference: The original Irish immigrants who settled here in the late 1800s grew row upon row of cabbages on their front lawns. **Riverdale,** Toronto's only inner-city farm, is at the eastern edge of the district (p. 125).

GREEKTOWN

Best for: Mediterranean restaurants, Greek pastries, Taste of the Danforth, concerts at the Danforth Music Hall

What you won't find: Museums, galleries

Neighborhood parameters: Danforth Avenue from Broadview Avenue to Greenwood Avenue

Across the Don Valley Viaduct, Bloor Street becomes the Danforth, which marks the beginning of Greektown. It's lined with old-style Greek tavernas and hip Mediterranean bars and restaurants that are crowded from

early evening into the night. The densest wining-and-dining area starts at Broadview Avenue and runs about eight blocks east.

Uptown

ST. CLAIR WEST / CORSO ITALIA

Best for: Italian food (hot tables, casual trats, upscale enotecas, cafes, and gelato shops), Artscape Whychwood barns

What you won't find: Nightlife

Neighborhood parameters: West from Christie Street to Dufferin Street

Until not long ago, this was a modest residential neighborhood where Torontonians would venture for some great Italian gelato or for a street party during the World Cup. Now the area and beyond is proving popular for its good cafes, fine Jamaican fare, and the **Artscape Whychwood Barns,** a century-old streetcar facility transformed into a mixed-use space shared by artists' studios, a farmer's market, community gardens, and an events space.

YONGE–EGLINTON

Best for: Youthful, low-key nightlife and Sunnybrook Park

What you won't find: Arts or culture

Neighborhood parameters: A two-block radius around the intersection of Yonge and Eglinton

Jokingly known as the "Young and Eligible," this bustling area is filled with restaurants—from neighborhood favorites to fine-dining destinations—as well as live-music pubs and nightclubs. To the east, it intersects with the 243-hectare (600-acre) Sunnybrook park system and the Ontario Science Centre.

TORONTO IN CONTEXT

Toronto is booming. Canada's biggest city and the country's economic epicenter has a population of 6.9 million in the greater metropolitan area. Each year, that population expands with about 115,000 new arrivals. Only 49% of those new Torontonians come from the local maternity wards; the rest were born outside of Canada. The city's sheer cultural diversity—more than 230 different nationalities call Toronto home—is what ultimately gives pulse to the place.

TORONTO TODAY

The city draws on its vast international pedigree to give it shape and definition: The polyglot Toronto *is* the Toronto story. And it's changing at a rapid pace.

There's a lot that's new about this place, which has its pros and cons. Although bike lanes, roads, and transit system struggle to keep up, the signs of growth are all around. The skyline downtown is a forest of cranes, as condo towers stretch upwards to 85 stories. There are marvelous new parks, new museums, and property values rising to new heights (asking locals if the bubble's soon to burst is an easy conversation starter in this town). Green initiatives include the Toronto Bike Share program and ever-improving waterfront playgrounds. An alternative foods movement is widespread.

The city is taking strides to reclaim its final frontier along the lakefront. After years of political dithering, visible progress is being made to rehab the city's derelict shipping and industrial past at the water's edge.

New developments include a revamped **Union Station** (p. 18), landscaped lakeside recreational trails, and the addition of multiple parks. The two crown jewels of the new waterfront are the whimsical, white-sand **Sugar Beach** opposite the Redpath Sugar refinery, and **Trillium Park**, an abandoned amusement park (Ontario Place) that has been transformed in a stunning ode to native flora.

North of the lake, traffic is congested at best—chaotic at worst—especially on weekdays. It's particularly bad in the core, but the highways aren't immune. As the suburbs continue to densify, developing their own personalities, the roads are only getting worse.

Gentrification has made an aggressive sweep over Toronto. As rents rise, colorful ethnic neighborhoods such as Parkdale (home to the city's largest Tibetan population) are being transformed, pushing eclectic and mom-and-pop businesses, and the people who run them, farther from the city center. Although much of downtown has been gentrified, there are some parts of Toronto, including downtown, where gangs rule. But the city remains one of the safest in the world, according to *The Economist*.

For better or for worse, the city's classic nickname, "Toronto the Good," tells just one part of the story these days. A local reporter has compared Toronto to a teenager (it's a young city, barely over 200 years). The comparison is apt: Toronto is exuberant, out for fun, a bit rambunctious, and sometimes a challenge to manage. The reward is that it's more interesting than merely nice.

LOOKING BACK AT TORONTO
Early Settlement in "Muddy York"

Over the past 15 millennia, the Huron-Wendat and Petun First Nations, the Seneca, and most recently, the Mississaugas of the Credit River have farmed, hunted, and lived in what is now Toronto. It wasn't until 1720 that the French established the first trading post along the Toronto Passage to intercept the furs that were being taken across Lake Ontario to New York State by English rivals. Fort Rouillé, built on the site of today's Canadian National Exhibition (CNE) grounds, replaced the trading post in 1751. When the 1763 Treaty of Paris ended the Anglo-French War after the fall of Québec, French rule in North America effectively ended, and the city's French antecedents were all but forgotten.

In the wake of the American Revolution, the Loyalists fled north, and the British decided it was time to carve a capital city out of the northern wilderness. Before any forts were built, the British needed to purchase the Toronto lands from the Mississaugas of New Credit. In 1787 the Crown purchased an area stretching from the Humber to the Don River along Lake Ontario for £1,700, 24 lace hats, 120 mirrors, some flannel, 96 gallons of rum, and sundry other trade items. The Toronto Purchase—deemed by the Mississaugas to be a land lease and not a purchase—remained in dispute for 223 years and was settled only in 2010.

In 1791, the British established Upper Canada (modern-day Ontario) as a province. Its first lieutenant governor, John Graves Simcoe, made Toronto its capital and renamed it "York" in honor of Frederick, Duke of York (one of George III's sons). Simcoe ordered a garrison built and laid out in a 10-block rectangle around Adelaide, Front, George, and Berkeley streets. The land

Turrono Today, Tkaronto Yesterday

The name Toronto comes from the Mohawk word *tkaronto*, which means "trees standing in water." Tkaronto referred to the narrows that connect lakes Couchiching and Simcoe, located 125km (78 miles) north of the present-day city. There, people fished using fishing weirs (made from stakes driven into the riverbed). In 1680, poor French cartography changed the name to Taronto and applied it to a nearby lake. Over the following centuries, the name was carried south down the portage routes and was ultimately applied to, what is today, the Humber River. The *Passage de Taronto* became the route that connected Lake Ontario with Lake Simcoe, and the French fort at the mouth of the Humber was named Fort Toronto. Today, you can tell a true Torontonian by how they swallow the middle of the Toronto. They all live in *Turrono*, not Toronto.

from Queen to Bloor was parceled out to government officials in an effort to mollify the Brits, who resented having to move to the mosquito-plagued, marshy outpost. York was notorious for its always-muddy streets, earning it the nickname "Muddy York."

By 1795, the hamlet had grown, and the first parliament buildings were erected. Simcoe also surveyed Yonge Street, which would eventually become the longest street in the world. The second Parliament meeting confirmed York as the capital of Upper Canada.

The War of 1812 & Aftermath

When America declared war on Britain in the War of 1812, President James Madison assumed that invading and holding Canada would be a simple matter. The opposite proved to be true. In April 1813, 2,700 American troops on 14 ships and schooners invaded York (population 625), looting and destroying the parliament buildings, the Fort York garrison, and much of the settlement. It was a pyrrhic victory: The Americans suffered heavy losses and failed to take any additional Canadian territory. In retaliation, British troops marched on Washington, D.C., in 1814 and burned all government buildings, including the White House.

Perhaps unsurprisingly, given the events of the war, York's ruling oligarchy shared a conservative pro-British outlook. Called the Family Compact, the group consisted of William Jarvis, a New England Loyalist who became provincial secretary; John Beverley Robinson, son of a Virginia Loyalist, who became attorney general at age 21 and, later, chief justice of Upper Canada; and Scottish-educated John Strachan, a schoolmaster who became an Anglican rector and, eventually, the most powerful figure in York. Anglo-Irish Dr. William Warren Baldwin, doctor, lawyer, architect, judge, and politician, laid out Spadina Avenue as a thoroughfare leading to his country house; the Boultons were prominent lawyers, judges, and politicians—Judge D'Arcy Boulton built a mansion, the Grange, which later became the core of the Art Gallery of Ontario and still stands today.

The Early 1800s Rebellion & Immigration

In 1834, the city was incorporated, and York became Toronto, a city bounded by Parliament Street to the east, Bathurst Street to the west, the lakefront to the south, and 400 yards north of Queen Street (then called Lot) to the north. Outside this area—west to Dufferin Street, east to the Don River, and north to Bloor Street—laid the "liberties," out of which the city would later carve new wards. North of Bloor, local brewer Joseph Bloor and Sheriff William Jarvis were already drawing up plans for the village of Yorkville. In 1827,

Muddy York

"Muddy York" was a subject of continuous complaint by early settlers. Just how muddy was the early settlement? One apocryphal story tells of a man who saw a hat lying in the middle of a street and went to pick it up. When he did, he found the head of a live man submerged in the muck below.

the first university, then called Kings College (later renamed the University of Toronto), opened. This was an intellectual achievement but also an aesthetic one, as the university added new and beautiful architecture.

As increasing numbers of immigrants arrived, demands arose for democracy and reform. Among the reformers were such leaders as Francis Collins, who launched the radical paper *Canadian Freeman* in 1825; lawyer and attorney general William Draper; and, most famous of all, fiery William Lyon Mackenzie, who was elected Toronto's first mayor in 1834.

More than anything else, immigration was changing Toronto. During the 1820s, 1830s, and 1840s, immigrants—Irish Protestants and Catholics, Scots, Presbyterians, Methodists, and other nonconformists—arrived in droves. Slavery was outlawed throughout the British Empire in 1833; by the 1840s, roughly 3% of Toronto's population was black. But the biggest change was the arrival of the Irish. In early 1847, Toronto's population stood at 20,000. That summer 38,560 Irish immigrants fleeing the Great Famine landed in Toronto, forever changing the city.

Canadian Confederation & the Late Victorian Era

During the 1850s, the building of the railroads accelerated Toronto's booming economy. By 1860, it was the trading hub for lumber and grain imports and exports. Merchant empires were founded, railroad magnates emerged, and institutions such as the Bank of Toronto were established. The foundations of an industrial city were laid: Toronto gained a waterworks, gas street lamps, and public transportation.

Despite its wealth, Toronto lagged behind Montréal, which had more than double Toronto's population in 1861. But under the Confederation of 1867, the city was guaranteed an advantage: As the capital of the newly created Ontario province, Toronto, in effect, controlled the minerals and timber of the north.

By 1891, Toronto's population had reached 181,000. The business of the city was business, and amassing wealth the pastime of such figures as Henry Pellatt, stockbroker and builder of Casa Loma; financier E. B. Osler; senator

The Toronto Rebellion

William Lyon Mackenzie, Toronto's first mayor, founded the *Colonial Advocate* newspaper to crusade against the narrow-minded Family Compact, the city's ruling group of oligarchs, calling for reform and challenging their power to such an extent that some of them broke into his office and wrecked presses before throwing his type into the lake. By 1837, Mackenzie, undaunted, was calling for open rebellion. The city's financial turmoil in the wake of some bank failures made his wish come true. On December 5, 1837, a few hundred rebels—armed mostly with pitchforks, pikes, and cudgels—gathered at Montgomery's Tavern outside the city (near modern-day Eglinton Ave.). Led by Mackenzie on a white horse, they marched on the city. But Sheriff Jarvis was waiting for them, and his militia crushed the rebellion. Mackenzie fled to the United States, but two other rebellion leaders were hanged (their graves are in the Toronto Necropolis). Mackenzie was later pardoned, returned to Toronto in 1849, and was elected to the Upper Canada legislature.

and president of the Bank of Commerce George Albertus Cox; and investment dealer Alfred Ernest Ames.

The boom spurred new commercial and residential construction. Projects included the first skyscrapers, such as the **Board of Trade Building** (1892) at Yonge and Front streets; George Gooderham's Romanesque-style **mansion** (1892) at St. George and Bloor streets (now the York Club); the **Ontario Legislative Building** in Queen's Park (1893); and the **city hall** (1899) at Queen and Bay streets. In the 1890s, electric lights, telephones, and electric streetcars—replacing their horse-drawn predecessors—appeared.

From Boom Town to the Great Depression

The Great Fire of 1904 destroyed 100 buildings, wreaking more than C$10 million (in 1904 dollars) in damage. Miraculously, no one died in the fire, the cause of which was never discovered.

Between 1901 and 1921, Toronto's population more than doubled to 521,893. The economy continued to expand, fueled by lumber, milling, mining, manufacturing, and, after 1911, hydroelectric power. Much of the new wealth went into construction, and three impressive buildings from this era can still be seen today: the **Horticultural Building** at the Exhibition Grounds (1907), the **King Edward Hotel** (1903), and **Union Station** (1914–20).

The booming economy and its factories attracted a wave of new immigrants—mostly Italians and Jews from Russia and Eastern Europe—who settled in the city's emerging ethnic enclaves. By 1912, **Kensington Market** was well-established, and the garment center and Jewish community were firmly ensconced around King Street and Spadina Avenue. Little Italy clustered around College and Grace streets. By 1911, some 30,000 Torontonians were foreign-born, and the slow march to change the English character of the city had begun.

As it became larger and wealthier, Toronto also became an intellectual and cultural magnet. Artists such as Charles Jefferys, J. E. H. MacDonald, Arthur Lismer, Tom Thomson, Lawren Harris, Frederick Varley, and A. Y. Jackson, most associated with the Group of Seven, set up studios in Toronto. Their first group show opened in 1920. Toronto also became the nation's English-language publishing center, and national magazines such as *Saturday Night* (1887) and *Maclean's* (1905) were launched. The **Art Gallery of Ontario,** the **Royal Ontario Museum,** and the **Royal Alexandra Theatre** all opened before 1914.

Women advanced, too, at the turn of the 20th century. In 1875, Jennie Kidd Trout became the first Canadian woman authorized to practice medicine. Trout was joined 5 years later by suffragette Emily Stowe, who obtained her medical license in 1880. In 1884, the University of Toronto began to accept women. The women's suffrage movement gained strength, led by Dr. Stowe, Flora McDonald Denison, and the Women's Christian Temperance Union.

But increased industrialization brought social problems as well, largely concentrated in Cabbagetown and the Ward, a large area that stretched west of Yonge Street and north of Queen Street. Here, people lived in crowded, wretched conditions: Housing was inadequate; health conditions were poor; and rag-picking, or sweatshop labor, was the only employment.

When Britain entered World War I, Canada was immediately pulled into it. Toronto became Canada's chief aviation center; factories, shipyards, and power facilities expanded to meet the needs of war; and women entered the workforce in great numbers.

The 1920s roared along, fueled by a mining boom that saw Bay Street become a veritable gold-rush alley. Then the Great Depression hit, and the only distraction from its bleakness was the opening of **Maple Leaf Gardens** in 1931. Besides being an ice-hockey center, it was host to large protest rallies during the Depression; later, it welcomed anyone, from the Jehovah's Witnesses to the Ringling Bros. Circus and the Metropolitan Opera.

As in the United States, hostility toward new immigrants was rife during the '20s. It reached a peak in 1923, when the Chinese Exclusion Act was passed,

"Toronto the Good"

Toronto's reputation for conservatism was well deserved. While the city was blessed with many beautiful churches, its nickname, "Toronto the Good," had less to do with religion and more to do with legislation against fun. This was, after all, the city that, in 1912, banned tobogganing on Sunday. As late as 1936, 24 men were arrested during a heat wave for exposing their chests…at the public city beaches! (At the time, the law stated that bathing suits were to cover men from neck to knees.) In 1947, cocktail lounges were approved, but it wasn't until 1950 that playing sports on Sunday became legal. Leopold Infeld, a University of Toronto physicist who worked with Einstein, famously said: "I dreaded the Sundays and prayed to God that if he chose for me to die in Toronto he would let it be on a Saturday afternoon to save me from one more Toronto Sunday."

which banned Chinese immigration. In the 1930s, anti-Semitism intensified (Canada accepted only 4,000 Jewish refugees out of the 800,000 seeking asylum). In August 1933, the display of a swastika at Christie Pits Park caused a battle between Nazis and Jewish men, who had been playing baseball before the riot broke out. As if things weren't bad enough, a polio epidemic struck in 1936.

World War II & Aftermath

Unlike World War I, Canada wasn't automatically bound to enter World War II by Britain's declaration of war. However, when the Canadian Parliament voted to declare war on Germany on September 10, 1939, the move was widely supported by Canadians.

The Second World War brought new life to Toronto—literally. Toronto men rushed to volunteer to serve while women took their place in the factories. Once again, the city became a major aviation center.

After World War II, prosperous Toronto continued to expand, especially into the suburbs. By the 1950s, the urban area had grown so large, disputes between city and suburbs were so frequent, and the need for social and other services was so great, that an effective administrative solution was needed. In 1953, the Metro Council, composed of equal numbers of representatives from the city and the suburbs, was established.

Mid- & Late 20th Century

Toronto became a major city in the 1950s, with the Metro Council providing a structure for planning and growth. The Yonge subway opened, and a network of highways was constructed. It linked the city to the affluent suburbs. **Don Mills,** the first postwar planned community, was built between 1952 and 1965; **Yorkdale Centre,** a mammoth shopping center, followed in 1964. American companies began locating branch plants in the area, fueling much of the growth.

The city also began to loosen up. While the old social elite continued to dominate the boardrooms, politics, at least, had become more accessible and fluid. In 1955, Nathan Phillips became the city's first Jewish mayor. In 1947, the Chinese Exclusion Act of 1923 was repealed. And after 1950, Germans and Italians were allowed to enter once again. Then, under pressure from the United Nations, people from Hungary, Yugoslavia, Portugal, and Greece poured in. Most arrived at Union Station, having journeyed from the ports of

Montréal's Loss, Toronto's Gain

In the 1970s, Toronto became the fastest-growing city in North America. For years, it had competed with Montréal for first-city status, but it was the election of the separatist Parti Québécois, in 1976, that boosted Toronto over the top. Montréal's loss was Toronto's gain, as English-speaking families and large companies chose Toronto over French-speaking Québec. The city overtook Montréal as a financial center as well, boasting more corporate headquarters. Its stock market was more important, and it remained the country's prime publishing center.

Halifax, Québec City, and Montréal. The 1960s brought an even richer mix of people—West Indians, South Asians, refugees from Chile, Vietnam, and elsewhere—changing the city's character forever.

In the 1960s, the focus shifted from the suburbs to the city. People moved back downtown, renovating the handsome brick Victorians so characteristic of today's downtown. Yorkville emerged briefly as the capital of hippiedom—the Haight-Ashbury of Canada. Gordon Lightfoot and Joni Mitchell sang in the coffeehouses, and a group called the Toronto Anti-Draft Programme helped many Americans fleeing the Vietnam War Draft settle in Toronto.

During the 1970s, the provincial government also helped develop attractions that would polish Toronto's patina and lure visitors, including **Ontario Place** (1971) and the **Metro Zoo** (1974). The **CN Tower** is another development from that era, and for more than 3 decades, it was the tallest free-standing structure in the world (now surpassed by the Burj Khalifa in Dubai). Unfortunately, in spite of strong efforts by preservationists, Toronto lost many historic buildings in the 1960s and '70s.

The 1980s were an interesting time in Toronto. On the one hand, the city fell into the habit of conspicuous consumption that seemed to define the oft-mocked era. Yorkville was transformed from hippie-coffeehouse central into a hive of chic boutiques. On a more positive note, previously neglected neighborhoods such as the Annex and Cabbagetown were revitalized, the grand mansions brought back to life by new waves of residents. People began to appreciate Toronto's historic architecture, working to restore it rather than tear it down as they had in the 1970s. The **Elgin** and **Winter Garden theaters** were fully renovated and reopened, as was the **Pantages Theatre** (now the **Ed Mirvish Theatre**). In 1986, Toronto's Mirvish family (of "Honest Ed's" fame) created Mirvish Productions, which (along with the now-defunct Livent group) ushered in a renaissance on the Toronto theater scene. There was also important new construction in the city: The **Roy Thomson Hall** opened in 1982, and **SkyDome** (now the **Rogers Centre**) debuted in 1989.

In the 1990s, the Greater Toronto Area (GTA) really began to boom, fueled in part by rising immigration to the city. In 1998, a megacity merger forced the former city of Toronto into a union with five previously independent boroughs, causing cuts in public services as the provincial government off-loaded transit and welfare costs to the city.

The 21st Century

The new century began with a renewal of the city's cultural inventory. At long last, the city got a purpose-built opera house, the **Four Seasons Centre for the Performing Arts,** which opened in 2006. Also, the **Royal Ontario Museum, the Art Gallery of Ontario,** the **Royal Conservatory of Music,** the **National Ballet School,** and the **Gardiner Museum of Ceramic Art** all underwent extensive renovations.

By 2008, Toronto had become North America's largest condo market, with towers going up all over the city. The trend continues unabated, and Toronto's future seems destined to become a city of high-rise living. In 2017, the market reached a new extreme: C$31 million for a penthouse suite in the Four Seasons hotel/condo tower.

Also on the rise are long-overdue efforts to reclaim the city's waterfront, where hotels, stadiums and theaters, bars, restaurants, and parks are being developed, including the whimsical and attractive **Sugar Beach,** at the foot of Jarvis Street (a reference to the Redpath sugar refinery, one of the last remaining industrial uses on the waterfront). There is no access to the lake from this beach, but a **new boardwalk** heads east to this burgeoning new East Bayfront neighborhood. The expansive **Sherbourne Common** is a welcome addition of green space on the site of a former industrial area—plus it claims to be the first park in Canada with a neighborhood-wide stormwater treatment facility as an integral part of its design. Even the Don River's banks have been rehabilitated, with trails to explore by foot or bike. Farther west, an old Ontario Place parking lot has been transformed into a lush, shoreline-hugging oasis called **Trillium Park.** The newly landscaped rolling hills are planted with dozens of native flowers and trees that hide serpentine paths that connect back to the main waterfront, the **Martin Goodman Trail.**

As the city grows, preservationists are stepping up to breathe life into Toronto's abandoned or derelict heritage structures. Three recent additions bridge past and present. **Artscape Wychwood Barns** is an artists' colony and local food resource center fashioned from streetcar repair barns from the 1920s. The **Toronto Railway Museum,** just a fly ball away from the Rogers Centre, is set in an old railroad roundhouse. And **Evergreen Brick Works** has transformed a quarry into a center for sustainable living.

Toronto continues to be very much a work in progress. As the skyline becomes more crowded, there's a noticeable increase in street life and energy as these rising condos fill up. The city's embrace of diverse and cosmopolitan cultures has helped shape what has become a dynamic and ever-changing scene.

ONTARIO LEGALIZES RECREATIONAL pot

In 2018, Ontario **legalized recreational marijuana.** Those 19 years of age and older can now smoke weed wherever tobacco smoking is permitted (this limits you to public places, private residences, and designated smoking hotel rooms). In Toronto, smoking isn't allowed in parks or on patios, and you could face serious fines if caught.

These days, the Province has become the biggest pot dealer in town. Ontarians get weed delivered right to their homes by placing orders on the online-only **Ontario Cannabis Store** (www.ocs.ca), which was the only place to buy weed legally at the time of legalization. As of April 2019, however, private pot retailers will be licensed to operate legally.

Prior to legalization, Toronto already had dozens of pot shops sprinkled about selling fancy toking devices, esoteric weed strains, and other Mary Jane–laced goodies, including chocolates, gummies, and more. Despite the city's old moniker, Toronto the Good, this town has been flouting the pot-smoking rules for years. Legalization just means that the variety and quantity of Amsterdam-like cafes will increase over the coming years.

TORONTO'S ARCHITECTURE

In the rush to grow up, the city demolished much of its past in the name of progress. Today Toronto is reinventing itself with bold new initiatives. As the city attempts to build up, rather than sprawl out, Toronto is emerging as a modern megacity, with almost half its residents residing in condos, not houses.

That said, the city's architectural history is still in evidence and made up of a wealth of architectural styles, from Gothic Revival churches to Romanesque civic buildings to the Modernist bank towers in the Financial District.

The Settling of York (1793–1837)

Early architecture in what was York and, after 1834, Toronto took its stylistic cues from England. The most notable style of the era was:

GEORGIAN These buildings are characterized by their formal, symmetrical design and by their classically inspired details, such as columns and pediments. There are few examples in Toronto, but an outstanding one is **Campbell House** at 160 Queen St. W. Built for Sir William Campbell in 1822 (he was a Loyalist and a chief justice of Upper Canada), it is currently a museum.

Early Victorian (1837–60)

The Victorian era in Toronto was a creative time in which many architectural styles were employed. There was a strong tendency to look at the styles of the past and reinterpret them for the present. The chief ones were:

GOTHIC REVIVAL This fanciful style emerged in England, reaching peak popularity in North America in the mid-19th century. Gothic Revival was inspired by medieval design, featuring pointed arches and windows, extensive ornamentation, and steeply pitched roofs; towers were often incorporated into the design. **St. James Cathedral** (p. 125), built between 1850 and 1853, is a perfect example of the style with its 93m-tall (305-ft.) spire and its Romantic-inspired stained-glass windows. **St. Michael's Cathedral;** the Toronto **Necropolis** (p. 132), a cemetery that was established in 1850; and **Hart House** (p. 118), at the University of Toronto, are further examples.

RENAISSANCE REVIVAL Buildings designed in this style tended to be large, impressive, and formal, with symmetrical arrangements of the facade, quoins (cornerstones that give an impression of strength and solidity), columns separating windows, and large blocks of masonry on the lowest floor. Toronto's **St. Lawrence Hall** (next to the St. Lawrence Market, p. 141), built in 1854, is a textbook example of Renaissance Revival.

Late Victorian (1860–1901)

Later in the Victorian period, Toronto was still being influenced by Britain, but the city was also becoming more original in its design:

RICHARDSONIAN ROMANESQUE Arguably old Toronto's most beloved architectural style. Toronto's Richardsonian Romanesque buildings were influenced by the American architect Henry Hobson Richardson. The style is immediately identifiable by its massive scale, rounded archways, decorative arcading, and large towers. The **Broadview and Gladstone hotels** are a Richardsonian Romanesque masterpiece, as is the **Old Toronto City Hall** (p. 22).

BAY-AND-GABLE Closely related to Gothic Revival architecture, this is a style that is considered unique to Toronto. It applies some of the decorative elements of Gothic Revival (such as sharp vertical lines) to single-family homes. Lots in 19th-century Toronto were oddly long and narrow, and the bay-and-gable style, with its steep roofs, large bay windows (often filled with stained glass), and extensive decorative gabling managed to fit into these lots perfectly. Excellent examples of bay-and-gable are found in **Cabbagetown,** as well as in the **Annex** and in **Little Italy.**

Early & Mid-20th Century (1901–70)

Toronto erected its first skyscraper in 1894—the Beard Building—but it has been demolished. In the first decades of the 20th century, the city became less interested in looking back at the past and more intrigued by the future. When the decision was made to create a new city hall in the 1950s, Torontonians voted down a classically designed city hall, eventually favoring a modern building based on the International Style (see below):

> ### Impressions
>
> *You build your stations like we build our cathedrals.*
>
> —The Prince of Wales, speaking at the opening of Toronto's Union Station in 1927

BEAUX ARTS Taking its name from the École des Beaux-Arts in Paris, this style was an idealization of classical Greek and Roman architecture. Toronto's most beloved example of Beaux Arts style is **Union Station** (p. 18), which was built between 1914 and 1920.

EARLY SKYSCRAPER The **Traders Bank Building,** which at 15 stories high was the tallest building in the British Commonwealth when it was completed in 1905, is one of the few still-standing skyscrapers from this era. It's located at the intersection of Yonge and Colborne.

INTERNATIONAL STYLE In the 1920s and 1930s, this was modern architecture. These stark, rectangular buildings were generally surfaced with glass and other lightweight industrial materials. The buildings were simple (at least, to the naked eye) in design. The **Toronto-Dominion Bank Tower,** at 66 Wellington St. W., was designed by Bauhaus director Ludwig Mies van der Rohe, perhaps the most famous of the Modernist architects. Completed in 1969, it is distinctive for its black steel structure and black-glazed glass.

Late 20th Century & Beyond (1970–Present)

Toronto architecture in the past 4 decades has veered from the postmodern to the eclectic. It's hard to group works together in a cohesive style, though they do share elements of whimsy and improbability. In the 1970s, a postmodern approach, in which classical or historical references were incorporated into the design of a building, became popular. There was a great deal of leeway in terms of the overall shape of a building, rather than using a simple rectangle. The **Toronto Reference Library** and the **Bata Shoe Museum** (p. 119), both designed by Toronto architect Raymond Moriyama, are two visually stunning counterpoints within walking distance of each other.

Toronto is basking in the afterglow of a cultural renaissance that saw major additions by leading architects to its key arts institutions over the past few years. The transformation elevated discussion in the public realm by adding controversy to the mix with some less-than-universally-accepted remakes of the city's beloved attractions.

Prime among them is Daniel Libeskind's crystal addition to the **Royal Ontario Museum** on Bloor Street. Love it or loathe it, it got people talking. Local boy Frank Gehry finally added his imprimatur to the cityscape with a favorable remake of the **Art Gallery of Ontario.** Another local, Jack Diamond, designed Canada's first purpose-built opera house, the **Four Seasons Centre for the Performing Arts,** whose exterior lights up University Avenue with its glass facade and whose interior provides wonderful sightlines and acoustics. And the newest addition, the **TIFF Bell Lightbox,** provides even more wattage to the Toronto International Film Festival with a gallery and year-round screening rooms on King Street West.

The **Sharp Centre for Design** (p. 184), which opened in 2005, still shocks many visitors. Best described as a checkerboard on colorful stilts, it was designed by English architect Will Alsop for the Ontario College of Art and Design and captures a sense of possibility and playfulness in contemporary architecture. (Alsop has since created two subway stations in the suburbs—Pioneer Village and Finch West—both of which feature cantilevered roofs, polished concrete, and playful pops of color.)

Other buildings appear frozen in time on the outside, but have been completely modernized inside, like **Maple Leaf Gardens.** Toronto's hockey shrine was at risk of being demolished after the Leafs decamped to the Scotiabank Arena, leaving the building vacant for over a decade. In 2012, Maple Leaf Gardens reopened after an unlikely duo—grocery chain Loblaws and Ryerson University—teamed up to preserve the Art Deco structure. The mixed-use facility is now Ryerson's new sports complex (yes, it still has an ice rink), with a grocery store on the street level.

The biggest trend in architecture in the city right now is one not always visible to the naked eye: sustainable design. LEED (Leadership in Energy and Environmental Design) buildings incorporate energy-saving systems such as green roofs, lake water to cool buildings instead of conventional air-conditioning, and new window glazing and shading techniques to prevent heat buildup. Some buildings on the vanguard of these principals include the **Evergreen Brick Works, One Cole** condominium in the renewed Regent Park, and new campus buildings at the **University of Toronto** and **George Brown College.**

Even City Hall, the Modernist marvel with a space-ship-style pod embraced by two curving towers, is being refashioned for these green-minded times with a wonderful garden on the elevated podium above the entrance.

Torontonians show up in films, television, music, and literature that's famous the world over, and their scientific, architectural, and political accomplishments have had a global impact. How many people on this list did you know were from Toronto?

- **Margaret Atwood** (b. 1939): Canada's most famous literary luminary is best known for her futuristic novel *The Handmaid's Tale*, which has been turned into a hugely successful small-screen series (filmed mostly in Toronto). Her body of work includes *The Edible Woman, The Robber Bride, Alias Grace,* and *Oryx and Crake.*

- **Jim Balsillie** (b. 1961) and **Mike Lazaridis** (b. 1961): Co-founders of Research in Motion, the firm in nearby Waterloo, Ontario, that invented the once-ubiquitous BlackBerry, the wireless handheld device. Both are billionaires.

- **Sir Frederick Banting** (1891–1941): Banting was the co-discoverer of insulin at the University of Toronto; in 1923, he was awarded the Nobel Prize for his life-saving research.

- **Samantha Bee** (b. 1969): The bawdy comedienne was a correspondent on *The Daily Show with Jon Stewart* before starting her own show *Full Frontal with Samantha Bee.*

- **John Candy** (1950–1994): The much-loved funnyman and Toronto native got his start in comedy with the local Second City troupe, playing a succession of crazy characters on "SCTV." In Hollywood, he made a succession of popular films that included *Only the Lonely, Uncle Buck,* and *Planes, Trains and Automobiles.* He was also a co-owner of the Toronto Argonauts football team.

- **Jim Carrey** (b. 1962): Before striking it rich in Hollywood with movies such as *The Mask, Ace Ventura: Pet Detective, Dumb and Dumber, The Truman Show,* and *Eternal Sunshine of the Spotless Mind,* Carrey lit up the stage at Toronto comedy clubs.

- **Michael Cera** (b. 1988): Hollywood's awkward straight man was born and raised in the suburb of Brampton, Ontario. His films include *Superbad, Juno,* and *Scott Pilgrim vs. the World,* and he appeared in the cult-hit television series *Arrested Development.*

- **David Cronenberg** (b. 1943): This director knows how to shock audiences—witness his 1996 film *Crash,* which explored violent injury fetishes and won the Jury Prize at the Cannes Film Festival. His eerie body of work includes *The Fly, The Dead Zone, Dead Ringers, Naked Lunch,* and *A History of Violence.*

- **Deadmau5** (b. 1981): The mouse ear–sporting EDM star Joel Zimmerman, better known as Deadmau5, is one of the few Toronto celebs who still call T.O. home. He can be seen driving around Toronto in his fleet of luxury cars. His Purrari, a Ferrari custom wrapped with Nyan cat, makes him particularly easy to spot.

- **Drake** (b. 1986): Maybe Aubrey Drake Graham shouldn't be on this list. He likely is the only famous person Toronto has produced who people actually realize is *from* Toronto. Drake is Toronto's number-one cheerleader (he's at most Raptors games) and has so much sway, he created a new nickname for Toronto overnight when he dropped the album *Views from the 6,* the cover of which features the pop star sitting forlornly atop the CN Tower.

- **Frank Gehry** (b. 1929): Arguably the world's most famous living architect, Gehry put Bilbao, Spain, on the map with the swooping titanium shape of its Guggenheim Museum.

In a more subdued way, Gehry refashioned the Art Gallery of Ontario to fit within the context of its residential neighborhood, where he grew up.

o **k-os** (b. 1972): His real name is Kevin Brereton, but he's better known as k-os in his work as a rapper, singer, songwriter, and producer. He frequently references places and events in Toronto in his songs.

o **K'naan** (b. 1978): This Somalia-born poet, rapper, and singer gained global exposure for writing "Wavin' Flag"—the anthem became synonymous with the 2010 FIFA World Cup of Soccer. K'naan (known off-stage as Keinan Abdi Warsame) continues to win over fans with songs about the immigrant experience in Canada.

o **Meghan Markle** (b. 1981): Yes, she's American, but the Duchess of Sussex calls Toronto her second home. Before Prince Harry popped the question, she lived in the Annex for 7 years while working as an actress on the Toronto-filmed series *Suits*. She visits regularly, since she's close friends with Canadian "royalty" Ben and Jessica Mulroney, whose children were among the bridesmaids and pageboys at the royal wedding.

o **Lorne Michaels** (b. 1944): Ever wonder why *Saturday Night Live* has featured so many Canadian performers? That may have had something to do with the fact that the show's creator was born and raised in Toronto. Michaels has also produced SNL-alum movies such as *Wayne's World* and *Baby Mama,* and TV shows including *30 Rock*.

o **Mike Myers** (b. 1963): Myers became a celebrity when he starred on *Saturday Night Live* from 1989 to 1994, playing a series of characters that included metal-head rocker Wayne Campbell and German aesthete Dieter. On the big screen, Myers has struck gold writing and starring in such films as *Wayne's World* and *Austin Powers* (and their respective sequels).

o **Mary Pickford** (1893–1979): Known in the Jazz Age as "America's Sweetheart," this Academy Award–winning actress was born and raised in Toronto. While she made some memorable films, including *Little Lord Fauntleroy* and *Coquette,* her most important role was of movie magnate: In 1919, Pickford, her husband Douglas Fairbanks, and Charlie Chaplin founded the United Artists film studio.

o **Christopher Plummer** (b. 1929): He's usually remembered as the dashing Baron Von Trapp in *The Sound of Music,* but this versatile actor has played every role imaginable in a film career spanning more than 50 years. Born in Toronto, the Shakespearean-trained Plummer has returned to his roots many times at the nearby Stratford Festival.

o **The Weeknd** (b. 1990): When not making tabloid headlines for feuding with Justin Bieber, hip-hop artist The Weeknd (a.k.a. Abel Makkonen Tesfaye) is busy taking over the charts and winning Grammys (he's banked three so far). The Scarborough native was groomed by Drake, who was in the audience at The Weeknd's first live performance, held at Toronto's Mod Club in 2011.

o **Neil Young** (b. 1945): Before skyrocketing to superstardom with Buffalo Springfield, Young played Yorkville's Riverboat Coffee House—a stage that had seen its share of big names including Joni Mitchell and Gordon Lightfoot. Young was born in Toronto, but Omemee (the town he grew up in) takes center stage in his oeuvre.

TORONTO IN POPULAR CULTURE

As a stand-in for large American cities, Toronto has fueled a busy film-production industry but done little to attract the curious, since its streets and skyline most always depict some other place. That's still the case overall, but the city's reputation as always a bridesmaid, never a bride (when it comes to movie stardom) eroded somewhat with its top billing in the film adaption of the *Scott Pilgrim* graphic-novel series. *Scott Pilgrim vs. the World* put Toronto landmarks (including Casa Loma and the since–knocked-down Honest Ed's) on the international silver screen.

As a city on the page, however, Toronto can claim a rich legacy. It's home to many of the country's most prolific and acclaimed writers, which might be the reason for its literary stardom.

Margaret Atwood's *The Robber Bride* pays homage to Toronto with a story that covers 3 decades of life in the city. Some of her other novels—*The Edible Woman, Cat's Eye, Alias Grace,* and *The Blind Assassin*—also use Toronto as a backdrop. *In the Skin of a Lion,* by Michael Ondaatje, the celebrated author of *The English Patient,* is a moving love story that brings the city's landmarks to life. Anne Michaels' best-selling debut novel *Fugitive Pieces* is an intimate portrayal of two Holocaust survivors grappling with their war-defined pasts against a Toronto backdrop. Carol Shields, the Pulitzer Prize–winning author who died in 2003, set her final novel, *Unless,* in Toronto's streets.

WHEN TO GO

Toronto is a city with four distinctive seasons. Autumn is a particularly good time to visit: The climate is brisk but temperate, the skies are sunny, the trees are a riot of color, and the cultural scene is in full swing. Another great time to see the city—if you don't mind a dusting of snow—is early winter in December, with holiday festivities for everyone. Spring is pretty, although rainy and cool days can make for a moody stay. Midsummer can be oppressive with heat, but the city has plenty of parks and other places to cool down (like the Toronto Islands). Really, the only time the city can seem unwelcoming is on a windy February day when the temperatures demand thick parkas and multiple layers. In fact, bone-chilling days are less frequent as the planet

---

Don't Forget the Sunscreen

Because of Canada's image as a land of harsh winters, many travelers don't realize that summer can be scorching. "The UV index goes quite high, between 7 and 10, in Toronto," says Dr. Patricia Agin of the Coppertone Solar Research Center in Memphis. A UV index reading of 7 can mean sunburn, so don't forget to pack sunscreen and a hat, especially if you're planning to enjoy Toronto's many parks and outdoor attractions.

warms: You could call it a boost for Torontonians and the city's visitors—at least, for now.

Never mind what the calendar says; these are Toronto's true seasons: **Spring** runs from late March to late May (though occasionally there's snow in April); **summer,** June to early September; **fall,** mid-September to mid-November; and **winter,** late November to sometime in March. The highest recorded temperature is 105°F (41°C); the lowest, –27°F (–33°C). The average date of the first frost is October 13; the average date of last frost is May 4. The windblasts from Lake Ontario can be fierce, even in June. Even in summer, bring a light jacket; brief, intense storms are common.

Toronto's Average Temperatures °F (°C)

	JAN	FEB	MAR	APR	MAY	JUNE	JULY	AUG	SEPT	OCT	NOV	DEC
HIGH	28 (–2)	29 (–2)	39 (4)	52 (11)	65 (18)	73 (23)	79 (26)	77 (25)	68 (20)	56 (13)	44 (7)	33 (1)
LOW	15 (–9)	15 (–9)	24 (–4)	35 (2)	45 (7)	54 (12)	60 (16)	58 (14)	50 (10)	39 (4)	31 (–1)	20 (–7)

Holidays

Toronto celebrates the following holidays: New Year's Day (January 1), Family Day (third Monday of February), Good Friday (March or April), Victoria Day (Monday on or before May 24), Canada Day (July 1), Civic Holiday (first Monday in August), Labour Day (first Monday in September), Thanksgiving (second Monday in October), Remembrance Day (Only banks and government offices close on November 11), Christmas Day (December 25), and Boxing Day (December 26).

Toronto Calendar of Events

JANUARY

Interior Design Show, Metro Toronto Convention Centre. Since 1999 design aficionados have been visiting this 3-day convention, which celebrates design and architecture with fascinating exhibits and interesting speakers. For details, go to https://toronto.interiordesignshow.com. Mid-January.

Winterlicious, citywide. Baby, it's cold outside, but Toronto's restaurants really know how to heat things up. Roughly 220 of the city's finest eateries offer prix-fixe lunch ($23–$33) and dinner menus ($33–$53). Late January through early February. **Note:** Bookings open early January; spots fill up fast at such hot-ticket restaurants as Canoe.

FEBRUARY

Canadian International AutoShow, Metro Toronto Convention Centre. Every year, almost 300,000 auto fanatics pilgrim here for a 10-day automobile show to ogle the futuristic alternative energy vehicles and souped-up exotics on display. For more, go to www.autoshow.ca.

Kuumba Festival, Harbourfront Centre. One of Toronto's longest-running festivals celebrating black history and the black community, Kuumba brings photographers, comedians, speakers and performers together. For details, visit www.harbourfrontcentre.com.

Lunar New Year Celebrations, various sites in the city. Festivities include traditional and contemporary performances of Chinese, Korean, and Taiwanese opera, dancing, music, and more. Harbourfront often has excellent performances throughout the 2-week fete. For more information on the lineup, visit www.harbourfrontcentre.com.

Rhubarb Festival, Buddies in Bad Times Theatre. Canada's longest-running new works festival has been putting Canada's most boundary-pushing theater in front of audiences for the past 4 decades. For details, go to www.buddiesinbadtimes.com.

MARCH

Blue Jays Season Opener, Rogers Centre. Turn out to root for your home-away-from-home team. For tickets, visit www.toronto.bluejays.mlb.com. Late March to early April.

Canada Blooms, Enercare Centre. At this time of year, any glimpse of greenery is welcome. Canada Blooms treats visitors to a sprawling series of indoor gardens and flower displays, seminars with green-thumb experts, and competitions. For information, visit www.canadablooms.com. Second or third week of March.

One-of-a-Kind Craft Show, Enercare Centre. More than 500 crafts artists from across Canada display their unique wares at this craft show. Visit www.oneofakindshow.com. Late March to early April; check for exact dates.

St. Patrick's Day Parade, downtown. Toronto's own version of the classic Irish celebration. Call ✆ 416/487-1566 or visit www.stpatrickstoronto.com. March 17. Some years held on different days.

Toronto ComiCon, Metro Toronto Convention Centre. Locals know that this 3-day fete has taken over the Convention Centre when X-Men, Pokemon, and Sailor Scouts are seen riding the streetcars next to the regular nine-to-fivers in suits. Anime lovers and fantasy geeks flock to Toronto for this event, which brings in celebs for panel discussions and fan meet-and-greets. For details, visit www.comicontoronto.com. Mid-March; check for dates.

Toronto Festival of Storytelling, various venues. This event celebrates international folklore with almost 100 storytellers imparting legends and fables from around the world. Go to www.torontofestivalofstorytelling.ca. Late March to early April; check for dates.

APRIL

Hot Docs Film Festival, citywide. North America's largest documentary festival has grown from a modest celebration to a 10-day extravaganza showcasing more than 240 films from some 40 countries. Visit www.hotdocs.ca. Late April to early May.

Shaw Festival, Niagara-on-the-Lake, Ontario. This festival presents the plays of George Bernard Shaw and his contemporaries, as well as modern works, too. Visit www.shawfest.com. Early April through first weekend of December.

Total Health Show, Metro Convention Centre. Founded in 1975, this 3-day event organizes panels and events with medical professionals, authors, alternative practitioners, organic farmers, and local chefs to talk about public and personal health issues. For information, visit www.totalhealthshow.com. Mid-April.

MAY

Canadian Music Week, citywide. Over the course of this 2-week music fest, more than 1,000 bands from Canada and abroad descend on the city to perform at 60 different venues. There's also an industry conference with workshops and talks. Go to http://cmw.net. Mid-May.

CONTACT Photography Festival, citywide. This annual month-long event shows the work of more than 500 Canadian and international photographers. For details, visit www.contactphoto.com. May 1 to 31.

Doors Open Toronto, citywide. Hugely popular, this weekend event invites city residents and visitors alike to tour some of Toronto's architectural marvels. Some of the more than 150 participating buildings aren't normally open to the public, and all are free of charge. Visit www.toronto.ca/doorsopen. Late May.

Inside Out, citywide. This 9-day LGBT film festival has nurtured plenty of new talent and supported many established artists. Check out www.insideout.ca. Late May through early June.

The Stratford Festival, Stratford, Ontario. Featuring a wide range of contemporary and classic plays, this festival always includes several works by Shakespeare. Check out the details at www.stratfordfestival.ca. Late April through early November.

Pedestrian Sundays, Kensington Market. Throughout the warmer months, Toronto's colorful Kensington Market is closed to cars. There are impromptu parades, buskers, snack vendors, and artists roaming the streets where cars once parked. Late May through to the end of October.

JUNE

Luminato, citywide. First launched in 2007, this 9-day arts festival has quickly become a highlight on the city's calendar. Featuring music, dance, theater, art, and educational programs, it really does offer something for the whole family. For information, visit www.luminato.com. Early to mid-June.

North by Northeast Festival, citywide. Known in the music biz as NXNE, this hot event features rock and indie bands at multiple venues around town. For information, visit www.nxne.com. Mid-June.

TD Toronto Jazz Festival, citywide. Jazz legends, ingénues, and up-and-comers perform at venues big and small. Recently, the 4-decade-old music fest centered around Yorkville, with pop-up stages and concerts taking place in funky bars and elegant halls such as Koerner Hall. Visit www.torontojazz.com for details. Late June/early July; dates vary.

Toronto International Dragon Boat Race Festival, Centre Island. More than 180 teams of dragon-boaters compete in the 2-day event, which commemorates the death of the Chinese philosopher and poet Qu Yuan. For information, visit www.dragonboats.com. Mid-June.

Pride Toronto, citywide. Celebrating Toronto's queer community, Pride features events, performances, symposiums, and parties. It culminates in an extravagant Sunday parade, one of the biggest in North America. For information, visit www.pridetoronto.com. Late June.

Toronto Fringe Festival, citywide. More than 100 troupes participate in this 11-day grassroots theater festival. Family-friendly works are presented under the FringeKinds! banner. For information, visit www.fringetoronto.com. Late June to early July.

JULY

Beaches International Jazz Festival, Queen Street East, east of Woodbine. Both local and international jazz artists turn out for this annual festival, which plays out over the month of July. All of the performances are free. For information, visit www.beachesjazz.com. Late July.

Canada Day Celebrations, citywide. Street parties, fireworks, and other special events commemorate the day. For information, visit the Tourism Toronto website at www.seetorontonow.com. July 1.

Caribbean Carnival, citywide. Toronto's version of Carnival, colloquially referred to as **Caribana,** transforms the city for an entire month. It's complete with traditional foods from the Caribbean and Latin America, ferry cruises, picnics, children's events, and concerts, and culminates with an epic parade. Visit www.torontocarnival.ca. Early July through early August.

Honda Indy, the Exhibition Place Street circuit. Formerly known as the Molson Indy, this is one of Canada's major races on the Indy-Car circuit. Away from the track, you'll find live music and beer gardens. For details, visit www.hondaindytoronto.com. Second weekend in July.

RBC Canadian Open, Hamilton Golf & Country Club, Hamilton. Formerly called the PGA Tour Canadian Open, Canada's national golf tournament has featured the likes of Greg Norman and Tiger Woods. Visit www.rbccanadianopen.com for more information. Early July.

Salsa In Toronto, citywide. This 3-week Latino festival culminates with Salsa on St. Clair, a riotous 2-day street party with dancing, vendors, and live music. See www.salsaintoronto.com for details. Mid-July; dates vary.

Summerlicious, citywide. It's just like January's Winterlicious event, except that you can dine alfresco. The prix-fixe menus are some of the best deals around. See www.toronto.ca for details and a complete list of participating restaurants. First 2 weeks of July.

Toronto Summer Music Festival, various venues in Toronto. Whether you're bonkers about baroque or ravished by the Russian composers, this celebration of classical music is sure to delight. There are concerts, master classes, lectures and more, all on a classic note, of course. Check it all out at www.torontosummermusic.com. Mid-July through early August.

AUGUST

BuskerFest, Woodbine Park. Jugglers, acrobats, mimes, magicians, musicians, and other street entertainers swarm this east end park for a 4-day stretch. For details, visit www.torontobuskerfest.com. Late August.

Canadian National Exhibition, Exhibition Place. It's an old-style touring amusement fair. One of the world's largest exhibitions, this 18-day extravaganza features midway rides, display buildings, free shows, and grandstand performers. The 3-day **Canadian International Air Show** (first staged in 1878) is a bonus. Visit www.theex.com for information. Mid-August through Labor Day.

Rogers Cup, Aviva Centre at York University. This international tennis championship is an important stop on the pro tennis tour. www.rogerscup.com. Early August.

Taste of the Danforth, Danforth Avenue, starting at Broadview Avenue. Toronto's Hellenic neighborhood puts on a weekend-long party in August. The major thoroughfare is transformed into a street party fueled by gyros, *loukoumades, spanakopita,* live music, and ouzo. Opa! Go to www.tasteofthedanforth.com. Early August.

SEPTEMBER

JFL42, citywide. This offshoot of the successful Montréal-based comedy festival **Just for Laughs** brings to town the world's top comics, alongside emerging talent. Visit www.jfl42.com for more information. Late September.

Toronto International Film Festival, citywide. The stars come out for one of the largest film festivals in the world. Almost 400 films from 80-plus countries are shown over 10 days. Outside of red-carpet season, award-winning artsy flicks are screened year-round at the TIFF Bell Lightbox. For information, go to www.tiff.net. Mid-September.

Word on the Street, Harbourfront Centre. This literati-loved event celebrates the written word with readings, discounted books and magazines, and children's events. Other major Canadian cities hold similar events throughout September. For information, visit www.thewordonthestreet.ca. Last weekend in September.

OCTOBER

International Festival of Authors, Harbourfront. Founded in 1980, this renowned 10-day literary festival is arguably the most prestigious in Canada. It draws the absolute top writers from around the world and at home, and has also proven to be an important stage for discovering new talent. Among the literary luminaries who have appeared are Salman Rushdie, Margaret Drabble, Thomas Kenneally, Joyce Carol Oates, A. S. Byatt, and Margaret Atwood. For information, visit www.readings.org. Late October through early November.

Nuit Blanche, citywide. Art takes over the street for this all-night art party. Installations pepper the town, and bars stay open until nearly dawn. For details, visit www.toronto.ca/explore-enjoy/festivals-events/nuit-blanche-toronto. Early October; some years late September.

Oktoberfest, Kitchener–Waterloo, about 1 hour from Toronto. This famed 9-day drinkfest features cultural events, plus a pageant and parade. For information, visit www.oktoberfest.ca. Mid-October.

Toronto Maple Leafs Opening Night, Scotiabank Arena. Torontonians love their hockey team, and opening night is always a big event. For tickets, visit www.nhl.com/mapleleafs/tickets. October.

NOVEMBER

Cavalcade of Lights, Nathan Phillips Square. This holiday celebration brings to life the skating rink at City Hall with a fantastic light show, performances, parties, and fireworks. Visit www.toronto.ca for more information. Late November through late December.

Royal Agricultural Winter Fair, Exhibition Place. The 12-day show is the largest indoor agricultural and equestrian competition in the world. Displays include giant vegetables and fruits, homey crafts, farm machinery, livestock, and more. A member of the British royal family traditionally attends the horse show; in 2010, it was a highlight when Prince Charles and Camilla cut the ribbon. Check www.royalfair.org for information. Mid-November.

Santa Claus Parade, downtown. A favorite with kids since 1905, it features marching bands, floats, clowns, and jolly St. Nick. American visitors are usually surprised that the parade's in November, but it's better than watching Santa try to slide through slush. For information, visit www.thesantaclausparade.com. Third Sunday of November.

Toronto Christmas Market, Distillery District. Toronto's pedestrian-only, redbrick Victorian neighborhood is transformed into a winter wonderland with a giant tree, singing elves, and a European-styled Christmas market, with vendors selling everything from pies to ornaments and slippers. For details, visit www.tochristmasmarket.com. Mid-November until late December.

DECEMBER

New Year's Eve at City Hall. In Nathan Phillips Square and in Mel Lastman Square in North York, concerts begin at around 10pm to usher in the countdown to the New Year. Visit www.toronto.ca for more information. December 31.

WHERE TO STAY IN TORONTO

4

Toronto's lodging landscape offers plenty of choice, from idiosyncratic inns to island B&Bs, conventional hotels to deluxe palaces. A recent boom in boutique properties has brought darling hotels such as the Kimpton St. George, the Broadview, and the Anndore House into the mix. On top of Toronto's 43,000 hotel rooms, the city's thousands of Airbnb rentals may offer a more authentic Torontonian experience for visitors. Whether you're a CEO who considers anything sub-penthouse to be slumming or you're on a student budget, Toronto is sure to have the right option to suit.

GETTING THE BEST DEAL

Want the secret for getting the hottest hotel deals in Toronto? **Visit during the chillier months.** Hotel prices here tend to rise in lockstep with the temperatures. Most of Toronto's big events (Pride, Caribana) also take place during the summer months, further pushing up the rates. The one exception is the town's eponymous film festival, TIFF, which draws star power from around the globe every autumn, filling up just about every hotel room in town. Do not try to negotiate a good deal around then (early Sept); hotel reservationists will laugh at you. I've heard them.

But do consider these other **money-saving tips:**

o Check out hotels that are **located away from big events** while you are visiting the capital. For instance, during TIFF, look at properties in Riverdale and Midtown. When the Leafs are playing home games at the Scotiabank Arena, consider hotels north of College Street, or west of Bathurst Street. In general, **hotels outside the downtown core** have lower rates.

o **Visit on a weekend.** Even popular hotels in the downtown core may be looking to fill rooms vacated by weekday business travelers. Ask about lower rates for weekend arrivals.

o **Check out money-saving package deals.** The website for the **Toronto Convention & Visitors Association** (www.seetoronto now.com) showcases packages with partnering hotels that include discounts on room rates, attractions, parking, and more. Plus, many online travel booking sites (Orbitz, Travelocity) offer air/ lodging packages that feature competitive room rates.

PRICE categories

Keep in mind that the prices in each review refer to the cost in Canadian dollars, using the following categories:

Expensive	C$290 and up
Moderate	C$150–$289
Inexpensive	Under C$150

- **Ask about special rates or other discounts.** You may qualify for substantial corporate, government, student, military, senior, trade union, or other discounts.
- **Book directly through the hotel.** You often get the best rate quoted. Also ask whether a room **less expensive than the first one** quoted is available.
- **Enroll in hotel loyalty programs.** It truly pays to enroll in the frequent-stay loyalty programs of big hotel chains. Members get perks like discounted rates, complimentary Wi-Fi, and early check-in and late check-out. You can also build points toward bonuses like a free night's stay or suite upgrades. And joining is free!
- **Subscribe to e-mail alerts.** Alerts from your favorite hotels or booking sites keep you informed of special deals.
- **Price match.** Many hotels will price-match deals you find online. Some will even give you extra bonuses like a free Wi-Fi upgrade.
- **Look into long-stay discounts.** If you're planning a long stay (at least 5 days), you might qualify for a discount. As a general rule, expect 1 night free after a 7-night stay. Likewise, if you come as part of a large group, you should be able to negotiate a bargain rate.
- Even if you haven't gotten the best deal possible on your room rate, **you can still save money on incidental costs.** Toronto hotels charge unbelievable rates for overnight parking—more than $45 a night at some hotels!—so if leave the car at home or find a parking lot. Generally speaking, the city-owned lots, marked with a big green "P," are the most affordable, but parking fines are a big money-maker for the city, so don't expect any handouts. More fees to avoid: Resist the **pricey minibar offerings,** and always ask if the hotel charges for **local calls.** Ask if the hotel charges a **resort fee,** and if so, what that covers.

Note: Ontario's **hotel tax** is a 4 percent on top of the 13 percent tax that people already pay for all goods and services.

DOWNTOWN WEST

This area encompasses a handful of neighborhoods, most of the city's more interesting hotels, and many top attractions, such as the CN Tower, AGO, and Scotiabank Arena.

Best for: A central location, plus the city's highest concentration of attractions. In a nutshell, it's all here. If you're on a shopping spree, big department stores and jewel-box boutiques are all around. If art, music, or theater is on

Toronto Hotels

DOWNTOWN NORTH
The Anndore House **13**
Annex Hotel **2**
Downtown Home Inn **14**
Four Seasons **12**
Kimpton Saint George
  Hotel **8**
Massey College **9**
The Only Backpackers Inn **15**
Victoria University at the
  University of Toronto **10**
Windsor Arms Hotel **11**

DOWNTOWN EAST
Bond Place Hotel **25**
Broadview Hotel **27**
Cambridge Suites Hotel **29**
Executive Hotel
  Cosmopolitan Toronto **30**
Hotel Victoria **31**
The Ivy at Verity **28**
Neill-Wycik Backpackers
  Hotel **16**
Pantages Hotel **24**
The Saint James Hotel **17**
Toronto Garden Inn B&B **26**

DOWNTOWN WEST
Baldwin Village Inn **19**
The Beverley Hotel **21**
Bisha **34**
Chelsea Hotel, Toronto **18**
Delta Hotels by Marriott
  Toronto **37**
The Drake Hotel **5**
Fairmont Royal York **36**
Gladstone Hotel **4**
Hôtel Le Germain
  Maple Leaf Square **38**
Hotel Ocho **20**
Hotel X **6**
Marriott Downtown at CF
  Toronto Eaton Centre **23**
Old Mill Toronto **1**
Planet Traveler Hostel **3**
The Rex Hotel **22**
Ritz-Carlton Toronto **35**
Shangri-La Hotel
  Toronto **33**
St. Regis **32**
Thompson Toronto **7**
Toronto Island Refuge **39**

BATHURST

Bloor St. W

PALMERSTON

Euclid Ave.

Manning Ave.

Herrick St.

Sussex Ave.

Harbord St.

Robert St.

Lippincott St.

Howland Ave.

Brunswick Ave.

Major St.

Ulster St.

College St.

Oxford St.

Augusta Ave.

Belleview St.

Nassau St.

KENSINGTON

Bathurst St.

Markham St.

Palmerston

Dundas St. W

Wales Ave.

Manning Ave.

Euclid Ave.

Claremont St.

Ave.

Alexandra
Park

ALEXANDRA
PARK

Gladstone
Ave.

Northcote Ave.

Beaconsfield
Ave.

Lisgar St.

Dovercourt St.

Argyle St.

Givins St.

Shaw St.

Crawford St.

Ossington
Ave.

Trinity-
Bellwoods
Park

Gore Vale Ave.

Bellwoods St.

Robinson St.

Carr St.

Queen St. W

Crawford St.

Shaw St.

Massey St.

Walnut Ave.

Niagara Ave.

Richmond St. W

Adelaide St. W

Portland St.

Dufferin St.

King St. W

Allan Lamport
Stadium Park

Liberty St.

Atlantic Ave.

Crawford St.

Strachan Ave.

King St. W

Stanley
Park

Tecumseth St.

Wellington St.

Niagara St.

Victoria
Mem. Sq.

Fraser Ave.

E. Liberty St.

Front St. W

Bathurst St.

Gardiner Expy.

Manitoba Dr.

Fort York

Exhibition
Place

Fleet St.

Fort York Blvd.

Coronation
Park

Remembrance Dr.

Princes Blvd.

Little
Norway
Park

Lake Shore Blvd. W

Ontario
Place

Budweiser
Stage

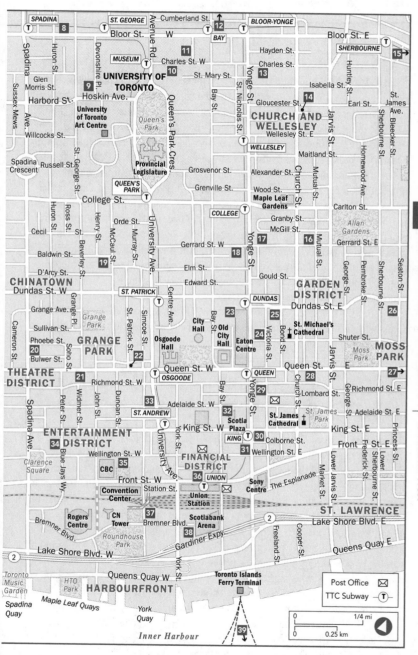

the agenda, you'll find it all at your doorstep. Ditto for great restaurants, trendy clubs, and top-drawer sports venues.

Drawbacks: All that activity can make this a busy and often noisy part of town.

Expensive

Bisha ★★ Millennial glitterati (aka influencers) flock to Bisha, which has become a nightlife hotspot with its two buzzy restaurants and glam bar, all located under its infinity pool–decked roof. According to design firm Studio Munge, the hotel aesthetic they created "celebrates the animals of the night that we are." Minimalism has been chucked to the curb; instead, Bisha embraces lavish maximalism: velvet walls, exotic marble, leather details, polished brass, and crown emblems aplenty, reminding visitors that this is a hotel tailored for modern royalty. The Gothic lobby, swathed in dark, reflective hues, has the feel of a very modish vampire queen's lair, and that nocturnal-bacchanalia motif is carried into the room decor. Stylish suites come with cloudlike beds swaddled in Frette linens. But this is not a hotel that invites guests to rest and recharge; it's a starting point for opulent adventures. Bathrooms are decorated to match the over-the-top theme with more marble, egg-shaped bathtubs, and heated floors. Luxe touches include toiletries by Stockholm's Byredo, minibars stocked with Veuve and CXBO chocolates, and a turndown service that delivers scrumptious rose-shaped Squish candies to make your dreams just a touch sweeter. Service is nightclub casual: No one holds the door for you, and that's worth noting since the double-height doors are a bear to push open with your suitcase in tow.

80 Blue Jays Way (at King St.). www.bishahoteltoronto.com. ⓒ **416/551-2800.** 96 units. $330–$370 double. Parking $50. Subway: St. Andrew, then streetcar 504 W to Blue Jays Way. Pets permitted. **Amenities:** 2 restaurants; 1 bar; outdoor pool; concierge; steam room; gym; room service; free Wi-Fi.

Fairmont Royal York ★★ Built by the Canadian Pacific Railroad in 1929, this massive hotel has 1,343 guest rooms and suites. A recent hotel-wide refresh has updated the rooms with flatscreen TVs and contemporary furnishings that are sleek, yet comfortable. Rose-scented Le Labo toiletries make every bathroom smell like a spa, even if the snug washrooms are slightly underwhelming. This is certainly not the case in the palatial suites, however. When visiting Toronto, Queen Elizabeth II takes up residence in the hotel's 16th-floor **Royal Suite,** which boasts two bedrooms, three washrooms, and a formal 12-seat dining room. Most of the hotel's weekday guests, though, are business travelers who appreciate the 2-minute underground stroll to Union Station. The Royal York is a popular spot for conferences and weddings thanks to its dozens of boardrooms and ballrooms, but my favourite amenity is open to all: The opulent, two-story lobby is all Art Deco splendor. The hotel pays attention to accessibility, and some guest rooms have been specially designed for wheelchair users, the hearing impaired, and the visually impaired. The hotel is also a leader in eco-friendly initiatives. Not only are the faucets, lights, and laundry facilities optimized for maximum efficiency, but guest-room amenities are donated to Clean the World, an organization that sanitizes and recycles hotel soaps, shampoos, and conditioners and then distributes them to homeless shelters across Canada.

100 Front St. W. (at York St.). www.fairmont.com/royalyork. ✆ **416/368-2511.** 1,343 units. $250–$319 double. Packages available. Parking $59. Subway: Union. Pets permitted. **Amenities:** 5 restaurants; 2 bars/lounges; babysitting; concierge; gym; hot tub; skylit indoor pool; children's wading pool; sauna; steam room; massage services; room service; business center; Wi-Fi $16/day (free for Le Club loyalty program members).

Hôtel Le Germain Maple Leaf Square ★★

The second Toronto outpost of the Quebec-based boutique hotel chain Le Germain has doubled down on its sporty, Scotiabank Arena–adjacent location. Designer Lemay Michaud's jock-approved theme is palpable in the corridors (accent lights locked to the home team's colors). Inside the rooms, the sports motif is still subtly present: Above every bed hangs photographer Matthew Plexman's gigantic black-and-white prints of muscled Leaf and Raptor players working out. The bedrooms are inviting and bright, fitted with ultra-soft bamboo-cotton sheets and featuring waterfall showerheads and sumptuous beds. The brand's flair is evident throughout, although the look is more postindustrial, with painted concrete walls and balconies. It's a perfect location for anyone with tickets to the big game (some rooms even face a giant screen over the Scotiabank Arena's entrance), but if you're not a fan, the frenetic game-time energy here might not be for you. Le Germain is particularly excellent at catering to families, providing pint-sized guests with everything from miniature robes to stuffed animals and bath toys. *Tip:* If you find a lower rate online, contact the hotel and they'll pledge to beat that rate by 10 percent.

75 Bremner Blvd. (at York St.). www.germainmapleleafsquare.com. ✆ **416/649-7575.** 167 units. $280–$380 double. Parking $49. Subway: Union Station. Pets permitted. **Amenities:** Lounge/bar; babysitting; concierge; gym; room service; free Wi-Fi.

Hotel X ★★★

This freshly completed 28-story hotel has some of the best amenities in the city. Jocks will appreciate the spectacular health club with high-tech machines that count reps while giving performance feedback. The three-story complex also boasts a spinning studio, two yogic sanctuaries (one hot, one not), a saltwater pool, nine squash courts, four tennis courts, a golf simulator, and a heap of motivating classes. If that isn't enough, a second heated saltwater pool is situated on the top of the main hotel tower; it's half outdoors, half indoors, and entirely fabulous. Parents, meanwhile, can drop the children off at the **Kids Play Centre** for a while—perhaps to make use of that fab gym. Wee ones (as young as 3 months) will be lavished over, while the older set can play ball hockey, basketball, and video games. Families also make great use of the 56-set screening room, where G-rated flicks are enjoyed with popcorn. Other stand-out amenities include an onsite **art gallery** dedicated to painter Neil Dankoff. The entire hotel is decorated with over 750 stunning Neil Dankoff landscape photos, so wandering the halls feels a bit like walking through an extended exhibition. Rooms have some of the best views in Toronto (and the floor-to-ceiling windows let you take it all in). To the east, downtown twinkles sans obstruction; to the south, Lake Ontario looks close enough to dive into. Although the hotel is well located for those with tickets to events at BMO Field or the Budweiser Stage, being situated on the Exhibition Place grounds means downtown is a 15-minute GO ride away. To make your stay seamless, Hotel X has two Audi SUVs on call to chauffeur guests (on a first come, first served basis) around downtown.

111 Princes' Blvd. (at Lakeshore Blvd.). www.hotelxtoronto.com. ✆ **647/943-9300.** 404 units. $275–$400 double. Parking $30. Subway: Union, then streetcar 509 W to Manitoba Dr., S on Strachan Ave., W on Princes' Blvd. Pets permitted. **Amenities:** 2 restaurants; 2 lounges; 2 cafes, 5 bars; 2 pools; spa; steam room; 7 squash courts; golf simulator; 4 indoor tennis courts; hot yoga studio; spinning studio; Pilates reformer studio; art gallery; cinema; gift shop; historical site; Kids Play Centre; nano-brewery and beer garden; room service; screening room; spa; free Wi-Fi.

The Ritz-Carlton ★★   This is Ontario's first Ritz, and the brand's reputation for elegance and five-star service does not disappoint. From the moment you enter the dramatic lobby, the ambition to impress is all around. Sip a sophisticated cocktail in one of the lounges, and luxuriate in the spacious rooms. The excellent on-site **spa** has an adjoining lap pool and a polished gym, too. To gild the lily, upgrade your reservation to Club status, and you'll get access to the 20th-floor lounges, which include a generous breakfast, hors d'oeuvres, and alcoholic beverages as well as a designated Club member concierge. Although the service is top-tier, the too-beige rooms have a dated look (there hasn't been a much in terms of updating since the hotel opened in 2011). The views of Lake Ontario, though, remain intact, at least for now, until more new high-rises block the vistas.

181 Wellington St. W. www.ritzcarlton.com. ✆ **416/585-2500.** 267 units. $520–$700 double. Parking $50. Subway: Osgoode. Pets permitted. **Amenities:** 2 restaurants; bar; concierge; gym; indoor lap pool; room service; spa; free Wi-Fi.

Shangri-La Hotel Toronto ★★★   Zhang Huan's breathtaking sculpture *Rising* defines the glittering exterior of this 66-story hotel-condo. The abstract, glass-straddling dragon swarmed by doves is part of the building; these peace-bestowing birds continue into the lobby, denoting a tonal shift. Inside, the Shangri-La is a peaceful respite from the tumult of the city. The chic lobby, with its extra-long fireplace, is the place to relax over live music. The Shangri-La brings Hong Kong panache to Toronto, showcasing over 480 Wang Xu Yuan lithographs, as well as museum-caliber vitrines containing priceless ancient artifacts. Design details, too, pull on an Asian theme: Cherry blossoms adorn wallpaper and consoles, while Chinese tracery patterns are found on doors, knobs, and carpets. The furniture, too, looks Qing Dynasty regal. Opulent details include raw silk-upholstered walls, white-oak millwork, and marble from around the world—the iron-red-striped black marble from Madagascar is particularly mesmerizing. Rooms are amply sized (starting at 49 sq. m/525 sq. ft.) and come equipped with every possible technological bell and whistle. Drapes, lights, and heating can be controlled through the wall-mounted panels or via the tablet, which can also be used to summon an ice bucket, checkout quickly, or order a dog walker. Bedside clocks come with all possible charging dongles and Bluetooth connectivity. Sun-drenched marble bathrooms are spectacular, but the best luxuriating happens on the fifth floor. There, you'll find the Turkish-inspired **Miraj Hammam** and the spectacular glass-encased saltwater pool. Between the lush tropical plants, waterfall feature, and private cabanas, the place feels more Bali beach resort than downtown Toronto.

188 University Ave. (at Adelaide St.). www.shangri-la.com/toronto. © **647/788-8888.** 202 units. $420–$580 double. Valet parking $50/24 hrs. Subway: Osgoode. Pets permitted. **Amenities:** 3 restaurants; 1 bar; 1 lounge; gym; yoga studio; spa; pool; hot tub; steam room; sauna; concierge; room service; babysitting; dog walking; free Wi-Fi.

St. Regis ★★★ The original St. Regis opened in 1904 in New York's Midtown neighborhood. Eight years later, the hotel's founder, John Jacob Astor IV, would die on the *Titanic,* sinking to the bottom of the Atlantic with the full knowledge that he was the richest man on a sinking unsinkable ship. To this day, the hotel still performs rituals adored by the Astors—perhaps more than any other luxury hotel brand, the St. Regis places an emphasis not only on keeping its traditions alive, but honoring its founders. Champagne is opened with a sabre and pomp for the daily sunset sabrage; on weekend afternoons high tea is served; and each property hosts Midnight Suppers. Bedding, towels, and robes are adorned with a diamond pattern, a nod to Caroline Astor's jewel fixation. Although the St. Regis heritage defines the brand, this is its first foray into the Canuck market, and many of the design details are nods to either Toronto or Canada. The bronze fireplace in the **Astor Lounge,** for instance, is inspired by the character of Queen Street, while the ceiling feature in the lobby references Ontario's topography. One thing St. Regis guests can't buy is time, which is why butlers are there to make guest stays effortless. Butlers unpack luggage, press clothes, arrange transport, obtain impossible reservations, and take care of any of the annoying planning that eats away at the day. At the end of all guests' stays, the butlers will even pack guests' bags for them. The hotel has fast become a favorite with the A-list set, who rave about the 189-sq. m (2,035-sq. ft.) John Jacob Astor Suite. Even standard rooms are a generous 51 sq. m (550 sq. ft.). All rooms have touch-control panels that automate everything from the lights to the curtains at the swipe of a finger. Pillowtop mattresses are swaddled in Italian linens. Bathrooms in the suites come with luxurious tubs and mirror-set flatscreens; some even boast excellent views. Leaving the comfort of your ultra-luxe room to dine in the 31st-story restaurant **Louix Louis** might seem like an onerous task, but trust me, it's worth it. The restaurant's dark spirit list is one of the deepest in the city, with over 750 bottles on offer, and the Franco-American food is top-tier.

325 Bay St. (at Adelaide St.). www.marriott.com/hotels/travel/yyzxr-the-st-regis-toronto. © **416/306-5800.** 258 units. $480–$700 double. $50 parking. Subway: King. Pets permitted. **Amenities:** Restaurant; cafe/bar; lounge; babysitting; butler service; concierge; gym; pool; hot tub; room service; spa; free Wi-Fi.

FAMILY-FRIENDLY hotels

○ **Chelsea Hotel, Toronto.** This perennial family favorite lures 'em in with a **Family Fun Zone,** a multi-room play area with live bunnies, a video arcade, and the only indoor waterslide in downtown Toronto. Family-specific suites have been designed with creative corners where kids can draw and play. These spacious suites—they start at 56 sq. m (600 sq. ft.)—also come with private balconies where parents can take a moment to themselves while the wee ones are occupied. See p. 65.

○ **Four Seasons Hotel Toronto.** A hop and a skip from the Royal Ontario Museum, this hotel has its own attractions, including a grotto-like pool that makes you feel like you're in Tahiti . . . even in February. Upon arrival, room service brings the kids complimentary cookies and milk. The concierge and housekeeping staff can also arrange babysitting services. See p. 73.

○ **Hotel X.** You can play together in one of the two saltwater pools or drop off the tykes for babysitting at the **Kids Play Centre,** a 279-sq.-m (3,000-sq.-ft.) facility with a basketball court, multiple gaming stations, and a craft corner. The high school set who no longer need nannying will enjoy the TenX health club facilities where they can take tennis and squash lessons. In the evenings, there are frequent family-friendly movie screenings in the cinema. See p. 61.

○ **The Ritz-Carlton.** The Ritz has some of the most creative kids programming out of any hotel in Toronto. The **Ritz Kids Night Safari,** for instance, sets up a tent in the suite, which comes with a lion plush toy, an on-theme activity book, and a night light, so that the little ones can imagine they're out camping in the wilds of the Okavango Delta. Children with a culinary bent might prefer the **Culinary Creators Experience.** For this, budding Gordon Ramsays are invited into the Ritz-Carlton kitchens, where they get to help create a liquid nitrogen ice cream sundae, which they then get to eat, of course. See p. 62.

○ **Le Germain Maple Leaf Square.** This boutique Canadian chain remains true to its superior standard of thoughtful service, even for pint-sized guests, with special touches such as child-sized bathrobes and special linens with kid-friendly patterns. See p. 61.

Thompson Toronto ★ This boutique New York import made a splash when it opened in Toronto in 2010. Topped by an infinity pool with an enviable CN Tower view, the Thompson quickly became the place to celebrate. Despite hosting many a glitzy fete, it wasn't until 2016 that the Thompson's status as *the* celebratory hotel was cemented. That was the year the NBA made the Thompson its official hotel for All-Star Weekend. Fans swarmed the hotel hoping to spy LeBron in his 5XL Thompson robe, but King James was likely too busy playing pool with pal Chris Paul in the penthouse's games room to sign autographs. Even standard rooms are chic, yet comfortable. The service is attentive, but not cloying, and the King West location, at the epicenter of

Toronto's clubbing district, is a welcome launching point for seeing the groovier parts of the city. It's also a short walk from the theater district.

550 Wellington St. W. (at Bathurst St.). www.thompsonhotels.com. © **888/550-8368** or 416/640-7778. 105 units. $230–$350 double. Valet parking $50. Subway: St. Patrick, then streetcar 505 W to Bathurst St. Pets permitted. **Amenities:** 2 restaurants; bar; lounge; babysitting; concierge; dog walking; gym; outdoor pool; room service; free Wi-Fi.

Moderate

The Beverley Hotel ★ The Beverley is so small that when you Google "pod hotels Toronto," this is a top hit. Despite its Lilliputian dimensions—the whole place weighs in at a whopping 669 sq. m (7,200 sq. ft.)—this is no pod property. With its fetching interior design, welcoming staff, and convenient Queen West location, the teeny Beverley is keen to prove that bigger isn't always better. This 18-room hotel attracts an international crowd that's unphased by petite rooms—the largest of which, cheekily named the XL room, maxes out at 30 sq. m (322 sq. ft.). Architect Steven Fong's sleek masculine aesthetic makes the most out of tight layouts. Flatscreens descend from the ceiling, while headboards decked out with black-and-white Queen West graphics do double-duty as art pieces. Volia! Tablets are found in every room and act as digital concierges plugging you into the city.

335 Queen St. W. (at Beverley St.). www.thebeverleyhotel.ca. © **416/493-2786.** 18 units. $190–$230 double. No on-site parking, but $25 for a nearby lot with in-out privileges. Subway: Osgoode, then streetcar 501 W to John St. **Amenities:** Restaurant/bar; concierge; free Wi-Fi.

Chelsea Hotel, Toronto ★ For Toronto's youngest tourists, the Chelsea is a favorite spot to stay when visiting the city. The four-story, 50m (130-ft.) corkscrew waterslide is a major draw, while parents appreciate the **Kid Centre,** which provides supervised activities (painting, playtime with the resident rabbits, educational games) for toddlers through preteens. The high-school set has a space to themselves, too, kitted out with pool tables, video games, and foosball. Grown-up amenities include **Deck 27,** an adults-only lounge with a panoramic view of Toronto. Rooms are basic and serviceable, if a touch dated.

33 Gerrard St. W. (at Yonge St.). www.chelseatoronto.com. © **416/595-1975.** 1,590 units. $150–$210 double. Additional adult $20. Children 17 & under stay free in parent's room. Parking $35. Subway: College. Pets permitted. **Amenities:** 2 restaurants; bar; babysitting; children's center; concierge; gym; hot tub; 2 pools (1 for adults only); sauna; free Wi-Fi.

Delta Hotels by Marriott Toronto ★★ This soaring, 46-story skyscraper was completed in 2014, the first purpose-built high-rise hotel to join Toronto's skyline in decades—until Hotel X stole this distinction in 2018. Although the brand may be American, Delta's new hotel celebrates all things Canada. The art, for example, is 100 percent Canuck: Pieces by Aleksandra Rdest, Jennifer McGregor, Hyun Chul Kim, and Teresa Aversa grace the walls. The public spaces local touches as well. A colorful Toronto mural spans the length of the equally vibrant lobby. Even the event rooms are named after

Toronto neighborhoods. Fresh, modern rooms with floor-to-ceiling windows are spacious, clean, and bright. Those who love to luxuriate in bubble baths will appreciate the corner units with deep soaker tubs that overlook the lake below.

75 Lower Simcoe St. (at Bremner Blvd.). www.marriott.com/yyzdl. © **416/849-1200.** 459 units. $220–$290 double. Parking $45. Subway: Union. Pets permitted. **Amenities:** Restaurant; bar; hot tub; pool; room service; free Wi-Fi.

The Drake Hotel ★★   The Drake is better known for its restaurant, rooftop bar, and subterranean music venue (the **Drake Underground**) than the guest rooms above. Nevertheless, solo travelers and couples appreciate the snug but cleverly designed rooms, where open-concept layouts make the most of the scant square footage. Exposed bathrooms are separated from the sleeping area by frosted glass. The artsy Drake is brimming with art installations, such as Luke Siemens' *Untitled Contraception*, which is hidden on the third-floor rooftop, visible only through a lone window. Trendy locals think of the Drake less as a hotel than a destination to dine, drink, dance, and listen to music-scene up-and-comers. In fact, this is one hotel where you're more likely to meet city residents than other visitors. *Note:* The Drake is currently under expansion with plans to open 32 more rooms by 2020.

1150 Queen St. W. (at Beaconsfield Ave.). www.thedrakehotel.ca. © **416/531-5042.** 19 units. Limited free parking available. $209–$270 double. Subway: Osgoode, then streetcar 501 W to Beaconsfield Ave. **Amenities:** 2 restaurants; cafe; 2 bars; access to local health club; free bicycle rental; free Wi-Fi.

The Gladstone Hotel ★★   This lovely Victorian redbrick hotel, opened in 1889, is the longest continually operating hotel in the city. Those first guests probably wouldn't know what to make of the arty offerings of the Gladstone today. When artist Christina Zeidler and her architecturally inclined family (her father, Eb, designed the Eaton Centre and Ontario Place) took over in 2005, they transformed the place while preserving its heritage features, including the charming birdcage elevator. The hip public rooms are now a hive of cultural activity, with offerings ranging from burlesque shows to indie bands, and the **Melody Bar** hosts the city's most colorful karaoke. No two rooms here are alike; artists have been given free reign over the decor. Epicureans will love Bob Blumer's food-decorated suite, outfitted with images of doughnuts, the Pillsbury DoughBoy, and Mr. Peanut as well as a mini kitchen quipped with a bar set and panini press; while pointillists will love Leif Harmsen's Pixel Ceiling. If contemporary art isn't your thing, the Victorian Billio room, furnished with the Gladstone's original antiques, might be a perfect fit. *Note:* If you're a light sleeper, this may not be the place for you.

1214 Queen St. W. (at Gladstone Ave.). www.gladstonehotel.com. © **416/531-4635.** 37 units. $200–$239 double. Parking $25. Subway: Osgoode, then streetcar 501 W to Gladstone Ave. **Amenities:** Restaurant; cafe-bar; access to local health club; free Wi-Fi.

Hotel Ocho ★   In 2012, 110 years after this textile factory was built, the four-story building was completely transformed from an industrial workplace into a fetching 12-room hotel. The reno brought the place back to its studs, but kept the brick-and-beam charm intact. Sun-drenched rooms look over

Chinatown, outfitted with simple-yet-timeless furnishings from design firm Dialogue 38. Bathrooms done up in dark granite are a nice contrast to the white-washed rooms. The onsite restaurant is a popular spot for weddings (the industrial-chic backdrop being de rigueur for Pinterest-loving brides these days). If you're staying on a weekend, ask whether any nuptials are planned during your stay—you may find the inconvenience of being pushed out of the common areas irksome. Hotel Ocho is good-value booking during the week-days. Despite being incredibly centrally located (the hotel is serviced by two streetcar lines, and is a stone's throw from both the AGO and Kensington Market), the area is fairly quiet at night, save for the careening streetcars.

195 Spadina Ave. (at Pheobe St.). www.hotelocho.com. © **416/593-0885.** 12 units. $160–$260 double. No parking on premises, municipal lots nearby. Subway: Spadina, then streetcar 510 S to Queen St. W. **Amenities:** Restaurant-bar; free Wi-Fi.

Marriott Downtown at CF Toronto Eaton Centre ★ It's a shopa-holic's dream: a hotel in a mall. And not just any mall, but downtown's mega shopping complex, the **Eaton Centre.** Because of its location, this is a fine choice for determined sightseers. This hotel duly caters to the tourist crowd: The knowledgeable concierges can help facilitate day-trip planning and other activi-ties. One caveat is that the area immediately surrounding the Eaton Centre is pickpocket heaven. On the upside, it's always busy in this neighborhood, so you won't want for company. Also, in summer, nearby **Yonge-Dundas Square** (p. 163) offers summer-time open-air concerts and films.

525 Bay St. (at Dundas St.). www.marriott eatoncentre.com. © **416/597-9200.** 461 units. $170–$300 double. Parking $36. Subway: Dundas. **Amenities:** Res-taurant; lounge; concierge; health club; hot tub; indoor rooftop pool; room service; Wi-Fi $11/day but free for Mar-riott Rewards members.

> **For Travelers in Need**
>
> If you should suddenly find yourself without a place to stay in Toronto, call the **Travellers' Aid Society of Toronto** (www.travellersaid.ca; © **416/366-7788**). The organization can help you book last-minute accommodations and can also assist in crisis situations. Travellers Aid maintains a booth at Union Station.

Inexpensive

Baldwin Village Inn ★★ If only there were more small, affordable, family-run hotels in Toronto like the Baldwin. This charming, friendly bed-and-breakfast is located on the equally charming Baldwin Street, steps away from trendy Queen West, Kensington, and Chinatown. It's a historic, con-verted house with six rooms that are well-cared for; bathrooms are shared, and there's a homey eat-in kitchen and a small garden in back. Reservations are a must. The owners, Roger and Tess, have four other inns scattered about the downtown, each with its own charms, and some equipped for long stays. See the inventory here: **www.urbannorthinans.com**.

9 Baldwin St. (at McCall St.). www.baldwininn.com. © **416/591-5359.** 6 units. $100–$125 double. Extra person $15. Rates include breakfast. Subway: St. Patrick. **Ameni-ties:** Lounge; free Wi-Fi.

Planet Traveler Hostel ★ Canada's most eco-conscious hostel is located deep in the heart of historic Kensington Market and steps from Little Italy with sleek, clean rooms and attractive common areas. You can chill out and enjoy the stunning view from the rooftop terrace or join in with one of the nightly communal activities designed to allow the solo traveler to easily make new friends and lasting memories. Planet Traveler employs a variety of environmentally friendly methods such as geothermal heat transfer and solar power to let you explore one of North America's most vibrant cities without having to worry about your carbon footprint.

357 College St. (at August Ave.). http://theplanettraveler.com. ✆ **647/352-8747.** 15 6-bed dorms, 11 private rooms. Dorm beds from $44/dorm bed; private rooms from $93. Rates include continental breakfast. Parking $10. Subway: Osgoode, then streetcar 506 W to Augusta. **Amenities:** Lounge; rooftop bar; computers; coin-operated laundry; free Wi-Fi.

The Rex Hotel ★ Light sleepers should not even consider a night at this hotel, located atop one of the city's most revered jazz and blues clubs. Every week, two dozen or so different acts grace the stages below, and the sultry

THE SKINNY ON short-term rentals

Taking the lodging world by storm, short-term vacation rentals—**Airbnb** (www.airbnb.ca), **Flip Key** (www.flipkey.com), **HomeAway** (www.homeaway.ca), and **VRBO** (www.vrbo.com)—offer thousands of unique options in Toronto for travelers looking to experience living like a local. It's particularly valuable for visitors interested in immersing themselves in neighborhoods outside the downtown core, like the Danforth, Roncesvalles, Leslieville or Parkdale. Options range from renting a room in someone's apartment to letting out entire Victorian homes. Airbnb even has the option to book with a "Superhost"—hosts who are recognized for the extraordinary experiences they provide for their guests—which can be like having your own personal tour guide.

These short-term rentals are great for visitors who want a more intimate and authentic Toronto experience—and can also be a great way to save money, especially if your rental has self-catering facilities. On the down side, the boom of platforms such as Airbnb has placed a great strain on Toronto's long-term rental stock (rents are at an all-time high, with vacancies hovering below 1 percent). As a result, Toronto's city council has sought to put restrictions on short-term rentals. The measures would limit how many days a year a home can be listed for rent and would also limit what types of domiciles can be rented out. Currently, these reforms are working their way through the courts, with a verdict expected by late summer 2019.

Note: Many condo boards have moved to ban Airbnb and its ilk. This can cause some awkwardness for vacationers should they find themselves renting in a building with tensions brewing between vacationers and residents. If you're looking to stay in a condo building, ask upfront if short-term stays are allowed—you don't want to feel as if you're being forced to tiptoe around.

Tip: Airbnb sets itself apart from the short-term-rental herd by offering "Experiences" as well as rentals. Experiences offer unique, one-of-a-kind outings that include everything from photography lessons to dive-bar crawls.

sounds travel up (it's particularly noisy in the rooms with shared bathrooms). The postage-stamp-sized accommodations are clean, however, and decently upkept, and the staff are top-drawer humans: happy to help with a heavy bag or snag a coveted dinner reso, and genuinely keen to know how your day is going. Although the noise sounds like a drawback, the Rex is ideal for night owls and music lovers who need a budget-friendly place to lay their heads. The frivolity below simmers down by the witching hour, earlier on weekdays. The Queen West location means the AGO, top galleries, and cool neighborhoods are all within walking distance, and the onsite music is a delightful way to kick off a night on the town.

194 Queen St. W. (at University Ave.). www.therex.ca. © **416/598-2475.** 30 units. $115–$155 double. Subway: Osgoode. **Amenities:** Restaurant; lounge; concierge; free Wi-Fi.

Toronto Island Refuge ★★   For a memorable, out-of-the ordinary stay, consider a few nights at this darling bed-and-breakfast on the Toronto Islands. The cottage community of Algonquin's Island is just a 10-minute ferry ride from downtown, but it feels worlds away from the urban tumult. The alluring amenities are the islands themselves: sandy beaches, clay tennis courts, and acres upon acres of lush parkland. Toronto Island Refuge is one of the few year-round B&Bs here. The two sunny bedrooms are located at the back of the owners' home, and are decently private. They come with a shared bathroom, a kitchenette, and a promise from the owners not to rent out the second room, even if you only end up needing the single bed. Remember if you're out late on the mainland, the last ferry back to Ward's Island departs around 11pm. If you miss it, you'll have to hire a water taxi to get back to the island.

18 Omaha Ave. (on Algonquin Island). www.refugeonti.com. © **416/203-1023.** 2 units. $145–$180 double. Ferries leave from docks at the bottom of Bay St. Subway: Union, then streetcar 509/510 to Queen's Quay. No parking; cars not permitted on the Toronto Islands. **Amenities**: Free Wi-Fi.

DOWNTOWN EAST & THE EAST END

The east end is on the rise with an evolving strip of cutting-edge design and furniture stores, the attractive Distillery District, historic Corktown, and well-trod Little India and the Danforth. East of the Don River, Riverdale and the Danforth offer visitors a chance to see Toronto's quieter, neighborly side.

Best for: Exploring off the beaten path.

Drawbacks: Things tend to be more spread out here, so be prepared to travel to eat, play, and sleep.

Expensive

The Broadview Hotel ★★   Built in 1891 as the offices for Dingman's soap factory, this handsome Richardson Romanesque building has taken on many permutations over its centuries-spanning history. It spent the last few decades hidden under sun-bleached ads for the strip club that occupied the space. After a 3-year gut job preserved the historic exteriors and completely modernized the interiors, the ex-flophouse is unrecognizable. Inside are cheeky nods toward the building's past: pinup-girl wallpaper in the washrooms, art installations made from the building's old fire escapes, and the old neon NO VACANCY sign that illuminates the rooftop terrace. The guest rooms are done up with bespoke furniture that draws inspiration from a mishmash of 20th-century styles. Atop the minibars, which are stuffed with local craft beers and artisanal snacks, sits a turntable with a dozen albums, ranging from Miles Davis to Caribou. The glass-pyramid addition, which created a seventh floor atop the building, offers one of Toronto's best sunset views, looking west onto the silhouetted skyline. Locally crafted, natural bath products by Graydon Skincare make bath time glorious.

106 Broadview Ave. (at Queen St. E.). www.thebroadviewhotel.ca. © **416-362-8439.** 58 units. $285–$350 double. No on-site parking. Pets permitted. Subway: Broadview, then streetcar 501 S to Queen. **Amenities:** 2 restaurants; cafe-bar; rooftop bar; babysitting; business center; room service; free Wi-Fi.

The Ivy at Verity ★★   Tucked into the top floor of a restored 1850s chocolate factory, this jewel-box boutique hotel consists of just four rooms. Each of the spacious suites is luxuriously appointed with ultra-comfy Hastens handcrafted beds, supple Rivolta Carmignani linens, and a private terrace overlooking the charming courtyard of **George,** the excellent French restaurant adjoining the hotel. Bathrooms are equally opulent, with soaking tubs, heated floors, marble finishes, and organic toiletries. The hotel is part of the Verity Club—a private women's club with a spa, fitness facilities, public rooms, and lounges—and many of the club's services are available for hotel guests to use. The place is overwhelmingly feminine (and only women are allowed in the fitness facilities), but men are welcome.

111d Queen St. E. (at Jarvis St.). www.theivyatverity.ca. © **416/368-6006,** ext 300. 4 units. $260–$360 double. Rates include breakfast. No parking. Subway: Queen. **Amenities:** Restaurant; honor bar; concierge; fitness facilities; pool; room service; spa; free Wi-Fi.

Moderate

Cambridge Suites Hotel ★   The emphasis at this all-suite hotel is comfortable home-away-from-home amenities, which makes it popular for extended stays. The smallest suite is a generous 51 sq. m (550 sq. ft.), and at the other end are deluxe duplexes. Rooms are equipped with desks and charging stations, as well as fully kitted-out kitchens with a fridge, microwave, and cookware, plus coffee and tea. Penthouse suites come with hot tubs, and some have views.

15 Richmond St. E. (at Yonge St.). www.cambridgesuitestoronto.com. © **800/463-1990** or 416/368-1990. 230 units. $180–$350 suite. Parking $27. Subway: Queen. **Amenities:** Restaurant; bar; babysitting; concierge; gym; access to large health club nearby; room service; sauna; hot tub; free Wi-Fi.

Executive Hotel Cosmopolitan Toronto ★   This all-suite hotel is tucked away on quiet Colborne Street, just off Yonge Street. Floor-to-ceiling windows allow guests to take in the expansive cityscape that fans out around the tower. Suites above the 21st floor have excellent views. In the summer, balconies let in fresh air and invite guests to relax. Find some inner tranquility at the onsite spa, or do it yourself with an impromptu yoga session (every room comes equipped with a yoga mat—a nice touch). This is an excellent choice for long-stay budget-conscious travelers; rooms come with petite kitchens and some even have washers and dryers. Furnishings are basic and beds are serviceable, but the central location (near the theater, entertainment, and shopping districts) is a draw.

8 Colborne St. (Yonge St.). www.cosmotoronto.com. ✆ **416/350-2000.** 80 suites. $155-$250 suite. Rates include continental breakfast. Valet parking $45. Subway: King. **Amenities:** Restaurant; concierge; bicycle rental; gym; hot tub; room service; spa; free Wi-Fi.

Hotel Victoria ★   In a landmark downtown building near the Hockey Hall of Fame, the Victoria retains a few glamorous touches from its past, such as crown moldings and marble columns in the lobby. It's Toronto's second-oldest hotel (built in 1909), although the rooms are much newer, furnished with sleek modern furniture and Netflix-connected flatscreens. The cramped bathrooms do feel a touch dated, though. On the plus side, the hotel's personal service and attention are a bonus not often found in budget accommodations. The lack of on-site parking makes unloading a bear; however, nearby city parking lots are reasonably priced.

56 Yonge St. (at Wellington St.). www.hotelvictoria-toronto.com. ✆ **800/363-8228** or 416/363-1666. 56 units. $160-$280 double. Parking in nearby garage $30. Subway: King. **Amenities:** Restaurant; business center; access to nearby health club; free Wi-Fi.

Pantages Hotel ★★   Architecture enthusiasts will be wowed by this Moshe Safdie–designed postmodern limestone building. Inside, the interiors are undergoing a slate of updates to keep rooms fresh. Bathrooms feature rainfall showerheads, Nest soaps, and cozy robes. Floor-to-ceiling windows offer views of historic Massey Hall to the south; for those who want to see the skyline, ask for something above the 10th floor. This hotel straddles the divide between moderate and inexpensive categories. When the price slips below $200 a night, a double here is more than worth it. Select suites have kitchenettes, and some even have laundry facilities, an excellent perk for longer-staying visitors.

200 Victoria St. (at Shuter St.). www.pantageshotel.com. ✆ **416/362-1777.** 111 units. $130-$299 double. No on-site parking. Subway: Queen. **Amenities:** Restaurant/lounge; business center; gym; relaxation room; room service; free Wi-Fi.

The Saint James Hotel ★   The uninspired beige-on-beige color scheme of the lobby looks like the interior decorator decided that Instragram's sepia filter was an aesthetic worthy of emulating. Maps and vintage photos of Old Toronto salvage the design, which is both functional and compact. Questionable color scheme aside, the rooms are decently commodious (considering the price

Bed & Breakfasts in Toronto

A B&B can be an excellent alternative to standard hotel accommodations. The **Downtown Toronto Association of Bed and Breakfast Guest Houses** (*C* **647/ 654-2959;** www.bnbinfo.com) has listings for most of metro Toronto, not just downtown.

point), and the staff are affable. Thoughtful touches like a welcome package of fruit gummies, chips, and water bottles are appreciated, while the comfy beds, in-room coffeemakers, and contemporary washrooms are all pluses. The Freshii-provided complimentary breakfast appeals to health nuts, but don't expect custom omelets: this is chia-seed country.

26 Gerrard St. E. (at Yonge St.). www.thesaintjameshotel.com. *C* **416/645-2200.** 36 units. $135–$185 double. Rates include complimentary breakfast. Off-site parking $20. Subway: College. Pets permitted. **Amenities:** Restaurant; concierge; free Wi-Fi.

4 Inexpensive

Bond Place Hotel ★★ The location is right—a block from the Eaton Centre, around the corner from the Canon and Elgin theaters—and so is the price. A recent refresh has given these shoebox-sized rooms an IKEA feel. The pine millwork is very econo-Scandinavian. Still, the rooms are clean and the service friendly. The only drawbacks are the aged air-conditioning units, which are awfully noisy. A more intensive renovation may be completed by the time you read this, with local design firm Ciccone Simone doubling down on the Nordic aesthetic. Public spaces too, are undergoing a serious facelift. The hotel was purchased by the same group that owns the Anndore House, so expect cool cachet once the renos are completed.

65 Dundas St. E. (at Bond St.). www.bondplace.ca. *C* **416/362-6061.** 285 units. $127– $200 double. Off-site parking $25. Subway: Dundas. **Amenities:** Restaurant; concierge; gym; Wi-Fi $10/day, or free if you book directly through the hotel.

Toronto Garden Inn B&B ★ Walking distance from bucolic Riverdale Farm (p. 199), along a quiet residential row of redbrick Victorians, is this seven-room bed-and-breakfast. The rooms are decorated in theme with the era it was built (circa 1890s): stately sleigh beds, damask throws, and Persian rugs. The century-old house creaks underfoot, but that only adds to the allure. In a more modern building, the wear would make the place seem tired; here it feels apropos. The best room is the Trillium, which takes up the top floor of the house (that means no footsteps overhead) and has its private en suite and terrace. The fridge is perennially stocked with juices, snacks, and breakfast fodder. Although the B&B is technically located in Cabbagetown, known for its gorgeous historic homes, this particular pocket can be dodgy at night. Savvy urbanites will be unphased, but if you prefer your neighborhoods well-gentrified, this area may not suit your tastes.

142 Seaton St. (at Sherborune St.). www.torontogardeninn.ca. *C* **866/945-1999.** 7 units. $69–$149 double. Rates include breakfast. No parking. Subway: Dundas, then streetcar 505 E to Sherbourne St. **Amenities:** Communal kitchen; garden deck; free Wi-Fi.

DOWNTOWN NORTH

Most of the hotels in Downtown North are located in or near Yorkville and the Annex.

Best for: High-end shopping along Mink Mile and in Yorkville. It's a pretty area to stroll around, and it's also home to a handful of fine-art galleries, the ROM, and a number of good restaurants and bars.

Drawbacks: It's expensive.

Expensive

The Anndore House ★★ The Anndore House is serious about making its guests feel as if they are staying in a home away from home. The Studio Munge–designed ground level feels like a house—a fabulously opulent home, that is, owned by a bootlegging magnate with a taste for leather, velvet, tempestuous color schemes, and fire-cooked delicacies. A living room area animated by a flickering fireplace is situated just off of the open-concept restaurant **Constantine** (famed for Chef Craig Harding's flame-cooked plates that pull from all corners of the Mediterranean). Even the homey entrance to the hotel feels less transactional than interactional. Concierges do not stand behind a tall counter, but greet guests at check-in like old friends. Service is courteous, prompt, and efficient. Upstairs, the rooms marry the Soho loft look with '50s panache. Crosley turntables spinning eclectic LPs, working replica rotary phones, vintage-looking red kettles, and pin-up-inspired artwork by artist Merve Özaslan aren't kitschy but delightfully nostalgia-inducing. Details like Balkan rugs, leather bucket chairs and whitewashed brick walls add warmth to the suites, making them feel like well-curated apartments. Beds, in 350-threadcount custom sheets, can be ordered with a firm or plush mattress. Pillows, similarly, come in a wide variety of sizes and stuffings. For guests who need a bit of extra pampering, the hotel has partnered with KX Yorkville to offer in-room spa services that range from restorative massages to hangover-eliminating IV therapy treatments.

15 Charles St. E. (at Yonge St.). www.theanndorehouse.com. ℂ **416/924-1222.** 115 units. $200–$400 double. Parking $35. Pets permitted. Subway: Yonge-Bloor. **Amenities:** Restaurant; bar; lounge; cafe; barber shop; bicycle rental; concierge; off-site gym; room service; free Wi-Fi.

Four Seasons Hotel Toronto ★★★ In 2012, the Four Seasons decamped from its original building—the first Four Seasons in the world—and moved into this elegant new flagship property crowned by one of the most sought-after condo towers in town (the asking price for the penthouse? $36 million). The airy, light-filled hotel rooms have birch and limestone details, not to mention luxurious beds outfitted with the Four Seasons' patented mattresses that promise a slumber deeper than Sleeping Beauty's. Spa-like, sunshine-steeped bathrooms with hinoki-macadamia scented soaps are divine. Better yet, though, is the top-tier service. Guests' whims are catered to before they even step into the opulent Yabu Pushelberg–designed lobby. A database of preferences ensures that those with glasses have lens wipes in their rooms. Even pillow preferences are logged and accommodated, while caffeine addicts will find extra coffee pods already stocked. Children and pets, too, are lavished over, with special robes and plushies for the wee ones and a bed and treats for Fido. Here, no detail is *not* agonized over. Even the minibar is curated with interesting treats like Prosecco-flavored Squish gummies. Other perks include the complimentary house car, which transports guests around town. Amenities—including one of the city's top spas, a Michelin-star-powered restaurant overseen by Daniel Boulud, and a grotto-reminiscent pool—are excellent.

60 Yorkville Ave. (at Bay St.), www.fourseasons.com/toronto. © **416/964-0411.** 259 units. $570–$700 double. Parking $55. Pets permitted. Subway: Yonge-Bloor. **Amenities:** Restaurant; bar/lounge; business center; concierge; gym; indoor pool; room service; free Wi-Fi.

Windsor Arms Hotel ★★ The Windsor Arms once held the only five-star status in town, but it's had its ups and downs. Today it's known as a dignified destination with just 28 suites. The spacious rooms—ranging from 51 to 144 sq. m (550–1,550 sq. ft.)—appeal to the country-club set, who appreciate things like crown moldings, Persian rugs, mahogany furniture, and ornate decorative touches like a baby grand piano (each room is decorated with a musical instrument). The hotel is refined without being showy. Everything from the buttery Molton Brown moisturizer to the high-thread-count Frette linens is intended to pamper guests. A saltwater pool with a poolside fireplace, part of the excellent spa, is a bonus. The **restaurant** is equally high end, and the afternoon tea suitably elegant.

18 St Thomas. (at Yorkville Ave.). www.windsorarmshotel.com. © **416/971-9666.** 28 units. $410–$500 double. Parking $45. Pets permitted. Subway: Bay. **Amenities:** Restaurant; 2 lounges (serving high tea); concierge; gym; hot tub; indoor pool; room service; free Wi-Fi.

Moderate

Annex Hotel ★★ A residential neighborhood favored by students (it's close to U of T) and the artistically inclined, the Annex is known for its cheap-and-cheerful restaurants and stately Victorian manses. It had few good hotel options, until recently. Launched in 2018, the Annex Hotel offers a cross between a boutique hotel and an Airbnb rental. Check-in happens online, and there is no check-out; guests simply close the door behind them and walk away. Instead of key cards, each guest logs into an online portal and is given a key code to access their rooms (in case of cellphone malfunction, I recommend scrawling the code on a piece of paper as a failsafe). The hotel boasts that it has no televisions, no phones, no parking lot, no gym, and no front desk. This is a space designed by millennials, for millennials. Need ice? Text the attendant on duty. Need an extra towel? There's a help-yourself closet in the hall. Although there's no concierge, the hotel hosts hangouts in the lobby (also a cafe-bar open to the public) and is happy to help with locally informed itineraries and insider recommendations. Rooms, decorated by hot local design firm StudioAC, have an industrial-loft allure, but the frosted-glass washrooms provide little privacy. Toiletries (Malin+Goetz) and beds (firm-yet-yielding mattresses) are top-tier. *Note:* You need a different key code after hours to access the main door; make sure you know this in advance; sifting through your inbox late at night is less than ideal.

296 Brunswick Ave. (at Bloor St.). www.theannex.com. © **647/277-1179.** 24 units. $150–$200 double. Nearby municipal parking lot ($4/hr). Subway: Spadina. **Amenities:** 2 restaurants; cafe-bar.

Kimpton Saint George Hotel ★★   When local design darlings Mason Studio were fashioning Toronto's first Kimpton Saint George, they began by looking at heritage homes, not other hotels. The resulting interiors—which saw a weary Holiday Inn completely transformed into a boutique gem—pulls from the residential architectural features that define the history-steeped Annex neighborhood. Arches were added to doorways and hallways, and the motif even carries into the stylish gym, where arch-shaped mirrors line the walls. During the intensive reno, the number of suites was nearly doubled—what had previously been two guest rooms become one. Rooms have a mid-century modern appeal, with polished brass light fixtures and thoughtful touches like in-room record players that come with a small selection of albums curated by **Sonic Boom** (p. 156). For those who don't appreciate the crack and pop of vinyl, the Bluetooth-ready Leff Amsterdam Tube speaker is both visually and aurally pleasing. Frette linens and robes are great, but the bathrooms in the suites, with ultra-deep soaker tubs and Atelier Bloem bath amenities, are rave-worthy. The hotel has serious artsy cred, too: More than 700 artworks, 95 percent of which were created by Canadian artists, hang throughout the hotel, as well as two murals (a forest scene in the lobby by Tisha Myles and a giant owl on the building's exterior by BirdO).

280 Bloor St W. (at St George). www.kimptonsaintgeorge.com. © **416/968-0010.** 188 units. $230–$350 double. Subway: St. George. Pets permitted. **Amenities:** Restaurant; lounge; free bicycles; concierge; gym; room service; free Wi-Fi.

Old Mill Toronto ★   Tucked along the lush banks of the Humber River, a 35-minute subway ride from downtown, this Arts and Crafts–style hotel was built to resemble a stately Tudor cottage. Parts of the sprawling property are occupied by a 200-year-old former gristmill, but the rooms feel less 1800s and more 1980s luxury. The old-money aesthetic won't appeal to everyone, but it has its charms, including rooms done in heavy, lustrous fabrics: box-pleated curtains with complementary bed skirts and tufted arm chairs. The ample square footage of the rooms, the four-poster mahogany beds, Jacuzzi tubs, and views over the ravine below are all boons. As are the silent nights: Expect to hear little but crickets chirping at midnight, not sirens. Old Mill is also located

BUDGET-FRIENDLY SUMMER OPTIONS

From September to early May, the dorms at the University of Toronto and at Ryerson University are full of students. But in summer, many of these rooms are rented out to budget-minded travelers. If you don't mind your in-room amenities on the spartan side, you can save a lot of money this way—and get a great downtown location, too.

o **Massey College:** Tucked away on a quiet street on the University of Toronto downtown campus sits the very attractive Massey College, designed by renowned architect Ron Thom. It's a small, exclusive graduate college, and the summer residence program offers a handful of tasteful, sparse rooms—all set around a beautiful courtyard. Personal touches are a bonus: The porter greets you upon arrival with your own key to the gate as well as a welcome package. You can use the public rooms, such as the library, and breakfast is included with the rate (lunch vouchers can also be purchased). Book a double suite, and you'll have a sitting area, private bathroom, and wood-burning fireplace. Rooms are available from May through late August. Not suitable for children under 6 years of age (4 Devonshire Place; www.massey college.ca; ℂ **416/946-7843;** rooms from $87; rates include breakfast).

o **Neill-Wycik Backpackers Hotel:** During the school year, this is a

student residence. Some young academics stay through the summer, when the place morphs into a guesthouse. Rooms have beds, chairs, desks, but no air-conditioning or TVs (although there is a TV lounge). Housekeeping offers towel and linen changes. Groups of five bedrooms share two bathrooms and one kitchen with a refrigerator and stove. The hotel has three patios with BBQs, on the fourth, fifth, and 23rd floors. It's less than a 5-minute walk to the Eaton Centre (96 Gerrard St. E.; www.torontobackpackers hotel.com; ℂ **800/268-4358** or 416/977-2320; $35 dorm bed, $55 single; $80 double; $120 quad; rates include breakfast).

o **Victoria University at the University of Toronto:** A steal for this very expensive neighborhood (just a 2-minute walk from tony Yorkville). Victoria University offers simple rooms with plain furnishings (a bed, desk, and chair are standard), but the surroundings are splendid. Many of the rooms are in Burwash Hall, a 19th-century building that overlooks a peaceful, leafy quad. Guests are provided with linens and towels but must provide their own toiletries (140 Charles St. W.; www. vicu.utoronto.ca; ℂ **416/585-4524;** $77 single, $103 double [2 twin beds]; rates include breakfast)

on the northwest end of downtown, making the taxi ride to the airport substantially cheaper. The buffet brunch can be hit or miss; high tea in the handsome rooms is splendid.

9 Old Mill Rd. (Bloor St. W.). www.oldmilltoronto.com. ℂ **416/232-3707.** 57 units. $190–$280 double. Subway: Old Mill. **Amenities:** Restaurant; concierge; gym; room service; spa; free Wi-Fi.

Inexpensive

Downtown Home Inn ★ This freshly renovated seven-room B&B is walking distance from the Gay Village, the Mink Mile, and the ROM. Rooms are bright with pops of color from fun wallpaper and floral duvets (of the fresh, contemporary variety, not the staid grandma type). Breakfasts are a DIY affair with everything on offer from cereals and toast to fruit, yogurt, cheese, deli meats, and eggs. The operators are fairly hands-off, so don't expect too much one-on-one attention. But if a clean, centrally located spot is what you're after, this affordable bed-and-breakfast tucked into a leafy cul-de-sac is sure to please.

2 Monteith St. (Church St.). www.downtownhomeinn.com. © **647/342-1010.** 7 units. $74–$145 double. Rates include breakfast. No parking. Subway: Wellesley. **Amenities:** Communal kitchen; free Wi-Fi.

The Only Backpackers Inn ★ The under-30 set keen to make friends and revel all night is the target demographic for this hipster-approved hostel. Located atop a funky cafe-bar in Greektown, the place can get raucous on weekends. Most of the carousing, though, takes place at the bar, which draws 'em in with an excellent selection of craft beers and board games. The unfussy dorm rooms (bunk beds, lockers) are made cheerful by pastel walls and colorful, eclectic bedding. It takes about 30 minutes to get downtown via transit, but the subway is spitting distance from the hostel's front door, making it's easy to move around town.

966 Danforth Ave. (at Donlands Ave.). www.theonlyinn.com. © **416/463-3249.** 24 beds. Beds $37–$42. Subway: Donlands. **Amenities:** Restaurant; bar; communal BBQ; communal kitchen; free Wi-Fi.

WHERE TO EAT IN TORONTO

Torontonians are obsessed with food. From street food to Michelin-caliber tasting menus, this town has something to sate any craving and every budget. The city's rich multicultural makeup ensures a kaleidoscopic banquet. Immigrants have flooded the food scene with authentic eats from around the globe, while second-generation chefs have doubled down on the Toronto melting pot by rehabilitating the f-word. Here, fusion isn't a gimmick; it's a culinary expression of the Toronto experience.

It's true: Toronto doesn't have an iconic dish. Montreal has poutine. Philly has cheesesteak. Chicago has deep-dish pizza. Halifax has donair. Bruges has waffles. But in Toronto you can get all of the above and every other geographically specific food your hunger hankers after.

The late culinary icon Anthony Bourdain himself wasn't immediately enamored with Hogtown upon touchdown. On his show *The Layover,* he quipped that Toronto's "not a good-looking city." But after 30-some hours eating and drinking his way through our less-than-handsome streets, he was romanced by what Toronto had to offer. He drank potent cocktails at secret bars, hidden in the back of strip malls. He ate dim sum that rivals the *har gow* in Guangzhou. Tasted some of the most decadent, artery-clogging poutine in Canada (sorry, Quebec). And met boundary-pushing chefs making creative, unpretentious food from Ontario-sourced ingredients. These chefs aren't afraid to fuse multiple culinary heritages on a single plate.

Successive waves of immigrants have left their imprints all around Toronto. Toronto has six Chinatowns, two Koreatowns, two Italian neighborhoods (Little Italy and Corso Italia), two Portuguese areas (one on Dundas West and one up by Dupont), a Greek strip (along Danforth), an Indian Bazaar, a Caribbean concentration (along Eglington West), and even a Polish avenue (Roncesvalles) that abuts the Tibetan section of West Queen West. All are fun to explore—they often have great markets (where you'll find specialty ingredients), as well as ethnic bakeries, cafes, and hot tables.

But gentrification is having its effects on the city's multicultured dining scene. Climbing rents have pushed unpretentious authentic eats into the suburbs. Mom-and-pop shops serving their home country's cooking are growing rarer in the core. Adventurous foodies would do well to explore some of the strip malls in North Toronto. Hit the suburbs and you'll find Balkan nodes, Persian clusters, Jewish neighborhoods, a Japanese mall, and more.

Older, more established ethnic enclaves like Little Italy have been undergoing a second round of gentrification. While some of the old guard remains, Sicilian pastry shops are now shoulder to shoulder with vegan cafes, upscale taco joints, fried chicken counters, and tapas restaurants. The new generation of chefs isn't necessarily opening Italian restaurants in Italian neighborhoods—chef-owners opening creative new spots are driven by rent, not tradition.

You'll find great Greek in Little Portugal (p. 88), while over in Greektown lies some of the city's best Neapolitan pizza (**Pizzeria Libretto**, p. 110). Of course *pastel de nata* is still found in Little Portugal and gyros on the Danforth—but just know there is fabulous food from everyplace all over Toronto, and nothing here is fettered to any particular neighborhood. All this to say, if Toronto was a culinary paint-by-numbers, the restaurants here refuse to color within the lines.

PRACTICAL MATTERS

Reservations

Whenever you can, book ahead if you're planning to dine at one of Toronto's top restaurants. That said, many of the hottest spots do not accept reservations for dinner. It's common for diners to arrive early, leave their name and phone number at the door, and skip out for a stroll or a drink until their table is ready.

Dining Hours

Restaurant hours vary. Lunch is typically served from noon to 2pm; dinner begins around 6pm—the busiest window is 7pm to after 9pm, especially on weekends when two seatings are standard at the best restaurants. Reservations are recommended when accepted.

Tipping

The standard tip in Toronto calculates as 15 percent, although 20 percent is pretty common if service has been above average. Groups of six or more can anticipate an automatic added service charge of 18 to 20 percent—and diners are not expected to leave an additional amount. Keep in mind that your bill will also include a 13 percent HST tax (which stands for a "harmonized sales tax"). It all adds up to a good 30 percent hike to the menu prices. Also, wine and other alcoholic beverages tend to be pricey in part because the provincial government levies high taxes and also because restaurateurs often charge as high as a 50 percent markup. Some establishments let you bring your own and add a corkage fee.

MONEY-SAVING TIPS ON DINING

While traveling, it can be a challenge to keep your belly full without emptying your wallet. With some smart planning, you can eat like royalty without leaving town like a pauper. Here are five savvy ways to cut down on dining costs while visiting Toronto.

○ **Dine during Toronto's restaurant weeks:** Every February and July, Toronto hosts 2-week-long food events: **Winterlicious** and **Summerlicious.** More than 200 restaurants participate, offering discounted three-course lunch and dinner prix-fixe menus for $23 to $53. The most coveted reso? A chance to dine at Canoe (p. 84) on a dime. Check **www.toronto.ca** for details.

○ **Nosh on market foods:** At the **St. Lawrence Market,** for example, dozens of vendors sell delicious prepared foods (Carousel Bakery's $6.45 peameal bacon sandwiches are legendry; p. 23), as well as stuff that's easy to assemble into a picnic table feast. The market has seating on the lower level and outside in the warmer months. **Kensington Market** is jam-packed with small vendors peddling some of the best cheap eats in the core. Embark on a Kensington snack parade (p. 23) and feast on delights under $5 from Mexico, the Caribbean, Portugal, Hungary, and Hawaii.

○ **Book a stay with self-catering facilities:** Having your own kitchen can help keep costs down, so choose accommodations that have self-catering facilities—be it an Airbnb or a suite outfitted with a kitchenette. Stock up on grocery fixings at **No Frills** and **FreshCo,** which offer great value and are some of the cheapest grocery chains in town. **Loblaws** and **Metro** are a bit fancier, with more prepared foods and higher prices.

○ **Look for lodgings where breakfast is included.** Breakfast included in your room rate can fortify you for a day of sightseeing. A growing number of long-stay properties have full breakfast buffets, and bed-and-breakfasts are known for delicious home-cooked options.

○ **Dine amid the college kids.** Although you won't find many early-bird specials in Toronto, you can score some amazing lunch deals in neighborhoods near the colleges and universities. Around U of T, at Bloor and Spadina, for instance, a half-dozen Japanese joints offer sushi combo lunches for less than $8.

o **Check out the latest lists of cheap eats.** Local publications such as **BlogTO** (www.blogto.com) and **Toronto Life** (www.torontolife.com) update their best-of-cheap-eats lists regularly, giving you a cheat sheet of sorts on where to score the best-value nosh in town.

o **Check out the deals on Groupon** (www.groupon.com). Select Toronto, and then scroll through the savings under the Food & Drink tab. Keep in mind that not all the restaurants offering discounts are winners, so be sure to cross-check the reviews on both Google and Yelp. Don't forget to read the fine print. A reservation specifying that you have a Groupon voucher is usually required; blackout dates are also common.

DOWNTOWN WEST

This is where you will find Toronto's highest concentration of great restaurants. **Little Italy,** which runs along College Street, has a mix of old-school trattorias, buzzy new restaurants, and snack bars; the streets of **Chinatown,** which radiate from Spadina Avenue, are lined with brightly lit, busy eateries; and **West Queen West, Dundas West,** and **Ossington Avenue** are littered with interesting chef-owned gems.

Very Expensive

Akira Back ★ JAPANESE   What happens when a pro snowboarder ditches the half-pipe for the kitchen? In this case, chef Back opened a Michelin-starred restaurant in his native Korea. Lucky for us, Back has brought his upscale Japanese-Korean fusion to Toronto. The menu strikes a delicate balance between irreverent (one of the maki features Pop Rocks; another is laced with chipotle) and traditional (the sashimi would impress even a sushi master, and includes delectable sea delicacies such as urchin, flounder, and botan shrimp). Even the cocktail card abides by the Asian-fusion theme. Flavors like yuzu, Thai chili, and green tea are combined with Pacific spirits such as Hibiki Harmony.

In the Bisha Hotel, 80 Blue Jays Way. www.akirabacktoronto.com. © **437/800-5967.** Main courses $28–$49. Mon–Sun 5–10pm. Subway: St. Andrew, then streetcar 504 W to Blue Jays Way.

Alo ★★★ FRENCH   Canada's most acclaimed restaurant sits on the top floor of a gorgeous redbrick Victorian. Alo's entrance, though, is neither grand nor obvious. It's tucked on the side of the building, sharing an unappealing foyer with a piercing studio. As the cramped elevator chugs up to the third floor, you begin to wonder what the fuss is about. Then the doors open onto the sumptuously decorated dining room, and you're immediately transported away from the bustle of Toronto below. Those lucky enough to snag one of the few extended tasting-menu seats at the Chef's Table have views of the open

Downtown West Restaurants

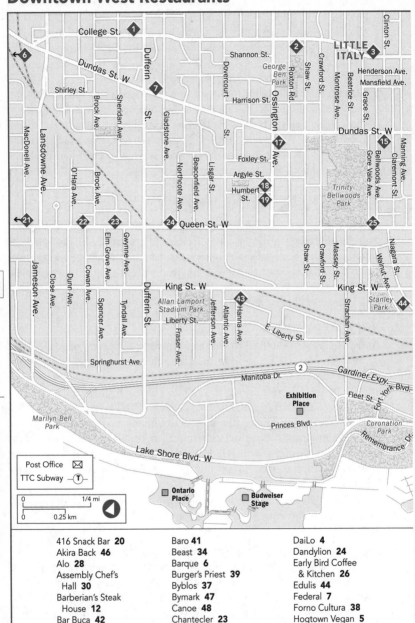

416 Snack Bar **20**
Akira Back **46**
Alo **28**
Assembly Chef's
  Hall **30**
Barberian's Steak
  House **12**
Bar Buca **42**
Bar Isabel **2**

Baro **41**
Beast **34**
Barque **6**
Burger's Priest **39**
Byblos **37**
Bymark **47**
Canoe **48**
Chantecler **23**
Cosmic Treats **13**

DaiLo **4**
Dandylion **24**
Early Bird Coffee
  & Kitchen **26**
Edulis **44**
Federal **7**
Forno Cultura **38**
Hogtown Vegan **5**
Kiin **32**

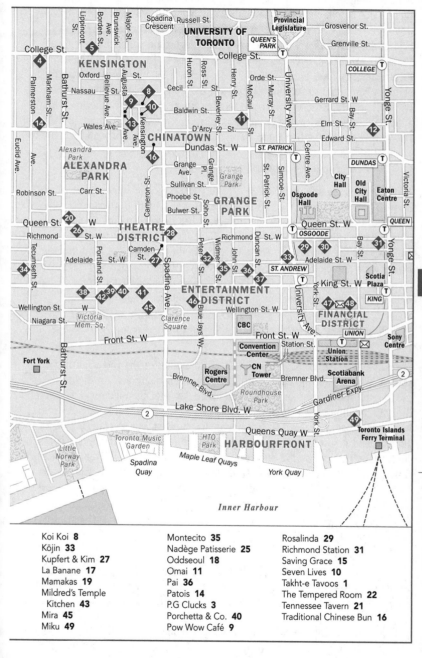

Koi Koi **8**
Kōjin **33**
Kupfert & Kim **27**
La Banane **17**
Mamakas **19**
Mildred's Temple
  Kitchen **43**
Mira **45**
Miku **49**

Montecito **35**
Nadège Patisserie **25**
Oddseoul **18**
Omai **11**
Pai **36**
Patois **14**
P.G Clucks **3**
Porchetta & Co. **40**
Pow Wow Café **9**

Rosalinda **29**
Richmond Station **31**
Saving Grace **15**
Seven Lives **10**
Takht-e Tavoos **1**
The Tempered Room **22**
Tennessee Tavern **21**
Traditional Chinese Bun **16**

kitchen as furrow-browed chefs agonize over the angle of a garnish. Every plate coming out of chef-owner Patrick Kriss's kitchen is close to perfect—there is no such thing as good enough at Alo, which is why this tasting-menu-driven restaurant isn't just one of the best in the country, it's also one of the best in the world. Every day, the six-course dégustation changes. It's always French in execution, but shaped by what's in season. The food is not trendy or theatrical à la Alinea but thoughtful in its preparation. To snag a coveted reservation here, plan to set multiple alarms; the 2-month block is usually gone within 72 hours. Reservations open the first Tuesday of every other month at 10am (EST). For those without a reso, the more casual sister restaurant **Aloette** downstairs on the first floor is also an excellent alternative; walk-ins only.

163 Spadina Ave. www.alorestaurant.com. © **416/260-2222.** Tasting menus $105–$165. Tues–Sat 5pm–1am. Subway: St. Andrew, then streetcar 504 W to Spadina Ave.

Barberian's Steak House ★ STEAKHOUSE   We believe that steak-houses, like steaks and good wine, are better when aged. Barberian's is anything but trendy. This family-run restaurant has been preparing some of the city's best beef since 1959, and every Canadian prime minister since John Diefenbaker has dined here. Some have come for the thick-cut porterhouses; others were attracted by Barberian's impressive 30,000-bottle wine cellar. Art connoisseurs should be sure to check out the collection of Group of Seven paintings displayed throughout the sprawling cottage.

7 Elm St. www.barberians.com. © **416/597-0335.** Main courses $23–$38 lunch, $35–$71 dinner. Mon–Fri noon–2:30pm and 5pm–midnight; Sat–Sun 5pm–midnight. Subway: Dundas, then walk N up Yonge St. to Elm St.

Bymark ★★ AMERICAN/BISTRO   In the heart of the financial district, this favorite among the corner-office set has seen many a seven-figure deal close over the course of lunch. Chef Brooke McDougall's food is very Toronto, abiding by no single geographic anchor, with a menu ranging from steaks and snazzy seafood to internationally inspired fare. A cheeky plate of Fogo Island cod tempura with mango-vinaigrette-dressed cucumber slaw is just as fabulous as a by-the-book Italian bowl of rabbit ravioli. Even the steak tartare gets a multicultural infusion in the form of a kimchi kick. But it's the burger topped with Brie de Meaux, shaved truffles, and grilled porcinis (well worth the $40 price tag) that has built a diehard following.

66 Wellington St. W. © **416/777-1144.** www.bymark.mcewangroup.ca. Main courses $29–$32 lunch, $30–$46 dinner. Mon–Fri 11:30am–3pm and 5–9pm; Sat 5pm–midnight. Subway: King, then walk W to Bay St.

Canoe ★★★ CANADIAN   The panorama from the 54th floor of this iconic bank tower is stunning, but as the many regulars can attest, the food is so good you might forget all about the views. In the heart of the Financial District, Canoe looks down on the towers of downtown and farther south still to the idyllic Toronto islands. The Canadian cuisine, such as Nunavut caribou and Quebec foie gras, is handled with delicacy and expert technique. The daytime vibe is corporate; evening is more romantic.

54th floor, Toronto Dominion Tower, 66 Wellington St. W. www.oliverbonacini.com. ℗ **416/ 364-0054.** Main courses $23–$37 lunch, $39–$62 dinner. Mon–Fri 11:45am–2:30pm and 5–10:30pm. Subway: King, then walk W to Bay St., then S to Wellington St. W.

Edulis ★★ SPANISH   Down a leafy residential street, tucked into the bottom of a postwar A-frame, is one the city's most competent kitchens. The room could pass for a Catalonian cantina: bentwood chairs, flickering candles, encaustic tile accents, and a few Catholic icons hung on the walls for good measure. Edulis is a labor of love from husband-and-wife team Michael Caballo and Tobey Nemeth. The latter charms guests in the dining room while her husband helms the kitchen, producing glorious plates inspired by the Basque, Catalonian, and Occitan regions. Order à la carte, or lean into the experience and let Chef Caballo decide on the feast—he does extraordinary things with mushrooms and seafood. Although the food changes regularly, a few standout items—like the hay-roasted Chantecler chicken carved tableside—are frequent guest stars.

169 Niagara St. www.edulisrestaurant.com. ℗ **416/703-4222.** Tasting menus $65–$85. Wed–Sat 6–10:30pm; Sun noon–3pm. Subway: Bathurst, then streetcar 511 S to Niagara St.

Miku ★★ JAPANESE   A cheerful Japanese greeting echoes from the open kitchen as a line of sushi chefs welcomes guests between slicing sashimi. Flame-torched fish *(arburi)* is the specialty here, though the raw bar is a great place to start any meal. Arburi is the antithesis of wasabi-and-soy-dunked plain-jane nigiri. Here, each blow-torched piece is carefully paired with its own special sauce and garnish to create deep flavors in every one-bite morsel. A pressed prawn, for example, comes with a tuft of lime zest and a lick of pickled plum sauce. The modern, 7,000-square-foot dining room is animated with murals painted by Japanese street artist Hideki Kimura.

10 Bay St. #105. www.mikutoronto.com. ℗ **647/347-7347.** Main courses $25–33 lunch, $35–$150 dinner. Mon–Fri 11:30am–10pm; Sat–Sun noon–10pm. Subway: Union Station, then streetcar 509 E to Queens Quay.

Yasu ★★★ JAPANESE   "What do you think this is?" asks one of the masters behind the counter. You take the *shirako nigiri* in your mouth. The sea-broth-flavored custard tastes unlike any part of fish you can name. After you swallow, you're told it's a cod organ. Later you Google *shirako,* only to discover that cod sperm is an absolutely delicious delicacy. Osaka-born sushi master Yasuhisa Ouchi tells each piece of fish he cuts to "taste good" before he presses the flesh into a much-fussed-over round of rice. Fans of the documentary *Jiro Dreams of Sushi* will be delighted by the omakase at this 16-seat Annex restaurant, where diners are treated to the whims of the chefs. The 2-hour affair includes some familiar seafood delights (fatty tuna, mackerel, Hokkaido scallop) but often ventures into esoteric territory. Thumb-sized firefly squid, sakura shrimp that actually look like cherry-blossom petals, and *ankimo* (monkfish liver) are seasonal highlights. This is not sushi for California-roll junkies.

81 Harbord St. www.yasu-sushibar.com. ℗ **416/477-2361.** Omakase set menu $135. Mon–Sun 6–11pm. Subway: Spadina, then streetcar 510 S to Harbord St.

Expensive

Bar Isabel ★★★ SPANISH   Restaurateur Grant van Gameren has the Midas touch. Every place he's opened has received rave reviews. Including this vibrant Spanish room, famous about town for its whole grilled octopus. Since opening in 2013, Bar Isabel has sold over a million dollars' worth of the stuff, it's that good. Some of the tapas here is by-the-book Barcelona *(jamón croquetas, patatas bravas);* other plates are pure van Gameren, like smoked sweetbreads with raw tuna and persimmon brown butter. Although the food is serious, van Gameren doesn't take himself too seriously. Jokes pepper the menu. Cocktails have cheeky names like Hank Hill, a refreshing summer bracer named after the Texan cartoon dad from "King of the Hill."

797 College St. www.barisabel.com. ✆ **416/532-2222.** Tapas $4–$22; large sharing plates $24–$72. Mon–Sun 6pm–midnight. Subway: Ossington, then bus 63 S to College St.

Byblos ★★ MIDDLE EASTERN   Tucked into the first two floors of a 170-year-old building is a restaurant with a name that banks more history than its exposed wood beams. At 10,000 years old, Byblos, Lebanon, is the world's oldest still-inhabited city. Chef Stuart Cameron poured through enough books to fill an ancient library while figuring out Byblos' menu. The resulting food travels to just about every nation the Ottomans ever conquered (including Lebanon), borrowing flavors and techniques from across the region. Start in Turkey with some *pide;* the wood-fired Turkish flatbread come in a half-dozen variations, including a halloumi-truffle option, which is intended to be shared, though often bogarted. Then, over to Egypt for *dukkah*-rubbed lamb ribs with a side of crispy Israeli artichokes accompanied by a preserved lemon–labneh dipping sauce. Dinner is best finished in Greece with *loukoumades*. The Greco doughnuts come with burnt honey ice cream—the perfect balance of sweet, rich cream with just a hint of ashy finish to punctuate the end of perfect meal. *Note:* Byblos opened a second location Uptown in late 2018 (2537 Yonge St.; ✆ **416/487-4897**).

11 Duncan St. www.byblostoronto.com. ✆ **647/660-0909.** Small plates $17–$19; large sharing plates $17–$75. Mon–Wed and Sun 5–10pm; Thurs–Sat 5–11pm. Subway: St. Andrew, then walk W on King, turn R on Duncan St.

The F-Word

Local chefs are unbound by rules when it comes to what they put on the plate. Here, fusion cooking has been rehabilitated. The f-word no longer denotes the icky, messy mash-ups popular in the '80s. In Toronto, fusion has become an earnest expression of an experience lived. In a city where almost half the residents speak a language other than Canada's mother tongues, where your neighbors on both sides might be from opposite ends of the world, fusion is just a part of life. Try Jamaican-Chinese at Patois (p. 92), Korean-American at Oddseoul (p. 95), New Chinese at DaiLo (p. 86), Korean tacos at Barrio Coreano (p. 101), or a Columbian-Canadian mashup at Kōjin (p. 87).

Chantecler ★★★ FRENCH Named for Canada's only heritage breed of chicken, Chantecler's menu is appropriately bilingual, though most dishes—gougères versus cheese puffs, for instance—do sound better in French, and the food at this narrow Parkdale bistro is decidedly Franco. The quaint dining room looks into the open kitchen, where tattooed young chefs execute the classics—duck confit, chicken ballotine—effortlessly. The best plates aren't plucked from *Larousse Gastronomique,* however. Seasonal one-offs, like butter-poached Gulf shrimp with pickled persimmon in a red pepper beurre blanc, are standouts.

1320 Queen St. W. www.restaurantchantecler.com. ✆ **416/628-3586.** Small plates $11–$17; large sharing plates $21–$89. Thurs–Tues 6pm–2am; closed Wed. Subway: Dufferin, then bus 29 S to Queen St. W.

DaiLo ★★★ INTERNATIONAL Chef-owner Nick Liu has christened his cooking style New Asian Cuisine. For Liu, that means he is pulling from Korean, Thai, and Chinese traditions, and executing plates with modern French flair. The menu oscillates between fun food (a Big Mac *bao* that stuffs pork, beef, house-processed cheddar, pickles, and special sauce into a steamed bun) and serious plates. A Mongolian grilled lamb neck, for instance, is tender with sweet notes from the Chinese five-spice rub; the share-friendly dish comes on a table-sized board, flanked by pickled cucumber celery, chili-chive pancakes, and hoisin dipping sauce—requiring some assembly. Occasionally Liu shows off his fine-dining pedigree. An heirloom tomato and prawn salad, made with vegetables grown by Liu's parents, looks like a Rothko painting. Head upstairs to **LoPan** for funky drinks and dim sum–inspired snacks.

503 College St. www.dailoto.com. ✆ **647/341-8882.** Small plates $6–$17; large sharing plates $18–48; set menu $65. Tues–Sun 5:30–11pm. Subway: Bathurst, then streetcar 511 S to College Street, then walk W to Palmerston Blvd.

Kōjin ★★ INTERNATIONAL At Kōjin—named after the Japanese god of the hearth—chef Paula Navarrete is not afraid to play with fire. Kōjin is dedicated to introducing Southern Ontario ingredients to flames. Here, hardwood doubles as both cooking fodder and decor. The parilla (an adjustable Argentinian grill) is stoked for hours. After the fire dies, the embers are used to slow-roast salt, tomatoes, peppers, and more, imbuing everything with a robust smokiness. Chef Navarrete worked her way up the Momofuku food chain, starting as a line cook at celeb chef David Chang's Noodle Bar. Six years later, she was the executive chef in charge of reimagining Momofuku's upscale Toronto outpost. The food has David Chang moments, like an XO sauce–flavored steak tartare served with all dressed chips, but the menu is Navarrete's biography on a plate: born in Columbia, finished in the melting pot of Toronto.

In the Shangri-La Hotel, 190 University Ave. https://kojin.momofuku.com. ✆ **647/253-8000.** Main courses $25–$29 lunch, $25–$78 dinner. Mon–Fri 11:30am–2pm and 5:30–10pm; Sat–Sun 5:30–10pm. Subway: St. Andrew, then walk N on University Ave.

La Banane ★★ FRENCH   In French, the idiom *"avoir la banane"* means to sport a happy smile. Every patron leaving this modern bistro is sure to head home with a huge, contented grin. The 80-seat Ossington dining room—done up in marble and gold—features art from Canadian superstars such as Douglas Coupland and Talia Shipman. The real showstopper, though, is the crustaceans stacked neatly behind the glass of the raw bar. Pull up a seat at the stone counter and watch with awe as cooks build towering trays of cockles, crabs, lobsters, and oysters. It's easy to imagine one of these silver towers waltzing through a Jay Gatsby fete. Francophiles will appreciate the unapologetically French menu: bass *en croute* comes to the table whole, the handsome fish braided in dough, while duck breast with charred endives in a prune jus is cooked to pink perfection. End dinner with a bang by ordering a hand-painted Ziggy Stardust Disco Egg, which, when smashed, reveals hand-rolled Peruvian truffles flavored with apricots, ancho chilies, and coffee beans.

227 Ossington Ave. www.labanane.ca. ⓒ **416/551-6263.** Main courses $30–$39. Sun–Wed 6–11pm; Thurs–Sat 6pm–midnight. Subway: Ossington, then bus 63 S to Dundas St. W.

Mamakas ★ GREEK   Owner Thanos Tripi named his Ossington restaurant "Mother" in Greek because the food here evokes nostalgic pangs for the Aegean Sea. It's the food Tripi grew up eating. Nothing is overly complex. A sea bass special is perfection, thanks to grassy, cold-pressed olive oil and not a second too many on the grill. Grilled lamb chops with tzatziki aren't redefining Greek, but refining it. The plating is thoughtful and the flavors punchy. On weekends, it is nearly impossible to score a table at the last minute in this sliver of a whitewashed dining room.

80 Ossington Ave. www.mamakas.ca. ⓒ **416/519-5996.** Main courses $19–$39. Mon–Sun 5:30–10:30pm. Subway: Ossington, then bus 63 S to Argyle St.

Montecito ★ AMERICAN   *Ghostbusters* director Ivan Reitman's Entertainment District restaurant has served dinner to the red-carpet who's-who. On one night it's Atom Egoyan chatting with friends in a corner; on another, Sandra Bullock, Richard Gere, or Jennifer Hudson can be found enjoying Chef Matt Simpson's seasonal menu. The 330-seat, two-level space is opulent. Two giant screens play a pastoral Californian scene shot by Reitman. It's as if you're looking out the window into the sunny, warm Montecito countryside—even when Toronto is gray and frostbitten. Although the menu abides by California farm-to-table principles (uncluttered plates that put the ingredients at the forefront), the kitchen is strict about promoting a Canada-first policy, sourcing only from Canuck producers. On the dessert card you'll find the only tie-in to Reitman's oeuvre: the Stay Puft Marshmallow Baked Alaska.

299 Adelaide St. W. www.montecitorestaurant.ca. ⓒ **416/599-0299.** Main courses $19–$26 lunch, $26–$39 dinner. Mon–Wed 11:30am–11pm; Thurs–Fri 11:30am–1am; Sat 4pm–1am; Sun 11am–11pm. Subway: St. Andrew, then streetcar 504 W to John St.

Richmond Station ★★★ CANADIAN   In 2012, "Top Chef Canada" winner Carl Heinrich catapulted to stardom after sweeping the competition with his smart, seasonally driven cooking. Shortly after the show wrapped up, Heinrich opened this low-fuss restaurant. The wooden tables and subway-tiled-walls read casual, though the food is anything but. Even a humble burger is something to ooh and ah over. Stuffed braised short ribs are swaddled in a cloud-light milk bun. There's a reason it's consistently named one of the best stacks in the city. There's not an ounce of locavore sanctimoniousness present, though the kitchen's dedication to knowing everything about the ingredients is impressive. Servers will happily tell you what the cow you're eating ate and where it was pastured.

1 Richmond St. W. www.richmondstation.ca. ℭ **647/748-1444.** $45 lunch prix fixe. Dinner main courses $24–$31. Mon–Sun 11am–10:30pm. Subway: Queen.

Moderate

Bar Buca ★★ ITALIAN   Mornings start early at this sleek, 38-seat cafe bar. Come 7:30am, well-tailored yuppies pop in for house-baked pastries (cornetti, pistachio cream–stuffed bombolone) and espresso drinks. Later on, the kitchen kicks into high gear, churning out elegant Italian plates made for sharing. Even the most basic dishes are knocked up a notch at Bar Buca: Meatballs are made with goat and ricotta, cacio e pepe gets an umami kick from uni, and burrata is stuffed to bursting with pesto. Brunch is particularly imaginative and great value. Bar Buca has a **second location** at 101 Eglinton Ave. E (ℭ **416/599-2822**).

75 Portland St. www.buca.ca/bar. ℭ **416/599-2822.** Brunch $9–$18; small plates $9–$21. Mon–Wed 7:30am–midnight; Thurs–Fri 7:30am–2am; Sat–Sun 8am–midnight. Subway: St. Andrew, then streetcar 504 W to Portland St.

Baro ★ LATIN AMERICAN   A turn-of-the-20th-century textile factory has been transformed into a three-story Latin temple. On the ground floor is Baro, a 4,000-square-foot dining room decked with a rain forest's worth of plants, Mexican-tile-topped tables, and elegant brass and marble accents. Here, modelesque influencers knock back $15 cocktails with names like Bermuda Triangle, a gin-based drink that goes down so easy you might just get lost after a few. Chef Steve Gonzalez isn't afraid to blend traditional Latin recipes with foreign flavors. A ceviche, for instance, has a Japanese bent, combining ponzu-marinated hamachi with watermelon, shiso, and edamame. Upstairs is **Pablo's Snack House,** a sepia-toned lounge serving a curtailed version of Baro's menu in a chic '70s setting. Tucked at the back of this upper level is **Escobar,** a speakeasy that cheekily requires an ever-changing password for entry.

485 King St. W. www.barotoronto.com. ℭ **416/363-8388.** Mon–Tues 5pm–midnight; Wed–Fri 5pm–2am; Sat–Sun 11am–3pm and 5pm–2am. Brunch $8–$23; main courses $18–$38. Subway: St. Andrew, then streetcar 504 W to Spadina Ave.

Dandylion ★ CANADIAN   Less is more is the mantra at this restrained, chef-owned restaurant. There are no flashy signs announcing Dandylion, just a small menu posted in a leaded glass window. The menu, which changes daily, could pass for a series of haikus. It has three starters (one veg, one fish,

PLANT-POWERED dining

Vegetarians and vegans are well looked after by Toronto's many veg-friendly restaurants. Here are seven of my favorite spots that serve innovative, flavor-packed veg nosh that's sure to delight herbivores and omnivores alike.

o **Awai** (2277 Bloor St. W.; www.awai.ca; ✆ 647/643-3132): This darling Bloor West Village room is worth the trip to the west end. The ever-changing tasting menu comes in two formats: five courses and eight courses. Every plate is a riot of colors, fresh seasonal flavors, and textures (tofu skins, rare and wonderful mushrooms, and fresh pasta). Gregarious staff go the extra mile here. In warmer months, garnishes and herbs are grown in the lush garden out back, picked to order.

o **Cosmic Treats** (207 Augusta Ave.; ✆ 647/352-2207): There's no shortage of veggie food in Toronto's artsy **Kensington Market.** Cosmic Treats has all the vegan variations of the junky treats you crave: jalapeño poppers, fried cheese sticks, even "chicken" pot pie. Don't skip out on dessert: I'm obsessed with their ever-so-creamy cashew-based ice cream.

o **Fresh on Front** (47 Front St. E.; https://freshrestaurants.ca/pages/our-history; ✆ 416/599-4442): Long before kale was trendy, Fresh was preaching the values of plant-based eating. Almost 30 years later, Fresh is still, well, keeping it fresh. With five locations in Toronto serving organic, fresh squeezed juices and scrumptious composed plates that range from hearty (almond-grain burger garnished with onion rings) to healthy (salads that can win you friends—to prove Bart Simpson wrong).

o **Kupfert & Kim** (140 Spadina Ave., ✆ 416/504-2206; 181 Bay St., ✆ 416/601-1333; and four other locations; www.kupfertandkim.com):

Worker bees in a rush to grab a nourishing lunch with a minimal carbon footprint head to this quick-service eatery for superfood-packed bowls of bitter greens, nuts, seeds, and heritage grains. The to-go packaging is compostable, and nearly all the ingredients are organic.

o **Hogtown Vegan** (382 College St., ✆ 416/546-7900; 1056 Bloor St. W., ✆ 416/901-9779; www.thehogtownvegan.com): At Toronto's number-one destination for vegan junk food you'll find poutine and fried clams (shiitake mushrooms), alongside burgers (soy), Ruebens (Seitan), and fish 'n' chips (tempeh). The artery-clogging brunch is well loved by local vegheads; get here early or risk waiting up to 40 minutes for a table.

o **Planta** (1221 Bay St.; www.plantarestaurants.com; ✆ 647/348-7000): Chef David Lee made a name for himself in Toronto as one of the chefs who brought three-star caliber dining to what was once a staid eating town. When he left the world of champagne carts and $75 porterhouses, many were surprised that he opened a vegan place. Planta offers the same high-end service Lee is known for, plus a menu of fabulously accessible plant-based nosh. The pizzas with nut-based cheeses are good enough to sate even the pickiest critic—be they vegan, vegetarian, or pizzaterian.

o **Rosalinda** (133 Richmond St. W.; www.rosalindarestaurant.com; ✆ 416/907-0650): The plant-strewn solarium-like room transports diners away from Toronto's financial district. Here you'll find the spice, zest, and freshness of Mexican food with none of the animal products and zero pretension. Must-tries include the young coconut ceviche and the jackfruit pibil taco with crispy taro root.

one meat), a triplet of mains (abiding by the same format as the appetizers), and a trio of desserts to finish. The field-to-fork food changes depending on what local farmers are harvesting that week. Autumn might see a schmaltz-braised chicken served with celery root and rye, while spring is a lighter affair: raw trout, fava beans, and cucumber juice. The food, like the restaurant, is paired down to the essentials. Jason Carter has been called a chef's chef, making gimmick-free food that's intended to be eaten, not Instagrammed.

1198 Queen St. W. www.restaurantdandylion.com. © **647/464-9100.** Main courses $22–$26. Tues–Sat 5:30–10:30pm. Subway: Dufferin, then bus 29 S to Queen St. W.

Kiin ★★★ THAI   Chef Nuit Regular has been the driving force behind Toronto's Thai craze. At Khao San Road, there were lines out the door for her Northern Thai curries. Here, she's delving into more delicate fare. Throughout the menu are nods to Royal Thai cuisine, a rare form of Thai cooking differentiated by its beauty (with an emphasis on adding color, texture, and ornament to what would otherwise be common Thai dishes). Vibrancy is key: Dumplings are dyed purple with butterfly pea flowers, and rice is turned bright yellow with turmeric. Even the drinks are visual treats. A padan ice tea, for instance, is ombre, shifting from dark indigo to a mossy green. The 35-seat room is particularly pretty on weekends. During brunch, the marble-tiled space becomes a warm, sun-drenched dream, made all the more delightful as plates of coconut waffles whizz past.

326 Adelaide St. W. www.kiintoronto.com. © **647/490-5040.** Brunch $12–$20; dinner main courses $14–$28. Mon–Wed 5–10pm; Thurs–Fri 5–11pm; Sat–Sun 11am–3pm & 5–11pm. Subway: St. Andrew, then streetcar 504 W to John St.

Mira ★★★ PERUVIAN   Down a redbrick alley that connects King to Wellington Street, a trail of flickering lanterns leads to the back door of an office building. No, this isn't a speakeasy; it's a posh Peruvian restaurant. The sleek, 75-seat space was inspired by Lima's Miraflores neighborhood. Bright patterns, warm woods, and backlit mirrors overlaid with illustrations of gorgeously tattooed women set the dimly lit scene. The kitchen delights with creative ceviches (there are six on offer), unusual cuts (the jalapeño-stung beef heart is tender, yet lean), and imported South American ingredients like purple corn, yuca, and lucuma, a maple-flavored fruit found in the desserts and a few of the impressive house cocktails. The entrance is in the back of the building by way of the alley.

420A Wellington St. W. www.mirarestaurant.com. © **647/951-3331.** Main courses $17–$58. Mon–Thurs 5–11pm; Fri–Sat 5–midnight; Sun 5–11pm. Subway: St. Andrew, then streetcar 504 W to Spadina Ave.

Omai ★★ JAPANESE/KOREAN   This newcomer to Baldwin Village's cute strip of rowhouse restaurants has won a legion of ardent fans with its Japanese-Korean izakaya-style bar snacks. Chef-owner Edward Bang has Michelin training (he's worked the vaunted kitchens at NYC's Eleven Madison Park and Blue Hill at Stone Barns), but his food isn't the least bit pretentious. Of the 10 *temaki* (hand rolls) on offer, the Hokkaido Scallop with compressed green apple and crème fraîche is a standout. Hot plates like chanterelle-cheddar croquettes or eight-spice deep-fried chicken demand a sake chaser.

3 Baldwin St. www.omairestaurant.ca. ☎ **647/341-7766.** Main courses $24–$25 lunch, $22–$36 dinner. Tues–Thurs noon–3pm and 5–10pm; Fri noon–3pm and 5–midnight; Sat 5pm–midnight; Sun 5–10pm. Subway: St. Patrick, then walk N on McCaul St. W to Baldwin St.

Patois ★★ INTERNATIONAL   Craig Wong is pure Toronto. Three generations ago, his family decamped from Guangzhou, China, and settled down in Jamaica, which has a thriving Chinese-Jamaican community. Four decades ago his parents decided to move once more, this time to Toronto. Wong grew up in the ethnic hodgepodge of Scarborough, a diverse GTA suburb, then moved to France where he worked his way through the country's top kitchens before returning home to open his own restaurant. During his time under Michelin-starred Alain Ducasse, Wong learned heaps about high-end gastronomy, but perhaps he learned the most about himself. When opening Patois, he wanted to ditch the pomp of haute cuisine. This place is pure fun: cocktails in sparkler-adorned pineapples, pool floaties hanging from the ceiling, thumping hip hop, and a crushable menu. The food is inspired by the Jamaican-Chinese fusion Wong grew up eating. Think succulent rotisserie jerked chicken with *lap cheong* dirty rice.

794 Dundas St. W. www.patoistoronto.com. ☎ **647/350-8999.** Main courses $12–$20. Tues–Thurs 5–11pm; Fri–Sat 5–midnight; Sun 5–11pm. Subway: Bathurst, then streetcar 511 S to Dundas St. W.

Piano Piano ★★★ ITALIAN   For 25 years, this Annex room was home to Splendido, one of Toronto's top dining rooms, where nights began with Champagne carts and caviar, and ended with scotches old enough to legally drink scotch. In 2016, owner Victory Barry decided it was time for a refresh. With its bubblegum-pink exterior covered in a mural of multicolored roses, Barry is inviting guests to figuratively smell the roses, or literally smell the rosé, your choice. The restaurant's name is borrowed from the Italian phrase *"piano piano va lontano,"* which translates to "slowly slowly we go further." By this, Barry means, don't rush through life; stop and enjoy the little moments, like a good pizza dinner shared with friends over a few bottles of vino. The food isn't masquerading as authentic Italian. Barry likes to joke that it's New Jersey Italian. Here, the fancy red sauce fare is a far cry from boring baked ziti. The pastas are all house-made, the pizza dough takes days to proof, and the proteins are impressive. The veal parmesan, for instance, comes on the bone. The choice cut is then wrapped in sopressata before it's dredged in breadcrumbs and fried to perfection. When it comes to the table, slathered in San Marzano tomato sauce, the *fior di latte* still bubbling, you know you're now ruined for all other veal parms.

88 Harbord St. www.pianopianotherestaurant.com. ☎ **416/929-7788.** Main courses $17–$24 lunch, $24–$29 dinner. Mon–Thurs 11am–3pm and 5–10pm; Fri–Sat 11am–3pm and 5–11pm; Sun 11am–3pm & 5–10pm. Subway: Spadina, then streetcar 510 S to Harbord St.

BETTER THAN BREAKFAST, NOT QUITE lunch

Torontonians take their brunch very, very seriously. So be warned: If you're headed to a buzzed-about brunch spot, get there early. Most restaurants don't take reservations for the in-between meal, and it's not uncommon to while away an hour waiting for a table. Here are seven of the best brunch bets in town.

- **Beast** (96 Tecumseth St.; $\mathcal{C}$ **647/352-6000**): Best start popping Lipitor before the coffee arrives, because this meat-centric restaurant makes deliciously artery-clogging plates. A bowl of crispy pigs' ears tossed with feta and topped with a poached egg is uncomplicated perfection. Brunch served only on weekends.

- **Barque** (299 Roncesvalles Ave.; $\mathcal{C}$ **416/532-7700**): Southern barbeque and brunch collide at this smokehouse. Brunch served only on weekends.

- **Early Bird Coffee & Kitchen** (613 Queen St. W.; $\mathcal{C}$ **647/348-2473**): Healthful breakfast bowls and *shakshukas* (eggs poached in a spicy tomato sauce) are popular, but the eggs benny (topped with a beet-brightened hollandaise) is the top seller. Brunch served 7 days a week.

- **Federal** (1438 Dundas St. W.; $\mathcal{C}$ **647/352-9120**): Astronaut Chris Hadfield never actually said that the foie gras–topped French toast at this understated Dundas West eatery was "out of this world," but that *is* his go-to order when grabbing brunch here. Brunch served 7 days a week.

- **Mildred's Temple Kitchen** (85 Hanna Ave. #104; $\mathcal{C}$ **416/588-5695**): Get the Mrs. Biederhof's Legendary Light and Fluffy Blueberry Buttermilk Pancakes; they live up to their over-the-top name. Those of the savory persuasion (and an ample appetite) can't go wrong with the Manhandler, an open-faced 6-ounce flatiron steak sandwich topped with a duo of fried eggs. Brunch served 7 days a week.

- **Pow Wow Cafe** (213 Augusta Ave.; $\mathcal{C}$ **416/551-7717**): Ojibway chef Shawn Adle's poached-egg-topped frybread is addictive and goes well with cedar tea, an interesting alternative to coffee. What it lacks in caffeine punch, it makes up for with a piney pucker that cuts through the heavy food. Brunch served 7 days a week.

- **Saving Grace** (907 Dundas St. W.; $\mathcal{C}$ **416/703-7368**): The short menu is supplemented by blackboard-scrawled specials like polenta waffles topped with lime-whipped cream and pomegranate coulis. Brunch served 6 days a week. Closed Tuesdays.

- **Takht-e Tavoos** (1120 College St. W.; $\mathcal{C}$ **647/352-7322**): Food writer Ruth Reichl raved about the *kalleh pacheh* (a sheep-hoof soup) at this Persian brunch spot. Less adventurous eaters can opt for more familiar breakfast options like sunny-side-up eggs with halloumi cheese. Brunch served 5 days a week. Closed Mondays and Tuesdays.

Inexpensive

416 Snack Bar ★★ INTERNATIONAL   This broody Bathurst Street room is perennially at capacity. Outside, stylish 20-somethings queue and wait patiently for seats to free up. Inside, the decor is stripped down: corrugated aluminum wainscoting here, a bit of weathered wood there, and some exposed ducts, all made romantic with taper candles in antique silver holders. The seating, mostly communal, facilitates making new friends. The setup also lets guests get a sneak peak of the many five-bite snack options on offer. The ever-changing menu is nomadic, pulling from around the world, mixing and mashing cuisines with gusto. On one night there's a falafel double-down (a play on the KFC special), the next, a Thai chicken satay skewer.

81 Bathurst St. www.416snackbar.com. ✆ **416/364-9320.** Bar snacks $5–$15. Mon–Thurs 5pm–2am; Fri–Sun noon–2am. Subway: Bathurst, then streetcar 511 S to Queen St. W.

Assembly Chef's Hall ★★ INTERNATIONAL Forget everything you thought you knew about food courts. This upscale food hall includes stalls from 17 of the city's hottest chefs. It has everything from a very Tokyo standing-only omakase option (Tachi) to superfood snacks (Nutbar), Thai street food (Little Khao), and a beer hall. The sprawling, Adelaide-facing patio gets slammed by the after-work crowd. If you've got a group of friends who can't make up their mind about where to eat, come here.

111 Richmond St. W. www.assemblychefshall.com. ✆ **647/557-5993.** Prices vary depending on vendor. Mon–Wed 11:30am–11pm; Thurs–Fri 11:30am–midnight; Sat 4pm–midnight; Sun 11am–11pm. Subway: Osgoode, then walk S to Richmond St. W.

Burger's Priest ★ AMERICAN The no-nonsense Toronto-born burger joint was founded by a wannabe pastor who quit studying theology to begin flipping burgers. The name, to him, is innocent and playful, connoting his reverence and passion for the patty (although he does have a secret menu where burgers have names like "the religious hypocrite"—that would be a veggie burger with bacon). For years, Torontonians would pilgrimage to Burger's Priest's lone east-end spot, where the menu was displayed on a hymn board, and the secret menu was no more than a rumor. They came for the unfussy griddled burgers made from fresh, never-frozen beef served on a buttered bun. Now, the secret menu is online and Burger's Priest has a dozen locations around the GTA. But the burgers are still A1.

212 Adelaide St. W. www.theburgerspriest.com. ✆ **647/347-7757.** Burgers $8–$15. Mon–Wed 11am–9:30pm; Thurs 11–2am; Sat 11am–4am; Sun 11am–8pm. Subway: St. Andrews, then walk N on University Ave. to Adelaide St. W. Plus five other downtown locations.

Forno Cultura ★★★ ITALIAN It's captivating to watch the waltz of bakers behind the glass as they create tomato-topped focaccias and too-pretty pastries. Cream-filled *sfogliatelle* (imagine a horn-shaped croissant) are great to ogle, but best when enjoyed with an espresso. While the *dolce* are tempting, it's the shop's breads that locals rave about. Loaves made from long-fermented sourdough are sold whole and turned into forearm-sized sandwiches. The prosciutto di parma with *fior di latte* and arugula on ciabatta can feed two, amply. This is a popular postwork spot for a glass of wine and a plate of charcuterie.

609 King St. W. www.fornocultura.com. ✆ **416/603-8305.** Sandwiches and pizzas $8–$14. Tues–Sat 7:30am–9:30pm; Sun 8am–6pm. Subway: St. Andrew, then streetcar 504 W to Portland St.

Koi Koi ★ JAPANESE   Sake initiates and sake snobs alike will appreciate the drink list at this funky Kensington Market spot. The dozens of Japan-imported rice wines are listed by number on the menu (to avoid awkward mispronunciations) and come with tasting notes. Some taste of adzuki beans, others of tart green apples. All taste great when paired with a *katsu sando*—a big-in-Japan breaded pork sandwich.

170 Baldwin St. www.koikoibar.com. ✆ **647/343-4618.** Bar snacks $10–$14. Mon–Thurs 5pm–1am; Fri 5pm–2am; Sat 12:30pm–2am; Sun 5pm–1am. Subway: Spadina, then streetcar 510 S to Nassau St.

Oddseoul ★★ KOREAN/INTERNATIONAL   American classics collide with Korean flavors at this Ossington snack bar. It may sound confusing, but it works. The Loosey, a fresh take on the Pennsylvania sliced-bread hamburger, is a postmodern Big Mac pretender. It has the familiar crunch of iceberg, onion, and dill pickle, but the special sauce has been upgraded: a kimchi-zinged hollandaise that soaks into the thick-cut challah bread. The griddled patty (half fatty brisket, half lean rib eye) holds the precarious stack together, though eating it elegantly is near impossible. Luckily, between the dim lights and thumping bass, no one's likely to notice. They're too busy knocking back boozy cocktails to care.

90 Ossington Ave. No website. No phone. Bar snacks $5–$14. Mon–Sat 6pm–2am. Subway: Ossington, then bus 63 S to Argyle St.

Pai ★★★ THAI   Jeff Regular met his wife, Nuit, while riding an elephant in Thailand. He was traveling, and she was a local nurse who loved to cook and wanted to face her elephant fears. Shortly after that fateful meeting, the two decided to open a low-key restaurant together in the small town of Pai, in Northern Thailand. They're bringing those bold Thai flavors to Toronto in a raucous underground room that's buzzing with energy. Green curry served in a young coconut is delicate but bold. The braised beef in the *gaeng masaman*—a curry that's rich (from the peanuts) and tart (thanks to the tamarind)—is so tender it succumbs to the shadow of your fork before it melts in your mouth.

18 Duncan St. www.paitoronto.com. ✆ **416/901-4724.** Main courses $13–$16. Mon–Sat 11:30am–10pm; Sun 3–10pm. Subway: St. Andrew, then walk W on King St. W to Duncan St.

P.G Clucks ★ AMERICAN   According to the *National Post,* this takeout counter fries up the best bird in all of Canada. Boneless leg meat gets a double brine (first in a lemon-herb mixture, then in buttermilk), before it's double-dredged and fried to extra-crispy perfection. Diners can opt for the tender morsels one of two ways: classic or Nashville hot. Purists will say the classic sammy—made with coleslaw, pickles, and buttermilk ranch on a white bun—is the menu's best bet, but off-menu ordering is always fun. Honey-dipped fried chicken on a honey cruller with fermented jalapeño sauce is spicy, savory, yielding, crunchy, and sweet, all in one synapse-delighting bite.

610 College St. www.pgclucks.com. ✆ **416/539-8224.** Sandwiches $8–$11; combos $3 more. Tues–Sat noon–11pm; Sun noon–8pm. Subway: Queens Park, then streetcar 506 W to Grace St.

Porchetta & Co. ★★ ITALIAN Porchetta & Co. has quadrupled its capacity with a King West outpost. The original, five-seat, pork-slinging kitchen is still building porcine stacks on Dundas West, but owner Nick auf der Mauer's comparatively palatial new location proves that bigger is better—mostly because local craft beer is on offer at the new spot. The expanded menu, which includes sides like a chicharron-topped kale Caesar, is also a plus. The house special—a slice of slow-roasted porchetta slathered in truffle sauce, crunchy mustard, and hot sauce, finished with a flurry of parm, and served on a Thuet bun that's chewy, yet yielding—is still the best thing on offer. Heck, it might be the best sandwich downtown.

545 King St. W. www.porchettaco.com. ✆ **647/351-8844.** Main courses $9–$14; Mon–Wed 11:30am–10pm; Thurs–Sat 11:30am–11pm; Sun 11:30am–10pm. Subway: St. Andrew, then streetcar 504 W to Portland St. One other location.

Seven Lives ★ MEXICAN The cooks at this Tijuana-style taco joint don't skimp. Tacos are loaded to bursting, which is why two soft corn tortillas are necessary (for architectural stability). Even then, eating one of these flavorful pockets is near impossible—they're just that overloaded. Veteran Seven Lives customers know to grab a fork for the first few bites. Seafood is the focus here: chili-spiked cheesy shrimp, grilled octopus, and deep-fried baja fish, all good choices. The often sold-out ceviche, which comes on a guac-loaded tostada, is the best in Kensington Market. Don't try and fight for one of the half-dozen seats (the room becomes a zoo at peak times). Instead, grab lunch to go and enjoy the Mexican eats under the shade of one of Bellevue Square Park maple trees. Cash only.

69 Kensington Ave. No website. ✆ **416/803-1086.** Tacos $4–$7. Mon–Sun noon–8pm. Subway: Spadina, then streetcar 510 S to Nassau St.

Tennessee Tavern ★★★ POLISH/SLAVIC A live Balkan brass band brings a frenetic enthusiasm to evening dining. Even eating a platter of pickles becomes thrilling. Heck, everything's more fun with a trilling trumpet soundtrack. The eclectic Parkdale room—filled with a mix Soviet tchotchkes and religious icons—makes for the perfect backdrop to eat your weight in pierogis, which is actually possible on All You Can Eat Pierogi Sundays. After supper, the place turns even more raucous, aided in part by the lengthy list of *rakija* (Balkan fruit brandy). Avoid the plum stuff (it tastes like rubbing alcohol), and limit yourself to one order of the cherry brandy—it goes down too easy.

1554 Queen St. W. www.tennesseetavern.ca. ✆ **416/535-7777.** Brunch $13–$17; main courses $7–$17. Mon–Thurs 6pm–midnight; Fri 6pm–2am; Sat 11am–2am. Subway: Dundas West, then streetcar 504 S to Sorauren Ave.

Traditional Chinese Bun ★★ CHINESE This Chinatown hole in the wall has a basement entrance that looks more like an abattoir than a restaurant. It doesn't instill great dining confidence. But the food more than makes up for the uninviting atmosphere. Everything is made in house, from the dumplings

roast **OF THE TOWN**

Toronto has heaps of great cafes slinging single-origin flat whites, but the best spots to grab a cup of joe roast their own beans. These five roasters supply most of the other cafes in town and have cute coffee shop fronts to boot.

- **Balzac's Coffee Roastery** (Building 60, 55 Mill St.; *©* **416/207-1709**): This airy cafe invites lounging upstairs in the loft living room or downstairs near the roaster. Beans are fresh-roasted and then micro-roasted on the premises for super freshness.
- **Ezra's Pound** (238 Dupont St.; *©* **416/929-4400**): You can sit down to warm croissants, a light lunch, or just plain great coffee—organic and fair trade—where Wi-Fi invites lingering in the pretty space. This place is more tranquil than most coffee bars.
- **De Mello Palheta** (2489 Yonge St.; *©* **647/748-3633**): The roasts might have silly names like Dancing Goats (from Brazil's Serras de Minas) or Dead Man Walking (a blend of Ethiopian and Brazilian beans), but the

Aussie expats who run this North Toronto spot are serious about their coffee.

- **I Deal Coffee** (Nassau St.; *©* **416/364-7700**): Eccentric Market regulars camp out on the sunny patio where an impromptu jam session isn't out of the question. Buy a pound of fresh-roasted beans and get a free espresso-based drink on the house.
- **Propeller Coffee** (50 Wade Ave.; *©* **416/479-3771**): Grab a crema-capped espresso and tuck into one of the communal tables, which look into the glass-encased roasting room where the alchemical coffee magic happens—in small batches, of course.
- **Reunion Island Coffee Bar** (385 Roncesvalles Ave.; *©* **905/829-8520**): Oakville's 20-year-old roastery opened a bright, minimalist room on Roncesvalles where their beans are sold by the pound and turned into foam-feather-finished lattes. Bean heads will swoon over the Modbar espresso system.

to the hand-pulled *biangbiang* noodles. Specialties include lamb dishes from Shaanxi and Sichuan plates with high Scoville counts. The potato noodles, which taste like a ramen-gnocchi love child, are phenomenal.

536 Dundas St. W. www.chinesetraditionalbuns.ca. *©* **416/299-9011**. Main courses $9–$17. Mon–Sun 11:30am–11pm. Subway: Spadina, then streetcar 510 S to Dundas St. W.

DOWNTOWN EAST
Very Expensive

Cafe Belong ★★ CANADIAN   The Evergreen Brick Work's only restaurant abides by the institution's eco-foundations with a mandate to use only ethically raised meats and sustainably sourced ingredients. Locavaores will delight in chef Brad Long's seasonally driven plates, which often feature foraged elements like garlic scapes and beechnuts. You can't get more low carbon in terms of your food's impact when the sumac is picked from a nearby hillside and the honey comes from the bees across the parking lot.

In the Evergreen Brick Works, 550 Bayview Ave. www.cafebelong.ca. ℰ **416/901-8234.** Brunch $12–$26; main courses $21–$32 lunch, $22–35 dinner. Mon–Tues 11:30am–3pm; Wed–Fri 11:30am–9pm; Sat 10am–10pm; Sun 10:30am–3pm. A free Evergreen Brick Works shuttle bus departs regularly from the parkette on Erindale Ave., north of the station, east of Broadview Ave.

Expensive

Biff's ★★ FRENCH   For over 15 years, concert goers have been heading to this modern French bistro for their pre-show dinners (it's directly across from the Sony Centre for the Performing Arts). The kitchen has mastered the big bistro hits: steak tartare, duck confit, escargot, beef bourguignon. Offerings are rounded out with a few unexpected Parisian departures including Quebecois tourtière and a Portuguese-inspired salad topped with octopus and chorizo.

4 Front St. E. www.biffsbistro.com. ℰ **416/860-0086.** Main courses $19–29 lunch, $25–$37 dinner. Mon–Wed 11:45am–10pm; Thurs–Fri 11:45am–10:30pm; Sat 5–10:30pm; Sun 5–9pm. Subway: King, then walk S to Front St. E.

Carbon Bar ★★ BARBECUE   Barbecue is usually a casual affair. Not here. The room reads more upscale bistro than backyard cookout (tufted, maroon leather booths; exposed brick; double-height ceilings). BBQ purists will want to stick to the St. Louis–cut pork ribs and brisket, but Carbon Bar's lighter fare deserves a hat tip, too. Bourbon-marinated chicken is sweet and succulent and best enjoyed with one of the on-theme cocktail creations like the Pit-Fired Old-Fashioned made with house-smoked bourbon.

99 Queen St. E. www.thecarbonbar.ca. ℰ **416/947-7000.** Main courses $17–$25 brunch, $24–$38 dinner. Mon–Wed 4–10pm; Thurs–Sat 4–11pm; Sun 10:30am–2:30pm and 5–10pm. Subway: Queen, then streetcar 501 E to Church St.

Moderate

Madrina ★ SPANISH   A Victorian grain mill has been transformed into a tapas bar that would easily fit into a Catalonian town. Exposed stone walls are adorned by backlit art that's reminiscent of Picasso. Design house Studio Munge has done up the space in wood on wood on wood, a Pantone book's worth of warm tones. Rather than read the wine list, look around the room; every wine on offer—all Spanish—doubles as decoration. Catalan import Chef Ramón Simarro is making modern tapas that reimagines tapas.

In the Distillery District, 2 Trinity St. www.madrinatapas.com. ℰ **416/548-8055.** Lunch main courses $16–$24; dinner tapas $5–$28. Mon–Tues 5–10pm; Thurs and Sun noon–10pm; Fri–Sat noon–11pm; closed Wed. Subway: Union, then bus 121 E to the Distillery District.

Terroni ★ ITALIAN   In 1992, Terroni was one of the first trattorias to bring A-class Italian to Toronto. Fast-forward almost 4 decades, and it's still making

Downtown East Restaurants

Balzac's Coffee Roastery **19**
Biff's **16**
Cafe Belong **2**
Carbon Bar **8**
Carrousel Bakery **18**
City Betty **4**
The Civic **9**

Descendant **12**
Eastside Social **11**
Fresh on Front **17**
George Street Diner **13**
Kanpai Snack Bar **1**
Pinkerton Snack Bar **6**

Pizzeria Libretto **3**
Real Jerk **5**
Roselle **15**
Ruby Watchco **10**
The Senator **7**
Soma **20**
Terroni **14**

Post Office ⊠
TTC Subway — Ⓣ

some of the best Neapolitan-style pizzas in town. With two dozen pies on offer, there's something for every taste (whether you like red or white, a classic Margherita, or loaded with toppings), which is why this kitchen has a strict no-substitutions policy. The house-made pastas never disappoint. Service is prompt, though this place is known for serving a little attitude with a side of arancini.

57 Adelaide St. E. www.terroni.com. © **416/203-3093.** Main courses $16–$21. Sun–Thurs 11am–10pm; Fri–Sat 11am–11pm. Subway: King, then walk N to Adelaide St. E.

The Senator ★ AMERICAN   A stone's throw from the neon ads of Yonge-Dundas Square, Toronto's oldest restaurant is still in operation. This quaint squeeze of a diner retains its yesteryear charm, though little remains of the original 1929 incarnation. But classic comfort foods such as meatloaf, fried liver, and chicken pot pie never go out of style. Upstairs, the second-floor **wine bar** might be a new addition, but thanks to its Belle Époque vibe, it feels like it's been around a while. Head up after dinner for great vino and live music.

249 Victoria St. www.thesenator.com. © **416/364-7517.** Main courses $16–$26 lunch, $20–$32 dinner. Downstairs diner: Mon 7:30am–2:15pm; Tues–Wed 7:30am–7:45pm; Thurs–Fri 7:30am–8:45pm; Sat 8am–8:45pm; Sun 8am–2:15pm. Upstairs wine bar: Thurs–Fri 5:30pm–midnight; Sat–Sun 9:30am–3pm. Subway: Dundas, then walk E to Victoria St.

Inexpensive

Carrousel Bakery ★ SANDWICHES   The St. Lawrence Market has heaps of tasty things to sample, but there's a reason for the permanent queue at this bakery. Tourists and locals alike line up for the peameal bacon sandwiches: thick slices of peameal bacon and a dollop of grainy mustard on a plain, fresh-baked roll. It's simple perfection that's been dubbed the most iconic sandwich in town. Cash only.

In the St. Lawrence Market, Upper Level, stall #42, 92 Front St. E. © **416/363-4247.** www.stlawrencemarket.com/vendors/vendor_detail/56. Tues–Thurs 8am–6pm; Fri 8am–7pm; Sat 5am–5pm. Subway: Union, then walk E on Front St. E.

Kanpai Snack Bar ★ TAIWANESE   Like Toronto, Taiwan is a cultural melting pot, an island nation where Japanese, Fujian, and mainland Chinese foods collide into nuanced deliciousness. This chic, lo-fi Cabbagetown room isn't concerned with authenticity. Owner Trevor Lui likes to say, "When Taipei meets Toronto, Kanpai happens." Taiwanese-spiced fried chicken, for instance, is fried on the bone because Lui thinks the American-style fried bird is juicier (and just better) than the pounded poultry filet that's popular in Taiwan. Exceptional cocktails with cheeky names go down easy.

252 Carlton St. www.kanpaisnackbar.com. © **416/968-6888.** Mon–Thurs 5pm–11pm; Fri 5pm–midnight; Sat 11am–midnight; Sun 11am–10pm. Snacks $6–$15. Subway: Castle Frank, then the 65 bus S to Carlton St.; or College Station, then streetcar 506 E to Parliament St.

DOWNTOWN NORTH

Very Expensive

Actinolite ★★★ CANADIAN   Toronto food critic Chris Nuttall-Smith has called Actinolite one of the most essential places to eat in Ontario, if not in Canada. There's a purity to the restaurant's food-driven directive: to show off Southern Ontario's landscape through cooking. In spring, expect fresh foraged ramps and fiddleheads. In summer, sorrel and marigolds are snagged from the garden out back. Crops are preserved into pickles, jellies, and more, only to return to the menu in different incarnations. Ramps come back months later, this time adding pickled punch. Chef Justin Cournoyer is a slow-food evangelist. "For everything there is a season. Even meat," he once told me. This is why summer menus are vegetable-powered splendors, while winter is a heartier affair.

971 Ossington Ave. www.actinoliterestaurant.com. ✆ **416/962-8943.** Tasting menu $105. Tues–Sat 6–10pm. Subway: Ossington, then bus 63 N to Hallam St.

Joso's ★★ MEDITERRANEAN   Entering its fifth decade, Joso's is one of the oldest still-serving restaurants in Yorkville—and the grand dame of Toronto seafood is looking good for her age. If this upscale spot for Dalmatian-style grilled fish seems familiar, that's because it graced the cover Drake's *Take Care* album. Toronto's best-known rapper isn't the only celeb to covet the cuttlefish-ink risotto here. Barbra Streisand, Mariah Carey, and Mick Jagger are but a few of the A-listers who've stopped by over the years.

202 Davenport Rd. www.josos.com. ✆ **416/925-1903.** Main courses $28–$68. Mon–Fri 11:30am–2pm and 5:30–9:30pm; Sat 5–10pm. Subway: Dupont, then bus 26 E to Avenue Rd.

Expensive

Barrio Coreano ★ KOREAN/MEXICAN   Korean ingredients marry Mexican comfort food at this 75-seat Bloor West room that plays fast and loose with culinary borders. A corn tortilla, for example, is stuffed with bulgogi shrimp, while a K-Mex salad combines Korean cabbage with avocado, corn, and *queso fresco* in a ginger sesame dressing. The funky space abides by the distressed-chic aesthetic: neon lights, purposefully peeling paint, tabletops made from salvaged bowling lanes, rusting seats that were imported from an Indian cricket stadium. It sounds dingy, but when these elements are polished and combined, the space is quite glam in its own tetanus-tempting way.

642 Bloor St. W. www.playacabana.ca/barrio. ✆ **416/901-5188.** Main courses $13–$21. Tues–Thurs 5–10pm; Fri 5pm–1am; Sat noon–1am; Sun noon–10pm. Subway: Bathurst, then walk W on Bloor St. W.

Constantine ★★ MEDITERRANEAN   Summer 2018 marked Toronto's pyro phase: the city became obsessed with flame-cooked fare, and Constantine was at the forefront of the zeitgeist. An elegant dining room fans out around the open kitchen, where chefs in crisp uniforms tend the fires. There are two here: one blazes under the parilla (where Cornish hens and rib eyes

Downtown North Restaurants

St. Clair Ave. W.

St. Clair Ave. W

ST. CLAIR WEST

Dufferin St.

Westmount Ave.
Northcliffe Ave.
Lauder Ave.
Glenholme Ave.
Oakwood Ave.
Robina Ave.
Winona Dr.
Atlas Ave.
Arlington Ave.
Rushton Rd.
Pinewood Ave.
Wychwood Ave.
Kenwood Ave.
Vaughan Rd.
Ragland Ave.
Tichester Rd.

Rosemount Ave.
Oakwood Ave.
Alberta Ave.
Greensides Ave.
Benson Ave.
Rushton Rd.
Christie St.
Wychwood Ave.

Ellsworth Ave.
Hocken Ave.
Helena Ave.
Alcina Ave.

Bathurst St.
Hilton Ave.
Wellshill Ave.
Lyndhurst Ave.
Nina St.

Tyrell Ave.

Wychwood Park
Burnside

Bristol Ave.
Bartlett Ave. N
Salem Ave. N
Westmoreland Ave. N
Dovercourt Rd.
Delaware Ave. N
Somerset Ave.
Ossington Ave.
Shaw St.

Davenport Rd.

Hillcrest Dr.

Hillcrest Park

Davenport Rd.

Austin Terr.

Walmer Rd.
Kendal Ave.

Albany Ave.
Bridgman Ave.

Dufferin St.

Geary Ave.

Hammond Pl.

Dupont St.

Gladstone Ave.
Bartlett Ave.
Salem Ave.
Westmoreland Ave.
Dovercourt Rd.
Delaware Ave.
Concord Ave.
Ossington Ave.

Hallam St.

Yarmouth Rd.

Vermont Ave.

Vermont Square

Clinton St.
Christie St.
Albany Ave.
Lippincott St.
Howland Ave.
Kendal Ave.

Wells St.
Jean Sibelius Square

Dovercourt Park

Essex St.

Olive Ave.
Follis Ave.

Pendrith St.

Shanly St.

Barton Ave.

Markham St.

Leeds St.

Christie Pits Park

London St.

DUFFERIN

Bloor St. W.

OSSINGTON

CHRISTIE

BATHURST

Bloor St. W

DUFFERIN

Havelock St.
Rusholme Rd.
Dovercourt Rd.
Delaware Ave.
Concord Ave.
Ossington Ave.
Roxton Rd.
Shaw St.
Crawford St.
Montrose Ave.
Grace St.
Clinton St.
Manning Ave.
Euclid Ave.

Herrick St.

Sussex

Dufferin Grove Park

Bickford Park

Harbord St.

PALMERSTON

Harbord

Ulster St.

Palmerston Ave.
Bathurst St.
Markham St.
Lippincott St.
Howland Ave.
Brunswick Ave.
Major St.

College St.

Oxford St.

KENSINGTON

0   1/4 mi
0   0.25 km

TTC Subway — T

Actinolite 13	Joso's 15	Pukka 3
Annabelle Pasta Bar 7	Kŭ-kŭm Kitchen 2	Scaramouche 8
Barrio Coreano 19	Lasa 4	Schmaltz Appetizing 10
Bar Begonia 11	Little Sister 1	Shunoko 5
Bar Reyna 16	Parallel 9	The Stop Market Café 6
Big Crow 12	Piano Piano 21	Sugo 17
Black Camel 14	Planta 19	Tacos El Asador 18
Constantine 20	The Pomegranate 23	Yasu 22

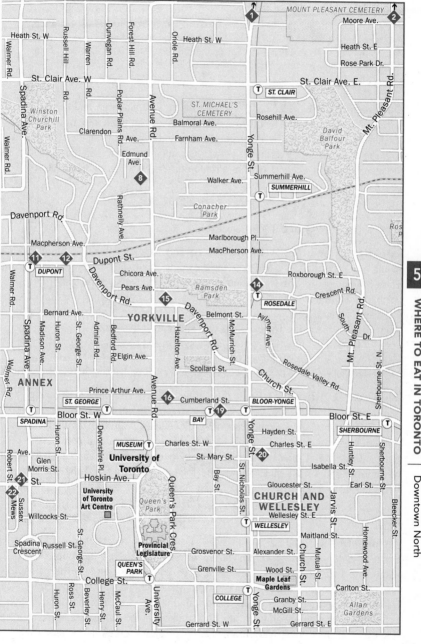

roast); the other is a wood-fired brick oven where fennel is caramelized, eggplant is roasted, and pizzas are made. As Chef Craig Harding tells me on a visit: "This is the hearth of our home."

In the Anndore House, 15 Charles St. E. www.constantineto.com. © **647/475-4436.** Breakfast $6–$17; brunch $12–$21; main courses $14–$25 lunch, $14–$35 dinner. Mon–Wed 7am–11pm; Thurs–Fri 7–1am; Sat 8am–1am; Sun 8am–10pm. Subway: Bloor-Yonge, then walk S on Yonge St., E on Charles St. E.

Moderate

Bar Begonia ★★ FRENCH   The room is very Montmartre and the food is pure Paris. You almost feel the urge to slip on a beret while ordering duck confit rillette with crusty baguette, cornichons, and mustard. Push the charade over the edge, and order a flute of grower's champagne. Annex literati swarm the place late on weekends, swirling Prohibition-era cocktails as Serge Gainsbourg croons in the background.

252 Dupont St. www.barbegonia.com. © **647/352-3337.** Brunch $10–$17; main courses $16–$32. Mon–Wed 5–11pm; Thurs 5pm–midnight; Fri 5pm–2am; Sat 11am–3pm and 5pm–2am; Sun 1am–3pm and 5pm–2am. Subway: Dupont.

Bar Reyna ★★ MEDITERRANEAN   This unapologetically feminine haunt for Yorkville's see-and-be-seen crowd is fabulously decorated. The glass-covered patio, with white umbrellas hanging from above and lush tropical plants below, is a great place to savor a fruity cocktail like Her Royal Highness, a cardamom- and rosewater–infused grapefruit bracer served in a giant copper pineapple. The evenings turn sultry with live jazz.

158 Cumberland St. www.barreyna.com. © **647/748-4464.** Brunch $12–$22; main courses $16–$36. Mon–Wed 11am–11pm; Thurs 11am–1am; Fri–Sat 11–2am; Sun 11am–4pm. Subway: Bay, then walk N on Bellair St., W on Cumberland St.

Big Crow ★★ BARBECUE   In the warmer months, Big Crow is like a big backyard BBQ, where the drinks are endless and you never need to clean a dish. The menu of smoked and charcoal-grilled meats is summer through and through (rainbow trout with maple-roasted Brussels sprouts and pecans is a personal favorite). Come late autumn, the outdoor spot goes through a winter metamorphosis. In ski-chalet mode, the food gets heartier and the smoke wafts a little longer.

176 Dupont St. www.roseandsonsbigcrow.com. © **647/748-3287.** Main courses $16–$27. Mon–Sat 5–11pm; Sun 5–10pm. Subway: Dupont, then walk E on Dupont St.

Parallel ★★★ MIDDLE EASTERN   On an industrial stretch, a block north of Dupont, great food things are happening between the auto-body shops and fish wholesalers. Parallel, a 2018 addition to the strip, is built around a single ingredient: sesame butter. Made on site, it's whipped into hummus, served with herb falafels, and found in the salad dressings. Tahini is turned electric pink with beets, it's also smoked (in the fattoush salad), and it's even steamed into latte form. The family-run restaurant is entirely open-concept. Walk up to the mezzanine for a great view of the sesame press and the indoor herb garden.

217 Geary Ave. https://parallelbrothers.com. © **416/516-7765.** Brunch $12–$14; main courses $12–$14 lunch, $15–$25 dinner. Tues 11am–5pm; Wed–Thurs 11am–10:30pm; Fri–Sat 11am–11:30pm; Sun 10am–4pm. Subway: Dufferin, then bus 29 N to Dupont St.

The Pomegranate ★★ PERSIAN   Colorful textile wall hangings and hammered copper chandeliers transport diners to Tehran. Ask for a table by the tiled fountain, where calico-colored fish glide and splash. The stews are the culinary highlight. Many plates come in both carnivore and vegetarian permutations. The *fesenjān* (an hours-long simmered delight of walnut and pomegranate paste), for instance, can be ordered with either chicken or oyster mushrooms.

418 College St. www.pomegranaterestaurant.ca. © **416/921-7557.** Main courses $12–$18. Tues–Thurs 5–9pm; Fri–Sat 5–10pm; Sun 5–9pm. Subway: Bathurst, then streetcar 511 S to College St.

Inexpensive

Annabelle Pasta Bar ★ ITALIAN   Every day a different trio of house-made pastas is on offer at this romantic trattoria. One day it's buckwheat orecchiette smothered in goat ragù, the next it's pappardelle with zucchini and mint or lamb Bolognese rigatoni, all priced at $10. Located in a narrow, two-story Davenport Village house that looks as if it was decorated by a 27-year-old thrift-store junkie, the trattoria has a casual, convivial ambience. The expansive negroni list is more interesting than the overpriced Italian wines. Service is hit or miss, but the value and quaint setting more than make up the difference.

909 Davenport Rd. annabellerestaurant.com. No phone. Main courses $10–$13. Mon–Wed noon–10pm; Thurs noon–11pm; Fri noon–midnight; Sat 10am–3:30pm and 5pm–midnight; Sun 10am–3:30pm and 5–10pm. Subway: Bathurst, then bus 7 N to Davenport Rd.

Schmaltz Appetizing ★★ JEWISH   Six types of fish are cured daily at this small Dupont bagel shop. Beet-root Pacific salmon gravlax and Acadian sturgeon are standouts. Those averse to fish will appreciate deli staples like chopped liver and egg salad. Although the focus here is on sandwiches, the shop offers a few grocery items: mustards, pickles, flavored cream cheeses, cured fish by the pound, as well as desserts. Black-and-white cookies are on theme, but it's the dessert bars—one is layered with chocolate, coconut, walnuts, and caramel atop a graham cracker foundation—that are the stuff of dreams. Good coffee.

414 Dupont St. www.schmaltzappetizing.com. © **647/350-4261.** Bagel sandwiches $7–$12. Mon–Sun 8am–7pm. Subway: Bathurst, then bus 7 N to Dupont.

Sugo ★ ITALIAN   If the Genovese crime family was based in Toronto instead of New Jersey, this is where they'd come for eggplant parm with a side of meatballs. This red-sauce joint is a favorite among the boxing community.

The kitchen hires up-and-coming young fighters who prep no-fuss pasta plates between sparring bouts. On the walls are framed pictures of famed fighters (George Chuvalo, Muhammad Ali, and others) along with local legends. This Bloorcourt spot is a great place to carb-load, watch the fight, and play a few rounds of foosball.

1281 Bloor St. W. www.sugotoronto.com. © **416/535-1717.** Main courses $10–$13. Mon–Sat 11:30am–9:30pm. Subway: Lansdowne.

Tacos El Asador ★ MEXICAN   A cheery yellow room serving a mix of Salvadorian and Mexican food in the heart of Koreatown. Everything, including the corn tortillas, are made from scratch at this well-loved spot for tacos, papusas, and enchiladas. Good for families.

689 Bloor St. W. © **416/538-9747.** Main courses $6–$9. Mon–Fri noon–9pm. Subway: Christie.

MIDTOWN & UPTOWN

Georgian mansions and sprawling lawns are pretty, but monied neighborhoods like Davisville and Summerhill, despite their denizens' deep pockets, don't have the density to support a robust restaurant row (though a few upscale gems are scattered around). Recently, exciting food things have been happening farther west: St. Clair West has become the hottest new dining destination in town, thanks to still-cheap rent and a revamped, speedy streetcar link. Restaurants in this section can be found on the "Downtown North" map on p. 102.

Very Expensive

Scaramouche ★★★ FRENCH   Chef Keith Froggett and maitre d' Carl Corte have been quietly perfecting one of the city's finest restaurants for over 30 years. The formal dining room, best for special occasions, is nicely complemented by the adjoining casual pasta bar and grill. Located in a tony apartment building in Midtown, it has beautiful views over the city.

1 Benvenuto Place. www.scaramoucherestaurant.com. © **416/961-8011.** Main courses $31–$56. Mon–Thurs 5:30–9:30pm; Fri–Sat 5:30–10pm. Subway: Museum, then bus 5 N Edmund Ave. R on Edmund Ave., then L on Benvenuto Place.

Expensive

KŬ-kŭm Kitchen ★★ INDIGENOUS   Odawa chef Joseph Shawana's Davisville restaurant is one of the few places in the city serving bold, exciting Indigenous plates. Of all the excellent game meats on the menu (and there are many, including elk, boar, venison, rabbit, and bison), the (lawfully hunted) harp seal from northern Quebec and Labrador is the most interesting. Raw seal is an acquired taste, like liver from a cow with a proclivity for open-water swimming, and this is the only place in Toronto that serves it. Seared seal loin, by comparison, is accessible and oh so delicious: tender yet lean, with iron-y depth. Dessert here is more than just a sweet afterthought. A sweetgrass crème brûlée is intriguingly herbal and just sweet enough. KŬ-kŭm has a well-priced Ontario wine selection. Non-alcoholic options like a house-made cedar soda are also worth trying.

581 Mt Pleasant Rd. www.kukum-kitchen.com. ℂ **416/519-2638.** Main courses: $22–$32. Wed 5–10pm; Sun 3–9pm. Subway: St. Clair, then bus 74 E to Belsize Dr.

Moderate

Little Sister ★★ INDONESIAN   What Indian curry is to England, Indonesian *rendang* is to the Netherlands. For centuries, the Dutch claimed the Indonesian Archipelago as a colony, profiting from the spice trade. Today, Indonesian food remains popular in the Netherlands, and at Little Sister, Chef Michael van den Winkel is serving up the spice-rich cuisine with a focus on the street foods that are popular in Jakarta and Surabaya today. The Midtown room looks into the leaded-glass-encased kitchen, meant to evoke the street-hawker stalls of Kaki Lima. Cocktails are richly flavored with spices and herbs. The gin-based Ubud Hangout, for instance, blends cilantro, black pepper, and jalapeño together for fabulous depth.

2031 Yonge St. www.littlesisterto.com. ℂ **416/488-2031.** Small plates $7–$16. Sun–Mon 4:45–9:30pm; Tues–Wed 4:45–10pm; Thurs–Sat 4:45–11pm. Subway: Davisville, then walk N up Yonge.

Pukka ★★ INDIAN   At this modern Indian bistro, the kitchen is taking electric Indian flavors and upgrading the presentation. *Saag paneer* is reimagined: Here, two slices of house-made cheese are seared, then stuffed with tomato-braised spinach and garnished with pea flowers. Vegetable *pakoras* look like fancy curly fries (the type of fries the Queen Mum would be seen eating). Offering many vegetarian and vegan offerings, it's a great pick for a demanding group, and it's also good for families. Pukka has an exciting wine list and a sommelier keen to chat about pairing spice with different grapes.

778 St Clair Ave. W. www.pukka.ca. ℂ **416/342-1906.** Main courses: $17–$35. Sun–Thurs 5–10pm; Fri–Sat 5–10:30pm. Subway: St. Clair West, then streetcar 512 W to Arlington Ave.

Shunoko ★★★ JAPANESE   Chef Jun Kim dropped out of high school when he realized he wanted to dedicate his life to sushi. He respected his chef father's culinary skills, but he knew that he couldn't learn from a man whom he has called the "Korean Gordon Ramsay." Instead, he left Toronto and moved back to his native Korea to learn from his uncle, one of the first generation of Korean sushi chefs dedicated to the Japanese craft. After years of perfecting his skills (apparently, learning to make great sushi starts with killing your own fish), Kim has opened this St. Clair West restaurant. The minimalist space (whitewashed bricks, pine beams) brings focus to the food. Wasabi is the real stuff, grated by hand; soya sauce is made in-house. And the sushi is playful. Of course, the nigiri and sashimi are very good, but Kim has fun with the maki. A spicy tuna-avocado maki rolled in popped rice and topped with toasted coconut is anything but orthodox. The omakase here is a great value.

1201 St Clair Ave. W. www.shunoko.com. ✆ **647/748-7288.** Sushi/sashimi sets $14–$35. Mon–Sat noon–3pm and 5–10pm. Subway: Dufferin, then bus 29 N to St. Clair W.

Inexpensive

Black Camel ★★ SANDWICHES   The brisket sandwiches are so good here, they disappear in under 5 minutes, despite taking 5 days to make. Beef from the Butcher Shoppe is left to marinate in a sweet spice rub for 3 days, before it's slow-roasted overnight for up to 14 hours. The sloppy mess—best when swimming in the house molasses BBQ sauce with a pile of caramelized onions—is well contained by the Portuguese bun. The bun must be magic: it sops up the sauce without every getting soggy. Although the brisket and the pulled pork often make best-of blogger lists, all seven of the sammies on offer at this tiny shop are stellar. Cheerful service.

4 Crescent Rd. ✆ **416/929-7518.** www.blackcamel.ca. Sandwiches $7.50–$10; sides $2.20–$5.75. Mon–Fri 7am–8pm; Sat–Sun 11am–8pm. Subway: Rosedale.

Lasa ★★ FILIPINO   This peppy, fast-casual eatery has some excellent cheap options. An order of six *lumpia,* spring rolls stuffed with hoisin-spiced pork sausage, is $6, while a duo of pork skewers (marinated in a 7-Up and soy blend) is also $6. Filipino classics are intended to be shared, though a bowl of braised oxtail-and-peanut stew called *kare kare,* which is fall-off-the bone splendor, might get bogarted despite its hefty size. Good for families.

634 St Clair Ave. W. www.lasabylamesa.com. ✆ **647/343-1110.** Main courses $12–$18. Tues–Sun noon–9pm. Subway: Bathurst, then bus 7 N to St. Clair W.

The Stop Market Café ★★★ CANADIAN   The **Wychwood Barns Farmer's Market** (which runs Sat mornings) is a great place to grab a piece-meal breakfast, but the best-kept secret is hidden in Barn 4. There, the Stop, a community hub with an anti-hunger mandate, serves wholesome breakfasts made from market ingredients brought in from local farms that very morning. The breakfasts include quiches, sandwiches, frittatas, and pancakes, but are always changing based on what's being grown in Ontario that week. Make sure to pop into the greenhouse after your meal. In winter, the scent of dirt and orange blossoms keeps the January blues at bay.

In Artscape Wychwood Barns, 601 Christie St. www.artscapewychwoodbarns.ca. ✆ **416/653-3520.** Breakfasts and sandwiches $7–$10. Sat 8am–12:30pm. Subway: Bathurst, then bus 7 N to St. Clair W.

THE EAST END

The general theme along the Danforth has long been Greek, although today you'll find more variety: Good pubs, bars, restaurants, and lounges line the busy thoroughfare. You can still come for good and middling (but cheap) Greek, too. Farther south on Gerrard Street, just west of the Indian Bazaar, a crop of cool snack bars have opened. Restaurants in this section can be found on the "Downtown East" map on p. 99.

Expensive

The Civic ★ CANADIAN   When chef John Sinopoli was asked to helm the kitchen at the Broadview Hotel's flagship restaurant, he decided to dig into the culinary culture of the Broadview's heyday. The resulting menu is rooted in turn-of-the-20th-century trends, executed through a modern lens. Oysters Rockefeller and chicken liver parfait are a few of the anachronistic items on offer. The mains are timeless; confit wild boar shank and roasted Mennonite chicken never go out of style. The glamorous, 100-seat dining room, with tufted maroon banquettes, Victorian wallpaper, and cool blue accent walls, could double as a "Boardwalk Empire" set. The most coveted seats are on the rooftop terrace. The 360-degree glass facade, topped with a pyramidal skylight, boasts sweeping views of downtown and the Don River.

In the Broadview Hotel, 106 Broadview Ave. www.thebroadviewhotel.ca/food-drink. html. ✆ **416/362-8439.** Brunch $14–$25; main courses $26–$42. Tues–Wed 6–10pm; Thurs–Fri 6–11pm; Sat 10am–3pm and 6–11pm; Sun 10am–3pm.

Ruby Watchco ★★★ CANADIAN   Ruby Watchco offers one exquisite prix-fixe dinner nightly featuring four courses and main ingredients supplied by local purveyors. Celebrity chefs Lynn Crawford and Lora Kirk work closely with farmers, and the mutual respect is evidenced in the truly inspired results. Service is warm and attentive.

730 Queen St. E. www.rubywatchco.ca. ✆ **416/465-0100.** Prix-fixe 4-course menu $56. Tues–Sat 6pm–10pm. Subway: Broadview, then streetcar 504 S to Queen St. E.

Moderate

City Betty ★★ BISTRO   This female-powered kitchen bills itself as a seven-season kitchen with bicoastal influences from New York and California powered by Southern Ontario ingredients. Vegetables are treated with particular reverence, with the kitchen regularly finding rare heritage varietals even your gardening-happy grandfather has never heard of. Watercolor-like murals, decorative crystals, and antique mirrors evoke a delicate splendor on an otherwise uninspiring eastern stretch of the Danforth—an area that is on the cusp of becoming Toronto's next restaurant row to watch.

1352 Danforth Ave. www.citybetty.com. ✆ **647/271-3949.** Brunch $10–$17; dinner main courses $13–$32. Wed 5–9pm; Thurs–Fri 5–10pm; Sat 10am–3pm and 5–10pm; Sun 10am–3pm & 5–9pm. Subway: Greenwood.

Descendant ★★ AMERICAN   You can find just about any style of pizza in Toronto. Whether you're hankering for thin-crust wood-fired or a New World pie drowning in cheese, the city's pie slingers have you covered. At this Leslieville parlor, the Detroit-style pizzas start with the dough. It's proofed for 2 days before being set into a well-oiled square pan and then layered from edge to edge with pepperoni, cheese, and, finally, tomato sauce on top (that's why these Motor City pies are sometimes called upside-down pizzas). The resulting crust is crunchy and caramelized on the bottom, with a gorgeous airiness. The beer and cider list includes Ontario craft brews such as Beau's.

1168 Queen St. E. www.descendantdsp.com. © **647/347-1168.** Pizzas $19–22. Tues–Sun 11:30am–10pm. Subway: Queen, then streetcar 501 E to Jones Ave.

Eastside Social ★ SEAFOOD   This neighborhood haunt with its stylish maritime decor (it's more vintage cool than seaside kitsch) is where locals come to hang out with "Restaurant Makeover" star Cherie Stinson. The TV celeb handles the dining room, which she decorated, while the kitchen sends out fresh-caught seafood plates inspired by global coastal spots from Normandy (*moules frites*) to Hawaii (ahi tuna poke), Portugal (house-cured sardine crostinis), and New England (clam chowder). This 52-seat spot is unpretentious, fun, and laidback.

1008 Queen St. E. www.eastsidesocial.ca. © **416/461-5663.** Main courses $18–$29. Mon–Thurs 6pm–midnight; Fri–Sat 6pm–1am. Sunway: Queen, then streetcar 501 E to Carlaw Ave.

Pizzeria Libretto ★ ITALIAN   To eat your pizza "libretto style" means pinching the crust in such a way that it folds the slice shut, almost like closing a book. (Libretto, after all, means "booklet" in English.) It's a necessary strategy when eating the floppy Neapolitan pizzas pulled from the wood-fired oven at this Danforth pizzeria. The food is textbook Neapolitan: pizzas, salads, and *assaggini* such as burrata, beef carpaccio, and buttermilk-fried calamari. Pizzeria Libretto has four other locations; check the website for addresses.

550 Danforth Ave. www.pizzerialibretto.com. © **416/466-0400.** Main courses $13–$19. Sun–Thurs 11:30am–10pm; Fri–Sat 11:30am–11pm. Subway: Chester.

Inexpensive

George Street Diner ★★ DINER   This diner is a dead ringer for the soda shop Archie Andrews and his Riverdale pals frequent in the famed comic series. With its soda fountain bar seats and red vinyl booths, stepping into the George Street Diner transports you away from the skyscraping Toronto of today to a simpler time, an era of meatloaf mains and milkshakes. Many think that the wallet-friendly prices equal standard greasy diner fare. This is not the case. The George Street kitchen places an emphasis on organic ingredients and seasonal produce. So while classics like club sandwiches, burgers, and grilled cheeses are on offer, there are many healthful options, too, including a fabulously fresh fattoush falafel salad. For breakfast, the banana chocolate chip French toast is a crowd-pleasing belt-buster. Or you could be healthy and order the house-made granola, but where's the fun in that?

129 George St. © **416/862-7676.** thegeorgestreetdiner.blogspot.com. Breakfast $8–$14; main courses $8.50–$13. Mon–Fri 7:30am–4pm; Sat–Sun 8:30am–3:30pm. Subway: Queen, then streetcar 501 E to Jarvis, then 1 block W to George St.

Pinkerton Snack Bar ★ INTERNATIONAL   Just west of the Gerrard Indian Bazaar, a clutch of hip cafes and restaurants has opened. Pinkerton was one of the first to bring Queen West cocktail culture to Gerrard East. Handsome bearded specimens man the bar at this raucous east end destination for

Ontario ciders, craft beers, and creative cocktails. The Asian-influenced small plates, like a Korean *chijimi* pancake topped with braised pork shoulder, are rave-worthy.

1026 Gerrard St E. No website. ☏ **416/855-1460.** Bar snacks $7–$11. Wed–Sun 6pm–2am. Subway: College, then streetcar 506 E to Marjory Ave.

Real Jerk ★ JAMAICAN Drake must love combining food and music; this is the second Toronto restaurant to make a Drake cameo (after Joso's, see p. 101). In the music video for "Work," the Real Jerk doubles as a Caribbean dancehall where Drizzy and Riri get lost in a crowd of smoke, bass, and pulsating bodies. Most nights, though, this is a great family spot for traditional Jamaican plates such as pepper shrimp, banana fritters, roti, and jerk chicken.

842 Gerrard St. E. ☏ **416/463-6055.** www.therealjerk.com. Main courses $8–$24. Mon–Wed 11:30am–10pm; Thurs 11:30–12:30am; Fri 11:30–1am; Sat noon–1am; Sun 2–10pm. Subway: College, then streetcar 506 E to Carlaw Ave.

UPTOWN

This area is too large to be considered a neighborhood, stretching as it does from north of Eglinton Avenue to Steeles Avenue. While it doesn't have the concentration of restaurants that the downtown area enjoys, a number of stellar options make the trip north worth your while.

Very Expensive

Auberge du Pommier ★ FRENCH The charming maître d' welcomes guests into this stone cottage, his Basque accent setting the mood for an enchanting experience. The lush terrace, with its retractable glass roof, could pass for a St. Tropez patio (the servers speaking to one another in French only perfects the illusion). Inside the circa-1860 woodcutters cottages—the two Victorian buildings were fused together to create Auberge du Pommier—fireplaces are animated by flickering candles. In colder months, the half-dozen hearths roar with crackling fires. The space is understated, with white tablecloths, Victorian tchotchkes (a brass duck on a mantle here, a porcelain dog on a windowsill there), and deep, comfortable dining chairs scrawled with whimsical French sayings that when read together become a poem about being lost in the woods. The food here invites diners to get lost in France's terroir. Seasonal tasting menus move through the French appellations. A summer Champagne menu, for instance, takes inspiration from the region's less famous, but equally delectable food. À la carte options take a modern approach to French favorites. A lobe of seared foie gras, for example, is served in a delicate but bitter cocoa tart that's filled with sweet corn, quince marmalade, pickled chanterelles, apple, and Sauternes jus. It's unapologetically modern French food, in a historical setting, that's worth the excursion to North York.

4150 Yonge St. www.aubergedupommier.com. ☏ **416/222-2220.** Tasting menu $115; main courses $19–$37 lunch, $39–$48 dinner. Mon–Thurs 11:45am–2:30pm and 5:30–9pm; Fri 11:45am–2:30pm and 5:30–9:30pm; Sat 5:30–9:30pm. Subway: York Mills, then walk N on Yonge St.

Expensive

Fisherman Lobster Clubhouse ★ CHINESE   Tanks of toddler-sized king crabs set the scene as hungry patrons wait for their tables to be ready. Moderation has no place at this Chinese banquet hall, so come with an appetite. Mountains of steamed, baked, deep-fried, and pan-fried crustaceans are delivered to excited tables, while a flurry of smartphones snap photos of the over-the-top feasts. Lobsters are purchased by weight, with the still-pinching specimens brought to the table for inspection before being cooked. It's dinner *and* a show. Even with a reservation, be prepared to wait a few minutes for a table; the restaurant becomes a madhouse at peak times. Service is wanting, but most come for the spectacle and the massive quantities of seafood, not charming banter (or lack thereof). Cash only.

4020 Finch Ave. E., Scarborough www.flctoronto.com. ℰ **416/321-0250.** Meals served family-style; expect about $60–$80 per person. Mon–Sun 11am–11pm. Subway: Finch, then bus 39B to Milliken Blvd. By car: Take DVP N to the 401, follow signs for 401 E, exit at Kennedy Rd., follow Kennedy Rd. to Finch Ave. E.

One ★★★ CANADIAN   Canada has produced few big-name celebrity chefs. Mark McEwan, whose dapper grin has become synonymous with the "Top Chef Canada" series, definitely qualifies. But long before he became a TV darling, McEwan was wooing local diners with his exquisite food. At One, located inside the five-star Hazelton Hotel, McEwan caters to the crème de la crème of Toronto society. The Yabu Pushelberg–designed room—with its pony-hair, brass, and leather details—is elegant yet understated. Here, the dishes have reached near-mythological status. The Lobster Spoons, Nova Scotian tail meat poached in butter and vermouth until tender, can't be so much as tweaked—there would be a revolt. Other favorites include a slow-braised beef short rib that's ready to melt at the shadow of a fork, and perfectly cooked steaks made from PEI-raised cattle and served with decadent sauces like foie gras bordelaise. If there's one thing you should never skip at One, it's dessert. The in-house pastry chef creates such delectable confections as a dulce de leche tart with a peanut butter crust, sliced bananas, and Chantilly cream. In summer, One's patio is among the best in town, less for the vista than the people-watching. Lean back with an Aperol spritz, graze on steak tartare, and take in the show.

116 Yorkville Ave. ℰ **416/961-9600**. www.one.mcewangroup.ca. Breakfast $10–$28; brunch $14–$30; main courses $22–$36 lunch, $26–$60 dinner. Daily 7:30am–11pm. Subway: Bay.

Moderate

Diwan ★ MIDDLE EASTERN   Along a mostly barren stretch of North York, there's an architectural gem: architect Fumihiko Maki's stunning Aga Khan Museum. The cubist structure, clad in sandblasted white Brazilian granite, was designed to capture as much light as possible. Inside, the restaurant Diwan (Persian for "meeting place") is no exception to the architect's sun-driven design. The sunny room—decorated with hand-carved 18th-century

WHERE TO EAT IN TORONTO

SWEET TREATS: TORONTO'S BEST dessert CAFES

I've got a serious sweet tooth. To my mind, dessert should be its own food group. Here are some of my recommendations for the city's most delicious places to satisfy a sugar craving and do some people-watching at the same time.

- **Baker & Scone** (693 St. Clair Ave. W.; *416/657-2663*): Few people lust after a scone—typically, the British sweet treat is a high-tea afterthought. But not for those who have visited Baker & Scone. The scones at this sweet Provence-reminiscent Midtown cafe defy the physics of baking: They're flakey yet pillowy and somehow still crumbly in all the right ways.

- **Dufflet Pastries** (787 Queen St. W.; *416/504-2870*): On menus around town, you'll sometimes see mention of "desserts by Dufflet." It's an institution: popular for everything from butter tarts to berry pies or three-tiered cakes heavy with icing and rich with flavor. The cafe also serves light fare.

- **Nadège Patisserie** (780 Queen St. W.; *416/203-2009*): Every confection in the glass display case of past master Nadège Nourian's Trinity Bellwoods cafe-cum-patisserie is worth ogling. Perfect chocolate sphere cakes with mirror glazing, a rainbow of macarons. and croissants in a half-dozen permutations (the pecan is particularly toothsome). Midsummer, seats on the park-flanking patio are near impossible to snag.

- **Millie Patisserie & Creamery** (12 Oxley St.; *416/596-0063*): This Japanese-inspired shop is best known for its cheese tarts and soufflé cheesecakes, but the mille crêpe cakes are particularly spectacular. It took owner Christinn Hua 9 months and more than 100 attempts to perfect the recipe. The resulting cakes, stacked 25 silk-thin layers

high, are unbelievably delicate. The best of the bunch is the matcha cake, which balances bitter green tea with sweet cream.

- **Roselle Desserts** (362 King St. E.; *416/368-8188*): "DESSERT MAKES YOU HAPPY," reads the text scrawled across the wall of this gem of a shop. A bite of the banana cream pie éclair banishes bad thoughts, creating a moment of pure bliss, which tastes of cream and rum-caramelized bananas, in case you didn't know. Just about any of the pretty French pastries here is sure to bring you mouthfuls of delight.

- **SOMA Chocolate** (In the Distillery District, 55 Mill St.; *416/815-7662*): Owners David Castellan and wife Cynthia Leung run the best chocolatier in town. Beans are carefully sourced from far-flung locales for fair-trade and organic certifications, with flavor a factor above all. Then, in this micro-factory where the process is on view, the beans are roasted, turned into paste (which is where most chocolatiers begin their work), and spun into beautiful truffles, exquisite bars, irresistible (chocolate) cakes, cookies, and more. In summer, have a gelato. In winter, don't miss the house specialty, the picante Mayan hot chocolate. Plenty to take away, too.

- **The Tempered Room** (1374 Queen St. W.; *416/546-4374*): Creative non-nine-to-fivers with asymmetrical haircuts populate this hip Parkdale haunt. The display is divided into savory (quiches, sandwiches, *croque monsieurs*) and sweet. Viennoiseries are flakey perfection, particularly the almond croissants. Traditional French pastries are very good, but the seasonal creations like rhubarb and pink peppercorn tart are always magnificent.

Damascene panels—is a bright delight. The menu invites guests to eat their way through Islam's culinary history. The peripatetic menu wanders across the Islamic world from Iran to Turkey, North Africa, and Malaysia. The prix-fixe menus are inspired by the Aga Khan Museum's special exhibits.

In the Aga Khan Museum, 77 Wynford Dr., North York. www.agakhanmuseum.org/diwan. © **416/646-4670.** Main courses $14–$24; prix-fixe menus $35–$40. Tues–Thurs 11:30am–2:30pm; Fri–Sun 11:30am–5pm. Subway: Eglinton, then bus 34 E to Don Valley Pkwy, then walk N to Wynford Dr. By car: Take DVP to Don Mills Road N exit, merge onto Don Mills Rd., then turn right onto Wynford Dr.

Inexpensive

Banh Mi Boys ★ VIETNAMESE   At brothers David, Philip, and Peter Chau's North York Banh Mi Boys outpost, they're slinging fancy Vietnamese submarines made on crusty baguettes. Sandwich fillings include duck confit and squid, alongside classic toppings such as grilled pork. The menu is not strictly updated Vietnamese, though. A Korean take on poutine (which piles kimchi, mayo, and pulled pork on top of fries) is a favorite with the voracious student crowd that frequents this sandwich shop.

2365 Yonge St. www.banhmiboys.com. © **647/345-3585.** Sandwiches $5.50–$8; sides $2.75–$6. Mon–Fri 11am–10pm; Sat 11am–9pm; Sun noon–7pm. Subway: Eglinton, then walk N on Yonge. Three other locations.

Tsujiri North York ★★ JAPANESE   North York has become a the next go-to destination for Asian-based franchises. Among the newcomers to this up-and-coming restaurant row is Tsujiri, a 155-year-old Japanese tea brand known for its green teas and icy, drinkable matcha-based desserts. Upstairs, you'll find the only Tsujiri location outside of Japan to serve hot food. Savory options include matcha soba, wobbly matcha pancakes, as well as healthy salad bowls.

4909 Yonge St. www.tsujiri.ca. © **647/341-6622.** Main courses $12–$13. Subway: Sheppard-Yonge, then walk S down Yonge St. One other location.

EXPLORING TORONTO

Toronto has a wealth of diverse attractions. If your pleasure is simply getting to know the city, head to Toronto's downtown core, and you're off to the races: The many things to do, see, and taste in the city's bustling downtown heart together offer an easy Introduction 101 to Toronto. The major museums, art galleries, and sports venues are here; plus, given the residential nature of the heart of the city, these top attractions are located in neighborhoods also worth exploring.

THE TOP ATTRACTIONS

Downtown West

Art Gallery of Ontario ★★★ MUSEUM   If you go to only one major attraction while you're in Toronto, let it be the AGO. After its 2008 top-to-bottom renovation—and reinvention—by Toronto-born Frank Gehry, the AGO emerged from its scaffolding cocoon as a bona fide wonder. Gehry's vision is throughout; the fabulous, circular floating staircase is especially impressive. Some rooms have skylights, adjusted every day to best display the works (to spectacular effect with Lawren Harris's paintings of the Arctic). Gorgeous **Galleria Italia** lets you view the scene on Dundas Street down below while you take a break from the art. Most of all, there's a dramatic increase in the amount of viewing space. Gehry's work is inspired yet practical, a rarity in today's starchitect-driven renovations of public spaces.

There's a lot to see: The collection numbers nearly 95,000 pieces and growing.

Local media magnate the late Ken Thomson donated his beautiful and extensive collection of paintings, carved miniatures, medieval triptychs, and model ships to the AGO. The **Thomson Collection** is central to the gallery: Alone, it spans 2,000 works and includes an unparalleled cache of great Canadian art—think the Group of Seven, David Milne—and international drawings, such as Peter Paul Rubens' masterpiece *The Massacre of the Innocents*. (One note: Thomson believed that art should be allowed to speak for itself, in other words, unencumbered by the usual explanatory and identifying tags; instead, a palette identifies the artists.)

Area of detail

Dupont St.
Bloor St. W
Yonge St.
Avenue Rd.
Spadina Ave.
Bathurst St.
Dufferin St.
Ossington Ave.
College St.
Dundas St. E
University Ave.
Queen St. W
King St. W

UNIVERSITY OF TORONTO
QUEEN'S PARK
College St.
DISCOVERY DISTRICT

Oxford St.
Spadina Ave.
Huron St.
Cecil St.
Henry St.
Orde St.
McCaul St.
Murray St.
University Ave.

Nassau St.
Augusta Ave.
Baldwin St.
Baldwin St.
Beverley St.
St. Andrews St.

Kensington Pl.
Kensington Ave.
6 D'Arcy St.
CHINATOWN
Dundas St. W
Centre Ave.
Chestnut St.
ST. PATRICK

Wales Ave.

Alexandra Park
ALEXANDRA PARK
Grange Ave.
Grange Pl.
7
Grange Park
GRANGE PARK
St. Patrick St.
Simcoe St.

Robinson St.
Carr St.
Ryerson Ave.
Augusta Ave.
Cameron St.
Sullivan St.
Phoebe St.
Stephanie St.
Soho St.

Wolseley St.
Bulwer St.

9
Palmerston Ave.
Bathurst St.
Richmond St. W
THEATRE DISTRICT
Camden St.
Peter St.
Widmer St.
John St.
Duncan St.
Simcoe St.
Richmond St. W
OSGOODE
York St.

Adelaide St. W
Brant St.
Portland St.
Spadina Ave.
ST. ANDREW

King St. W
Mercer St.
ENTERTAINMENT DISTRICT
Emily St.
University Ave.

Wellington St. W
Wellington St. W
Niagara St.
Victoria Mem. Sq.
Clarence Square
Blue Jays W.
10
Front St. W

Front St. W
Convention Center
Station St.

11
13 **14**
Bremner Blvd.

Gardiner Expy.
Rogers Centre
12
Roundhouse Park
Bremner Blvd.

Lake Shore Blvd. W
2

15
Queens Quay W
17 Toronto Music Garden
HTO Park
Queens Quay W
18
HARBOURFRONT

Little Norway Park
16
Spadina Quay
Maple Leaf Quays
York Quay

Stadium Rd.

Inner Harbour

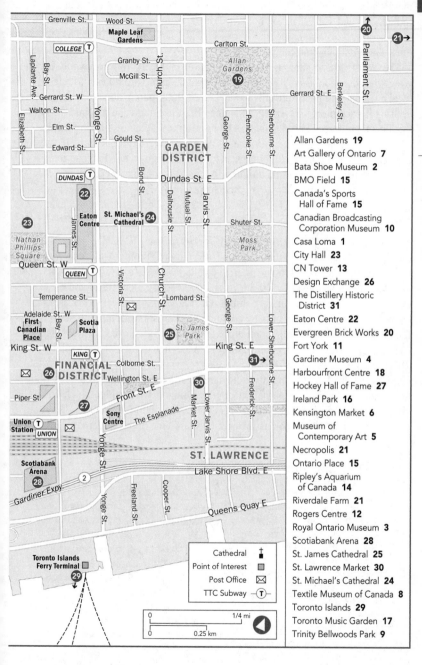

Allan Gardens **19**
Art Gallery of Ontario **7**
Bata Shoe Museum **2**
BMO Field **15**
Canada's Sports
  Hall of Fame **15**
Canadian Broadcasting
  Corporation Museum **10**
Casa Loma **1**
City Hall **23**
CN Tower **13**
Design Exchange **26**
The Distillery Historic
  District **31**
Eaton Centre **22**
Evergreen Brick Works **20**
Fort York **11**
Gardiner Museum **4**
Harbourfront Centre **18**
Hockey Hall of Fame **27**
Ireland Park **16**
Kensington Market **6**
Museum of
  Contemporary Art **5**
Necropolis **21**
Ontario Place **15**
Ripley's Aquarium
  of Canada **14**
Riverdale Farm **21**
Rogers Centre **12**
Royal Ontario Museum **3**
Scotiabank Arena **28**
St. James Cathedral **25**
St. Lawrence Market **30**
St. Michael's Cathedral **24**
Textile Museum of Canada **8**
Toronto Islands **29**
Toronto Music Garden **17**
Trinity Bellwoods Park **9**

And there's far more to see. The AGO's European collection ranges from the 14th century to the French Impressionists. The museum's collection of Indigenous and Canadian art holds treasures from historical paintings and Inuit sculpture to contemporary works by Norval Morrisseau, Kent Monkman, Tim Pitsiulak, and Suzy Lake.

The AGO is also famous for its collection of Henry Moore sculptures, which number more than 900. (The artist gave them to Toronto as a tribute to local citizens' enthusiasm for his work: In the 1960s, public donations helped to bring his sculpture *The Archer* to Nathan Phillips Square, an inspired move that cost then-mayor Philips his job.) In addition to displaying rotating exhibits of works from its collection, the AGO hosts a variety of historical and contemporary temporary exhibitions and installations by Canadian and international artists throughout the building. All in all, a topnotch experience.

317 Dundas St. W. www.ago.net. © **416/977-0414.** $19.50 adults; $16 seniors; $11 students (w/ID) and children 6–17; free for children 5 and under. Wed 6–9pm. Tues and Thurs–Sun 10:30am–5pm; Wed and Sat 10:30am–9pm. Closed Dec 25. Subway: St. Patrick.

Art Museum at the University of Toronto ★★ MUSEUM   In 2014, the Justina M. Barnicke Gallery and the University of Toronto Art Centre were federated. Steps from each other, these two galleries forged a new, joint identity. Located in **Hart House,** the Barnicke is a two-room gallery that features an ever-changing series of monthly exhibits. Occasionally, historical works are on show, but the focus is on works by contemporary artists working with various media. Pieces from the collection are scattered throughout the hallways and rooms in Hart House (it's a public building, so feel free to wander and explore). To access the University of Toronto Art Centre, you must enter via the University College quad, an Oxford-style cloistered garden that in itself is a work of art. Inside, you'll find a gallery housing the **Malcove Collection,** which consists mainly of Byzantine art dating from the 14th to the 18th centuries. There are early stone reliefs and an assortment of icons. One of the Malcove's gems

SAVING ON admission costs

The major museums are pricey in Toronto, especially when compared with the smart and progressive freebie programs in cities like London. The ROM and AGO are particularly expensive, with a $20 admission for adults and additional charges for special exhibitions. The list below will help you save on admission fees. Just keep in mind that these free or discounted times do change, so check before you visit.

○ **Art Gallery of Ontario:** Free admission every Wednesday from 6 to 9pm

○ **Aga Khan Museum:** Free admission every Wednesday from 4 to 8pm

○ **Bata Shoe Museum:** Pay-what-you-can admission every Thursday from 5 to 8pm (suggested donation is $5)

○ **Gardiner Museum:** Half-priced admission every Friday from 4 to 9pm; free admission every Tuesday for students (with ID).

○ **Textile Museum of Canada:** Pay-what-you-can admission every Wednesday from 5 to 8pm was painted by a German master in 1538: Lucas Cranach the Elder's *Adam and Eve*. The rest of the Art Centre is devoted to temporary exhibitions.

Justina M. Barnicke Gallery is located in Hart House, 7 Hart House Circle. www.utac. utoronto.ca. © **416/978-8398.** University of Toronto Art Centre is located in University College, 15 King's College Circle. © **416/978-1838.** Free admission. Tues–Fri noon– 5pm; Sat noon–4pm. Closed all statutory holidays. Subway: St. George or Museum.

Bata Shoe Museum ★ MUSEUM

Imelda Marcos, eat your heart out. This modern museum houses the shoe-magnate Bata family's 10,000-item collection. The attractive building, designed by Raymond Moriyama, suggests a whimsical shoebox. The main gallery, "All About Shoes," traces the history of footwear, beginning with a plaster cast of some of the earliest known human footprints that date to 4 million B.C. You'll come across such specialty shoes as spiked clogs used to crush chestnuts in 17th-century France, Elton John's 12-inch-plus platforms, and well-worn sandals that once graced the feet of former Canadian Prime Minister Pierre Trudeau. One display focuses on Canadian footwear fashioned by the Inuit, while another highlights 19th-century ladies' shoes. The second-story galleries house changing exhibits, which have taken on some serious topics, such as a history of foot binding in China.

327 Bloor St. W. (at St. George St.). www.batashoemuseum.ca. © **416/979-7799.** $14 adults; $12 seniors; $8 students (w/ID); $5 children 5–17; free for children 4 and under. Mon, Tues, Wed, Fri and Sat 10am–5pm; Thurs 10am–8pm; Sun noon–5pm. Subway: St. George.

City Hall ★ ARCHITECTURE

The city's fourth city hall, it was built between 1958 and 1965 in modern sculptural style. It's the symbol of Toronto's postwar dynamism, although not everyone felt that way when it was completed. According to Pierre Berton, Frank Lloyd Wright said of it, "You've got a headmarker for a grave and future generations will look at it and say: 'This marks the spot where Toronto fell.'" The truth is quite the opposite— this breathtaking building was the first architectural marker of an evolving metropolis. Finnish architect Viljo Revell won a design competition that drew entries by 510 architects from 42 countries, including I. M. Pei. The building has a great square in front with a fountain and pool; people flock here in summer to relax, and in winter to skate. The square's namesake, Nathan Phillips, was Toronto's first Jewish mayor.

City Hall also has some art worth viewing. Look just inside the entrance for *Metropolis,* which local artist David Partridge fashioned from more than 100,000 common nails. You'll need to stand well back to enjoy the effect. Henry Moore's sculpture *The Archer* stands in front of the building—thanks to Mayor Phil Givens, who raised the money to buy it through public subscription after city authorities refused. The gesture encouraged Moore to bestow a major collection of his works on the Art Gallery of Ontario (see p. 115). Two curved concrete towers, which house the bureaucracy, flank the Council Chamber. From the air, the whole complex supposedly looks like an eye peering up at the heavens.

Recently, the pretty, elevated walkways were opened to the public after decades; they're a good way to get a close look at the buildings and check out the street scenes below.

100 Queen St. W. www.toronto.ca. ✆ **416/338-0338.** Free admission. Self-guided tours Mon–Fri 8:30am–4:30pm. Subway: Queen, then walk W to Bay St.

CN Tower ★ ATTRACTION The CN Tower may no longer be the world's tallest freestanding structure (thanks, Burj Dubai), but it's still an impressive attraction—even if it's something that most locals agree is better to visit than to live with.

However you approach Toronto—on an island-airport flight or on the highway—the first thing you see is this slender structure. Glass-walled elevators glide up the 553m (1,814-ft.) tower, first stopping at the 346m-high (1,136-ft.) **LookOut** level. (The truly fearless can ride up in one of the three vertiginous glass-floored elevators, which the CN Tower opened in 2008.) Walk down one level to experience the **Glass Floor,** which is great for a dizzying face-plant: Through it, you can see all the way down to street level. Take comfort: The floor won't break. The glass can withstand the weight of 35 adult moose.

Above the LookOut is the world's highest public observation gallery, the **SkyPod,** 447m (1,465 ft.) above the ground. From here on a clear day, the sweeping vista stretches across Lake Ontario to the south and across the cityscape to the north. Atop the tower sits a 102m (335-ft.) antenna mast: It took 26 days, with the aid of a giant Sikorsky helicopter, to complete the operation.

For a 35th-anniversary celebration, the **EdgeWalk** opened in summer 2011. An elevated, narrow platform 116 stories above ground, it circles around the perimeter of the tower's main pod and claims to be "the world's highest full-circle hands-free walk." Thrill-seekers, locked into harnesses that are attached to an overhead rail and pulley system, head off for a gravity-defying walk. It's definitely not for vertigo sufferers. It also comes with the dizzying fee of $225.

301 Front St. W. www.cntower.ca. ✆ **416/868-6937.** General admission $38 adults; $34 seniors; $28 children 4–12 (extra fees apply to visit SkyPod level). Daily 9:30am–10:30pm. Closed Dec 25. Subway: Union, then walk west on Front St.

Design Exchange ★ MUSEUM Located in the old Stock Exchange Building, the Design Exchange—or DX, as it prefers to be known—has become an important Canadian design museum. It features work from a range of disciplines, from architecture to fashion, landscape design to interactive media design. Engaging exhibits have previously included *Northern Touch*—a survey of Made in Canada housewares, furniture, lifestyle objects, and gadgets—and *Evolution*, an exhibit that delved into biomimicry, designs that mimic nature (think mussel-inspired soy adhesives and breathing buildings).

234 Bay St. www.dx.org. ✆ **416/363-6121.** Free general admission; some special exhibitions extra. Wed–Fri 9am–5pm; Sat and Sun noon–4:30pm. Subway: King.

Gardiner Museum ★★ MUSEUM It's a rarity: a museum dedicated to the ceramic arts. There's plenty to see here, from pre-Columbian artifacts to Canada's most important collection of European porcelain, all housed within

When the frost starts to linger in late November, Toronto's **52 skating rinks** open for the season, which runs into March. With its civic backdrop, **Nathan Phillips Square,** 100 Queen St. West (http://nathanphillipssquareskaterentals. com; daily 10am–10pm; 2-hr. skate rentals: $10 adults, $5 children 12 and under), is one of the city's most enticing ice rinks. The reflecting fountain is transformed as the water becomes ice, and the concrete arches above are festooned with festive lights. Down by the water, the **Natrel Rink** at the **Harbourfront Centre,** 235 Queens Quay West (www.harbourfront centre.com/venues/natrelrink; Sun–Thurs 10am–10pm, Fri–Sat 10am–11pm; 2-hr. skate rentals: $13 adults, $8 students), is the city's second best rink; if it weren't for the sometimes whipping wind that comes off the lake, this would take top place. The chill, though, is easily combatted when you're grooving to the tunes at the regular DJ Skate Nights. If that's not enough to warm your bones, **Boxcar Social** (www. boxcarsocial.ca/harbourfront), a charming rinkside bar that looks down onto the ice, is a great place for some warming tea (or something a bit stiffer) between rink loops. Helmets are available for rent at both rinks.

one of the city's architectural gems. It's clearly a collection curated with passion. Among the highlights are a re-created 18th-century dessert table and a whimsical collection of *commedia dell'arte* figures. Special exhibitions are on display throughout the year. Free guided tours are given every day at 2 pm.

111 Queen's Park. www.gardinermuseum.com. ✆ **416/586-8080.** $15 adults; $11 seniors; $9 students (w/ID); free for visitors 18 and under. Mon–Thurs 10am–6pm; Fri 10am–9pm; Sat and Sun 10am–5pm. Closed Jan 1 and Dec 25. Subway: Museum.

Harbourfront Centre ★★ CULTURAL COMPLEX   This cultural center encompasses a four-hectare (10-acre) strip of waterfront land, once-abandoned warehouses, charming piers, and an old smokestack. The center, which opened in 1974, is a stunning urban playground and one of the most popular destinations for locals and visitors alike—a great place to spend time strolling, picnicking, gallery-hopping, biking, shopping, and sailing.

Harbourfront has several venues devoted to the arts. The **Power Plant** is a contemporary art gallery with some excellent and often edgy shows; behind it is the **Harbourfront Centre Theatre.** At the **Craft Studio,** you can watch artisans blow glass, throw pots, and make silkscreen prints. You can buy their works at the **Harbourfront Centre Shop.**

More than 4,000 events take place annually at Harbourfront, the biggest of which are two literary gems: the **Forest of Reading** series in June and the **International Festival of Authors** in October. Other happenings include dance, theater, art exhibitions, music, film, children's programs, multicultural festivals, and marine-themed events. Harbourfront is best in summer but a great destination year-round, especially when wintertime activities like the pretty ice-skating rink open for cold-weather fun. In midwinter, the winds blowing off Lake Ontario can be wicked, so dress warmly.

235 Queens Quay W. www.harbourfrontcentre.com. ✆ **416/973-4000.** Subway: Union, then LRT to Queen's Quay or York Quay.

A Real Deal

You can save a lot of money visiting Toronto's attractions by purchasing a **Toronto CityPASS.** See the CN Tower, Ripley's Aquarium of Canada, Casa Loma, the Ontario Science Centre, the Royal Ontario Museum, and the Toronto Zoo for $88 adults, $59 kids 4 to 12. Each booklet of tickets is valid for 9 days from the time the first one is used. **Note:** Buyers have the option of either the zoo or the science center, but not both. It is available for purchase online at **www.citypass.com**, and also at any of the aforementioned attractions that accept the CityPASS.

Ireland Park ★ PARK In 1847, Toronto was a city of 20,000—until 38,000 Irish immigrants arrived that summer. On June 21, 2007, this memorial to the Irish Famine was opened at Éireann Quay by Mary McAleese, president of Ireland. The park was inspired by Rowan Gillespie's "Departure" series of famine figures, which stand on Dublin's Liffey quayside, depicting Irish emigrants looking out to sea. There are seven figures in Dublin and five in Toronto's new park: They reach out to one another across the sea. The figures in Ireland Park were also created by Gillespie, and they are called the "Arrival" series. There is also a memorial in the park to the more than 1,100 people who died just after their arrival; as their names are discovered, they are inscribed in a limestone wall. Although it's tucked away, it's a worthwhile trek to find it and pause to think on this key time in history. At Bathurst St. and Queens Quay W. (across from Bathurst Quay). www.irelandpark foundation.com. © **416/601-6906.** Free admission. Daily dawn–11pm. Subway: Union, then the streetcar 509 W to Dan Leckie Way, then walk W to Bathurst St.

Ripley's Aquarium of Canada ★★★ AQUARIUM Underwater marvels from around the world are divided into 10 galleries at Canada's largest aquarium. The Great Lakes' deep-dwelling denizens get their due in the first exhibit where prehistoric-looking paddlefish and sturgeon prowl. After being impressed by the macrofauna that lives in Lake Ontario, check out the crazy Canadian creatures that call the Atlantic and Pacific oceans home. The Giant Pacific Octopus isn't quite kraken-sized, but he's impressive nonetheless, as are the extremely rare electric blue lobsters. Then hop over to the other side of the world (minus the jet lag), and get lost among the Indo-Pacific coral reef residents. The **Rainbow Reef** gallery is the aquarium's most diverse exhibit, with over 100 species of colorful fish with funky names like the unicorn surgeon, Picasso triggerfish, and harlequin tusk-fish. From there, a moving sidewalk carries you through the **Dangerous Lagoon,** a 90m (295-ft.) underwater tunnel where green morays, giant groupers, sharks, and sea turtles sail past. Other highlights include **Planet Jellies,** an entire hall dedicated to stinging plankton, and the **Discovery Centre,** where budding marine biologists can crawl through underwater tunnels into transparent viewing bubbles that put you smack-dab in the middle of a clownfish school—it's about as close as you can get to hanging out with Nemo and his pals without a SCUBA certification. 288 Bremner Blvd. www.ripleyaquariums.com/canada. © **647/351-3474.** General admission $33 adults; $23 seniors and children 6–14; $12 children 3–5; free for children 2 and under; $5 off after 7pm. Daily 9am–11pm (check website for the occasional early closures). Subway: Union, then walk west on Front St.

Textile Museum of Canada ★ MUSEUM   This museum is internationally recognized for its collection of historic and ethnographic textiles and related artifacts; although, due to its specialized nature, it's really suited to those with a keen interest in the wide world of fabrics. It has fine Oriental rugs and tapestries from all over the world, a gallery that presents the work of contemporary artists, and the museum, which is so small that only a fraction of the collection is on display at any given time. The space is vibrant and interesting.

55 Centre Ave. www.textilemuseum.ca. © **416/599-5321.** $15 adults; $10 seniors; $6 students and children 5–14; free for children 4 and under. Daily 11am–5pm; Wed 11am–8pm. Subway: St. Patrick.

The Toronto Islands ★★★ PARK/GARDEN   In under 10 minutes, an 800-passenger ferry delivers you to 245 hectares (605 acres) of island parkland crisscrossed by shaded paths and quiet waterways—a glorious spot to walk, bike, picnic, feed the ducks, putter around in boats, picnic, or soak up the sun. Of the 14 islands, the two major ones are **Centre Island** and **Ward's Island.** Originally, the land was a peninsula, but in the 1800s, storms shattered it into islands. Ward's is more residential (about 600 people live on the islands), while Centre Island is the most popular with tourists—in no small part because of the **Centreville Theme Park** (www.centreisland.ca; © **416/203-0405**), an old-fashioned amusement park that's been in business since 1966. You won't see the usual neon signs, shrill hawkers, and greasy hot-dog stands here. Instead, you'll find a turn-of-the-20th-century village complete with a Main Street; tiny shops; a firehouse; and the **Far Enough Farm,** where the kids can pet lambs, chicks, and other barnyard animals. The kids will also love trying out the antique cars, fire engines, old-fashioned train, authentic 1890s carousel, flume ride, and aerial cars. Cafes, pizza joints, and even a beer-and-BBQ restaurant provide the fuel. An all-day ride pass costs $26.50 for 1.2m (4 ft.) tall and under, $35.35 for those taller than 1.2m (4 ft.); a family pass for four is $114. Centreville is open from 10:30am to 6pm daily from mid-May to Labor Day, and weekends in early May and September.

You can also rent bikes and boats in season on Centre Island. Bikes can be rented at the family-owned **Toronto Island Bicycle Rental** (www.torontoislandbicyclerental.com), which offers not only single and tandem bikes ($9–$16/hr.) but two- and four-seater quadracycles ($18–$32/hr.); deposit required.

SLEEPING WITH THE fishes

Pack your PJs and grab your sleeping bag for a unique sleepover opportunity under the cover of 2.9 million liters (766,100 gallons) of water at **Ripley's Aquarium of Canada**. The **Overnight Reef Adventures** are fun for the whole family. The experience starts with fish-themed craft-making, followed by a scavenger hunt through the aquarium, and then a round of underwater "Jeopardy." After a late-night snack, the crew hunkers down for the night in the Dangerous Lagoon's shark tunnel. Watch with awe as the ocean's most prolific predators soar across the ceiling. After a night of fish-filled dreams, wake up to breakfast with more time to explore the exhibits. The cost is $99 per person (www.ripleyaquariums.com/canada).

Rent canoes, kayaks, and pedal boats at the blue-painted **Toronto Island Boat House** (www.torontoisland.com/boathouse.php).

Centre Island. Round-trip ferry fare $7.80 adults, $5.20 seniors and youths 14–16; $3.20 youths 2–14; free for children under 2. Ferries leave from Jack Layton Ferry Terminal at the bottom of Bay St. Subway: Union Station, then the streetcar to Queen's Quay.

Downtown East

The Distillery District ★★★ NEIGHBORHOOD
This was home to the Gooderham and Worts Distillery, founded in 1832 and once Canada's largest distilling company. In 2003, the 45-building complex (empty save the film crews that used it as a set) was reinvented as a historic district with galleries and cafes inhabiting the industrial Victorian buildings. A miller named James Worts, who immigrated from Scotland in 1831, built the first building on the site: a windmill intended to power a grain mill (the millstone he brought with him is still on display). His brother-in-law, William Gooderham, soon joined him in the business. In 1834, Worts' wife died in childbirth, and in despair, Worts drowned himself in the mill's well. Gooderham took over the business and adopted Worts' son, who eventually joined the business.

The charming complex is an excellent example of 19th-century industrial design. Most of the buildings were made with Toronto's own red brick; you'll see it in everything from the buildings to the streets themselves. One exception is the mill building, which is stone.

The Distillery District has launched an ambitious program of events throughout the year, including a Christmas market, an outdoor art exhibition; and a farmer's market, which takes place on summer weekends. It's also home to the **Soulpepper Theatre Company,** the **Sandra Ainsley gallery,** and top chocolatier **Soma,** as well as a handful of pubs and patios.

55 Mill St. www.thedistillerydistrict.com. © **416/367-1800.** Free admission. Subway: King, then a streetcar E to Parliament St.

Evergreen Brick Works ★★★ CULTURAL COMPLEX
Be prepared: You have to hike it here on foot over a lush path, take a shuttle from Broadview subway station, or drive and pay for parking. Once the home of the city's founding brick factory, it has been reinvented by the dynamic Evergreen foundation (national in scope; its business is to "green" cities) to include a farmer's market that runs year-round on Saturday mornings, a Sunday artisans market, a cafe and restaurant featuring local goods under the **Cafe Belong** moniker, marshlands, a beautiful park, and thoughtful exhibits that take advantage of the unique setting of age-old kilns—this is where Toronto's signature red bricks were once formed. A taste of past and present, the Brick Works is proving to be one of the city's most attractive locales for brilliant events. There are programs for families, parties for grown-ups, and much more.

550 Bayview Ave. http://ebw.evergreen.ca © **416/596-1495.** Free admission. Subway: Broadview Station, then free shuttle bus to the site (see website for schedule). By car: From downtown, take River St. just N of Gerrard St. to Bayview Ave., then follow Bayview Ave. to the site.

Riverdale Farm ★★ ATTRACTION   Situated on the edge of the Don Valley Ravine, this 7.5-acre working farm is located right in the city. Small tots enjoy watching the cows, pigs, turkeys, and ducks—and can get close enough to pet some animals, such as the rabbits. Because this really is a working farm, you'll see all of the chores of daily life, such as horse grooming, cow and goat milking, egg collecting, and animal feeding. Originally this was the site of Toronto's first zoo, which opened in 1890. At the turn of the century, throngs of locals would come to gawk at the ocelots, monkeys, and elephant. Today, the only wild animals about can be found in the ravine, where 3km (1 mile) of trails knot through a forest filled with ponds, home to herons, turtles, and the wild cousins of the geese that live on the farm.

201 Winchester St. (at Sumach St.). http://riverdalefarmtoronto.ca. ✆ **416/392-6794.** Free admission. Daily 9am–5pm. Subway: Castle Frank, then bus no. 65 S on Parliament St. to Wellesley St. and walk 3 blocks E to Sumach St.

St. James Cathedral ★★★ ARCHITECTURE   This Gothic Revival Anglican cathedral is home to Toronto's oldest congregation, founded in 1797. The first church built here in 1807 was constructed out of wood. In 1818, the building was enlarged, and a bell tower—which did double duty as York's fire bell as well as its church bell—was added. In 1833 the wooden church was replaced with a neoclassical stone building that would, somewhat ironically, catch fire twice, once in 1839, and then in 1849 when the building was completely destroyed by the great fire of 1849. The present building was begun in 1850 and completed in 1875, though services resumed in the chapel in 1853. It boasts the tallest steeple in Canada (and second tallest in North America after New York's St. Patrick's Cathedral). Inside is a Tiffany-style window in memory of William Jarvis, one of Toronto's founding fathers.

In addition to being a great work of architecture, St. James is a good place to stop and rest for a bit. Unless there's a service going on, it doesn't draw much of a crowd, so it feels like a private oasis in the middle of downtown. St. James hosts free organ recitals every Tuesdays at 1pm and Sundays at 4pm. The adjoining park is pretty, too, especially in summer months. Free concerts also take place in the park from June through September, on Thursdays from 7 to 9pm.

106 King St. E. www.stjamescathedral.on.ca. ✆ **416/364-7865.** Free admission. Sun–Fri 7am–5:30pm; Sat 9am–3pm. Subway: King.

Downtown North

Casa Loma ★★ CASTLE   A kitschy glitch in the city's skyline to locals, this castle on a hill offers an inspiring view of the sweep of the city. But while you can admire the view for free, it's worth visiting the interior of the castle, too. The elegant rooms and period furniture are appropriately grand. If you're up for it, climb the towers (one Norman, one Scottish, both great).

Sir Henry Pellatt, who built Casa Loma between 1911 and 1914, had a life-long fascination with castles. He studied medieval palaces and gathered materials and furnishings from around the world, bringing marble, glass, and paneling from Europe; teak from Asia; and oak and walnut from North America. He imported Scottish stonemasons to build the massive walls that surround the site.

Wander through the majestic Great Hall, with its 18m-high (59-ft.) hammer-beam ceiling; the Oak Room, where three artisans took 3 years to fashion the paneling; and the Conservatory, with its elegant bronze doors, stained-glass dome, and pink-and-green marble. The castle encompasses battlements and a tower; Peacock Alley, designed after Windsor Castle; and a 1,800-bottle wine cellar. A 244m (801-ft.) tunnel runs to the stables, where Spanish tile and mahogany surrounded the horses.

The tour is self-guided; pick up an audiocassette, available in eight languages, upon arrival (it's included in the price of admission).

After the castle closes, **Escape Casa Loma** (www.escapecasaloma.com) takes over the grounds. This series of escape games—based loosely around the castle's history—bring riddle solvers to sections of Casa Loma that are closed to visitors on the regular tour. The unfinished underground pool, which has been turned into a musky cinema where you'll be briefed on the rules of the game, sets the tone for an immersive quasi-historical experience. Tickets are $40 to $46.

1 Austin Terrace. www.casaloma.org. © **416/923-1171.** $30 adults; $25 seniors and children 14–17; $20 children 4–13; free for children 3 and under. Daily 9:30am–5pm (last entry at 4pm). Closed Dec 25. Subway: Dupont, then walk 2 blocks N.

Museum of Contemporary Art Toronto Canada ★★★ MUSEUM

Like a teenager telling his mom he's no longer Billy, he's William, MOCCA is now going by MOCA, or simply, the Museum of Contemporary Art (they dropped the C for Canadian from their acronym). This name change comes with a 2018 relocation. Toronto's largest collection dedicated to the art of today has moved into new home: a former automotive factory that manufactured aluminum parts for both world wars. On the heels of a renovation that's glorifying the city's industrial past while contributing to the gentrification of a traditionally blue-collar neighborhood, MOCA's first display, fittingly, engages with architectural colonial legacies. Andreas Angelidakis's *Demos* invites people to rearrange 74 stone-like building blocks into collaborative constructions.

158 Sterling Rd. museumofcontemporaryart.ca. © **416/530-2500.** $10 adults; $5 seniors; $5 students (w/ID); free for people 18 and under. Mon, Wed, Thurs, Sat, Sun 10am–5pm; Fri 10am–9pm. Subway: Landsdowne, walk west on Bloor Street, then south down Sterling.

Ontario Legislature ★ LANDMARK

At the northern end of University Avenue, with University of Toronto buildings to the east and west, lies Queen's Park, a lovely green place in the heart of the city. Embedded in its center is the rose-tinted sandstone-and-granite Ontario Legislature, which has stood here since 1893. *New Yorker* comic writer Bruce McCall labeled it an example of "Early Penitentiary" style, but many find it stately and attractive. Be sure to call ahead before you visit to make sure that the building will be open to the public that day. Try to take the afternoon "Art & Architecture" tour—it's free, but advance reservations are required to participate (visit the website for details; times vary). If you're interested in observing the Ontario Legislature in session, the public is welcome to watch as laws and policies are made. With Doug Ford—ex–Toronto mayor Rob's brother—as Premier, the shows at Queen's Park have been more dramatic than a "Jerry Springer" episode. Shortly after Ford was elected, the official opposition, the New Democratic Party, was kicked out of the Ontario Legislature for banging on tables in protest of the Premier's decision to slash Toronto's city council in half.

111 Wellesley St. W. (at University Ave.). www.ontla.on.ca. © **416/325-7500.** Free admission. Mon–Fri 8am–6pm; Sat–Sun 9am–4:30pm. Call for tour information and reservations. Subway: Queen's Park.

Royal Ontario Museum (ROM) ★★ MUSEUM   This is Canada's largest museum, with 13 million objects in its collections. The massive and controversial 2007 renovation by starchitect Daniel Libeskind has had mixed reviews from visitors and locals: Some love it; others decry the design. The new crystal wing, the **Michael Lee-Chin Crystal,** which houses seven galleries, hangs out over Bloor Street, with peek-a-boo views to the street below. But best to focus on the content here, rather than the renovation. Fortunately, there's plenty to see, with particular strengths in natural history and world cultures.

Don't miss the Chinese galleries, which feature an intact Ming tomb and the magnificent *Paradise of Maitreya* mural; wonderful galleries exploring the ancient world (Egypt, Nubia, Greece, Byzantium, and Bronze Age Aegean are standouts); dazzling dinosaurs (including one of only three complete Barosaurus skeletons on display in the world); a newly improved **Bat Cave** (a very popular draw for kids); and galleries devoted to biodiversity in the animal kingdom. The hands-on **CIBC Discovery Gallery** invites children to dress up in medieval garb and dig for dino bones (a hit with would-be paleontologists). The four totem poles are remarkable, too, as are the mummies. On Fridays though summer and during the warmer weeks of spring and fall, the museum runs **ROM Friday Night Live,** an evening affair (that goes until 11:30 p.m.) with music and drinks to accompany the displays.

100 Queen's Park. www.rom.on.ca. © **416/586-8000.** $20 adults; $17 seniors; $16.50 students (w/ID) and youth 15–19; $14 children 4–14; free for children 3 and under. Sat–Thurs 10am–5:30pm; Fri 10am–9:30pm. Subway: Museum.

North Toronto

Aga Khan Museum ★★ MUSEUM   When the Aga, spiritual leader of Shiite Ismaili Muslims, was looking for a place to build a museum dedicated to Islamic arts and objects, he was enamored by Toronto's pluralism. In a letter the Aga Khan penned in 2008, he said that the impetus behind the museum was "to bridge the growing divide of misunderstanding between East and West." In Japanese architect Fumihiko Maki's stunning building, you'll find gorgeously lit galleries—the modernist structure was designed to pull in as much natural light as possible—with exhibits that showcase over 1,000 objects from the Aga Khan's personal collection. The ever-changing displays (only 300 items are taken out at a time), span from artifacts from the 8th century to contemporary art being produced in Pakistan today. There's nowhere near the isolated museum to grab lunch; however, the on-site restaurant **Diwan** has excellent Middle Eastern, North African, and South Asian offerings meant to showcase the flavors of the Islamic nations.

77 Wynford Dr., North York. www.agakhanmuseum.org. © **416/646-4677.** $20 adults; $15 seniors; $12 students (w/ID) and youth 14–17; $10 children 6–13; free for children 5 and under. Tues 10am–6pm; Wed 10am–8pm; Wed–Sun 10am–6pm. Closed Dec 25. Subway: Broadview, then the 100A Flemingdon Park bus north to 100 Wynford Drive

stop. By car: Take DVP N to Eglinton, exit onto Eglington heading E, R onto Gervais Dr. followed by a R onto Wynford Dr.

Toronto Zoo ★★★ ZOO   At 283 hectares (700 acres) of parkland, it's one of the largest zoos in the world, with some 5,000 animals representing more than 500 species, plus an extensive botanical collection. Five indoor tropical pavilions—including Africa, Indo-Malaya, Australasia, Malayan Woods and the Americas—and extensive outdoor habitats house the resident critters.

One popular attraction is the **African Savanna.** It re-creates a market bazaar and safari atmosphere. Visitors trek through Kesho National Park past such special features as a bush camp, a white rhino, and several watering holes. This much-loved exhibition includes the **African Rainforest,** one of the most popular sights at the zoo and the largest indoor gorilla exhibit in North America. Another hit is **Splash Island,** where kids enjoy the cool mist as they explore and learn about which plants and animals live in different bodies of water in Canada.

In 2017, the Toronto Zoo opened a state-of-the-art **Wildlife Health Centre.** This is the first facility of its kind in Canada and is where important veterinary, nutritional physiology, conservation, and wildlife research efforts take place. Visitors can catch behind-the-scenes glimpses into this important work from the public viewing gallery.

Ten kilometers (6¼ miles) of walkways offer access to all areas of the zoo. Be prepared to walk long distances, but during the warmer months, the Zoomobile takes visitors around the major walkways to view the animals in the outdoor paddocks. The zoo has restaurants, a gift shop, first aid, and a family center. Visitors can rent strollers and wagons, and borrow wheelchairs. The African pavilion has an elevator for strollers and wheelchairs. There are several parking areas and plenty of picnic tables.

2000 Meadowvale Rd. www.torontozoo.com. © **416/392-5900.** Admission rates and hours change seasonally; visit website for current pricing and hours of operation. Last admission 1 hr. before closing. Closed Dec 25. Subway: Bloor-Danforth line to Kennedy, then bus no. 86A N. By car: From downtown, take Don Valley Pkwy. to Hwy. 401 E, exit on Meadowvale Rd. and follow signs.

Ontario Science Centre ★★ MUSEUM   Since this pioneering interactive science museum opened in 1969, generations of Toronto's kids, and their offspring, have proven loyal fans. It's not surprising: The hands-on approach to exploring the wide world of science is absolutely thrilling. With more than

ZIPLINING THROUGH THE ZOO

The **Toronto Zoo** is located in the heart of the scenic Rouge Valley, which is home to white-tailed deer, rabbits, turtles, salamanders, and dozens of bird species, big and small. Now, zoo-goers can whip across the valley on an ecologically themed **zipline,** down the 300m (984-ft.) cable, which ends in an adrenaline-jolting drop-off. At speeds exceeding 40km (25 miles) per hour, it might be hard to spy the red-shouldered hawk in the canopy, but that's what the ATV ride back to the Indo-Malayan Pavilion is for.

800 exhibits, there is an abundance of things to touch, push, pull, or crank. Test your reflexes, or balance, or heart rate, or grip strength; watch frozen-solid liquid nitrogen shatter into thousands of icy shards; study slides of butterfly wings, bedbugs, fish scales, or feathers under a microscope; land a spaceship on the moon; see how many lights you can turn on or how high you can elevate a balloon using pedal power. The fun goes on and on.

In addition, the city's only **planetarium,** an **IMAX Dome** cinema, and a collection of small theaters showing assorted documentaries and slide shows are located here. A 2006 addition, the **Weston Family Innovation Centre,** offers a hands-on focus on problem-solving, with such activities as mixing music, making stop-motion films, and creating your own designer footwear. There are also some outdoor improvements, including a music-making water garden. The food is much less exciting, though the center has two restaurants and three cafes on site. This is one Toronto attraction that always seems to be busy (blame school groups), so arrive early to see everything. Make no mistake: The OSC provides a full day's entertainment.

770 Don Mills Rd. (at Eglinton Ave. E.). www.ontariosciencecentre.ca. © **416/696-3127.** OSC $22 adults; $16 seniors and children 13–17; $13 children 3–12; free for children 2 and under; IMAX tickets extra. Mon–Fri 10am–4pm; Sat 10am–7pm; Sun 10am–5pm. Subway: Yonge St. line to Eglinton Ave., then 34 Eglinton bus E to Don Mills Rd. By car: From downtown, take Don Valley Pkwy. to Don Mills Rd. exit and follow signs.

HISTORIC BUILDINGS

Fort York ★ HISTORIC SITE   For those interested in history—especially military history—this is a treat. This historic base was established by Lt. Gov. John Graves Simcoe in 1793 to defend "little muddy York," as Toronto was then known. Americans sacked it in April 1813, but the British rebuilt that same summer. Fort York was used by the military until 1880 and was pressed back into service during both world wars.

You can tour the soldiers' and officers' quarters; clamber over the ramparts; and in summer, view demonstrations of drills, music, and cooking. If you can, try to visit on Victoria Day, Canada Day, or Simcoe Day, when lots of pomp, pageantry, and special demonstrations is planned.

250 Fort York Blvd. www.fortyork.ca. © **416/392-6907.** $14 adults; $10 seniors; $8 children 13–18; $6 children 6–12; children 5 and under free. Jan 2–May 23 Mon–Fri 10am–4pm, Sat–Sun 10am–5pm; May 24–Sept 5 daily 10am–5pm; Sept 6 to Dec 31 Mon–Fri 10am–4pm, Sat–Sun 10am–5pm. Subway: Bathurst, then streetcar S to Fort York Blvd.

Spadina Museum Historic House & Garden ★ HISTORIC SITE This circa-1866 mansion with spectacular seasonal gardens reopened in 2010 after an extensive, expensive renovation. The result is worth a visit: Now run year-round by the City of Toronto, the museum gives visitors a sense of domestic life in Toronto in the 1920s and '30s. The garden is also themed: It's a Victorian-Edwardian masterpiece. The Austin family occupied the house from 1866 to 1980, and successive generations modified and added to the house and its decor. An annual Gatsby-themed party fills the grounds with flappers every June. The party is more than Prohibition-era cocktails and costumes; croquet, silent-film screenings, and dancing make this a memorable celebration of pre–Depression decadence. It sells out quickly.

285 Spadina Ave. www.toronto.ca/spadinamuseum. ☏ **416/392-6910.** $10 adults, C$8 seniors and children 13–18, $6 children 6–12, free for children 5 and under. Jan–Apr Sat, Sun and holiday Mon noon–5pm; Apr–Sept Mon–Sun noon–5pm; Sept–Jan 12 Tues–Fri noon–4pm, Sat, Sun, and holiday Mon noon–5pm. Closed Dec 25, Dec 26, Jan 1 and Good Friday. Subway: Dupont.

PARKS, GARDENS & LAKES

Downtown West

LAKE ONTARIO ★★★

In the 1950s, the Gardiner Expressway severed Toronto from the lake. For decades, the waterfront went underutilized, but recent efforts to revitalize the area have yielded new parks, a multi-purpose trail, and the **Bentway,** a park that runs under the Gardiner inviting people to engage with a previously unsavory space. Spanning from Exhibition GO Station to Spadina Avenue, the Bentway makes walking down to the lake a delight. Once at the waterfront, there's tons to do. The DIY way to see the waters is to rent a kayak or canoe and discover the coastline. It's ill-advised for novice paddlers to traverse the channel during peak times—the water traffic can get congested. If you're keen to explore the islands by boat, it's best to rent a sailboat. **Gone Sailing Adventures** (www.gonesailingadventures. com; ☏ **416/240-0202**) offers a 3-hour circumnavigation of islands for $150. Lake Ontario is also stocked with plenty of great eating fish. Fishing charters like **Epic Sport Fishing** (www.torontofishingtours.com; ☏ **416/688-4662**) have all the equipment and know-how needed to make for a breezy day of casting (and if you ask nicely, they might tour you around the islands in the fishing boat).

Toronto Music Garden ★ Toronto is a city of gardens, but this one along Toronto's waterfront is a favorite of many locals. Cellist Yo-Yo Ma and landscape designer Julie Moir Messervy created the Toronto Music Garden to invoke Bach's "The First Suite for Unaccompanied Cello." The prelude is represented by the undulating curves of a riverscape; the *allemande* by a forest grove that's filled with wandering trails; the *courante* by a swirling path through wildflowers; the *menuett* by a pavilion of formally arranged flower-beds; and finally the *gigue,* with giant grass steps that lead you back to the real

---

Music Alfresco

The **Toronto Music Garden** hosts some of the city's best summer concerts. From late June to mid-September, you can count on listening to live music here every Thursday at 7pm and on Sunday at 4pm. Sometimes, you'll hear classical music—especially by the baroque composers—but the programs are rather eclectic. Recent offerings have included Spanish flamenco music and traditional Chinese melodies. All performances are free.

world. It's tough to translate the experience into words, but the music garden is a don't-miss spot if you visit Toronto in warm weather.

475 Queens Quay W. ℭ **416/338-0338.** Free admission. Daily dawn–dusk. Subway: Union, then the streetcar to Spadina.

Trillium Park ★★   A decommissioned Ontario Place parking lot has been turned into a splendid lake-skirting provincial park, complete with vertical landscaping that has brought rolling hills to the previously flat patch of asphalt. Various Ontario landscapes, including ravines, bluffs, and evergreen forests, inspired the design of the park, which is populated by thousands of native trees, flowers, and shrubs that in turn have attracted rare local birds to the area. Lucky joggers pass orioles, nuthatches, and cedar waxwings, who flit about the trees. While there is no playground per se, the dozens of gigantic boulders invite children to play, climb, and explore.

955 Lake Shore Blvd. W ℭ **416/314-9900.** Free admission. Daily dawn–dusk. Subway: Union, then bus 121 to Strachan Ave, followed by a 10-minute walk S.

Trinity Bellwoods Park ★   This gorgeous neighborhood park was originally part of a military reserve when Toronto was still a small town called York and the British troops were garrisoned at Fort York (p. 129). Eventually, parcels were sold to retiring officers, but in 1851, Bishop John Strachan bought up some of the land in order to found a college. Strachan was furious at the University of Toronto's decision to become a secular school, and he founded the Anglican Trinity College in 1852 (of course, Trinity is now part of the university, though it has kept its Anglican traditions). The buildings were torn down, but the impressive stone-and-wrought-iron gates that face Queen Street West still remain, and Victorian lampposts illuminate the main paths at night. Given the colorful neighborhood it's located in (West Queen West), it's no surprise that Trinity Bellwoods has hosted some interesting events, including an anarchist book fair and the odd drum circle. It's a family park, good for picnics and people-watching. Be on the lookout for the legendary albino squirrels who reside here—a coffee shop across the street is named in their honor.

Btw. Dundas St. W., Crawford St., Queen St. W. and Gore Vale Ave. ℭ **416/392-111.** Free admission. Daily dawn–dusk. Subway: Osgoode, then a streetcar W to Bellwoods Ave.

Downtown East

Allan Gardens ★   Toronto's first civic park is lackluster (and a bit dangerous after dark), but plant fanatics flock here en masse to enjoy the 1,486sq m (16,000-sq.-ft.) Victorian greenhouses. Inside are citrus trees, palms, cacti, and colorful tropical flowers including rare orchids and bromeliads. I love heading here in winter, when the ponds and waterfalls provide an escape from the bone-gnawing chill of the Ontario cold.

Btw. Jarvis, Sherbourne, Dundas and Gerrard sts. ℭ **416/392-1111.** Free admission. 10am–4:45pm. Subway: Dundas, then streetcar 505 W to Sherbourne St.

Downtown North

High Park ★   This 161-hectare (398-acre) park northwest of downtown was architect John G. Howard's gift to the city. He lived in **Colborne Lodge,**

which still stands in the park. There's a large lake here called **Grenadier Pond** (great for ice skating in winter); a small zoo; a swimming pool; tennis courts; sports fields; bowling greens; and vast expanses of green for baseball, jogging, picnicking, cycling, and more. The **Dream in High Park,** an annual Shakespearean offering in the open air, is staged each summer and draws crowds who often picnic on-site.

1873 Bloor St. W. www.toronto.ca/parks. Free admission. Daily dawn–dusk. Subway: High Park.

Necropolis ★   If you have a fascination with historic cemeteries, definitely make a stop here. Located in Downtown North East, this is one of the city's oldest cemeteries, dating to 1850. Some of the remains were originally buried in Potter's Field, where Yorkville stands today.

Buried here is William Lyon Mackenzie, leader of the 1837 rebellion, as well as those of his followers Samuel Lount and Peter Matthews, who were hanged for their parts in the rebellion. (Mackenzie himself went on to become a member of Parliament. Go figure.) Other notables buried in the 7.2-hectare (18-acre) cemetery include George Brown, one of the fathers of Confederation; Anderson Ruffin Abbott, the first Canadian-born black surgeon; Joseph Tyrrell, who unearthed dinosaurs in Alberta; and world-champion oarsman Ned Hanlan. Henry Langley, who designed the Necropolis's *porte-cochere* and the Gothic Revival chapel—as well as the St. James (p. 125) and St. Michael cathedrals—is also buried here.

200 Winchester St. (at Sumach St.). www.mountpleasantgroupofcemeteries.ca. © **416/ 923-7911.** Free admission. Daily 8am–dusk. Subway: Castle Frank, then bus no. 65 S on Parliament St. to Wellesley St. and walk 3 blocks E to Sumach St.

East End

Scarborough Bluffs ★★   On the eastern edge of Toronto is a natural wonder that's well worth a half-day visit. The Scarborough Bluffs are unique in North America, and their layers of sand and clay offer a remarkable geological record of the great Ice Age. Rising up to 90m (300 ft.) above Lake Ontario, they stretch out over 14km (8¾ miles). The first 46m (150 ft.) contains fossil plants and animals that were deposited by the advancing Wisconsin Glacier 70,000 years ago. It was because of the bluffs that Lady Elizabeth Simcoe, wife of the first Lieutenant Governor of Upper Canada (Ontario), decided to name the eastern suburb Scarborough. While rowing past the bluffs in 1793, she was reminded of the chalk cliffs of Yorkshire.

S of Kingston Rd. www.toronto.ca/parks. No phone. Free admission. Daily dawn–dusk. Subway: Victoria Park, then no. 12 Kingston Rd. bus to Brimley Rd. and about a 15-min. walk S along Brimley Rd. By car: From downtown, take Don Valley Pkwy. to Hwy. 401 E, exit on Brimley Rd. and drive S.

Toronto North

Toronto Botanical Garden ★★   Best visited during the late spring, summer and early autumn, the Toronto Botanical Garden is located entirely outdoors, which means blooms are dependent on the season. Divided into 17 different gardens, which range from native Carolinian Forest habitat to Renaissance-inspired formal gardens, if offers plenty to explore. Landscaping aficionados will be delighted by Dutch garden designer Piet Oudolf's **Entry Garden Walk,** planted in the New Wave Planting style. Oudolf allowed flowers and shrubs to self-seed for 3 years, creating sculptural "sophisticated meadows" that aren't just beautiful when blossoming, but striking well into late autumn. For budding botanists, the **Teaching Garden** includes demonstrations that teach youngsters how to sow seeds and harvest veggies. Younger ones might prefer meandering through the **Alphabet Garden,** where plants A through Z are planted.

777 Lawrence Ave. E. https://torontobotanicalgarden.ca. © **416/397-1341.** Free admission. Daily dawn–dusk. Closed all statutory holidays. Subway: Eglinton, then bus 54 N to Lawrence Ave.

Rouge Park ★★★ This is Canada's first national urban park, and it's still growing. Rouge Park will eventually encompass 79 sq. km (30 sq. miles) of parkland made up of rivers, beaches, wetlands, historic farms, and meadows. Once fully established, the park will be the largest urban protected area in North America, stretching from Lake Ontario in the south to the Oak Ridges Moraine in the north. Download the **Rouge App,** an interactive guide that provides hiking trail information as well as historical facts and useful tips on what poisonous plants look like, where they grow, and how to avoid them. Although Rouge Park is a great place to cross-country ski, camp, canoe, mountain bike, and hike, the park does not provide rentals.

Zoo Rd., Toronto. © **416/264-2020**. Free admission. Daily dawn–dusk. Subway: Union, then GO train to Eglinton GO, then bus 86A to Zoo Rd. By car: From downtown, take Don Valley Pkwy. to Hwy. 401 E, exit on Meadowvale Rd. and follow signs.

MARKETS

Toronto's markets are thriving. In summer and fall, dozens of **farmer's markets** operate throughout the city's residential neighborhoods and beyond, even at New City Hall. **Antiques** markets run year-round, and **open-air markets** such as Kensington are an integral part of the city's fabric. Make like a local and dive into the fray. In addition to the markets listed below, check out the smaller farmer's markets at the **Evergreen Brick Works** (p. 124) and at the **Wychwood Barns** (p. 108); both are open year-round.

Kensington Market ★★ This colorful, lively area should not be missed. You'll hear Caribbean, Portuguese, Italian, and many other languages and dialects as merchants spread out their wares. Think: squid and crabs in pails; local breads; cheese from around the world; apples, pears, peppers, ginger, and spices; West Indies mangoes; and salted fish from Portuguese dories. There's also lace, fabrics, and other colorful remnants. The **Kensington Brewing Co.** (www.kensingtonbrewingcompany.com) recently opened in the market, selling fresh crafted brews on tap and by the bottle.

Kensington Avenue itself is a treasure trove of **vintage clothing stores**. You'll see a lot of junk here, but amazing finds can be had at shops such as

Courage My Love (see p. 150). Many of the shops display their wares outdoors in decent weather, adding to the color and charm of the area.

Bounded by Dundas St., Spadina Ave., Baldwin St., and Augusta Ave. www.kensington-market.ca. Market open daily except Christmas and New Year's Day. Store hours vary. Subway: St. Patrick, then Dundas St. streetcar W to Kensington St.

St. Lawrence Market ★ This handsome food market occupies two buildings. The primary market, called the **South Market,** runs throughout the week in a vast building constructed around the facade of the city's second city hall, built in 1850. Vendors sell meat, fish, fruit, vegetables, and dairy products, as well as other foodstuffs. The second St. Lawrence building, the **North Market,** is currently being rebuilt (scheduled to reopen in 2021), but a temporary North Market has opened, confusingly enough, just south of the South Market at 125 The Esplanade. The temporary North Market continues to host Saturday farmer's markets and Sunday antique markets, where peddlers sell everything from naughty Victorian postcards to rare books. The South Market is closed Sundays and Mondays, with the North Market open Sundays from 7am to 5pm.

92 Front St. E. www.stlawrencemarket.com. ✆ **416/392-7219.** Tues–Thurs 8am–6pm; Fri 8am–7pm; Sat 5am–5pm. Subway: Union.

SPECTATOR SPORTS

BMO Field ★ SPORTS ARENA With a capacity of 40,000, this arena is home to Canada's national soccer team, as well as the popular Toronto FC. In 2016, the field also became the Toronto Argonauts football HQ, after renovations to the field lengthened the pitch to make it suitable for Canadian football. (During the update, an upper deck was added to the east grandstand, and a roof was erected over the seating areas.) Without a single pillar to block your view, there are no bad seats here.

BMO Field, 170 Princes' Blvd., Exhibition Place. www.bmofield.com. ✆ **416/815-540 ext. 4040**). Subway: Bathurst, then streetcar no. 511 S to end of line.

Hockey Hall of Fame ★★ MUSEUM Ice hockey fans will be thrilled by the artifacts collected here. They include the original Stanley Cup, a replica of the Montréal Canadiens' locker room, Terry Sawchuck's goalie gear, Newsy Lalonde's skates, and the stick used by Max Bentley. You'll also see photographs of the personalities and great moments in hockey history. Most fun are the shooting and goalkeeping interactive displays, where you can take a whack at targets with a puck or don goalie gear and face down flying sponge pucks.

In Brookfield Place, 30 Yonge St. (at Front St.). www.hhof.com. ✆ **416/360-7765.** $20 adults; $16 seniors; $14 children 4–13; free for children 3 and under. Mon–Fri 10am–5pm; Sat 9:30am–6pm; Sun 10:30am–5pm. For extended summer and holiday hours, see website. Closed Jan 1, Nov 12 and Dec 25. Subway: Union.

Lamport Stadium ★ STADIUM Apart from football, Canada doesn't sustain that many national sports leagues. Typically, we tend to play in the

ESPECIALLY FOR kids

Toronto is a town with plenty of great family attractions, from the idiosyncratic Ontario Science Centre to Paramount Canada's Wonderland theme park to the Toronto Zoo, one of the great zoos of the world. Following are our recommended suggestions for family fun and kid-oriented entertainment in Toronto:

- **Harbourfront:** Kaleidoscope is an ongoing program of creative crafts, active games, and special events on weekends and holidays. It also has a pond, winter ice skating, and a crafts studio. See p. 121.

- **Ontario Science Centre:** Kids race to be the first at this paradise of hands-on games, experiments, and push-button demonstrations—800 of them. See p. 128.

- **Toronto Zoo:** One of the best in the world, modeled after San Diego's—the animals in this 284-hectare (702-acre) park really do live in a natural environment. See p. 128.

- **Evergreen Brick Works:** For hands-on learning experiences in cooking, ecology, markets, and treats. See p. 124.

- **Casa Loma:** The stables, secret passageway, and fantasy rooms capture children's imaginations. See p. 125.

- **CN Tower:** Especially the 58-second ride to the top in the glass-floor elevator. See p. 120.

- **Fort York:** For its reenactments of battle drills, musket and cannon firing, and musical marches with fife and drum. See p. 14.

- **High Park:** Wide-open spaces, a fairy-tale kingdom–inspired playground, plus the chance to hang out with llamas. See p. 131.

- **Hockey Hall of Fame:** Who wouldn't want the chance to tend goal against Mark Messier and Wayne Gretzky (with a sponge puck), and to practice with the fun and challenging video pucks? See p. 134.

- **Riverdale Farm:** A working farm in the heart of the city flanked by a park and knotting trails that wind through wildlife-rich ravines. See p. 125.

- **Ripley's Aquarium:** Budding Jacque Cousteaus can see sea critters from around the world. The Pacific octopus is often shy, but his shark friends in the Dangerous Lagoon exhibit are more than keen to flash a jagged smile as they sail past. See p. 122.

- **Royal Ontario Museum:** The top hits are the Ancient Egypt Gallery featuring a real live (well, real dead) mummy and the Hands-On Biodiversity Gallery. See p. 127.

- **Toronto Islands–Centreville:** Riding a ferry to this turn-of-the-20th-century amusement park is part of the fun. See p. 123.

American leagues (like the NHL or MLB). Our newest Rugby League team, however, has taken this to the next level. The Toronto Wolfpack plays in the British Rugby Football League system, which means that the burly blokes have accrued some serious frequent-flier miles hopping the pond for games. When in town, they play here at Lamport Stadium, a casual affair with no real fixed seats. Tickets are cheap ($15–$60), and on a sunny day, it's a blast to take in the tackles as the crowd roars with pleasure.

1155 King St. W. www.toronto.ca. © **416/392-1366**. Subway: Dufferin, then bus 29 S to King.

The **Osborne Collection of Early Children's Books** is a treasure trove for bibliophiles of all ages. Located at the **Lillian H. Smith Branch** of the **Toronto Public Library** (239 College St.; www.torontopubliclibrary.ca/lillianhsmith.com; ☏ **416/393-7753**), the collection includes a 14th-century manuscript of Aesop's fables, Victorian and Edwardian adventure and fantasy tales, 16th-century schoolbooks, storybooks once owned by British royalty, an array of "penny dreadfuls" (cheap thrillers from the days when a paperback book cost a penny), and Florence Nightingale's childhood library. Special exhibits at the Osborne often feature whimsical subjects. Check website for hours.

Rogers Centre ★ STADIUM   This is home to the Toronto Blue Jays baseball team. The opening in 1989 of this stadium, then known as SkyDome, was a gala event. The stadium is an engineering feat, featuring the world's first fully retractable roof and a gigantic video scoreboard. It is so large that a 31-story building would fit inside the complex when the roof is closed.

1 Blue Jays Way. www.rogerscentre.com. ☏ **416/341-2770.** Subway: Union, then follow the signs and walkway.

Scotiabank Arena ★ SPORTS/ENTERTAINMENT COMPLEX   This multi-use complex is home to the Toronto Maple Leafs (hockey) and the Toronto Raptors (basketball). Longtime fans were crushed when the Leafs moved here in 1999 from Maple Leaf Gardens—the arena that had housed the team since 1931—but the Scotiabank Arena (previously called the Air Canada Centre) has quickly become a fan favorite; the center was designed with comfort in mind (seats are wide and upholstered). Seating is on a steeper-than-usual grade so that even the "nosebleed" sections have decent sightlines. When the teams are off the field (or ice), it becomes a concert venue.

40 Bay St. (at Lakeshore Blvd.). www.theaircanadacentre.com. ☏ **416/815-5500.** Subway: Union, then the LRT to Queen's Quay.

OUTLYING ATTRACTIONS

Paramount Canada's Wonderland ★ AMUSEMENT PARK   An hour north of Toronto lies what some say is Canada's answer to Disney World. The sprawling park features more than 200 attractions, including 70 rides, a water park, two play areas for tots (**KidZville** and **Planet Snoopy**), and live shows. Because the park relies on a local audience for most of its business, there are new attractions each year. Some of the most popular have been the **Leviathan,** Canada's biggest, fastest, and tallest roller coaster; the **Fly,** a roller coaster designed to make every seat feel as though it's in the front car (the faint of heart can't hide at the back on this one!); **Sledge Hammer,** a "menacing mechanical giant" that stands 24m (80 ft.) tall and hurls riders through accelerated jumps and free-falls; **Riptide,** a giant swing that executes 360-degree turns and makes riders feel immune to gravity (on hot days, water shoots up from the ground, soaking riders midair); and the **Xtreme Skyflyer,** a hang-gliding and skydiving hybrid that plunges riders 46m (153 ft.) in a freefall. The roller coasters range from the looping, inverted Flight Deck to the suspended Vortex.

The **Splash Works water park** offers a huge wave pool and water rides spread over 8.1 hectares (20 acres), from speed slides and tube rides to special scaled-down slides and a kids' play area.

9580 Jane St., Vaughan. www.canadaswonderland.com. © **905/832-8131.** Pay-One-Price Passport (includes unlimited rides and shows, but not special attractions or Kingswood Music Theater) $65 adults; free for children 3 and under; check website for specials and seasonal rates. June 1–June 25 Mon–Fri 10am–8pm, Fri and Sat 10am–10pm; June 26–Labor Day daily 10am–10pm; late May and early Sept to early Oct Sat and Sun 10am–8pm. Closed mid-Oct to mid-May. Subway: Yorkdale or York Mills, then GO Express Bus to Wonderland. By car: From downtown, take Yonge St. N to Hwy. 401 and go W to Hwy. 400. Go N on Hwy. 400 to Rutherford Rd. exit and follow signs. From the N, exit at Major Mackenzie Dr.

ORGANIZED TOURS

Bus Tours

The **Hop-On Hop-Off City Tour** offered by **City Sightseeing Toronto** (249 Queens Quay W.; www.citysightseeingtoronto.com; © **416/410-0536**) goes to such major sights as the Eaton Centre, City Hall, Casa Loma, Yorkville, Chinatown, Harbourfront, the Rogers Centre, and the CN Tower, and a ticket allows you to get on and off the bus over a 2-day period. Occasionally the bus outpaces the sites, however, creating a dissonance between the narrative and what you're seeing. But all is redeemed with the boat trip (included in the price of the ticket). Know that during peak holiday periods, the buses can be packed tighter than a sardine can, and queues can eat up too much of your day. These tours run daily starting at 10am and cost $38.05 adults, $34.51 seniors and students (w/ID), and $20.35 children 3 to 12; children 2 and under free.

Walking Tours

The joke-cracking **Tour Guys** (www.tourguys.ca; © **647/557-3249**) tour guides are keen to arm you with heaps of interesting Toronto facts during these free 90-minute walking tours. The tours range the gamut from by-the-book historical tours (a tour around Old Town promises that you'll "discover more about cholera than you probably want to") to a ghost walk through Toronto's most haunted downtown locations. There's even a tour through Queen West's Graffiti Alley that delves into the history of street art and gives you a glance into what Toronto's current graffiti culture's all about. Tours leave from various points around the city; check website for times and rendezvous locations. Tours are free, but make sure to tip the guide in cash.

Boat Tours

Hop aboard the *Oriole,* a Great Lakes steamship replica, for a 45-minute tour of Toronto's waterfront led by **Mariposa Cruises** (www.mariposacruises.com; © **416/203-0178**). On chilly days, it's best to huddle inside the cabin (skip this tour entirely if it's foggy or rainy), but when the weather's agreeable, climb one of the stunning wrought-iron staircases up to the canopied upper deck for the ultimate viewing experience. A GPS-triggered audio guide narrates points of interest as you sail past, while a screen displays historical images of Toronto. Cruises depart from Pier 6, 207 Queens Quay West. Tours run from May to mid-October and cost $25 adults, $18.25 students (w/ID), $16 children 5 to 15, children 4 and under free.

OUTDOOR PURSUITS

Toronto residents love the great outdoors, whatever the time of year. In summer, you'll see people cycling, boating, and hiking; in winter, they are skating or skiing and snowboarding out of town. Locals make great use of their parks system and waterways to escape the city without ever leaving T.O. proper.

Beaches

With a name like the **Beaches,** it's not surprising that this east end nabe has some excellent sandy shores. From Coxwell Avenue to Victoria Park, a charming boardwalk connects the beaches, starting at **Ashbridge's Bay Park,** which has a sizable marina. **Woodbine Beach** connects to **Kew Gardens Park** and is a favorite with sunbathers and volleyball players. Woodbine also boasts the **Donald D. Summerville Olympic Pool.** Snack bars and trinket sellers line the length of the boardwalk.

Many locals prefer the beaches on the **Toronto Islands.** The ones on **Centre Island,** always the busiest, are favorites with families because of such nearby attractions as **Centreville.** The beaches on **Ward's Island** are much more secluded. They're connected by the loveliest boardwalk in the city, with masses of fragrant flowers and raspberry bushes along its edges. **Hanlan's Point,** also in the Islands, is Toronto's only nude beach.

All of the Island beaches, plus four others in the Beaches, have earned Blue Flag status, an international eco-standard of water quality and cleanliness. For water-quality updates, visit www.app.toronto.ca/tpha/beaches.html.

Canoeing, Kayaking & SUPing

The **Harbourfront Canoe and Kayak School** (283A Queens Quay W.; www.paddletoronto.com; ☏ **800/960-8886** or 416/203-2277) rents canoes and kayaks; call ahead if you are interested in taking private instruction. You can also rent canoes, rowboats, and pedal boats on the **Toronto Islands** just north of Centreville from the **Boat House** (www.torontoisland.com/boathouse.php). Stand-up paddleboards can be rented on Ward's Island from **Toronto Island SUP** (www.torontoislandsup.com; ☏ **416/899-1668**), which also holds SUP yoga classes for truly advanced balancers who are keen to test their core strength while floating among the swans.

Cross-Country Skiing

Just about every park in Toronto becomes potential cross-country-skiing territory as soon as snow falls. Best bets are **Sunnybrook Park** and **Ross Lord**

TORONTO'S golf OBSESSION

Toronto is obsessed with golf: The city has more than 75 public courses within an hour's drive of downtown. Travelers who are really into golf might want to consider a side trip to the Muskoka Lakes. This area, just 90 minutes north, has some of the best golfing in the country at courses such as **Taboo Muskoka** (www.taboomuskoka.com) and the **Deerhurst Highlands** (https://deerhurst resort.com/golf). Here's information on some of the best golf courses in Toronto.

○ **Don Valley** (4200 Yonge St., south of Highway 401; www.donvalley proshop.com; tel] **416/392-2465**). Designed by Howard Watson, this is a scenic par-71 course with some challenging elevated tees. The par-3 13th hole is nicknamed the Hallelujah

Corner (it takes a miracle to make par). This course is considered a good place to start your kids.

○ **Humber Valley** (40 Beattie Ave., at Albion Road; www.humbervalley. com/golf; ○ **416/392-2488**). The relatively flat par-72 course is easy to walk, with lots of shade from towering trees. The three final holes require major concentration (the 16th and 17th are par-5s).

○ **Glen Abbey Golf Club** (1333 Dorval Dr., Oakville; www.glenabbey.ca; tel] **905/844-1800**). The championship course is one of the most famous in Canada. Designed by Jack Nicklaus, the par-73 layout traditionally plays host to the Canadian Open.

Park, both in North York. For more information, contact **Toronto Parks and Recreation** (www.toronto.ca/parks). Serious skiers interested in day trips to excellent out-of-town sites, such as **Horseshoe Valley,** can contact **Trakkers Cross Country Ski Club** (www.trakkers.ca), which also rents equipment.

Cycling

With biking trails through most of the city's parks and more than 70km (43 miles) of street bike routes, it's not surprising that Toronto has been called one of the best cycling cities in North America. Favorite pathways include the **Martin Goodman Trail** (from the Beaches to the Humber River along the waterfront); the **Lower Don Valley** bike trail (from the east end of the city north to Riverdale Park); **High Park** (with winding trails over 160 hectares/395 acres); and the **Toronto Islands,** where bikers ride without fear of cars.

The **Toronto Bike Share Network** (www.bikesharetoronto.com) is one of the most headache-free ways to rent a two-wheeled mount. A 3-day pass costs $15 and gives you access to 3,750 bikes scattered around town across at 360 stations. Returning the bikes at these stations means you don't need to worry about locks or being tethered to returning to the same bike—you can grab or return your bike to any station.

Be forewarned: Like many other North American cities, the tensions between cyclists and car drivers are mounting, so be on your guard, take it easy, and always take streetcar tracks at a perpendicular angle.

SHOPPING

For shopaholics to casual browsers, Toronto offers a dizzying range of choices. While there are enough buys offered by the numerous international brands in Toronto to pack a U-Haul with, Toronto also has a bustling arts-and-crafts community, with a wealth of galleries, custom jewelers, and artisans. Don't forget the local talent. If your passion is fashion, there are great Canadian labels such as Greta Constantine, Beaufille, Sentaler, Sid Neigum, and Comrags, for starters. Local arts and crafts are also abundant. Some of the best regional artisans are design-related, such as the eclectic collection at Swipe Design and Canadiana-with-cheek at MADE.

THE SHOPPING SCENE
The Neighborhoods
The quaint, sometimes junky shops of **Yonge Street** deal in touristy trinkets, antiques, and local book chains like Book City, while **Kensington Market** is all vintage racks, most of them loaded down with clothing. Top labels like Gucci and Chanel line **Mink Mile** along **Bloor Street West,** which borders tony **Yorkville** where luxe boutiques reign. **Downtown West** leads to locally designed and generally hip finds like Muttonhead (unisex wear, nothing to do with shepherding), Lilliput Hats on College Street, and Anice Jewllery on Ossington. An emerging design area along **King Street East,** in the heart of the historic Corktown neighborhood, promises dazzling showrooms featuring the latest in top brands. The city is also dense with ethnic pockets offering culinary delicacies and other delights, from **Little India** in the east to **Koreatown** in the West, **Little Italy**(s) north and south, and multiple **Chinatowns** to explore, as well as many more to suit your tastes.

Practical Matters
Stores usually open around 10am from Tuesday to Sunday. Smaller boutiques are often closed Mondays (some also take Tues off). Closing hours change depending on the day. Early in the week, most stores close at 6pm; on Thursday and Friday, hours can run to 8pm or 9pm; on Saturday, closing is usually at 6pm. Most stores are open on Sunday, though the hours may be restricted—11am or noon to 5pm is standard.

Note: All Toronto retailers charge shoppers for plastic bags; the charge for a plastic bag is C5¢. The move was intended to boost Toronto's eco-friendliness.

Almost every establishment accepts MasterCard and Visa, and a growing number take American Express.

Great Shopping Areas

DOWNTOWN

Chinatown The city's original Chinatown (there are six and counting) is in the heart of the city, steps away from Kensington Market and other shopping destinations. It is well worth a visit: You can peruse bins of touristy junk such as cheapo plastic toys and jewelry, or search out fine rosewood furniture, exquisite ceramics, homeopathic herbs, and a bounty of exotic foodstuffs. But don't try driving here: This is traffic purgatory and best navigated on foot.

Eaton Centre A downtown mall is a bit of an oddity, but this is one popular destination. Toronto's most famous shopping arcade has more than 200 international chain stores spread over four levels. Think: Banana Republic, Williams-Sonoma, Abercrombie & Fitch, and the Gap, plus two department stores, the Bay and Nordstrom, at either end of the block-long mall. The Eaton Centre is convenient, yet generally boring.

Kensington Between the charming cafes and cheesemongers are a half-dozen or more thrift stores. Rebelling teens love the army-surplus stores for clunky boots and camo gear. Fashionistas prefer to thrift through vintage shops. Exile has great prices, but demands sifting through piles, while King of Kensington, Courage My Love, and Flash Back have top-tier threads ranging from '40s ball gowns to '80s acid wash cutoffs.

The Junction It's a bit of a trek to get to this west-end neighborhood, but it's worth the 5-minute bus ride from Dundas West station. This is where restaurateurs come when they want to decorate Toronto's next top eatery. This is where Diane Keaton comes to antique when visiting Toronto. This is where you'll find everything from oddities (boar skulls at Latre) and high-end Japanese design (Mjolk) to art supplies (Articulations) and Fair Trade chocolate (Delight). The

Junction went dormant for nearly 100 years of Prohibition—the booze ban was lifted in 2001—as a result, many of the turn-of-the-20th-century window displays remain intact. It makes for a charming window-shopping experience.

St. Lawrence Market This market is a local favorite for fresh produce, and it even draws people who live a good distance away. The peameal bacon sandwiches are famous, but there's far more here than just food. There are Baltic amber traders, stalls dedicated to kitchen gadgets, and even pashmina purveyors and vendors who deal exclusively in kitschy souvenirs.

Queen Street West Queen Street West, between University Avenue and Bathurst Street, once *the* hip destination, is still a stomping ground for fashionistas in need of a fix. There's a mix of stores like the Gap and neighboring Canadian-based Le Chateau for budget fashions, M.A.C. Cosmetics, Kiehl's (originally of New York), and some fine local designer fare such as Hayley Elsaesser (the kind of boutique Dali would adore: psychedelic prints, melting sunglasses, neon walls).

The Underground City Subterranean Toronto is a hive of shopping activity for the multitudes working in the Financial District. While you won't find many shops down here that don't have an aboveground location, the Underground City is a popular retreat for winter's coldest days and for summer heat waves, and it's convenient for those who have little time to explore beyond.

West Queen West Queen Street West cool cred has shifted west of Bathurst. This is where you'll find a concentration of fashion talent, art galleries, and some of the best new restaurants. While you're at it, walk north (along Ossington) to the next major street, Dundas Street West, which is on the avant-garde of all fronts, from fashion to food.

MIDTOWN

The Mink Mile This strip of pricey Bloor Street real estate is bordered by Yonge Street to the east and Avenue Road to the west. It's where most of the top international names in fashion set up shop. If you're in the mood to see what Karl Lagerfeld is designing or to pick up a glittering bauble from Cartier or Tiffany, this is your hunting ground.

Yorkville One of Toronto's best-known—and most expensive—shopping neighborhoods, this is where you'll find art galleries of note like LUMAS, designer boutiques, major outlets such as Anthropologie and Whole Foods Market, and boutiques such as the Papery for curated stationery.

SHOPPING A TO Z
Antiques, Furniture & Housewares
ANTIQUES

Bernardi's Antiques ★ For more than 4 decades, this Davisville spot has been the go-to destination for collectors in the know. Repoussé sterling tea sets from the 1830s? They've got it. Louis XVI period porcelain? Pick your pattern. Art Nouveau desks? Of course—though lugging home a leather-topped table might be a bit precarious. For a carry-on-friendly souvenir, an early-20th-century Canadian painting might be your best bet. 699 Mount Pleasant Rd. www.bernardis antiques.com. ✆ **416/483-6471.** Subway: St. Clair, then bus 74 N to Soudan Ave.

Blackbird Vintage Finds ★★ Paula DiRenzo scours flea markets, garage sales and antique barns up north for only the most visually appealing artifacts. A rare Koh-I-Noor Cast Iron Pencil Sharpener, circa 1900, is about as useful as a paperweight, but its retro graphics make it a covetable ornament. The offerings are varied. Wool trapper blankets, bell jars displaying taxidermy, and century-old puppets take up shelf space beside Canadian-made products of today like Vancouver Candle Co. diffusers in scents such as Great Lakes and The North. In the Distillery District, 11 Trinity St. www.blackbirdvintage. com. ✆ **416/681-0558.** Subway: King, then streetcar 504 W to Parliament.

Cynthia Findlay Antiques ★ The vintage jewelry selection at this King West room is unparalleled: engagement rings to rival Kate Middleton's, cocktail rings made with emeralds, star sapphires, diamonds, rubies, and many more shiny baubles are sure to suit any taste from modern to Art Deco and Edwardian. 284 King St. W. www.cynthiafindlay.com. ✆ **416/260-9057.** Subway: St. Andrew.

Green's Antiques ★★ If walking by the stunningly maintained Victorian houses in Cabbagetown evokes a hankering for some pre-WWI antiques, pop into Green's. The family-run shop (passed down over three generations) carries everything from crystal chandeliers to Victorian side tables and bronze statues. 529 Parliament St. www.greensantiques.ca. ✆ **416/925-1556.** Subway: College, then streetcar 506 E to Parliament St.

Smash Salvage ★★★ Since 2008, this sprawling Junction showroom has been a not-so-well-kept secret among the city's best designers. Dealing primarily in oversized pieces that appeal to those keen on the distressed Industrial aesthetic, Smash Salvage is the place to find Depression-era marquee signs, printer's chests, and original Eames shell rocking chairs. 2880 Dundas St. W. www. smashsalvage.com. ✆ **416/762-3113.** Subway: Dundas West, then bus 40 W to Keele St.

FURNITURE

Klaus By Nienkämper ★★★ In 1965, Klaus Nienkämper, Sr., moved here from Germany with $36 in his pocket. Three years later, he became the first Torontonian to import contemporary European furniture. In the '80s, the importer established an eponymous line of locally made pieces that were streamlined, elegant, and timeless. Today, Klaus Nienkämper, Jr., presides over the same Corktown showroom. There are still Nienkämper pieces on display, alongside Tom Dixon lights, Moooi carpets, and Fogo Island chairs. 300 King St. E. www.klausn.com. ✆ **416/362-3434.** Subway: King, then streetcar 504 E to Ontario St.

MADE DESIGN ★★★ Owner Shaun Moore's well-curated collection of Canadian-designed crafts and furniture abides by a mostly avant-garde aesthetic. A Tapermoon Sky floor lamp by Zeed, for instance, looks like a Cubist cactus, while a Jeremy Hutch porcelain platter appears to be made from hundreds of white Lego pieces. Contemporary carpets with intriguing graphics (including one inspired by various heart-beat patterns) come in sumptuous materials like hand-tufted New Zealand wool. 70 Geary Ave. www.madedesign. ca. ✆ **416/607-6384.** Subway: Ossington, then bus 161 W to Geary Ave.

Morba ★★★ Those with Eames tastes and IKEA budgets will be delighted by the convincing replicas for sale at this Queen West establishment. Faux Tom Dixon pendant lights and Xavier Pauchard knockoffs share shelf space with curiosities (mounted deer heads, preserved beetles) and genuine designer items like Lütken's jellyfish-reminiscent glass bowls. 665 Queen St. www.morba.ca. ✆ **416/364-5144.** Subway: Queen, then streetcar 501 W to Bathurst St., or Bathurst, then streetcar 511 S to Queen St. W.

Mjölk ★★★ Specializing in Japanese and Scandinavian design, this Junction shop run by husband-and-wife team John and Juli Bake feels more like an art gallery than a store. Exclusive product collections explore the theme of daily rituals. This translates to wine openers meant to be displayed, not tucked in drawers, oak shaker tables imported from Denmark, and concrete toilet-brush holders that could pass for abstract sculptures. 2959 Dundas St. www.mjolk. ca. ✆ **416/551-9853.** Subway: Dundas West, then bus 40 W to Pacific Ave.

Go Where the Dealers Go

There are plenty of antiques stores in **Rosedale,** on that stretch of Yonge Street from Rosedale subway station to St. Clair Avenue. True bargain hunters gravitate to **Leslieville,** the stretch of Queen Street East between Carlaw and Coxwell avenues, where small antiques shops offer great finds that need a little bit of fixing up. **Parkdale** and the **Junction** also offer good selections of used-furniture and other bric-a-brac shops.

HOUSEWARES, GLASS & DESIGN

Bergo Designs ★★★ Get everything from kitchen basics (if you can call an $160 truffle slicer or an $145 breadbox basic) to funky items like a dachshund-shaped butter dish at this Distillery District shop. Kitchenware brands of note for sale here include Alessi, Bodum, Georg Jensen, and Seletti. In the Distillery District, 55 Mill St. www.bergo.ca. ✆ **416/861-1821.** Subway: King, then a streetcar E to Parliament St.

Cookery ★ Kitchen essentials—cast-iron pans, cutting boards, Dutch ovens, KitchenAids, along with heaps of other gadgets and gizmos that make cooking easier and more efficient—line the shelves of this cheery Roncesvalles shop. Check out the website for a list of classes taught in-store, like pasta for beginners, knife skills, and cheese-making. 303 Roncesvalles Ave. www.cookery-store.ca. ✆ **647/478-3873.** Subway: Dundas West, then streetcar 504 S to Grenadier Rd. 2nd location, 2588 Yonge St. ✆ 416/482-0188.

Hopson Grace ★★ For Martha Stewart wannabes, this Summerhill showroom is a must. An avid entertainer's dream store, Hopson Grace carries products with an emphasis on sustainability. The massive selection ranges from fun and quirky (a Donna Wilson TV tray with a cute anthropomorphic cat design) to stunning decorative decor. Vases made by wood-turner Jim Lorriman, for example, cost on average $1,000, but they are wooden works of art. 1120 Yonge St. www.hopsongrace.com. ✆ **416/926-1120.** Subway: Summerhill.

Placewares ★ Squeezed between fishmongers and produce vendors is one St. Lawrence Market stall that carries everything needed to throw the perfect dinner party, plus everything you'll need to neatly store the leftovers after the guests have gone. In the St. Lawrence Market, Upper Level, stall #29, 92 Front St. E. ✆ **416/363-4247.** Subway: Union, then walk E on Front St. E.

Tosho Knife Arts ★★ When Michelin-starred chefs visit Toronto, most make sure to stop by this Annex boîte renowned for its fancy Japanese blades. The knives come in five different types of steel (from Damascus to Honyaki), and knife handles are made from rare materials such as rosewood, ho wood, lacewood, and Madagascar ebony. 934 Bathurst St. www.toshoknifearts.com. ✆ **647/722-6329.** Subway: Bathurst.

Art

Bau-Xi Gallery ★★★ When artist Bau-Xi Huang immigrated to Vancouver at 23, he took a job at a cedar shingle mill. During the day, he'd work for less than minimum wage, while at night he'd create wall-sized abstract paintings. Despite winning numerous art prizes, Huang struggled to find a gallery that would display his large canvases, so he took a leave of absence from work to open his own gallery. The opening was a smashing success; unfortunately, Huang's boss fired him after reading about it in the paper. Without a job to return to, the young artist poured everything he had into the gallery. Today, Bau-Xi has grown into a tri-city art empire with a location in Vancouver, two galleries in Toronto, and the recent acquisition of the Foster/White Gallery in

Seattle. The first Toronto location (across from the AGO) has long been a cornerstone of the local arts community—painters Jack Shadbolt and Guido Molinari often hung out here, with the latter even helping landscape the backyard. 340 Dundas St. W. www.bau-xi.com. ✆ **416/977-0600.** Subway: St. Patrick.

Craft Ontario ★★ This octogenarian not-for-profit with a mandate to promote and nurture Ontario's craftsmen through mentoring and scholarships, has been hard hit by Etsy and its online ilk. After closing its Yorkville outpost (which had been visited by the likes of Christopher Plummer, Bill Clinton, Margaret Atwood, and others), Craft Ontario has consolidated its shop and gallery south on Queen. Even if crafty exhibitions like "Chromatic Geography: Natural Dyes in the 21st Century" don't tickle your fancy, the gift shop is full of one-of-a-kind wonders. 1106 Queen St. W. www.craftontario.com. ✆ **416/ 921-1721.** Subway: Bay station at Cumberland exit, then cross the road.

Nicholas Metivier Gallery ★★★ This Corktown gallery is one of the largest contemporary art showrooms in Canada. Artists represented by Nicholas Metivier include international heavyweights like photographers Chuck Close and Gordon Parks, as well as up-and-coming local talent such as painter Stephen Appleby-Barr, whose 2017 exhibit, "Corvidae," brought a collection of surreal human-animal hybrids together. 190 Richmond St. E. www.metivier gallery.com. ✆ **416/205-9000.** Subway: Queen, then streetcar 501 E to Jarvis St.

Olga Korper Gallery ★★ This impressive gallery is located in a former foundry and mattress factory, just north of busy Dundas West. The soaring ceilings allow for oversized installations that few other independent spaces in the city can accommodate. Natural light pouring down from the roof makes exhibits like John McEwan's life-size corten steel animal sculptures come to life. Olga Korper balances a roster of burgeoning talent with big names like Patterson Ewen and Will Alsop. 17 Morrow Ave. (off Dundas St. W.). www.olgakorper gallery.com. ✆ **416/538-8220.** Subway: Dundas West.

Stephen Bulger Gallery ★★ Since 1955, Stephen Bulger has exhibited the works of hyper-talented Canadian photographers, who create documentary-influenced prints. Stephen Bulger represents a huge range of talent, from local shutterbug Ruth Kaplan, who shoots serene nude bathers in black and white, to Gerry Deiter, who photographed the infamous 1969 bed-in staged by John Lennon and Yoko Ono in a Montreal hotel room. 1356 Dundas St. W. www. bulgergallery.com. ✆ **416/504-0575.** Subway: St. Patrick, then streetcar 505 W to Dovercourt Rd.

Audiovisual & Electronic Goods

Bay Bloor Radio ★★ Sol Mandlsohn opened a small radio shop in 1946. Seven-plus decades later, this is still the top spot for FM dials, though it sells far more than radios these days. High-fidelity turntables, top-tier headphones (in all the permutations, including in-ear, wireless, Bluetooth, noise-cancelling), speakers, projectors, flatscreens. You name it, odds are they've got it. In the Manulife Centre, 55 Bloor St. W. www.baybloorradio.com. ✆ **416/967-1122.** Subway: Bay.

Henry's ★ Whether you're looking for a new zoom lens fit for a safari or an ultra-fast SD card, this camera emporium is sure to have what you're hankering after. Photo geeks on a budget will be particularly impressed by the used camera lens selection. 119 Church St. www.henrys.com. ℂ **416/868-0872.** Subway: Queen.

Moog Audio ★★★ Sound engineers and DJs flock to this Montreal-based audio store (with two locations: one in La Belle Province, a second in T.O.). Bands and musicians such as Arcade Fire, Kid Koala, and Tiga all shop Moog for mixers, synthesizers, effect pedals, or even for new mics or amps. 442 Queen St. W. www.moogaudio.com. ℂ **416/599-6664.** Subway: Osgoode, then streetcar 501 E to Augusta Ave.

Books

Book City ★ For a small chain, Book City offers big discounts—many titles are discounted by 10 to 30 percent. The selection of international magazines is particularly good. Book City also has several branches around the city, including 2354 Bloor St. W (ℂ **416/961-4496**), 1950 Queen St. E. (ℂ **416/698-1444**), and 348 Danforth Ave. (ℂ **416/469-9997**). 1430 Yonge St. www.bookcity. ca. ℂ **416/926-0749.** Subway: St. Clair.

Glad Day Bookshop ★★★ In 2016, the world's oldest surviving gay bookstore moved into a larger space. It was a bold move in an era of shuttering shops. To make the math work, Glad Day wears many hats: it's still a bookstore selling top LGBTQ titles, but now it's also a cafe and restaurant serving diner nosh and locally roasted Propeller coffee. At night, the shop shifts into bar mode (the book stacks are on wheels so they can be pushed to the side to make room for dance parties). 499 Church St. www.gladdaybookshop.com. ℂ **416/901-6600.** Subway: Wellesley.

Monkey's Paw ★★★ This emporium for old and unusual books is home to the world's only Biblio-Mat: a randomized book vending machine. Pop in a toonie, and it spits out a surprise tome—maybe 250 pages about modern dance, or a slim paperback on Slavic demonology. There's no telling what you'll get, but that's half the fun. 1267 Bloor St. W. www.monkeyspaw.com. ℂ **416/531-2123.** Subway: Landsdowne.

Silver Snail ★ Toronto's premier comic-book store carries everything from dorky T-shirts to action figures and, of course, all the hot-off-the-press, must-have comics a self-avowed nerd could hope for. There's also an excellent cafe located in the store (**Black Canary Espresso Bar**), where you can curl up with a flat white and your recently purchased Marvel masterpiece. 329 Yonge St. www.silversnail.com. ℂ **416/593-0889.** Subway: Dundas.

Swipe Design ★★★ Looking for a gift for the aesthete in your life? This design and architecture shop is a must-visit for bookworms and shopaholics alike. The selection of obscure design books is impressive, but it's also easy to get distracted by the funky designer items on display. Adults will be delighted by a corkscrew-shaped Que Bottle that collapses for easy storage on the go, or the copper Stagg kettles that look like deer antlers; while the younger set go gaga over the handmade puppets and multi-surface markers that encourage drawing on walls. 401 Richmond St. W. www.swipe.com. ℂ **416/363-1332.** Subway: Queen or King, then streetcar 504 W to Richmond St.

Type Books ★★   Type is a love story—a love story about two people who both love books. Canadian books, specifically. Samara Walbohm and Joanne Saul met while studying CanLit in the '90s, and despite the doom and gloom of Amazon looming on the horizon, the academic duo dreamed of opening an eclectic bookshop where keen-minded readers could gather to discuss great novels. Since 2005, Toronto's most avid readers have been pilgrimaging here to stock their home libraries. 883 Queen St. W. www.typebooks.ca. ℂ **416/366-8973.** Subway: Osgoode, then a streetcar 501 W to Trinity-Bellwoods. 2nd location: 427 Spadina Rd. ℂ 416/487-8973.

University of Toronto Bookstore ★★   This is one of the best-stocked independent booksellers in town, with textbooks galore, fiction, nonfiction, medical tomes, and impressive collections of classics and Can Lit. As of year-end—that's May for college students—there's an annual blowout sale. In the Koffler Centre, 214 College St. www.uoftbookstore.com. ℂ **416/978-7900.** Subway: Queen's Park.

Department Stores

The Bay ★★   Striped Bay blankets evoke almost as much patriotic pride as the flag. It may sound silly, but this department store is more than twice as old as Canada. Founded in 1670, North America's oldest company far predates confederation. Back then, the British fur-trading company dealt primarily in pelts, not ladieswear and summer sales. In 1881, the Bay opened its first department store, and has since become an iconic Canadian retailer with 90 locations scattered about the country. The Bay has also been generating news in fashion circles with its reinvention from conservative to cutting-edge. Celebrity fashion editors and designers come to visit and endorse the collections of frocks and more. 176 Yonge St. (at Queen St.). www.thebay.com. ℂ 416/861-9111. Subway: Queen. 2nd location at 2 Bloor St. E. (at Yonge St.). ℂ **416/972-3333.** Subway: Yonge/Bloor.

Holt Renfrew ★★   "Say, what's the dividing line between upper-middle-middle class and lower-upper-middle class?" asks a character in an Edward Albee play. If *Zoo Story* had been set in Canada, the answer would have been the latter shops at Holts, the former at The Bay. The Canadian equivalent of Saks, the upscale retailer was founded in 1837 as a Quebec City fur shop that provided Queen Victoria with her luxe pelts. Today, Holts remains a favorite among the city's upper crust; you'll find all the big-name designers here, including Manolo Blahnik, Balenciaga, Roger Vivier, Valentino, and Prada, among many, many others. The department store anchors the **Holt Renfrew Centre** (www.holtrenfrewcentre.com), a small underground concourse holding a range of shops (Zara, Gap, Aritzia, Fossil) that trend downscale, price-wise.

Holt Renfrew Centre connects with the **Manulife Centre**, packed with even more posh shops, including William Ashley and Indigo Books, and the **Hudson's Bay Centre**, yet another retail complex, holding the Bay Department Store (see above) and some 45 specialty shops. Holt Renfrew Centre, 50 Bloor St. W. www.holtrenfrew.com. © **416/922-2333.** Subway: Yonge/Bloor.

7 Fashion

Toronto has all of the requisite big-name European boutiques along Bloor Street West, between Yonge Street and Avenue Road. You'll see **Hermès** at no. 100, **Gucci** at no. 130, **Prada** next door at no. 131, and **Louis Vuitton** at no. 150. But the listings below largely focus on shops particular to Toronto.

CLOTHING FOR CHILDREN

Advice from a Caterpillar ★★ To ensure that their collection of designer baby togs is ahead of the Toronto trends, the owners of this Rosedale boutique make frequent jaunts to Paris. Designer brands in mini sizes include Stella McCartney and Nellystella. Advice from a Caterpillar carries far more than wardrobe essentials, though. At this one-stop shop you'll find everything to decorate your nursery, from ultra-soft merino wool knit blankets to crocheted butterfly chairs sized for the preschool set, as well as clothes for mom, too. 8 Price St. www.advicefromacaterpillar.ca. © **416/960-2223.** Subway: Summerhill.

Mini Mioche ★ Most clothing companies this size don't have a mission statement, but Canadian-made kids apparel brand Mini Mioche was founded with the mandate to offer the world's best ethically made, premium organic fashion basics for babies and kids. The well-constructed children's threads are a favorite among Queen West's hip moms. 795 Queen St. W. www.minimioche. com. © **647/348-5883.** Subway: Queen, then streetcar 501 W to Tecumseth St.

CLOTHING FOR MEN & WOMEN

Muttonhead ★ These unisex clothes are smart enough to wear in the city, but are built to withstand backcountry camping adventures. The clothing, and even many of the fabrics they're made from, are crafted in the GTA under the supervision of Muttonhead co-founders, sisters Meg and Mel Sinclair. The duo is dedicated to offering a line of long-lasting, sweatshop-free wardrobe essentials. Since it was founded in 2009, Muttonhead has developed a global cult following. 337 Roncesvalles Ave. www.muttonheadstore.com. © **647/341-4415.** Subway: Dunas West, then streetcar 504 S to Grenadier. Second location: 2124 Queen St. E. © 647/348-2980. Subway: Main, then bus 64 S to Queen St.

Hayley Elsaesser ★★ If Lisa Frank and Ed Hardy banded together to design a clothing line for a Japanese cartoon universe, the result would be Hayley Elsaesser. The Toronto-based, Australia-educated designer has become a favorite among pop singers like Miley Cyrus and Katy Perry, who love Elsaesser's color choices (neon and pastels) and punchy prints. A recent collection included flip-phone, scorpion, dice, and cactus motifs. 695 Queen St W. www.hayleyelsaesser.com. © **416/223-4400.** Subway: Osgoode, then streetcar 501 W to Bathurst St.

KOTN ★★★ Founders Helali, Mackenzie Yeates, and Benjamin Sehl source directly from Egyptian farmers who grow what they think is the softest, most breathable cotton in the world. They're applying farm-to-table practices to clothes: buying at fair prices, and then transforming the raw material into fabric at a cut-and-sew factory outside Alexandria that they know pays fair wages. In an effort to stop the cycle of child labor, the Toronto-based company has even used their profits to build one (soon two) schools in the region. Since launching in 2015, the offerings have expanded from simple white T-shirts to include turtlenecks, dresses, and hoodies, all made from that same high-quality Egyptian cotton. 754 Queen St. W. www.kotn.com. ℂ **416/363-5656.** Subway: Osgoode, then streetcar 501 W to Niagara St.

CLOTHING FOR MEN

Gerhard Supply ★★★ Head to this Junction boutique for high-end menswear without an ounce of the pretension usually found at places peddling this price point. Owner Langton Willms is a delight. His well-curated selection focuses on Canadian-made apparel such as cashmere outerwear by Wings+Horns and heritage European brands. Italian-made leather hiking boots by Diemme are a dream to slip on your feet, perfect for scaling the Alps or trekking uptown for a coffee date. 2949 Dundas St. W. www.gerhardsupply.com. ℂ **416/797-1290.** Subway: Dundas West, then bus 40 W to Keele St.

Model Citizen ★ In 2004, Model Citizen opened as a silk-screening studio. Today, they still run silk-screening classes and sell T-shirts printed with funky custom designs like a Modigliani-reminiscent bullfighter in a neon pink matador outfit. But it's their collection of menswear that has voguish lads stopping in to browse the racks: floral ties and matching pocket squares from Pomp and Ceremony, Armour Lux long-sleeved marinières, and Deus Ex Machina jackets that scream *slip me on and ride off into the sunset.* 279 Augusta Ave. www.modelcitizentoronto.com. ℂ **416/553-6632.** Subway: Queens Park, then streetcar 506 W to Augusta Ave.

Serpentine ★★ Owners Paul Mailing and Stephen George have stocked their Yorkville boutique with brands that find the midpoint between avant-garde haute couture and rock-and-roll fashion (think distressed hoodies with opulent fur details). The room, done up with industrial-era antiques and arty murals, appeals to the broody modern *flaneur* keen to fill his closet with foreign labels from Italy, Spain, and Japan. 132 Cumberland St. www.theserpentine.net. ℂ **416/513-1818.** Subway: Bay.

CLOTHING FOR WOMEN

Canon Blanc ★★ A few months after moving to Toronto from Paris, Caroline and Matéo Masquelier opened a charming Queen West boutique specializing in small designers that reflect the multiculturalism of their adopted city. The sunny shop focuses on international artisans like Marie-Laure Chamorel—a Kenzo and Balmain alumna who creates flapper-inspired chokers from vintage lace, pearls, and ribbons—and Becksondergaard, a

HUNTING FOR vintage

In-the-know shoppers will tell you that Toronto has had a truly great vintage-shopping scene since the '70s. From couture and designer finds to simple smocks, collectibles to impulse buys—and if you're prepared to rummage—you can find it at the treasure troves below.

○ **Courage My Love** ★ Follow the wafting patchouli inside this long-standing Kensington thrift shop and you'll find an antique library catalogue with drawers and drawers full of buttons: wood, bronze, brass, bone, horn, and more. The front of the shop is dedicated to accessories and baubles (old and new), but head to the wings of the store where you'll find everything from '50s cocktail dresses to disco jumpers and cashmere button-downs. (14 Kensington Ave.; ℭ **416/979-1992;** subway: Spadina, then streetcar 510 S to Dundas St. W.)

○ **Divine Decadence Originals** ★★★ If you've ever wondered where Kate Moss shops for vintage glad rags when visiting T.O., it would be this Yorkville stalwart. For the past 30 years, fashionistas with a proclivity for dated duds come for silk Spanish caftans, black Chantilly lace ball gowns, and Yves St. Laurent evening dresses (made in the '70s but in such great condition they hardly look a day over 25). (128 Cumberland St., 2nd floor; www.divinedecadenceoriginals.com; ℭ **416/324-9759;** subway: Bay)

○ **Exile** ★ Named for the Rolling Stones song "Exile on Main Street," this Kensington shop was founded in 1975 with punk chutzpah. Don't expect a boutique experience. Shopping here demands a bit of cavalier spirit. It takes dedication to sift through the immense collection of clothes—not everything here is a gem, though between the ill-fitting leather bombers you may find the occasional Keith Richardsesque

Danish outfit known for their hand-printed scarves and eelskin bags. 679 Queen St. W. www.canon-blanc.com. ℭ **647/346-5060.** Subway: Queen, then streetcar 501 W to Bathurst.

Coal Miner's Daughter ★★★ Co-owner Krysten Caddy's great-grandmother was a real coal miner's daughter, but none of the cute frocks or stylish jumpers here scream modern-day miner. The look here is elegant, yet whimsical, with an emphasis on locally made garb (the shop's goal is to have no less than 80% Canadian brands). A few favorites include Birds of North America (for their vintage cuts with quirky prints) and Sara Duke (for her flouncy tops). 744 Queen St. W. www.coalminersdaughter.ca. ℭ **647/381-1439.** Subway: Osgoode, then streetcar 501 W to Niagara St. Second location: 87 Roncesvalles Ave. ℭ 647/381-1439. Subway: Dundas West, then streetcar 504 E to Marion St. Third location: 3023 Dundas St. W. ℭ 647/381-1439. Subway: Dundas West, then bus 40 W to Pacific Ave.

Comrags ★★ Designers Judy Cornish and Joyce Gunhouse create retro-inspired clothing that looks great on a range of body types. It's a label beloved for dresses, especially. Suits and coats are snazzy, too. 812 Dundas St. W. www.comrags.com. ℭ **416/360-7249.** Subway: St. Patrick, then streetcar 505 W to Palmerston Ave.

ston Ave.

jacket. The offerings skew newer. The younger set, who think the '90s are ancient, are sure to find some well-loved Levi's or an '80s prom dress to delight. A must-visit when putting costumes together; it even has a wall of wigs. (62 Kensington Ave.; www.exilevintage.com; *(C)* 416/595-7199; subway: Spadina, then streetcar 510 S to Baldwin St.)

o **Gadabout** ★★★ When a theater company is seeking out the perfect Edwardian bed coat for an upcoming production, they ask Victoria Dinnick, who is perhaps the most knowledgeable person in T.O. when it comes to pre-Reagan-era clothes. (Dinnick insists that anything post-1979 is just old, not yet vintage.) The shop is stuffed to the gills with curios, old games, vases, and other ephemera to keep even non-thrifters occupied. True fans of vintage clothing will swoon over the rare finds such as a

1930s Chinese silk wedding dress or a cat-printed '60s paper dress. The Victoria and Albert Museum in London has a paper dress from the same collection in its archives. (1300 Queen St. E; www.gadabout.ca; *(C)* 416/463-1254; subway: Queen, then streetcar 501 E to Alton Ave.)

o **I Miss You** ★★ Glad rags from all the big European fashion houses (Hermès, Cartier, Louis Vuitton, Gucci, Prada) along with local design darlings (Greta Constantine) line the shelves at this three-room Ossington shop. The selection isn't limited to dresses of a certain vintage; you're just as likely to find last season's hot-pink velvet Balenciaga knife boots as you are a pair of suede Chanel bellbottoms from the '80s. (63 Ossington Ave.; www.imiss youvintage.com; *(C)* 416/916-7021; subway: Osgoode, then streetcar 501 W to Ossington Ave.)

Lilliput Hats ★★ If you're a hat fan, Lilliput's is a must-visit for stunning designs made by owner Karyn Gingras. Her creations have been worn by Celine Dion and Whoopi Goldberg, among others. 462 College St. www.lilliputhats.com. *(C)* 416/536-5933. Subway: Queen's Park, then streetcar 506 W to Bathurst St.

Secrets From Your Sister ★ Thanks to Oprah, we know that the vast majority of women in North America are wearing the wrong bra size. That won't be true of you if you visit this store, which carries a terrific selection of bras to suit figures as dissimilar as Audrey Hepburn and Jayne Mansfield, and everything in between. 560 Bloor St. W. www.secretsfromyoursister.com. *(C)* 416/538-1234. Subway: Bathurst.

Trove ★ Trove started out primarily as a jewelry store, but expanded both in size and goods to now include groovy shoes, fun hats, and other accessories, plus a good selection of handbags. It's a bit of a trek out to the Junction (where Trove recently relocated to), but the entire strip along Dundas Street West is full of charming independent shops with everything from great menswear to fantastic antiques. 3036 Dundas St. W. (at High Park Ave.). www.trove.ca. *(C)* 416/766-1258. Subway: Bathurst.

SHOES (MEN'S, WOMEN'S & CHILDREN'S)

Getoutside ★   With its utilitarian shelving and lighting, this store doesn't look like much, but it stocks an amazing variety of sneakers from manufacturers around the world. 437 Queen St. W. www.getoutsideshoes.com. ℂ **416/593-5598.** Subway: Osgoode.

John Fluevog ★★   Famous for his Goth footwear, this Vancouver designer also creates shoes and boots in a kaleidoscope of colors. These shoes aren't for shrinking violets, but their funky chic will get your attention without having to stomp your feet. 686 Queen St. W. www.fluevog.com. ℂ **416/581-1420.** Subway: Osgoode, then streetcar 501 W to Niagara St.

Mephisto ★   These shoes are made for walking—particularly because they're made from all-natural materials. Devotees of this shop, now in its third decade, swear that it's impossible to wear out Mephisto footwear. 1177 Yonge St. www.ca.mephisto.com. ℂ **416/968-7026.** Subway: Summerhill. 2nd location, 100 King St. W. ℂ 416/703-2400.

Food & Wine
FOOD

The Cheese Boutique ★★★   While browsing aisles of cold-pressed olive oils and balsamic vinegars old enough to vote—before you even make it to the cheese and charcuterie counters—you'll be offered an espresso, and maybe a Belgian chocolate, to sate you while you explore the gourmet offerings at this foodie mecca. The expansive Swansea store carries just about every cheese a turophile could dream of, from Ontario water-buffalo fresco to obscure Scottish wheels. The cheese cave, with human-sized provolones hanging from the ceiling, is a must visit. The excellent in-house kitchen churns out restaurant-quality sandwiches, quiches, and salads, perfect for ready-made picnics in nearby High Park. 45 Ripley Ave. www.cheeseboutique.com. ℂ **416/762-7292.** Subway: Runnymede, then bus 77 S to Ripley Ave.

Kristapsons ★★   Since 1953, this family-owned shop has been crafting some of the best cold-smoked salmon in Ontario. Ardent fans argue that the lox is some of the best east of B.C. The Coho salmon has a hint of sweetness, and the 24-hour flameless smoking technique yields lox just oily enough to satisfy, without any unctuous, fishy aftertaste. There's a reason they sell almost a ton of this stuff every week. 1095 Queen St. E. www.kristapsons.com. ℂ **416/466-5152.** Subway: Queen, then streetcar 501 E to Caroline Ave.

Ontario Spring Water Sake Company ★★★   During a trip to Japan, Ken Valvur became obsessed with unpasteurized sake. To him, it tasted magical. However, he couldn't get it back home in Toronto (because it needs to be kept refrigerated, it's prohibitively expensive to import). So, to slake his raw sake cravings, in 2010 Valvur founded Toronto's first sake distiller. Tour the facility, try a variety of Junmai sakes, then finish at the bottle shop where you can browse the selection with a newfound appreciation for the Japanese

liquor. In the Distillery District, 51 Gristmill Lane. www.ontariosake.com. (C) **416/365-7253.** Subway: St. Andrew, then streetcar 504 E to Parliament St.

Sanko Trading Co. ★ Whether you're shopping for sushi-grade sea bream flown in from the Toyosu market in Tokyo that morning, or you're just hankering after a *mochi* snack, this Japanese purveyor of food, ceramics, and knives carries just about everything that's big in Japan. 730 Queen St. W. www.toronto-sanko.com. (C) **416/703-4550.** Subway: Osgoode, then streetcar 501 W to Niagara St.

SOMA Chocolatemaker ★★★ Thinking about purveyors of first-class chocolate delights, the mind is pulled to Belgium, Switzerland, and then France. Chocolate aficionados, though, know that some of the best chocolate bars in the world are coming out of Canada. After winning gold at the International Chocolate Awards, Soma has gained a legion of international fans who will pay top dollar for its single-origin bars. Whether you want something with raspberry tang (opt for a Madagascar bar), or have a craving for something rich and nutty (Venezuelan), Soma is sure to deliver. The collection of 26 types of truffles includes a pistachio crisp with the snap of a praline and a Maya dome (spicy hot chocolate infused with chili, ginger, orange peel, allspice, and cinnamon. In the Distillery District, 55 Mill St. www.somachocolate.com. (C) **416/815-7662.** Subway: King, then streetcar 504 E to Parliament St. 2nd location: 443 King St. W. (C) 416/599-7662. Subway: St. Andrew, then streetcar 504 W to Bathurst St.

The Spice Trader & The Olive Pit ★★ This contemporary apothecary shop doesn't deal in herbal remedies; it deals in fair-trade organic herbs, dried and blended in small batches. Neatly arranged tins contain esoteric spices like sumac berries, urfa pepper, and calamus root, alongside common kitchen staples. Even baking necessities like cinnamon are a cut above the grocery-store variety (Spice Trader only carries Sri Lankan Ceylon cinnamon, a more pungent, sweeter cinnamon, far superior to the thick cassia variety that's ubiquitous). 877 Queen St. W. www.thespicetrader.ca. (C) **647/430-7085.** Subway: Osgoode, then streetcar 501 W to Niagara St.

WINE

In Ontario, **Liquor Control Board of Ontario (LCBO)** (www.lcbo.com/lcbo/store-locator) outlets include small boutiques, big stores, and some (wine and beer only) locations at grocery or convenience stores. It's a government monopoly that rattles many a citizen who would prefer more choices. At least there's plenty on offer. Look for tastes you won't find easily elsewhere, such as locally produced wines (Niagara and Prince Edward County are producing exceptional vintages), as well as the popular ice wine, an intensely sweet dessert wine that has won awards the world over. There are LCBO outlets all over the city, and prices are the same at all of them.

The nicest shop is the **LCBO Summerhill** (10 Scrivener Sq.; (C) **416/922-0403;** subway: Summerhill). Built into a former train station, this outpost hosts cooking classes, wine and spirits tastings, and party-planning seminars. It's open Monday through Thursday 9am to 10pm, Friday and Saturday 9am to 11pm and Sunday 10am to 8pm.

Gifts & Unique Items

Beau and Bauble ★★ This charming Junction gem caters to girls of all ages, be they 12-year-olds with a penchant for lava lamps and hip printed backpacks, or well-heeled dames who like the Scandinavian frocks and on-trend sunglasses. The store is a dream to browse: No matter where you turn, there's something cute, glimmering, or gorgeous that catches the eye. It's an excellent spot to pick up interesting locally made jewelry as well as top-tier stationary and cards for every (and any) occasion. An ex-costumier who worked in London's West End, owner Kate Elia is an absolute pleasure. She's got a discerning eye, so ask her to pull a few items from the rack for you to try on, and she's sure to deliver. 3092 Dundas St. W. www.thebeauandbauble.com. ✆ **416/904-6136.** Subway: Dundas West, then bus 40 W to Quebec Ave.

Curiosa ★★ No, the door handle of this Parkdale shop isn't a portkey that's transported you into Ollivander's wand shop. This Harry Potter–inspired gift shop is decked with cauldrons stirring themselves, quills, wands, palmistry posters, bowtruckle pin badges, and other shiny treasures. Not everything is wizard-related, though. Muggles will appreciate the selection of puzzles, funky enamel pins, cool-looking hourglasses and compasses, and charming miniature antique reproductions of hot-air balloons. 1273 Queen St W. www.curiosasociety.com. ✆ **647/341-0394.** Subway: Dufferin, then bus 29 S to Queen St. W.

V de V ★★★ Imagine a cooler, independent Anthropologie and you've got V de V: a Montreal-based retailer that brought its effortlessly on-trend style to Ossington in 2016. Locals head here for the modestly priced midcentury modern furniture: sleek velvet sitting chairs, embroidered pillows, and sculptural side tables. The accessories are particularly funky: bathtub-shaped ring holders, hammered copper pendant lights, geometric glass-and-bronze terrariums and wee air plants to put inside them, as well as affordable twee jewelry and cute bucket and cross-body bags. Add to that candles, throws, rugs, and all manner of hooks, knobs, and shelves, and you've got a one-stop shop for a real home redo. 120 Ossington Ave. www.vdevmaison.com. ✆ **647/348-3381.** Subway: Ossington, then bus 63 S to Argyle St.

Teatro Verde ★ It's easy to get distracted by the vibrant blooms here— cases stuffed with magenta dahlias the size of dinner plates, flamingo pink pin-cushion proteas, and gigantic star-gazer lilies actually being arranged for the stars (Lady Gaga is a fan of the flowers here). While the flora impresses, it's the selection of gift-ready baubles that make gift giving a lilac-scented breeze. From copper milk jugs to pig-shaped porcelain punch bowls and stunning abstract vases, there's something for every taste (from eccentric to highbrow) and budget. Yorkville Village Shopping Center, 136 Yorkville Ave. www.teatroverde.com. ✆ **888/4-TEATRO** or 416/966-2227. Subway: Bay.

Likely General ★★ Owner Brooke Manning is an artist who has always had a collaborative bent. When opening her 21st-century general store (she carries everything from decorative macramé plant holders to fancy bath salts,

Australia-made watches and attractive stationary), she wanted to support the artistic work of women, non-binary people, and marginalized people. She's careful about where she sources products, and favors items made by humans, not machines. 389 Roncesvalles Ave. www.likelygeneral.com. ☏ **647/351-4590.** Subway: Dundas West, then streetcar 504 S to Howard Park Ave.

Health & Beauty

The Cure Apothecary ★★   The organic non-GMO Whole Foods demographic is ga-ga for the green beauty products sold at the Cure. Selection focuses on Canadian, Kiwi, Swedish, and American beauty brands that tout themselves as clean products that are just as good for the environment as they are for your skin. 719 Queen St. W. www.thecureapothecary.ca. ☏ **647/350-8274.** Subway: Bathurst, then streetcar 511 S to Queen St. W.

Gee Beauty ★   Well-heeled Rosedale mavens head here for youth-restoring treatments like skin tightening and blue light therapy. Their trust-funded daughters come for the fancy facials and eyelash extensions, and to keep their nails and brows on point. 2A Roxborough St. W. www.geebeauty.ca. ☏ **416/486-0080.** Subway: Rosedale.

Province Apothecary ★★   The Dundas West headquarters for the eponymous skincare brand delivers on its apothecary promises. Wooden shelves lined with jars of petals, roots, and leaves remind customers that the products here are all natural, derived from plant oils, waxes, and herbs. Owner Julie Clark, a certified holistic esthetician, will hand-blend ingredients to create face masks individually tailored to her clients' specific skin needs. The ready-made line is also great. 1518 Dundas St. W. www.provinceapothecary.com. ☏ **647/479-4854.** Subway: Dufferin, the bus 29 S to Dundas St. W.

Jewelry

Anice ★★★   Brittany Hopkins inherited many things from her grandmother Anice, including her infectious joie de vivre and her magpie-like love for anything shimmering and sparkly. At her wee Ossington shop, named after the aforementioned grandmother, she transforms vintage jewels (be they out-of-fashion family heirlooms or sweet antique finds) into swoon-worthy contemporary pieces. The custom creations often feature delicate chains and stunning details like sesame-seed-sized pearls. Hopkins often goes on exotic jewel hunts, bringing back treasures from places like Morocco and Spain, and transforms those into collections she sells in the store. 102 Ossington Ave. www.anicejewellery.com. ☏ **647/351-5526.** Subway: Ossington, then bus 63 S to Argyle St.

Jenny Bird ★   According to Jenny Bird, "The market does not need more soulless, short-lived fashion jewelry, nor does it need overpriced plated pieces," which is why the jeweler has sought to create fairly priced, well-made jewelry with an artistic flare. The resulting pieces are fashion-forward but extremely wearable. 174 Spadina Ave. www.jenny-bird.com. ☏ **647/346-2473.** Subway: Spadina, then streetcar 510 S to Queen St. W.

Made You Look ★★   More than 100 different artists sell their wares at this Parkdale shop. Rather than an owner curating the selection, up-and-coming jewelers rent space, which means there's no telling what you'll find from one visit to the next. The expansive selection ranges from affordable funky statement pieces (photo pedants depicting Toronto street signs) to delicate high-end jewels like a sapphire cluster rose-gold ring by Magnons. 1338 Queen St. W. www.madeyoulook.ca. ✆ **416/463-2136.** Subway: Dufferin, then bus 29 S to Queen St. W.

Leather Goods

Varsity Brown ★   A supporter of the slow fashion movement, leathersmith Matt Boston crafts bags, wallets, and belts that are durable enough to endure the test of time, and stylish enough to outlast any trend cycle. The Toronto-based company bills itself as a micro fashion house that combines heritage techniques with technological precision. 1107 Queen St. E. www.varsitybrown.ca. ✆ **647/523-9900.** Subway: Queen, then streetcar 501 E to Caroline Ave.

Music

Rotate This ★★★   When Prince popped by this record store, he had his bodyguard flip through the records for him. When Quentin Tarantino stopped by in the late '90s, the auteur was impressed by the film collection. After almost 30 years selling records, Rotate This remains a favorite among both local and in-the-know international collectors. The well-organized shop boasts an extensive collection of new and used titles, including many rare finds. *Tip:* Check out the concert tickets on sale here; they're cheaper than through the online distributors. 186 Ossington Ave. www.rotate.com. ✆ **416/504-8447.** Subway: Ossington, then bus 63 S to Dundas St. W.

Sonic Boom ★★   Canada's largest record store has tens of thousands of vinyl records, CDs, and DVDs for sale. The mix of new and used records means you might stumble on a rare funk 45, though this is a better place to find new pressings from your favorite Scandinavian black metal band. Even Top 40 pop starlets like Taylor Swift are issuing LPs these days, and you can find them here, sharing shelf space with broody shoe-gazer EPs. Budding audiophiles can set themselves up with everything they need to become a bona fide music snob in training, thanks to the modest selection of turntables, amps, and speakers. 215 Spadina Ave. www.sonicboommusic.com. ✆ **416/532-0334.** Subway: Spadina, then streetcar 510 S to Sullivan St.

Soundscapes ★★   Since 1999, Soundscapes has been helping fledgling bands kick-start music dynasties. Of Montreal and Feist both played intimate shows here when starting out. Today, the shop welcomes up-and-coming musicians to sell their albums among chart topping re-releases and LPs by indie darlings like Alvvays, Timber Timbre, The Sadies, and Austra. 572 College St. www.soundscapesmusic.com. ✆ **416/537-1620.** Subway: College, then streetcar 506 W to Manning Ave.

TORONTO ENTERTAINMENT & NIGHTLIFE

There's no lack of things to do in Toronto after the sun goes down. The city is a genuine mecca for top-notch theater, with some acclaimed productions actually premiering in Toronto before heading to Broadway or London's West End. Notable local performing-arts organizations include the Canadian Stage Company, the Canadian Opera Company, the National Ballet of Canada, Soulpepper, the Tafelmusik Baroque Orchestra and Chamber Choir, and the Toronto Symphony Orchestra.

Toronto's many dance and music venues also host the crème de la crème of Canadian and international performers. Some of the best entertainment is in Toronto's comedy clubs, which have served as training grounds for stars such as Jim Carrey, Mike Myers, Dan Aykroyd, and John Candy.

There's plenty going on at the Sony Centre for the Performing Arts, Four Seasons Centre for the Performing Arts, Roy Thomson Hall, Massey Hall, the acoustically perfect Koerner Hall, and at other theaters around town.

On the nightlife front, those of the hipster persuasion gravitate to Ossington Avenue, West Queen West, and Dunas West. Some spots to look for include the Dakota Tavern, Black Dice, The Fountain, Sweaty Betty's, Soso's and Majong Bar. For a night of bottle service, skintight dresses and house bass thuds, King West is your best bet. There, Uniun Nightclub, EFS, and Brasaii are popular weekend destinations for local weekend revelers.

MAKING PLANS For listings of local performances and events, check out *Toronto Life* (www.torontolife.com), as well as the *Toronto Star* (www.thestar.com). For up-to-the-minute lists of hot-ticket events, check out the free weeklies (and their informative websites) such as *Now* (www.nowtoronto.com), available around town in newspaper boxes and at bars, cafes, and bookstores. The city website **www.toronto.com** also boasts lengthy lists of performances. Events of particular interest to the gay and lesbian community are listed in *Xtra!* (www.xtra.ca), another free weekly available in newspaper boxes and many bookstores. **BlogTO**

(www.blogto.com/events) is also a great source for upcoming performances and events.

THE PERFORMING ARTS

Toronto's arts scene offers something for every taste year-round. The city's arts institutions are widely renowned, and top-notch international performers regularly pass through town.

Theater

Big-budget musicals—think *Wicked* and *Mamma Mia!*—continue to dominate Toronto's larger theaters, but a number of excellent boutique companies also exist. Many of the smaller troupes have no permanent performance space, so they move from venue to venue. A few festivals offer great times to drop in and capture the flavor of Toronto's theater life:

o **Luminato** (www.luminato.com): Innovative international arts festival in North America, featuring 2 weeks of performance, theater, media and visual arts, and programming. Early June.

o The **Summer Works Theatre Festival** (www.summerworks.ca): Canada's largest juried theater festival. Early August.

o The **Fringe Festival** (www.fringetoronto.com; ✆ **416/966-1062**): Two-week performance festival featuring more than 100 casts from Canada and beyond. Starting in early July.

LANDMARK THEATERS & PERFORMANCE VENUES

Ed Mirvish Theatre ★ This beautiful venue has had a tumultuous history. It got its start as the Pantages Theatre in 1920, and its opulent design (by the famous theater architect Thomas Lamb) was widely admired. But the theater's fortunes sank in 1929—not because of the stock-market crash, but because its owner was embroiled in a legal battle. Eventually, the gorgeous space was carved into six cinemas. It was rescued and dramatically renovated by the Livent production company, which then collapsed, and so the theater went dark for a long time. Eventually, Mirvish Productions, Toronto's leading theater promoters and owners of the Royal Alex and the Princess of Wales Theatre (both listed below), bought the theater and renamed it after the company's founder, Ed Mivish. In recent years, it has hosted such shows as *Mamma Mia!* and *Bat Out of Hell*.

244 Victoria St. www.mirvish.com. ✆ **416/593-0351.** Subway: Dundas or Queen.

Discount Tickets

Want to take in a show, but don't want to spend a bundle? Visit the **Today Tix** website (www.todaytix.com/x/toronto), which sells heavily discounted last-minute tickets. **What's On Tonight** (www.whatsontonight.ca) is another website selling day-of tickets; in addition, What's On Tonight offers **hipTIX,** where students between the ages of 15 and 29 can score $5 tickets for certain shows.

The Elgin and Winter Garden Theatre Centre ★

These landmark theaters first opened their doors in 1913, and the Centre is now a designated National Historic Site, owned and operated by the Ontario Heritage Trust.

Festivals Farther Afield

Don't forget that two major theater festivals—the **Shaw Festival** in Niagara-on-the-Lake (p. 213) and the renowned **Stratford Festival** in Stratford (p. 203)—are only an hour or two away.

Both the Elgin and the Winter Garden have been restored to their Edwardian gilded glory, and the theaters vie with the Royal Alexandra and the Princess of Wales Theatre (see below for both) for major shows and attention. The Centre has been deemed the last operating double-decker theater. The downstairs Elgin is larger, seating 1,539 and featuring a lavish domed ceiling and gilded decoration on the boxes and proscenium. Frescoes adorn the striking interior of the 984-seat Winter Garden. Suspended from the ceiling and lit with lanterns are more than 5,000 branches of beech leaves, which have been preserved, painted, and fireproofed. Both theaters offer everything from Broadway musicals and dramas to concerts and opera performances, with the Toronto International Film Festival utilizing the Elgin as a cinema.

189 Yonge St. www.heritagetrust.on.ca. ℂ **416/314-3718**. Subway: Queen.

Four Seasons Centre for the Performing Arts ★★★

Toronto's opera house, which opened in 2006, is a stunner. Designed by architect Jack Diamond of the renowned Toronto firm Diamond and Schmitt, it has a simple exterior, resembling a house of glass. Inside, in the tradition of truly grand opera houses, there are three stages: main, rear, and side. But the masterstroke in the Four Seasons Centre's design is its perfect acoustics. No small feat given that the structure is set on not one but two major thoroughfares, and a subway line rumbles beneath it. This is home to both the Canadian Opera Company (p. 166) and the National Ballet of Canada (p. 167).

145 Queen St. W. www.fourseasonscentre.ca. ℂ **416/363-8231** for tickets or 416/363-6671 for administration. Subway: Osgoode.

Princess of Wales Theatre ★★

This spectacular 2,000-seat, state-of-the-art facility was built for the Toronto run of *Miss Saigon,* with a stage large enough to accommodate the landing of the helicopter in that production. Later, it was home to *The Lion King, Hairspray,* and the ill-fated stage adaptation of the epic *The Lord of the Rings*. More recently, it has featured *The Book of Mormon*. Frank Stella, who painted 929 sq. m (10,000 sq.-ft.) of colorful murals, decorated the exterior and interior walls. People in wheelchairs have access to all levels of the theater (not the norm in Toronto).

300 King St. W. www.mirvish.com. ℂ **416/872-1212**. Subway: St. Andrew.

Royal Alexandra Theatre ★

John M. Lyle built this beloved theater in 1906 and 1907 at a cost of $750,000. In 1963, it was scheduled for demolition, but Ed Mirvish bought it for $200,000 and refurbished it. Named after Queen Alexandra, wife of Edward VII, the magnificent Beaux Arts structure is

Toronto Nightlife

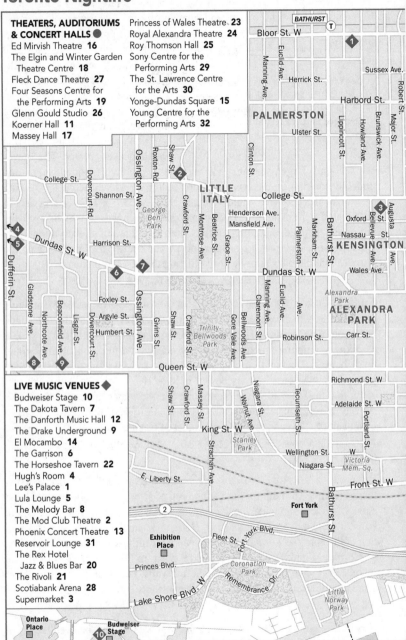

THEATERS, AUDITORIUMS & CONCERT HALLS ●
Ed Mirvish Theatre **16**
The Elgin and Winter Garden Theatre Centre **18**
Fleck Dance Theatre **27**
Four Seasons Centre for the Performing Arts **19**
Glenn Gould Studio **26**
Koerner Hall **11**
Massey Hall **17**
Princess of Wales Theatre **23**
Royal Alexandra Theatre **24**
Roy Thomson Hall **25**
Sony Centre for the Performing Arts **29**
The St. Lawrence Centre for the Arts **30**
Yonge-Dundas Square **15**
Young Centre for the Performing Arts **32**

LIVE MUSIC VENUES ◆
Budweiser Stage **10**
The Dakota Tavern **7**
The Danforth Music Hall **12**
The Drake Underground **9**
El Mocambo **14**
The Garrison **6**
The Horseshoe Tavern **22**
Hugh's Room **4**
Lee's Palace **1**
Lula Lounge **5**
The Melody Bar **8**
The Mod Club Theatre **2**
Phoenix Concert Theatre **13**
Reservoir Lounge **31**
The Rex Hotel Jazz & Blues Bar **20**
The Rivoli **21**
Scotiabank Arena **28**
Supermarket **3**

The Performing Arts

TORONTO ENTERTAINMENT & NIGHTLIFE

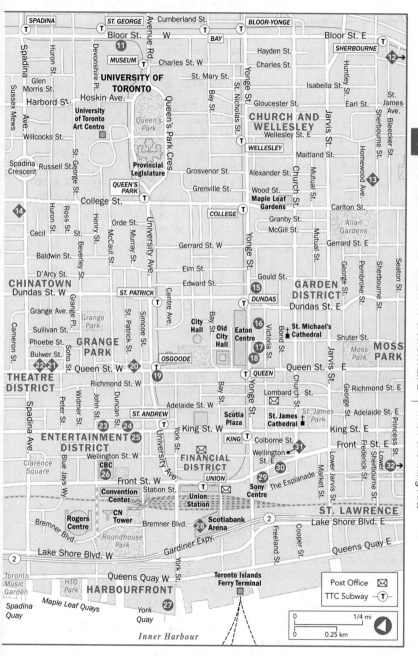

Edwardian down to the last detail. It abounds with gilt and velvet, and green marble lines the entrance foyer. Recent productions here have included the Canadian smash hit *Come From Away,* a musical based on the 38 planes forced to land in Newfoundland after the 9/11 attacks. Avoid the vertigo-inducing second balcony and the seats "under the circle," which don't have the greatest sightlines. Be forewarned that legroom is very limited here.

260 King St. W. www.mirvish.com. ✆ **416/593-4225.** Subway: St. Andrew.

Roy Thomson Hall ★★★   This important concert hall bears the name of newspaper magnate Lord Thomson of Fleet (a Canadian press baron who wound up taking a seat in the British House of Lords). Built between 1972 and 1982, and designed by Arthur Erickson, the building's exterior looks very Space Age. Inside, the mirrored effects are dramatic. Roy Thompson Hall is home to the **Toronto Symphony Orchestra** (p. 166). Since it opened, it has also hosted an array of international musical artists, including Yo-Yo Ma, Jessye Norman, and Kiri Te Kanawa. The hall was designed to give the audience a feeling of unusual intimacy with the performers—none of the 2,812 seats is more than 33m (108 ft.) from the stage. This is one of the few venues where you can feel happy in the nosebleed seats.

60 Simcoe St. www.roythomsonhall.com. ✆ **416/872-4255.** Subway: St. Andrew.

The St. Lawrence Centre for the Arts ★   For 3 decades, the St. Lawrence Centre has presented topnotch theater, music, and dance performances. The facade of the building is unattractive, but the theaters inside are comfortable (and there's more legroom here than, say, the Royal Alex). The Bluma Appel Theatre stages many Canadian Stage company (p. 164) productions, while the smaller Jane Mallet Theatre features the Toronto Operetta Theatre Company, among others. This is a popular spot for lectures, too.

27 Front St. E. www.stlc.com. ✆ **416/366-7723.** Subway: Union.

MAJOR CONCERT HALLS & AUDITORIUMS

Fleck Dance Theatre ★   Part of the sprawling Harbourfront Centre (p. 121) by the waterfront, this 446-seat theater (formerly the Premiere Dance Theatre) is specifically designed for dance performances and is where you can catch some of Toronto's leading contemporary dance companies. 207 Queens Quay W. www.harbourfrontcentre.com. ✆ **416/973-4000.** Subway: Union, then the LRT to York Quay.

Glenn Gould Studio ★   Located on the main floor of the Canadian Broadcasting Centre, this 341-seat radio concert hall offers chamber music, jazz, roots music, and spoken-word performances. Its name celebrates the great, eccentric Toronto pianist whose life was cut short by a stroke in 1982. 250 Front St. W. www.cbc.ca/glenngould. ✆ **416/205-5555.** Subway: Union.

Koerner Hall ★★   Opened in 2009, this is a jewel on Toronto's performing arts scene. Designed by the renowned KPMB Architects group, the concert hall seats 1,135 patrons. The centerpiece of the Royal Conservatory of Music's TELUS Centre for Performance and Learning, it has received rave reviews for its acoustics and attracted such international stars as Steve Reich, Frederica von Stade, Ravi Shankar, and Baaba Maal in genres ranging from jazz to blues to world music to classical. 273 Bloor St. W. www.rcmusic.ca. ✆ **416/408-2825.** Subway: St. George or Museum.

Massey Hall ★★   This landmark 1892 building is one of Canada's premier music venues. It has hosted now-legendary concerts from the likes of Charlie Parker and Neil Young, and its programming runs the gamut from classical to pop to rock to jazz. Recent visitors have included Norah Jones, Diana Krall, Jimmy Cliff, and Pat Metheny. *Note:* In July 2018, Massey Hall closed for a 2-year top-to-bottom reno that will improve amenities while restoring the building to its Victorian splendor. The revamp will add another 500-person venue to complex, which, once complete, will also include a high-tech recording studio. 178 Victoria St. www.masseyhall.com. ✆ **416/872-4255.** Subway: King.

Sony Centre for the Performing Arts ★★   In 2010 this building celebrated its 50th birthday with a $30-million facelift—quite the gift, but then this is quite the venue. Artists who have appeared in this storied venue range from Richard Burton and Liz Taylor to Bob Dylan, the Clash, and Radiohead. Star architect Daniel Libeskind, the man responsible for the Royal Ontario Museum's controversial crystal galleries (p. 127), designed the precipitous 58-story tower that now sits atop the theater. 1 Front St. E. www.sonycentre.ca. ✆ **416/872-2262.** Subway: Union.

Toronto Centre for the Arts ★   Built in 1993, this gigantic complex is a half-hour subway ride from downtown and located in a neighborhood with generally ho-hum food options. Best advice: Have a really early pre-theater dinner before making the trek (see the Downtown North section in the dining chapter [p. 101] for ideas). Programming is varied; one day the Tafelmusik presents a series of Vivaldi concertos; the next evening, a Montreal theater troupe visits to put on a gutsy rendition of the four-man play *Bad Jews.* 5040 Yonge St. www.tocentre.com. ✆ **416/733-9388.** Subway: North York Centre.

Yonge-Dundas Square ★   Toronto's open-air entertainment venue is across the street from the Eaton Centre. Summer is its liveliest season: Events include Yoga in the Square on Mondays, indie concert Fridays, and the odd movie to round out the mix. Events such as NXNE and Pride often host special free concerts here, too. When not in use for events, this is a public square where you can stroll or sit by the fountains. However, unless there is a specific event drawing you to YDS, it's not worth a visit in and of itself. Think of it as Times Square Lite™ (complete with crowds, pickpockets, and blinding neon billboards). 1 Dundas St. E. www.ydsquare.ca. ✆ **416/979-9960.** Subway: Dundas.

Young Centre for the Performing Arts ★★   This was once the home of the Gooderham and Worts Distillery, Canada's largest distilling company in the 19th century. The 45-building complex is an outstanding example of industrial design from the Victorian age (p. 39). In 2003, it was reinvented

A LITTLE CHURCH MUSIC

Everyone knows that a lovely party of churchgoing is listening to choir music—but in Toronto, several churches double as performance spaces for classical and opera ensembles. **Trinity-St. Paul's United Church,** at 427 Bloor St. W. (www.trinitystpauls.ca; ✆ **416/964-6337**), is home to Toronto's acclaimed Tafelmusik Baroque Orchestra & Chamber Choir (p. 166). **St. James Cathedral,** at 65 Church St. (www.stjamescathedral. on.ca; ✆ **416/364-7865**), hosts everything from solo performances of classical cellists to youth choirs from abroad, as well as its own high-quality 18-voice Cathedral Choir and organ recitals. **St. Patrick's Church,** at 141 McCaul St. (✆ **416/483-0559**), is where the **Tallis Choir of Toronto** (www.tallischoir.com; ✆ **416/286-9798**) often performs (its repertoire is mostly Renaissance and Tudor music).

as the Distillery District, which includes galleries, restaurants, and shops. The district also houses several performing-arts venues, including the Case Goods Theatre and the state-of-the-art Young Centre for the Performing Arts, home to Soulpepper. In the Distillery District, 50 Tank House Ln. www.thedistillerydistrict.com. ✆ **416/866-8666.** Subway: King, then a streetcar 504 E to Parliament St.

THEATER COMPANIES & SMALLER THEATERS

Buddies in Bad Times Theatre ★★   Proudly provocative, this not-for-profit company has been dedicated to queer theatrical expression since its founding in 1979. Buddies' artistic mandate is to develop and present voices that question sexual and cultural norms; the artist-in-residence program has produced many amazing voices contributing to this discourse. Controversial playwright Sky Gilbert helped build the theater's cutting-edge reputation. 12 Alexander St. www.buddiesinbadtimes.com. ✆ **416/975-8555.** Tickets $15–$50; pay-what-you-can admission to some performances. Subway: Wellesley.

Canadian Stage ★★   This company performs an eclectic variety of Canadian (from the likes of Michel Tremblay and Robert Lepage) and international plays. Their productions are often groundbreaking. They perform at the **Bluma Appel Theatre,** which seats 868, and the **Berkeley Theatre,** a more avant-garde, intimate (244-seat) space. Bluma Appel Theatre (St. Lawrence Centre): 27 Front St. E.; Berkeley Theatre: 26 Berkeley St. www.canadianstage.com. ✆ **416/368-3110.** Tickets $49–$111; Tues evening pay-what-you-can admission. $30 rush tickets and $29 tickets for individuals under 30. Subway for St. Lawrence Centre: Union; for Berkeley Theatre: King, then any streetcar 504 E to Berkeley St.

Factory Theatre ★★   Since it opened in 1970, the Factory Theatre has focused on presenting Canadian plays, from political dramas to over-the-top comedies. The theater likes to call itself "the home of the Canadian playwright." Performances showcase up-and-coming scribes, as well as such established playwrights as the internationally acclaimed George F. Walker, who has had nearly two dozen shows produced here. The options veer from experimental to traditional. 125 Bathurst St. www.factorytheatre.ca. ✆ **416/504-9971.**

Tickets $25–$50. Subway: St. Andrew, then any streetcar 504 W to Bathurst St. & walk S to Adelaide St.

Native Earth Performing Arts Inc. ★★★ A small company dedicated to performing works that express and dramatize the Indigenous experience in Canada, and to encouraging the use of theater as a form of communication within First Nations communities. Playwright Tomson Highway, author of *Dry Lips Oughta Move to Kapuskasing*, was one of the company's founders. The company also performs at other theaters around town. Performing primarily at the Aki Studio in Regent Park, 585 Dundas St. E., unit 250. www.nativeearth.ca. ✆ **416/531-1402.** Tickets $15–$30. Subway: Dundas, then streetcar 505 E to Sackville St.

Soulpepper ★★★ Founded in 1997, this artist-created classical repertory company began by presenting theatrical masterpieces of the 20th century. They've now commissioned a slew of successful plays, such as *Spoon River*, that have since toured abroad to great acclaim. Education and youth outreach are key parts of their mandate. The highly respected—and award-winning—group recently staged *Kim's Convenience* (later turned into a TV show because it was so well-received) and *Rose*, a new musical based on Gertrude Stein's *The World Is Round*. Performing at the Young Centre in the Distillery District, 55 Mill St. www.soulpepper.ca. ✆ **416/866-8666.** Tickets $36–$97; $20 for ages 22–29; select performances free for those 21 & under; $25 rush tickets. Subway: King, then streetcar 504 E to Parliament St.

Tarragon Theatre ★★★ Opened in 1971, Tarragon produces original works by such famous Canadian literary figures as Michel Tremblay, Michael Ondaatje, and Judith Thompson, alongside works from the likes of David Hare and David Mamet, as well as the occasional classic. There are two small theaters on-site—or three, if you count the 60-seat rehearsal hall, which is occasionally used for performances. 30 Bridgman Ave. www.tarragontheatre.com. ✆ **416/531-1827.** Tickets $30–$60; student tickets from $23. Subway: Bathurst, walk N to Bridgman Ave.

Theatre Passe Muraille ★★ This theater started in the late 1960s, when a pool of actors began experimenting and improvising original Canadian material. It continues to produce innovative, provocative theater by such contemporary Canadian playwrights as John Mighton, Daniel David Moses, and Wajdi Mouawad. There are two stages—the Mainspace seats 220; the more intimate (if rather uncomfortable) Backspace seats 70. 16 Ryerson Ave. www.passemuraille.on.ca. ✆ **416/504-7529.** Tickets $10–$38; reduced admission seniors and individuals 29 & under. Subway: Osgoode, then streetcar 501 W to Bathurst St.

Young People's Theatre ★★ Toronto is such a theater town that even tiny tots (and the rest of the family) get their own performance center. For more than 50 years, the always-enjoyable YPT has mounted whimsical productions such as *Jacob Two-Two Meets the Hooded Fang* (by the late, great Mordecai Richler) and children's classics like *Mary Poppins*. This theater company is particularly committed to diversity in its programming and in its artists. 165 Front St. E. www.youngpeoplestheatre.ca. ✆ **416/862-2222** for tickets or

416/363-5131 for administration. Tickets $15–$54. Check website for PWYC performances. Subway: King, then streetcar 504 W to Jarvis St. and walk S to Front St.

Classical Music & Opera

Canadian Opera Company ★★★   Performances take place in downtown Toronto at the Four Seasons Centre for the Performing Arts, Canada's first purpose-built opera house, which opened in 2006. Special $22 tickets for the under-30 crowd and discounted rush tickets are available, subject to availability. Visitors can also drop in to the **Richard Bradshaw Amphitheatre** for one of the 70-plus free concerts offered annually. Floor-to-ceiling windows allow for a spectacular view of the bustling city core. Regular building tours also offer backstage access, fascinating insight into the building's brilliant acoustic design, and a chance to snap some shareable selfies against the modern architectural backdrop. 145 Queen St. W. www.coc.ca. ℘ **416/363-8231** for tickets or 416/363-6671 for administration. Tickets $35–$350. Subway: Osgoode.

Tafelmusik Baroque Orchestra & Chamber Choir ★★★   This internationally acclaimed ensemble plays baroque compositions by the likes of Handel, Bach, and Mozart on authentic period instruments. The annual *Messiah* concerts always sell out. Visiting musicians frequently join the permanent performers. Concerts take place, primarily, at Koerner Hall (p. 162) and Trinity-St. Paul's United Church, 427 Bloor St. W. www.tafelmusik.org. ℘ **416/964-6337.** Tickets $30–$99. Subway: Yonge/Bloor.

Toronto Symphony Orchestra ★★★   The TSO has was revitalized under the direction of Peter Oundjian (to be replaced in 2020 by Spanish maestro Gustavo Gimeno) and the improved acoustics of their home venue. The orchestra performs anything from classics to jazzy Broadway tunes to new Canadian works at Roy Thomson Hall from September to June. 60 Simcoe St. www.tso.on.ca. ℘ **416/593-4828.** Tickets $26–$154. Subway: St. Andrew.

---

opera OBSESSED

It was big news back in 2006 when Toronto's opera house—the **Four Seasons Centre for the Performing Arts**—opened its doors. The irony was that Toronto, a city that had never had an opera house, was already a North American magnet for opera lovers. **The Canadian Opera Company** (see above) is just one reason to visit. Others include **Opera Atelier** (www.operaatelier.com; ℘ 416/703-3767), a renowned company that produces baroque operas (Monteverdi, Mozart, and Gluck are perennially popular). The **Toronto City Opera** (www.torontocityopera.com; ℘ **800/838-3006**) showcases some of the best emerging opera soloists in town with democratically priced tickets. Those hoping to experience some homegrown Canadian opera should seek out **Tapestry New Opera Works** (www.tapestryopera.com; ℘ 416/537-6066), which has been staging fantastic Canadian-written productions since 1995. For its 20th anniversary, Tapestry introduced Tap:Ex, a successful series that seeks to radically redefine opera through inspiriting collaborations with DJs, punk bands, and more.

Dance

Dancemakers ★ Now under the artistic direction of choreographer Amelia Ehrhardt, Dancemakers has, over the past 4 decades, gained international recognition for its provocative mix of stylized physical movement and theater. It is based in the Distillery District, in a state-of-the-art 98-seat performance venue. Case Goods Theatre in the Distillery District, 15 Case Goods Ln. www.dancemakers.org. ℂ **416/367-1800.** Tickets $20–$25.

National Ballet of Canada ★★★ Perhaps the most beloved and famous of Toronto's cultural icons is the National Ballet of Canada. English ballerina Celia Franca launched the company in Toronto in 1951 and served as director, principal dancer, choreographer, and teacher. Over the years, the company has achieved great renown. The legendary Canadian ballerina Karen Kain became its artistic director in 2005. The company shares the **Four Seasons Centre for the Performing Arts** (p. 159) with the Canadian Opera Company. Its repertoire includes the classics (you can always count on *The Nutcracker* every December) and works by luminaries such as George Balanchine, as well as Canadian choreographers. 145 Queen St. W. www.national.ballet.ca. ℂ **416/345-9595** for tickets, or 416/345-9686 for administration. Tickets $40–$265. Subway: Osgoode.

Toronto Dance Theatre ★ The city's leading contemporary-dance company was founded in 1968, bringing an inventive spirit and original Canadian dance to the stage. Christopher House has been the company's director since 1994. House's choreography is widely acclaimed and has earned him multiple awards. TDT tours internationally and often performs at Fleck Dance Theatre, Queen's Quay Terminal. 207 Queens Quay W. Office: 80 Winchester St. www.tdt.org. ℂ **416/973-4000** for tickets or 416/967-1365 for administration. Tickets $20–$40. Student and senior discount tickets start at $15.

Cinema

TIFF Bell Lightbox ★★★ During September, this glitzy cinema is ground zero for A-listers, who come to town for **TIFF,** Toronto's annual international film festival. The rest of the year, the red carpet is rolled up, and the TIFF Bell Lightbox becomes a great place to catch obscure 1950s Japanese films screened in 35mm, or the newest CanCon indie flick that's making international waves. Year-round programming includes more than artsy film screenings; there are also exhibitions, Q&As, seminars, and more. 350 King St. W. www.tiff.net/visit. ℂ **416/968-3456.** Tickets $14 adults; $11.50 seniors & students. Subway: St. Andrew, then streetcar 504 W to John St.

The Hot Docs Ted Rogers Cinema ★ Another successful festival that's found a brick-and-mortar home is Hot Docs. Now, the film festival dedicated to documentary flicks from around the world showcases biopics, docs, and Q&As year-round. Films span the gamut from flicks about flat-earthers to biopics about famed people (Buster Keaton, Bill Murray, Dame Judi Dench) and historical looks into seminal places such as Studio 54. 506 Bloor St. W. www.hotdocscinema.ca. ℂ **416/637-3123.** Tickets $11.50. Subway: Bathurst.

Pop & Rock Music Venues

Toronto is known for possessing one of the most active live-music scenes in North America. In addition to the previously mentioned Roy Thomson Hall and Massey Hall, these are the major pop and rock music venues. Ticket prices vary widely depending on both the venue and the act. Tickets are available through Ticketmaster (www.ticketmaster.ca; ✆ **416/870-8000**).

Scotiabank Arena ★   Better known as a sports venue—it's home to the Maple Leafs and the Raptors—the Scotiabank Arena (formerly the Air Canada Centre) also hosts popular musical acts. Neil Young has performed here, as have Tom Petty, Radiohead, and Lady Gaga. 40 Bay St. (at Lakeshore Blvd). www.scotiabankarena.com. ✆ **416/815-5500.** Subway: Union, then the streetcar to Queen's Quay.

Budweiser Stage ★   The pleasure of listening to music by the shores of Lake Ontario makes this a favorite summer spot. The amphitheater seats 9,000, the cheaper lawn section another 7,000. The Budweiser Stage regularly draws some of the biggest names in rock, pop, and country. Recent headliners have included Kings of Leon, Jimmy Buffett, Iron Maiden, Muse, and Dolly Parton. In 2018, the name was changed from the Molson Canadian Amphitheatre to its current name. Ontario Place, 909 Lakeshore Blvd. W. www.canadianamphitheatre.net. ✆ **416/260-5600.** Subway: Bathurst, then the Bathurst streetcar S to Exhibition Place (last stop).

Rogers Centre ★   The biggest venue in the city, the Rogers Centre is the home of the MLB Toronto Blue Jays. It's not used regularly for music concerts but occasionally draws superstars like U2 and AC/DC. This venue is about as intimate as a parking lot. If you're seated in the 400 or 500 levels, bring your binoculars; otherwise you'll be watching the show on the JumboTron. Speaking of which, steer clear of the seats next to the JumboTron, or you won't see anything at all. 1 Blue Jays Way. www.rogerscentre.com. ✆ **416/341-3663.** Subway: Union.

THE CLUB & MUSIC SCENE

A few tips before you head out for the evening.

- The **drinking age** in Ontario is currently 19, and most establishments enforce the law.
- Bars and pubs are **open daily from 11am to 2am**.
- Expect **long queues** on Friday and Saturday after 10pm at downtown clubs.
- During **special events** as the Toronto International Film Festival, Nuit Blanche, the North By Northeast Music Festival (NXNE), and Pride, a number of downtown bars are allowed to stay open until 4am.
- If you're out at **closing time,** you'll find the subway shut down, but late-night buses run along Yonge and Bloor streets. Major routes on streets such as College, Queen, and King operate all night.
- To find out **what's on,** see "Making Plans," earlier in this chapter.

Comedy Clubs

Toronto must be one heck of a funny place. How else to explain why a disproportionate number of comedians, including Jim Carrey and Mike Myers, hail from here. The city's comedy clubs are thriving.

The 9-day **Just for Laughs (JFL42)** (www.jfl42.com), Toronto's offshoot of Montreal's celebrated comedy festival **Just for Laughs,** delivers laughs every September with star comics as well as up-and-comers. The 2018 fest included headliners like Seth Meyers, Wanda Sykes, and Hannibal Buress. Individual tickets are $25 to $32 and festival passes run from $55 to $299 (VIP).

Comedy Bar ★★ This new kid on the comedy block has quickly proved popular. It stresses sketch and improv comedy over stand-up (it's co-owned by Gary Rideout, Jr., of sketch troupe the Sketchersons). 945 Bloor St. W. www.comedybar.ca. ℓ **416/238-7337.** Cover: Free to $12. Subway: Ossington.

The Rivoli ★★ While the Riv is also known for its music performances, the Monday-night **ALT.COMedy Lounge** is a huge draw. The Riv features local and visiting stand-ups, and is best known as the place where the comedy troupe Kids in the Hall got their start. Shows take place in the intimate 125-seat back room. 332–334 Queen St. W. www.altcomedylounge.com. ℓ **416/597-0794.** Cover: $10. Subway: Osgoode.

Second City ★ Sacred ground to comedy aficionados. This was where Mike Myers received his formal—and improvisational—comic training. Over the years, the legendary Second City nurtured the likes of John Candy, Dan Aykroyd, Bill Murray, Martin Short, Andrea Martin, and Eugene Levy. It continues to turn out talented young actors. The shows are always funny and topical, though the outrageous post-show improvs usually get the biggest laughs. Skip the bundle deal for the pre-show dinner at Wayne Gretzky's; **Pai** (p. 95) and **Byblos** (p. 87) are nearby and serve much better food. 51 Mercer St. www.secondcity.com. ℓ **800/263-4485** or 416/343-0011. Tickets $16–$57. Subway: St. Andrew.

Yuk Yuk's Toronto ★ Yuk Yuk's is Canada's original home of stand-up comedy. Comic Mark Breslin founded the place in 1976, inspired by New York's Catch a Rising Star and Los Angeles's Comedy Store. Famous alumni include Jim Carrey, Howie Mandel, and Norm MacDonald. Jerry Seinfeld, Robin Williams, Sandra Bernhard, and Bill Hicks have all headlined here. Tuesday is amateur night and is, correspondingly, cheap. 224 Richmond St. W. www.yukyuks.com. ℓ **416/967-6425.** Cover: $5–$20. Subway: Osgoode.

Live Music Venues

The Dakota Tavern ★★ This basement honky-tonk has quickly turned into a mecca for roots, bluegrass, and country rock in Toronto. High-profile singer/songwriters like Ron Sexsmith (a local resident), Serena Ryder, and John Doe (of X) have graced the small stage under the disco ball. Excellent Mexican and Southern-accented food is on offer, and barstools fashioned from wine barrels are a fun touch that pays homage to the Little Portugal locale. The bottomless bluegrass brunch on Sundays is an institution. 249 Ossington Ave. www.thedakotatavern.com. ℂ **416/850-4579.** Subway: St. Patrick, then streetcar 505 W to Ossington Ave.

The Danforth Music Hall ★   From 1919 until the 1970s, this Palladian building functioned as a first-run movie theater. As the Danforth neighborhood became progressively more Greek in the '60s, the theater began to lose its viability, and it was eventually sold and turned into a Greek-language cinema, before it ultimately transformed into a music-venue-cum-rep-house. After a serious renovation in the early aughts, the venue has become a full-time music hall. The gently sloping floor ensures great sightlines for both seated and standing concerts (both are accommodated here). St. Vincent, Metric, Iggy Azalea, Rihanna, and Justin Bieber have all performed at this midsized venue. 147 Danforth Ave. www.thedanforth.com. ℂ **855/985-5000** for tickets or 416/778-8163 for administration. Subway: Broadview.

The Drake Underground ★★   In the basement of the Drake Hotel, this venue was designed with flexibility in mind. It's a good thing, too, because the performers who appear here range from local and visiting musical acts in a wide variety of genres to burlesque artists. At the Drake Hotel, 1150 Queen St. W. www.thedrake.ca/thedrakehotel/underground. ℂ **416/531-5042.** Cover $5–$25. Subway: Osgoode, then streetcar 501 W to Beaconsfield Ave.

El Mocambo ★★   This world-renowned rock-'n'-roll institution hosted an infamous Rolling Stones show in the '70s, while the likes of U2 and Elvis Costello also graced its stage in their early years. Its famous neon sign blinked no more when the club closed for a few years. After trading hands a number of times, Dragon's Den star Michael Wekerle scooped up the property for a cool $3.6 million, then (rumor has it) invested another $10 million, tearing the place back to its studs. He brought famed record producer Eddie Kramer (who collaborated on albums with the Beatles, David Bowie, and The Kinks, to name a few) to help rebuild the space. 464 Spadina Ave. https://elmocambo.com. Cover will vary. Subway: Spadina, then streetcar 510 S to College St.

The Garrison ★   Since opening in 2009, this club has quickly become a valued member of Toronto's live music scene. A petite venue (capacity 300), it sports good sightlines and sound, and has a separate bar area up front if your ears need a break. It is co-owned and booked by scene veteran (Sneaky Dee's) and former rocker Shaun Bowring, and concentrates on local and visiting indie rock bands. 1197 Dundas St. W. ℂ **416/519-9439.** Cover free to $25. Subway: St. Patrick, then streetcar 505 W to Ossington Ave.

The Horseshoe Tavern ★★   Since 1947, this much-loved honky-tonk has played a crucial role in Toronto's music community. The country and blues sounds it showcased in the '60s and early '70s gave way to punk and New Wave, while its current booking policy primarily concentrates on modern rock and roots music styles. The Stones had a secret gig here in 1997, and the likes of Los Lobos, Wilco, and local heroes Blue Rodeo have also graced its stage. For over 2 decades, the free Nu Music Night every Tuesday has presented some real gems. The expanded room now holds 520, and a friendly and unpretentious atmosphere has remained constant. 368 Queen St. W. www.horseshoe tavern.com. ✆ **416/598-4226.** Cover free to $25. Subway: Osgoode.

Hugh's Room ★   Call this a folk supper club for baby boomers. Around since 2001, the 225-seat venue has good sound and sightlines (except at the bar) and decent food. The booking policy ranges from folk legends like Judy Collins and the Strawbs to emerging roots singer/songwriters. 2261 Dundas St. W. https://hughsroomlive.com. ✆ **416/533-5483.** Cover $10–$50 Subway: Dundas West.

Lee's Palace ★   Versailles this ain't, but ignore Lee's patina of grunge and focus instead on the excellent sightlines, high stage, and good sound. Such alternative-rock icons as Nirvana and Red Hot Chili Peppers have played the 600-capacity club, and indie rock remains the primary focus these days. Alt-rock DJs spin in the upstairs room, the **Dance Cave.** 529 Bloor St. W. www.lees palace.com. ✆ **416/532-1598.** Cover $5–$30. Subway: Bathurst.

Lula Lounge   Want to sip a well-mixed mojito or caipirinha, feast on fine Latin cuisine, and catch some great music without leaving your table? If so, make a date with Lula. Located on the outskirts of Little Portugal, this vibrant and spacious room is well worth the trek. It has the feel of a nightclub in pre-Castro Havana, while excellent sightlines and sound, and a capacity of 250, make it one of the city's best live music clubs. Latin sounds are a specialty, but a wide variety of world music is presented here. Country, jazz, rock, and classical artists have also performed at Lula, including Norah Jones, Jonathan Richman, and Canadian rock heroes Sloan. 1585 Dundas St. W. www.lula.ca. ✆ **416/538-7405.** Cover free to $30. Subway: St. Patrick, then streetcar 505 W to Dufferin St.

The Melody Bar ★   After the live music wraps up on Fridays and Saturdays around 10pm, this becomes Toronto's favorite karaoke bar. Skinny-jean-clad cool kids get silly with the mic, belting out '80s love ballades, Spice Girls hits, and heaps of Bowie, Queen, and Rolling Stones. When karaoke's not in session, you'll find local musicians, DJs, trivia nights, and open-mic events. At the Gladstone Hotel, 1214 Queen St. W. www.gladstonehotel.com. ✆ **416/531-4635.** No cover. Subway: Osgoode, then streetcar 501 W to Gladstone Ave.

The Mod Club Theatre ★   One of Toronto's best midsized live music venues, it's co-owned by Mark Holmes, former frontman of '80s rock faves Platinum Blonde. The Killers, Amy Winehouse, and Canadian favorites like Metric and Stars have all performed here; the concert hall morphs into a dance club later at night. 722 College St. www.themodclub.com. ✆ **416/588-4MOD** (416/588-4663). Cover $15 and up. Subway: Queen's Park, then streetcar 506 W to Crawford St.

Phoenix Concert Theatre ★★   The Phoenix is an old-school rock venue and has a loyal local following. It has showcased such legends as the New York Dolls, Patti Smith, and Gang of Four, while newer stars such as Grimes and the Raveonettes have also gigged here. On the weekends, it gets the crowds dancing with a mix of retro, Latin, alternative, and funk. 410

Sherbourne St. http://thephoenixconcerttheatre.com. ✆ **416/323-1251.** Tickets $10–$55. Subway: College, then streetcar 506 E to Sherbourne St.

Reservoir Lounge ★   This joint feels like a contemporary speakeasy. The cramped space—it seats only 100—is below street level, yet feels intimate rather than claustrophobic. Live jazz—Dixieland, vocal jazz, or swing—and Motown belts out 7 nights a week. Defunct elsewhere, the swing dance craze lives on here, as well-dressed hepcats show their moves. 52 Wellington St. E., lower level. www.reservoirlounge.com. ✆ **416/955-0887.** Cover varies, typically around $10. Subway: Union, then walk E to Church St.

The Rex Hotel Jazz & Blues Bar ★★   The busiest jazz club in the city, the Rex presents two or even three different acts daily, 7 days a week. A casual watering hole lacking the pretensions of some jazz joints, it has been drawing jazz fans since it opened in 1951. The decor hasn't changed much since the old days, but the sounds here range from the traditional to the cutting edge. The Rex features the city's best players and sometimes attracts international talent. 194 Queen St. W. www.therex.ca. ✆ **416/598-2475.** Cover up to $15. Subway: Osgoode.

The Rivoli ★★   It may not quite be the mainstay of the local music scene it once was, but Riv's Back Room now hosts an eclectic mix of performances, including roots, rock, jazz, comedy, and poetry reading. Tori Amos and Norah Jones made their Toronto debuts here, and Toronto comedy legends the Kids in the Hall also got their start here. Shows begin at 8pm and continue until 2am. Upstairs is a comfortable billiards room and bar. 332–334 Queen St. W. www.rivoli. ca. ✆ **416/596-1908.** Cover pay-what-you-can admission to $20. Subway: Osgoode.

Supermarket ★★   Kensington Market is famous for its food stores, so it seems appropriate that this new club is playing on the name. It offers a wide assortment of live jazz, soul, roots, and rock. Earlier in the evening, Supermarket is an affordable Asian fusion restaurant, and it occasionally hosts author readings and art events. 268 Augusta St. www.supermarketto.ca. ✆ **416/840-0501.** Cover: free up to $15. Subway: Spadina, then streetcar 510 S to College St.

DANCE CLUBS

Dance clubs come and go at an alarming pace in Toronto, and most of the big-box clubs are in fact on the outskirts of town. Be sure to check out the club listings in the free weekly *Now* (www.nowtoronto.com), or at **www.toronto life.com**, to keep up with the current hot spots. Those listed below have survived the ultra-competitive scene by presenting a consistent music policy and lively atmosphere. Most clubs don't have rigid dress codes, though "no jeans" rules are not uncommon. And remember, it's always easier to get in earlier rather than later in the evening when lines start to form. Several primarily gay and lesbian clubs attract a sizable hetero contingent; one notable destination is El Convento Rico (p. 179).

Crocodile Rock ★   There's something sweet about the fact that a club as untrendy and blue-collar as Crocodile Rock can survive in the heart of the entertainment district downtown. It caters to a slightly older crowd, for whom

'80s pop will never die. 240 Adelaide St. W. www.crocrock.ca. ℂ **416/599-9751.** Cover $5. Subway: St. Andrew.

The Piston ★★ The cozy front room, with its checkerboard floor and exposed brick attracts a mature crowd, who comes to listen to obscure Motown while knocking back local craft tall cans. The ambience changes gears in the much younger back room, the site of some of the city's best low-key dance parties. Fridays are Beam Me Up, a weekly disco night, Thursdays feature Sister Mister, a popular queer dance party, while Tuesdays are Indie Nights. Other popular monthly events include Juicebox (new wave), Synthesexer (electropop), and It's All Good, a '90s video dance party. 937 Bloor St. W. www.thepiston.ca. ℂ **416/532-3989.** Cover $5–$10. Subway: Ossington.

Sneaky Dee's ★★ The antidote to the glut of posh clubs that have been proliferating in Toronto, this long-established oasis of a dive bar boasts the city's best nachos, cheap beer, rowdy '90s-themed dance nights, and excellent live music. The graffiti-layered walls are a testament to the many generations of punks—both poseur and genuine—who have knocked back a pint or three at this well-loved watering hole. Arcade Fire, Feist, and the Dirty Projects all started their music careers with performances at Sneak's upstairs music venue, which rages until 2am. Downstairs, the Tex-Mex menu ain't fancy, but it's greasy enough to soak up a night's worth of reveling. The lower level bar is open until 3am on weekdays, 4:30am on weekends. 431 College St. http://sneaky-dees.com. ℂ **416/603-3090.** Cover up to $15. Subway: Queen's Park, then streetcar 505/506 W to Bathurst St.

Rebel ★ A favorite among the Gen Z cohort, this 4,180sq m (45,000 sq.-ft.) dance club plays a hip hop–heavy top-40 soundtrack to get the crowd moving. The two-story space, complete with a wraparound mezzanine, looks like a neo-Gaudí cathedral inside—if, that is, the Catalonian architect was obsessed with LEDs and theatrical lighting. Outside the venue, the views of the city skyline are absolutely breathtaking. Before trekking down to the waterfront, make sure to check the club's listings; concerts often take over the venue. 11 Polson St. www.rebeltoronto.com. ℂ **416/469-5655.** Cover: $15–$20. Subway: Union.

The Rock 'N' Horse Saloon ★ Why yes, that is a mechanical bull in the back corner with a bride-to-be about to be flipped off the rearing electric bovine. And, wait, did the servers just break out into a well-choreographed line dance? They sure as heck did, partner. This faux Southern saloon is as close as you're gonna get to Texas while dancing the night away in the heart of Toronto's Entertainment District. 250 Adelaide St. W. www.rocknhorsesaloon.com. ℂ **647/344-1234.** Cover: $15–$20. Subway: King.

Soso's Food Club ★★ Until 10pm, this is primarily a restaurant where stylish patrons slurp spicy biang biang noodles and other mainland Chinese delicacies, accompanied by copious amounts of sake chaser. As the night grows later, the vibe shifts, and the space becomes a riotous dance hall with a particularly aesthetically pleasing backdrop—think *Blade Runners* meets Wong Kar-wai.

The drink list is fabulous (Asian spirits and spices feature prominently), and the wines are mostly of the biodynamic variety. Music depends on who mans the DJ booth—Soso's owners are well-connected to the Berlin scene, so expect heavy-hitters spinning infectious beats. 1166 Dundas St. W. www.sosofood.club. ℂ **416/519-6661.** No cover. Subway: St. Patrick, then streetcar 505 W to Ossington Ave.

Uniun Nightclub ★　The 4m-tall (14-ft.) bronze metal arches that frame the dance floor make it feel as if you're reveling under a turn-of-the-century bridge. The time warp is made complete with gargantuan antique chandeliers, decorative apothecary bottles, and the odd taxidermy embellishment behind one of the many bars that flank the sprawling dance floor. At the tufted banquettes, groups with cash to burn sip fancy bottles of cognac and bubbly (a bottle of Ace of Spades is a casual $950). This disc-spinning pulpit attracts some of the best DJs around, with throngs of clubbers pilgrimaging here en masse to dance until the wee hours of the morning. 473 Adelaide St. W. www.uniun.com. ℂ **416/603-9300.** Cover: $15–$20; special DJs as much as $100. Only open Fri and Sat. Subway: St. Andrew, then streetcar 504 E to Portland St.

THE BAR SCENE

The current highly competitive night scene encompasses a flock of attractive bistros with diverse cuisine. You can enjoy cocktails, a reasonably priced meal, and in some, a game of pool in comfortable, aesthetically pleasing surroundings. Compared with dance clubs, the bars and lounges in Toronto are a pretty stable bunch.

Bars & Lounges

BarChef ★★★　A night at BarChef is two parts boundary-pushing mixology, one part theatricality, and a dash of enchantment. Owner Frankie Solarik's objective at this Queen West destination is to "create an experience involving all the senses: a visceral and emotional journey of taste, touch, smell, sound and sight." To achieve this lofty goal, Solarik (who is somewhere between an artist, a chemist, a magician, and a mix maestro) creates elaborate modernist cocktails that present a scene, not just an alcoholic mélange over ice. On one visit, the Illuminated Eucalyptus, a bowl nestled into a Japanese pebble garden vignette, is recommended. The quaff tastes of coconut with hints of creamed sake and bright green spice. On another visit, a recommended cocktail for two comes to the table looking like a bowl of ramen, complete with noodles and chopsticks. A warm mix of bourbon, Islay Scotch, rosemary syrup, and maraschino is poured over the bowl, tableside, thawing the "noodles" (actually a frozen gel made from cacao and green Chartreuse). The presentation enchants, while the perfect balance of sweet and bitter titillates taste buds. 472 Queen St. W. www.barchef.com. ℂ **416/868-4800.** Subway: Osgoode, then streetcar 501 W to August Ave.

Bar Raval ★★★　This might be the most stunningly gorgeous bar in Toronto. This true European-style cafe-bar is a fabulous spot for late-morning cappuccino and a flakey pastry or a for *cinq-à-sept* snack 'n' sip. After the sun sets, attractive creative professionals with money to burn knock back potent, fabulously crafted cocktails while snacking on *pinxos*. Restaurant impresario Grant van Gameren (who also owns Bar Isabel, Tennessee Tavern, and El Rey) is rumored to have spent almost a half-million dollars outfitting the room and its gorgeous wood millwork. The addition of a covered patio with rustic charms has increased sitting capacity threefold; inside, the limited barstools are a coveted commodity, though you do meet some interesting people when chatting around the wine barrel tables. 505 College St. www.thisisbarraval.com. ℭ **647/344-8001.** Subway: College, then streetcar 506 W to Bathurst St.

Birreria Volo ★ What was once an alleyway next to the Royal Cinema has been transformed into a beer-lover's paradise. (The two brick walls are actually the walls of the neighboring buildings, which explains why the space is oh-so-very narrow.) Brothers Julian and Tomas Morana pull 26 beers—the taps are labeled A through Z—with a focus on North American craft. Selection is varied, from a vermouth-oak-aged *saison* from Portland to a double IPA from Vancouver to a dry-hopped apricot sour-brewed in Toronto—the board is ever-changing. The impressive bottle selection skews European. Wild yeast–fermented brews brought in from Italy and Belgium feature prominently. Excellent Italian bar snacks include the fried chicken platters from **P.G Clucks** (p. 95) next door. 612 College St. www.birreriavolo.com. ℭ **416/498-5786.** Subway: College, then streetcar 506 W to Grace St.

Cold Tea ★★ There's no signage on the street indicating that the derelict Kensington Market mall might house one of the coolest bars in town. Instead, walk past the closed bric-a-brac dealers and look for the red light that shines above an industrial-looking door. Inside, you'll find a hip space, made even better by its excellent (usually esoteric) soundtrack and one of the best secret patios in Toronto. Small plates by **Juanmoto** are superb: The nosh is a hybrid of South American, North American, and Asian favors, which translates to teriyaki wings, wasabi-piqued steak tartare garnished with octopus, and silken tofu guacamole, all of which goes down easy with a local beer on tap. In the Kensington Mall, 60 Kensington Ave. ℭ **416/546-4536.** Subway: Subway: College, then streetcar 506 W to Augusta Ave.

The Communist's Daughter ★★ Not the easiest place to find (look for the Nazare Snack Bar sign), but well worth the quest. A tiny, laid-back spot with Formica tables, it possesses one of the city's best jukeboxes. There's excellent live music on Saturday and Sunday afternoons (jazz and country, respectively). 1149 Dundas St. W. ℭ **647/435-0103.** Subway: St. Patrick, then streetcar 505 W to Ossington Ave.

The Drake Lounge ★★ The bar at the Drake Hotel (see p. 66) is a perfect perch for sipping old-fashioneds and envisioning yourself in a glamorous bygone era. The Lounge is designed to evoke a mid-20th-century feel. It's dressed-up, grown-up fun, and it attracts a crowd of devoted locals and

DRINK WHERE YOU play

Toronto might be known as Canada's financial epicenter, but we don't always put work before play. In fact, sometimes we even double down on the play. Locals just love games, and Toronto has game bars of all different stripes. Whether you're keen for a bout of bocce, or you're more of an esoteric strategy-based board-game aficionado, Toronto is sure to have a game bar that will delight.

○ **The Ballroom** ★ (145 John St.; theballroom.ca; ✆ **416/597-2695**). On game night, hundreds of fans gather at this sporty destination to cheer on the home team. Over 5 dozen flatscreens promise that the action is never out of sight. Those who prefer to play, not watch, can avail themselves of the nine bowling lanes on the lower level and a second floor packed with game-bar standards including bubble hockey, foosball, and giant Jenga.

○ **Snakes & Lattes** ★ (489 College St.; www.snakesandlattes.com; ✆ **647/342-9229**). Board-game zealots, and even those whose gaming experience starts and stops at Monopoly, head to this funky gaming paradise, where the $5 admission gets you access to over 1,000 different games, and the ever-chipper staff (all game masters) will teach you the rules to any game you pluck from the well-organized shelves. An excellent selection of craft beer and ciders ensure that even if you're losing, you're probably having a great time. As the name suggests, this a great spot for non-drinkers, too.

○ **Dundas Video** ★ (831 Dundas St. W.; no website/no phone). This Dundas West dive bar feeds on '80s nostalgia. Old-school Nintendo consoles (N64, NES, and SNES) are hooked up to cathode-ray TVs. The no-frills room is undergrad chic: picnic tables, a few old movie-theater seats, and the odd unframed poster effuse the joint's *je ne care pas* attitude.

○ **Spin** ★★ (461 King St W.; toronto. wearespin.com; ✆ **416/599-7746**). You don't need Forrest Gump's table-tennis skills to enjoy this ping-pong "social club." The sleekly sprawling, 12,000-square-foot King West space boasts a dozen tables, which are best reserved in advance at peak bar times. Prices for a table vary from $15 for a weekday walk-in at 5pm to $70 for a prime Saturday-night booking. Potent cocktails and crushable snacks, such as shrimp toast and buffalo broccoli, make this a respectable bar in its own right.

○ **Track & Field Bar** ★★ (860 College St.; www.trackandfieldbar.com; no phone). Here, games generally played by your grandpa are cool again. Maybe that's why this large subterranean space is a top pick for birthday parties—it's got intergenerational appeal. Trendy kids born with a smartphone in hand sip complicated cocktails while playing leisurely lawn games like bocce ball and shuffleboard, as well as tabletop games like crokinole. The games are free to play for walk-ins, but the wait can be hours, so book in advance online for $40 to ensure you snag a lane.

suburbanites. At the Drake Hotel, 1150 Queen St. W. www.thedrake.ca. ✆ **416/531-5042.** Subway: Osgoode, then streetcar 501 W to Beaconsfield Ave.

The Lockhart ★★ Muggles hoping to sip on butterbeer should come to this Harry Potter–inspired bar, where the magic is in the presentation. The

Befuddlement Draught, for example, comes to the table ablaze (fire is, after all, listed as an ingredient on the drinks card). The snug room is well-decorated: "Potions & Elixirs" is painted on the brick wall behind the bar, and tables are made from the tops of traveling trunks (the sort you could easily imagine at the end of a bed in a Hogwarts dormitory). After 9pm there's almost always a line, so come early or prepare to queue. 1479 Dundas St. W. www.thelockhart.ca. ✆ **647/748-4434.** Subway: Dufferin, then bus 29 S to Dundas St. W.

The Fountain ★ The excellent, eclectic music ranges from Hank Snow crooning to obscure shoe-gazer tracks, but don't try and make any requests. The sassy bartenders here run the show. The small room is one of the few spots on quickly gentrifying Dundas West where the artistically inclined locals still gather, potent dark and stormies in hand, to make merry and forget the stresses of the day. The vibe here is witch chic: Think antique dolls that look ready to come to life, mounted owls, and a decorative church pulpit. The space doubles as a gallery, always showing a rotating roster of interesting local artists. Monthly tarot card readings are a big draw. 1261 Dundas St. W. ✆ **416/262-4986.** Subway: St. Patrick, then streetcar 505 W to Dovercourt Rd.

Get Well ★ The type of late 20-something who lists thrifting as a top hobby on a dating profile is likely to choose Get Well for a first date with their Tinder match du jour. The eclectic space is a mismatch of Formica tables, disco balls, depression-era lights; the bar is crowned by a golden phoenix with red glowing eyes. The draws are threefold: The craft beer list is more than respectable, the nostalgic video games are free and fun (think Frogger, Space Invaders, and pinball), and there's great pizza on offer from **Brooklyn Pizza.** The lines on weekends are decidedly less of a plus. 1181 Dundas St. W. www.getwellbar.com. ✆ **647/351-2337.** Subway: St. Patrick, then streetcar 505 W to Ossington Ave.

Mahjong Bar ★★ You'd be excused for walking by and thinking this Pepto-Bismol pink bodega was just a place to buy Korean cosmetics and hard-to-find instant ramen. Those in the know head to the curtained doorway, behind which is Mahjong Bar: a sumptuous room with a Hong Kong speakeasy vibe. 1276 Dundas St. W. www.mahjongbar.com. ✆ **647/980-5664.** Subway: St. Patrick, then streetcar 505 W to Dovercourt Rd.

Motel ★ Historic art pieces grace the walls, the Britpop and local content on the jukebox impresses, and the cozy place (capacity: 40) exudes a laid-back vibe. Guest bartenders and DJs will take care of your beverage and aural needs. Too bad you can't book a room. 1235 Queen St. W. ✆ **416/399-4108.** Subway: Osgoode, then streetcar 501 W to Gwynne Ave.

Sweaty Betty's ★★ This low-key, unpretentious place won't be to everyone's taste—a good thing, since the seating capacity is limited to roughly 60 people (and that includes the patio). Famous for its snarky bartenders, this is a great spot for meeting others, since the close quarters means you'll hear everyone else's conversations. 13 Ossington Ave. ✆ **416/535-6861.** Subway: Osgoode, then streetcar 501 W to Ossington Ave.

Pubs & Taverns

Allen's ★   Allen's is a great bar offering more than 150 beer selections and 278 single malts. Guinness is the drink of choice on Tuesday and Saturday nights, when folks reel and jig to Celtic entertainment. 143 Danforth Ave. www. allens.to. ℂ **416/463-3086.** Subway: Broadview.

The Caledonian ★★★   What's a pair of Scots to do when craving some good whisky and a Scotch egg, but they're a full red-eye away from home? Let Donna and David Wolff banish any homesickness at this homey Scottish pub. The convivial atmosphere takes work—the Wolffs chat with regulars, introduce new friends, and recommend Scotches based on your preferences (if you like peat, they've got the tipple for you; if you prefer sweet, they'll find the right well-aged match to sate). Whisky tasting flights range from introductory ($19 for three Highland quaffs) to advanced. The luxury flight, for example, is a steep $250, but includes a 25-year-old Bunnahabhain and a 30-year-old Balvenie. This is one of the few places in town that serves haggis. 856 College St. www. thecaledonian.ca. ℂ **416/577-7472.** Subway: Ossington, then bus 63 S to College St.

Dora Keogh ★   Comfortable and friendly, with a decidedly authentic atmosphere, this is a good spot for a hearty meal and a pint. But the real reason to come is the music. Saturday afternoons feature topnotch jazz, while traditional Celtic melodies are served up on Thursdays at 9pm and Sundays at 5pm by some of the city's best players. The sessions are becoming legendary, especially since famous fiddler Natalie MacMaster and members of the Chieftains have joined in. 141 Danforth Ave. www.dorakeogh.to. ℂ **416/778-1804.** Subway: Broadview.

Irish Embassy ★   Located in a stunning 1873 bank building in the Financial District, this pub fills up after the closing bell rings at the Toronto Stock Exchange. Guinness is just one of the many brews on tap, and the excellent pub-grub menu will help tide you over. 49 Yonge St. www.irishembassypub.com. ℂ **416/866-8282.** Subway: King.

Hemingway's ★★   Don't be fooled by its literary name. This Toronto institution has been a favorite among the sporty, party-loving set for decades. Although the many flatscreens play everything from hockey to football (American and European), Hemmo's is one of the few places in town that screens rugby games. After work, sports fans flock to this three-story Kiwi pub for a pint and a bite. In summer, the four patios are coveted by locals. Service is friendly. Deep-fried pub grub isn't the only nosh on offer; a few healthful salads round out the menu—this is Yorkville, after all. 142 Cumberland St. www.hemingways.to. ℂ **416/968-2828.** Subway: Bay.

Madison Avenue Pub ★   This is a favorite haunt of University of Toronto students, but older patrons will also feel welcome. Beer is the beverage of choice here, with more than 150 varieties available on tap. The original pub at 14 Madison Avenue has gobbled up its neighbors at 16 and 18, and now this spot is a huge complex with six separate British-style pubs and capacity for close to 2,000 people. 14 Madison Ave. www.madisonavenuepub.com. ℂ **416/927-1722.** Subway: Spadina.

The Queen & Beaver Public House ★★ Every good pub must have a competent kitchen. This British pub has a superb kitchen. Everything is made from scratch, even the breads and sausages. The full English breakfast is one of the most authentic, rib-sticking portions this side of the Atlantic. (The black pudding is simply fantastic.) The pub occupies a two-story Victorian that's been gorgeously decorated to match the era of the building. The drink card includes rotating cask beers, local ciders, and an excellent wine selection. 35 Elm St. www.queenandbeaverpub.ca. ✆ **647/347-2712.** Subway: Dundas.

The Queer Scene

Toronto's queer community is one of the largest of any city in North America, so the nightlife scene is diverse. It remains largely concentrated in the Gay Village, around Church and Wellesley streets, but popular new locales have recently opened in Parkdale. Queer women are generally served by monthly or semi-regular parties at various venues around town in lieu of a designated bar—listings for these parties can be found in the free weekly newspaper *Xtra!* (www.xtra.ca). *Xtra!* Is also a great resource for finding LGBTQ+ community–oriented events, seminars, and performances.

The Beaver ★★ The name probably tells you most of what you need to know. Located between the Gladstone and the Drake, and blessed with a great patio, this cozy watering hole has good food and on-point DJs that can read a room to keep parties going well into the night. 1192 Queen St. W. www.thebeaver toronto.com. ✆ **416/537-2768.** Subway: Osgoode, then streetcar 501 W to Gladstone Ave.

Crews & Tangos ★★★ Located in a Victorian house, this three-in-one club promises something for everyone. **Crews** is a gay bar for men and is known for its pubby atmosphere and drag shows, which start at 11pm. The dance floor and lounge of the upstairs **Tangos** bar gets wild on weekends. Then there's the **Zone,** which offers karaoke, drag queen and drag king shows, and dancing. 508 Church St. www.crewsandtangos.com. ✆ **647/349-7469.** Subway: Wellesley.

El Convento Rico ★★ The Latin beat beckons one and all—straight, gay, and otherwise—to this lively club. It has welcomed a diverse crowd for nearly a quarter-century. If you don't know how to salsa, meringue, or cha-cha, you can pick up the basics at the Friday-night dance lessons, but even if you don't learn, no one on the jam-packed dance floor will notice. A substantial hetero contingent comes out just to watch the fabulous drag queens—and don't be surprised if you encounter a bachelorette party in progress. Post-midnight shows, Friday and Saturday, are big draws. 750 College St. www.elconventorico. com. ✆ **416/588-7800.** Subway: Queen's Park, then streetcar 506 W to Shaw Ave.

Pegasus Bar ★ This relaxed pub draws a gay and lesbian crowd with its four professional-size billiard tables, trivia nights, video games, pinball machines, and gigantic TV (tuned to gay dramas). The staff is warm and welcoming. 489B Church St. www.pegasusonchurch.com. ✆ **416/927-8832.** Subway: Wellesley.

BREWTOPIA: TORONTO'S BEST BREWERY BARS

Toronto has a booming brewery scene. At last count, we were fast approaching nearly three dozen breweries. A number of these local craft-beer producers have onsite bars, many with excellent food, perfect for pairing with suds, be they barrel-aged, extra hopped, sour, or blended with wine.

o **Bellwoods Brewery** ★★★ (124 Ossington Ave; www.bellwoods brewery.com; no phone): In 2012, two budding brewers turned an old mechanic's garage into one of the city's top breweries. In summer, it's nearly impossible to nab a table on the white-picket fenced-in patio. There, social media influencers snap selfies of themselves sipping beers with names like Jelly King (a pineapple-grapefruit-tangerine sour) and Skeleton Key (a rum-barrel-aged imperial stout). Great, well-priced nibbles; try the grilled duck hearts and smoked buffalo sausage.

o **Blood Brothers Brewing** ★★★ (165 Geary Ave.; www.bloodbrothers brewing.com; ℂ 647/628-6062): An industrial stretch north of Dupont street has come alive with amazing restaurants, bars, and this top craft brewery. Here, brothers Justin and Brayden Jones make innovative beers. Every beer is perfectly balanced: The Shumei IPA begins

bitter, then finishes with pine punch, while the Paradise Lost sour balances salinity (from Maldon sea salt) with a crisp citrus quench from fermented yuzu juice.

o **Burdock** ★★ (1184 Bloor St W.; www.burdockto.com; ℂ 416/546-4033): At Burdock, first came the music-venue aspect (this is a great spot to catch indie and folk sets). Then, the restaurant component: The from-scratch nosh is superb—especially the bread made using 100-year-old French sourdough starter. Finally, the fermenting tanks were installed. But just because beer was the final addition, it doesn't mean it's an afterthought. The beers here are often made with interesting ingredients from Niagara farms and local forest foragers. The wine-blended saisons are among some of the most interesting brews fermenting in the city. Try the Black Ruby, a brett saison aged in Cognac barrels for 8 months with Cab Franc skins, then blended in a stainless tote, before being aged on black and red raspberries for a further 3 months.

o **Godspeed Brewery** ★★ (242 Coxwell Ave.; www.godspeedbrewery. com; ℂ 416/551-2282): In 2017, the *Toronto Star* called Godspeed's launch the "most anticipated brewery

---

Sailor ★★   This bar is attached to Woody's (see below) but has a livelier atmosphere; unlike Woody's, you won't see many women here. Every Thursday, there's a Best Chest competition; every Friday, the prize is for Best Ass. In the evening, a DJ spins an assortment of dance and alternative tunes. 465 Church St. ℂ **416/972-0887.** Subway: Wellesley.

opening of the year." The brewery was a long time in the making. Originally, owner Luc Lafontaine had planned to open a brewery in Tokyo with his Japanese wife, Eri Kuramasu. Unfortunately, Japanese business bureaucracy is a bear for an international entrepreneur, so the two moved back to Canada and opened Godspeed. The 100-seat brewery pairs easy-sipping suds with Japanese comfort food.

○ **Indie Alehouse Brewing Co.** ★
(2876 Dundas St. W.; www.indiealehouse.com; ☏ **416/760-9691**): Belgian sours, double IPAs, and English porters are the focus at this Junction brew house that likes to color outside the lines. "We're not fans of rules, beer style guidelines, or people telling us what we can or can't do," they proudly aver on their website. Leaning into their self-avowed iconoclast status, Indie Alehouse aims to brew beers aged in funky barrels and made with unusual ingredients. A lactose sour called Lemonade Stand is a summer favorite, while the über-hoppy Cockpuncher is bitter in a good way. The haute pub grub is creative and sating. Service can be inconsistent, though.

○ **Mill Street Brew Pub** ★ (21A Tank House Ln.; ☏ **416/681-0338**):

Situated in the historic site of an old brewery, this pub features an award-winning array of beers brewed in small batches (some are available only seasonally). The Tankhouse Pale Ale is a constant, with its five malts blended for a particularly complex flavor.

○ **Rorschach Brewing Co.** ★★
(1001 Eastern Ave.; www.rorschachbrewing.com; ☏ **416/901-3233**): After a day spent sunning on Toronto's east end beaches, jump off the westbound streetcar on the way back downtown and head here for a sundowner. All 16 taps pull draught that's been brewed in-house. The suds have on-theme psychotherapy-inspired names. An order of Positive Reinforcement begets a *festbier* (a popular Octoberfest frosty) with notes of warm spices, malt, and soft pretzels. Meanwhile, the Systematic Desensitization does anything but desensitize the palate; this blueberry lager (fermented with rice, lactose sugar, and a pinch of vanilla) tastes like liquid blueberry pie and will leave you hankering for seconds. While the beer names might be high-faluting, the food menu is a mix of globe-spanning crowd-pleasers like tacos, baos, wings, and flatbreads.

Woody's ★★★ A local institution, immortalized in the television series "Queer As Folk," Woody's is still the reigning men's bar in the village, welcoming women and heteros. Best Chest contests, drag shows, and DJs are all featured on different nights. It's a popular meeting spot, especially for weekend brunch. 467 Church St. (S of Wellesley St.). www.woodystoronto.com. ☏ **416/972-0887.** Subway: Wellesley.

WALKING TOURS OF TORONTO

Toronto is a great city for walking. The patchwork of dynamic ethnic neighborhoods, the impressive architecture, and the many parks all combine to encourage visitors to lace up and hit the streets. Along the way are small cafes and eateries for refueling or for taking a leisurely break. But because the city is such a sprawling place, you'll need to pick your route carefully…unless you're happy to wander.

The walking tours in this chapter aren't designed to provide an overview, but rather to guide you through the most colorful and exciting neighborhoods in the city, which feature worthwhile sights on almost every corner.

WALKING TOUR 1: CHINATOWN & KENSINGTON MARKET

START:	**St. Patrick subway station.**
FINISH:	**Queen's Park subway station.**
TIME:	**At least 2 hours. Depending on how long you want to linger at the Art Gallery of Ontario and at various stops, perhaps as long as 8 hours.**
BEST TIMES:	**Tuesday through Saturday during the day.**
WORST TIMES:	**Monday, when the Art Gallery is closed.**

This walk takes you through the oldest of Toronto's existing Chinatowns (the city's original Chinatown was on York St., between King and Queen streets, but skyscrapers replaced it long ago). Although at least six Chinatowns exist today, and most Chinese live in the suburbs, the intersection of Dundas Street and Spadina (pronounced spa-*dye*-na) Avenue is still a major shopping and dining area for the Asian communities.

Kensington has changed dramatically over the years. Originally a Jewish community, it then became home to Portuguese and other European immigrants, and then changed again as the bordering Chinatown expanded at the same time shopkeepers from the Caribbean, the Middle East, and elsewhere arrived. There are several Asian herbalists and grocers, as well as West Indian and Middle Eastern shops. Kensington Avenue has the greatest concentration of

Walking Tour: Chinatown & Kensington Market

1 St. Patrick's Church
2 Sharp Centre for Design
3 Art Gallery of Ontario
4 The Grange
5 Bau-Xi
6 Consulate General of Italy
7 The Herb Depot
8 Dragon City
9 Kai Wei Supermarket
10a Swatow
10b Rol San
11 Tap Phong Trading Company
12 B & J Trading Company
13 Plaiter Place
14 Tom's Place
15 CXBO Chocolate
16 Blackbird Bakery
17 Exile
18 Courage My Love
19 Bellevue Square Park
20 Kiever Synagogue
21 La Tortilleria
22 Perola Supermarket
23a Ideal Coffee
23b Ronnie's Local 069
24 Church of St. Stephen-in-the-Fields

vintage clothing stores in the city as well as some good grub and excellent cafes for refueling.

From the St. Patrick subway station, exit on the NW corner of Dundas St. and University Ave., and walk W on Dundas St. Turn right onto McCaul St. At no. 131, you'll see:

1 St. Patrick's Church

Built in 1861 for Toronto's Irish-Catholic community, this church became the base of German-speaking Catholics from 1929 to the late 1960s. Inside, you'll find some of the most beautiful stained glass in Toronto. The church is also a popular site for concerts.

Go back toward Dundas St. and walk W; looking S on McCaul St., you'll see:

2 Sharp Centre for Design

This is one of the city's more controversial contributions to the recent surge in new and bold architecture. Will Alsop's building, which is part of the Ontario College of Art & Design, looks like a checkerboard box on stilts. The Sharp Centre won a Worldwide Award from the Royal Institute of British Architects in 2004; they described it as "courageous, bold, and just a little insane." Admire the insanity from the outside; visitors are not allowed beyond the lobby, although it has a shop worth a look.

Continue W along Dundas St. On your left is the:

3 Art Gallery of Ontario

Renovated in 2008 by local boy Frank Gehry, who grew up around the corner, the AGO is arguably Toronto's best gallery. Visit for the stellar collection of paintings by Canadian legends and European masters, the best collection of Henry Moore sculpture in the world, the photography gallery, and much more. A recent gift from local collector and philanthropist Dr. Ydessa Hendeles added 32 Canadian and international contemporary artworks—the most significant single gift of contemporary art in the AGO's history.

Walk behind the AGO, following Beverley St. S. Behind the AGO, you'll find:

4 The Grange

This historic mansion was the original home of the Art Gallery of Ontario. Built in 1817, the Georgian mansion is still part of the AGO. Although there are tours of the kitchens, most of the building now houses the AGO's members club. In 2017, the surrounding Grange Park reopened after a $12.5-million makeover. The revitalized park fans out around Henry Moore's iconic, 8-metric-ton sculpture, *Large Two Forms*.

Retrace your steps to Dundas St. W. and cross so that you're on the N side of the street. On this block, you'll find:

5 Bau-Xi

This gallery, at 340 Dundas St. W., represents contemporary Canadian artists. It's been in business since 1965 and offers a worthwhile perspective on the current national art scene.

Walk W along Dundas St.; at the NW corner of Beverley and Dundas sts. is the:

6 Consulate General of Italy

It doesn't look like a government building: The rambling late-19th-century mansion, with its sandy-colored brick, quasi-Gothic windows and wrought-iron decoration, is a beauty. Too bad you can't go in.

You're now walking into the heart of Chinatown, with its grocery stores, bakeries, trinkets, and emporiums selling herbs and handcrafts.

What follows are some of my favorite stops along the stretch of Dundas St. between Beverley St. and Spadina Ave. On the S side, or the left side as you go W, is:

7 The Herb Depot

At 407–409 Dundas St., this market carries every herb under the sun. Many are a mystery, but the terrific English-speaking herbalists and acupuncturists on duty are happy to help. Several markets in Chinatown carry similar wares, but this one is the best bet for those who don't speak Chinese.

8 Dragon City

This small mall at 280 Spadina Ave. is notable for a few things. The pet-store **Downtown Pet Centre** is in the basement; they have emperor sharks, fancy *orandas,* and piranhas to watch in the aquariums, as well as a great collection of gear for your dog/cat/bird/fish at home. Dragon City also has Hui's Pharmacy, a Canada Post outlet inside Sun Wa bookstore, and free Wi-Fi throughout the building.

Cross Dundas St. and walk S on Spadina Ave.; at no. 253 is:

9 Kai Wei Supermarket

Look at all the different provisions—chili and fish sauces, fresh meat and fish (including live crabs and tilapia), preserved plums, chrysanthemum tea and other infusions, moon cakes, and large sacks of rice. There's also a great selection of Kasugai Japanese-made gummy candies and sweet rice snacks to keep you going.

10 Swatow and Rol San 🍽

For fine, reasonably priced food, a Chinatown favorite is **Swatow 10A** (309 Spadina Ave.; ℂ **416/977-0601**). If you don't mind lining up, head for the ever-popular all-day-and-all-night dim sum at **Rol San 10B** (323 Spadina Ave.; ℂ **416/977-1128**).

Continuing N, cross St. Andrews St. to reach:

11 Tap Phong Trading Company

This shop, at 360 Spadina Ave., stocks terrific wicker baskets of all shapes and sizes, as well as woks and ceramic cookware, attractive mortars and pestles, and other household items.

Cross Baldwin St., and on the N side of the street is:

12 B & J Trading Company

This shop, at 378 Spadina Ave., is a good place to pick up souvenirs, including painted chopsticks, fans, parasols, cushion covers, and satin slippers. **Mashion Bakery,** at 345 Spadina Ave., is an Asian bakery that features fluffy steamed barbecued-pork buns, deep-fried sesame balls, and pineapple bread.

Next door is:

13 Plaiter Place

At 384 Spadina Ave., Plaiter Place has a huge selection of wicker baskets, birdcages, woven blinds, bamboo steamers, hats, and other souvenirs.

Now double back to Baldwin Street. You're heading into the heart of the **Kensington Market** area, which is particularly rich with cultural diversity. Once, it was primarily a Jewish market; later, it became a Portuguese neighborhood. Today, it is largely Asian and Caribbean, but its past lives on in many ways.

Head back to Baldwin St. and walk W; you'll find:

14 Tom's Place

This traditional haberdasher—located at 190 Baldwin St.—is a place to haggle for a deal on good, Made-in-Italy men's shirts. The store also sells women's clothing, but it's mostly the men's suits and clothing that draw crowds.

Across the street is:

15 CXBO Chocolate

Located at 193 Baldwin St., this tiny temple to chocolate has some tasty, unusual offerings imagined by *Iron Chef* Brandon Olsen. Yuzu-sake is a personal favorite.

Across the street and down a few shops, look for:

16 Blackbird Bakery

At 172 Baldwin St. is one of the market's finest bakeries. Ask any chef in town and they'll tout Blackbird's baguette as one of the city's best: moist and airy with a perfectly crunchy crust. The sweets are also on point: rhubarb Danishes, lemon-almond polenta cakes and oh-so-perfect *canelés de Bordeaux* (little cakes with custardy interiors).

As you stroll S along Kensington Ave. and pass St. Andrews St., you will find a series of secondhand and vintage-clothing stores:

17 Exile

At 60 Kensington Ave., on the west side of the street, this store has good jeans, leather jackets, and assorted accessories.

18 Courage My Love

The best spot for cheap but chic vintage clothing is at 14 Kensington Ave. It stocks retro gowns and wedding dresses, suits, and accessories, as well as new jewelry and beads for do-it-yourself projects. The $5 rack out front (in nice weather) has some great deals; if you take some of these exquisite but damaged dresses and coats to a tailor, you can end up with beautiful, original pieces for a song.

When you reach Dundas St., turn right and walk 1 block to Augusta Ave. Turn right on Augusta Ave. As you walk N and cross Wales Ave., you'll find:

19 Bellevue Square Park

A favorite spot for modern hippies to kick back under the pine canopy, while kids frolic in the splash pads.

Stroll through the park; at the corner of Bellevue Ave. and Denison Sq., you'll find:

20 Kiever Synagogue

This building, at 28 Denison Sq, was completed in 1927. Architect Benjamin Swartz designed it with the Byzantine style in mind. The most striking features are the twin domes atop the building (sadly, the building isn't open to the public). The Kiever Synagogue was the first specifically Jewish building designated as a historic site by the province of Ontario.

Turn back toward Augusta Ave., and you'll see:

21 **La Tortilleria** 💭

This tiny spot—just a few stools inside and, weather permitting, tables out front—serves good corn tortillas made daily. Tacos and bottled drinks from Mexico round out the tiny menu (198 Augusta Ave.; ✆ **647/723-8760**).

Walk N on Augusta Ave. to:

22 Perola Supermarket

This store, at 247 Augusta Ave., is great for cassava and strings of peppers—ancho, *arbol, pasilla*—that are hung up to dry. Check out the bins of other exotic fruits and herbs, too.

Continue N along Augusta Ave. to Nassau St., turn W., and you'll find:

23 Refreshments 💭

Depending on the time of day, you might need a caffeine pick-me-up from local micro-roaster **Ideal Coffee** ㉓Ⓐ (84 Nassau St. ✆ **416/364-7700**), or perhaps a full-on break's in order. In which case, some local craft suds are best enjoyed at the lo-fi bar **Ronnie's Local 069** ㉓Ⓑ (69 Nassau St. ✆ **416/340-1110**), which also happens to have an excellent patio for people-watching.

Continue W along Nassau St., to Bellview Ave., follow Bellview Ave. N to College St., and you'll find:

24 Church of St. Stephen-in-the-Fields

This small but historically significant church has had to fight hard to ward off the condo developers circling Kensington Market. Ironically, the Anglican Diocesan Council wanted to sell its own church, and the local community—many of whom have no religious connection to the church—came together to save it. The building, built in 1858, is a lovely example of Gothic Revival architecture and contains some splendid stained-glass windows.

On College St., hop on an eastbound streetcar, which will deliver you to the Queen's Park subway station. The southbound train will take you downtown.

WALKING TOUR 2: WYCHWOOD

START:	**Dupont subway station.**
FINISH:	**Pain Perdu or Patachou on St. Clair West.**
TIME:	**2 to 4 hours.**
BEST TIME:	**Weekdays during business hours or Saturday mornings.**
WORST TIMES:	**Sundays, when many buildings are closed or reserved for weddings.**

This eclectic tour takes in the city archives; a castle; a stately home; a toll-keeper's house; and two artist enclaves, one in a sylvan glade, the other in a former public-transit parking lot. The castle is a tale in itself: Toronto's kitschy chateau, Casa Loma, is a museum and events destination, complete with Elizabethan-style chimneys, Rhineland turrets, secret passageways, and an underground tunnel. Built about 100 years ago, it was a dream-come-true for a wealthy financier who, in the long term, had greater architectural ambitions than cash.

The neighborhoods involved include busy Davenport; the magical parklike setting of Wychwood Park, with its stately homes; the pretty Hillcrest area, another residential gem; and finally, the new and very progressive development of an old barn for streetcars that was saved from ugly development by a brilliant partnership between Artscape, the city's primo art cooperative, and the Stop Food Community Centre, a leading activist organization that works to feed, with dignity, Toronto's poor. Any day of the week, stop by what's known as the Green Barns, and you might find ta screening of a topical documentary on food politics, an exhibit of resident artists' work, children from the nursery school playing outside, or the bustling year-round farmer's market.

From the Dupont subway station, walk N on Spadina Rd. under the train bridge and to:

1 City of Toronto Archives

This often-overlooked repository at 255 Spadina Rd. is the closest thing Toronto has to a museum of the city. Ongoing exhibits, largely photography-based, reflect events and themes in the city's past. The collection has more than 1 million images, dating from 1856.

Walk 100m (328 ft.) N to the top of Spadina Rd., at Davenport Rd., and look up at the zigzagging flight of stairs you are about to climb:

2 The Baldwin Steps

This part of Spadina Road ends at the base of a zigzagging flight of stairs that ascends the pre–Ice Age shoreline of the ancient Lake Iroquois. A public right-of-way that dates from the 1800s, the Baldwin Steps are a rare example in the city of a thigh-burning incline. The panoramic views of downtown and Lake Ontario are worth the effort. The steps are named after Robert Baldwin, a former premier of Ontario who owned land in this well-to-do neighborhood.

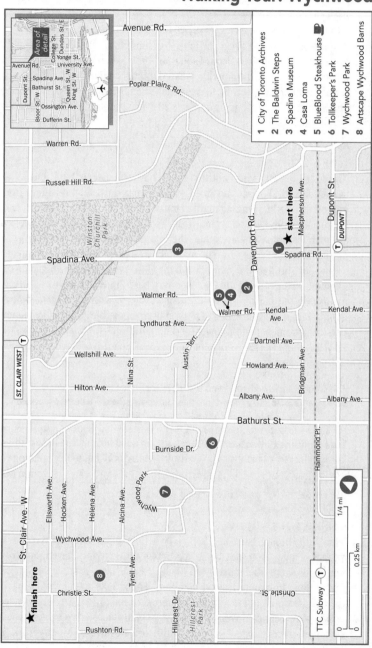

Area of detail

Avenue Rd.
Yonge St.
College St.
Dundas St. E
Dundas St. W
University Ave.
Spadina Ave.
Queen St. W
King St. W
Bathurst St.
Ossington Ave.
Dufferin St.
Bloor St. W
Dupont St.

1 City of Toronto Archives
2 The Baldwin Steps
3 Spadina Museum
4 Casa Loma
5 BlueBlood Steakhouse
6 Tollkeeper's Park
7 Wychwood Park
8 Artscape Wychwood Barns

Avenue Rd.

Poplar Plains Rd.

Warren Rd.

Russell Hill Rd.

Winston Churchill Park

Spadina Ave.

★ start here

Macpherson Ave.

Dupont St.

T DUPONT

1

T Spadina Rd.

3

Davenport Rd.

Walmer Rd.

5 4 2

Walmer Rd.

Kendal Ave.

Kendal Ave.

Lyndhurst Ave.

Dartnell Ave.

Austin Terr.

Wellshill Ave.

Nina St.

Howland Ave.

Bridgman Ave.

T ST. CLAIR WEST

Hilton Ave.

Albany Ave.

Albany Ave.

Bathurst St.

Burnside Dr.

6

Hammond Pl.

St. Clair Ave. W

Ellsworth Ave.

Hocken Ave.

Helena Ave.

Alcina Ave.

Wychwood Park

7

Wychwood Ave.

★ finish here

8

Tyrell Ave.

Christie St.

Christie St.

Hillcrest Dr.

Hillcrest Park

Rushton Rd.

TTC Subway — T

1/4 mi

0.25 km

9

WALKING TOURS OF TORONTO | Walking Tour 2: Wychwood

Continue on the path for 50m (164 ft.), with Toronto's turreted wonder, Casa Loma, on your left. Instead of visiting, though, turn right into the lush garden setting of a more subdued stately mansion:

3 Spadina Museum: Historic House & Gardens

The historic home of financier James Austin was occupied by the family for more than 100 years, from 1866 until 1980, when it became a city-run museum. In 2010, the interior was completely renovated and updated from a 19th-century setting to one focused on the interwar years, with an emphasis on decorations from the 1920s. The grounds are as sumptuous as the interiors.

It's just a hop, skip, and a jump across the street to a more exuberant neighbor:

4 Casa Loma

Sir Henry Pellatt, who built this faux chateau between 1911 and 1914, studied medieval palaces and then gathered materials and furnishings from around the world, bringing marble, glass, and paneling from Europe; teak from Asia; and oak and walnut from North America. He then imported Scottish stonemasons to build the massive walls that surround the 2.5-hectare (6¼-acre) site. The architect was local talent E. J. Lennox.

Wander through the majestic Great Hall, with its 18m-high (59-ft.) hammer-beam ceiling; the Oak Room, where three artisans took 3 years to fashion the paneling; and the Conservatory, with its elegant bronze doors, stained-glass dome, and pink-and-green marble. The castle encompasses battlements and a tower, and a 244m (801-ft.) tunnel runs to the stables, where horses were kept in rooms of Spanish tile and mahogany.

5 BlueBlood Steakhouse 🍴

The setting, tucked into a grand first-floor room that looks down onto the Casa Loma gardens, is magnificent. Leather tufted benches, staghorn chandeliers, a casual Dalí sculpture for decor (real, not a replica): This is opulence. Sir Henry Pellatt would approve…perhaps not that his estate now housed a steakhouse, but the sheer extravagance of it all. Steaks are aged for a minimum of 40 days, but cost far more than their age (1 Austin Tr. ✆ **416/353-4647**).

From Casa Loma, walk down Walmer Rd., then turn right along Davenport Rd. to Bathurst St. The NW corner of the intersection is home to one of the oldest structures in the city, a tollkeeper's cottage:

6 Tollkeeper's Park

This little home, built in 1835, is where hapless tollkeepers tried to extract pennies from passing horse-drawn traffic along Davenport Road until tolls were abolished in 1890. It's also a rare example of vertical (rather than horizontal) wood planking. The simple living conditions in the two-bedroom home attest to the terms of the office: Any uncollected tariffs were deducted from their pay. A small interpretive center, where costumed docents regale visitors with stories of life in Muddy York, is connected to the house.

Continue W on the N side of Davenport Rd. until you reach the sign for Wychwood Park Private Grounds:

7 Wychwood Park

Don't let the "private" sign deter you: Step through the stone gate to enter another world tucked into the heart of the city. The fortunate residents of this secret enclave like to keep the wooded setting to themselves; another sign just inside the gate—"DANGER DEEP WATER QUICKSAND"—is merely a ruse to deter visitors. Immediately ahead is a pond (often featuring the resident swan) and a fork in the road. The route to the left is a little shorter, but both are pleasant, taking you past many English-style Arts-and-Crafts homes designed by Toronto architect Eden Smith. Marmaduke Matthews envisioned an artist colony when he built the first home here in 1874, naming it after Wychwood Forest in Oxfordshire, England. This early example of a planned community retains its natural landscaping and bucolic setting.

Exit Wychwood Park at the N end and walk N on Wychwood Ave. 2 blocks until you get to:

8 Artscape Wychwood Barns

It's hard to imagine, as you come out at the top of these winding, tree-lined roads, that a TTC streetcar repair barn operated here until the 1990s. Now, it's one of the city's most successful transformations of industry into arts space. Artscape Wychwood Barns opened in 2009; attractions include studios for the 2 dozen artists-in-residence, ongoing exhibits of new work, and archival images of the old barns. The Stop Food Community Centre, a leading activist organization that fights poverty and pushes political agendas on the food front, runs the food side of the space with a bake oven, greenhouse, community kitchen, and classroom on-site. There are lots of events to check out, from movies to fab dinners/fundraisers. (www.thestop.org). A bustling Saturday farmer's market is complete with picniclike prepared foods, such as butternut squash empanadas and some of the best fish tacos anywhere. If the weather cooperates, sit outside with a bite to eat and watch the parade of dogs, kids, farmers, and shoppers. Kick back: You've earned it.

Walk 2 blocks N to St. Clair Ave. W., where there are plenty of great cafes and restaurants:

WALKING TOUR 3: ST. LAWRENCE & DOWNTOWN EAST

START:	**Union Station.**
FINISH:	**King subway station.**
TIME:	**2 to 3 hours.**
BEST TIME:	**Saturday, when the St. Lawrence Market is in full swing.**
WORST TIME:	**Sunday, when it's closed.**

At one time, this area was at the center of city life. Today, it's a little off center, yet it has historic and modern architectural treasures and a wealth of history in and around the St. Lawrence Market.

1 Union Station

Check out the interior of this Classical Revival beauty, which opened in 1927 as a temple to and for the railroad. The shimmering ceiling, faced with vitrified Guastavino tile, soars 27m (89 ft.) above the 79m-long (259-ft.) hall.

Across the street, at York and Front sts., stands the:

2 Fairmont Royal York

The venerable railroad hotel is a longtime gathering place for Torontonians. It was the home of the famous Imperial Room cabaret and nightclub, which was one of Eartha Kitt's favorite venues. The hotel was once the tallest building in Toronto and the largest hotel in the British Commonwealth. Check out the lobby, with its coffered ceiling and opulent furnishings. One floor up on the mezzanine is a new **gallery** of black-and-white photographs that cover the hotel's long and illustrious history.

3 The Royal York ☕

Okay, you're just getting started, but it would be a missed opportunity not to stop in for a bite at one of the many good dining options at the **Royal York** (p. 60). The roof garden, where the hotel grows its own mint for mojitos, is also home to several honeybee hives. Expect an eco-conscious menu.

As you leave the hotel, turn left and walk E on Front St. At the corner of Bay and Front sts., look up at the stunning:

4 Royal Bank Plaza

The two triangular gold-sheathed towers rise 41 floors and 26 floors, respectively. A 40m-high (131-ft.) atrium joins them, and 68kg (150 lb.) of gold enhances the mirrored glass. Webb Zerafa Menkes Housden designed the project, which was built between 1973 and 1977.

Cross Bay Street and continue east on Front Street. On the south side of the street is the impressive sweep of **One Front Street,** the attractive main post office building.

On the N side of the street is:

5 Brookfield Place

Go inside to view the soaring galleria. Skidmore, Owings, and Merrill, with Bregman + Hamann, designed it in 1993. The twin office towers connect through a huge glass-covered galleria five stories high, spanning the block between Bay and Yonge streets. Designed by artist-architect Santiago Calatrava, it links the old Midland Bank building to the twin towers.

Walking Tour: St. Lawrence & Downtown East

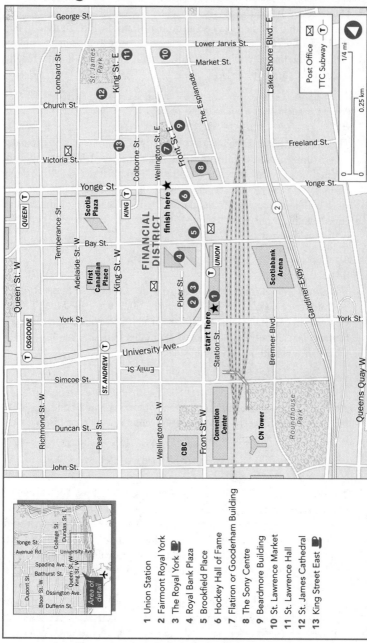

1 Union Station
2 Fairmont Royal York
3 The Royal York
4 Royal Bank Plaza
5 Brookfield Place
6 Hockey Hall of Fame
7 Flatiron or Gooderham Building
8 The Sony Centre
9 Beardmore Building
10 St. Lawrence Market
11 St. Lawrence Hall
12 St. James Cathedral
13 King Street East

On Front St., turn left and continue to the NW corner of Yonge and Front sts., stopping to notice the:

6 Hockey Hall of Fame

The ornate old building may be a surprise—built in 1885, it used to be a Bank of Montreal. Inside, the banking hall rises to a beamed coffered ceiling with domed skylights of stained glass. If you're a hockey fanatic, this is your shrine (p. 134).

From here, you can look ahead along Front St. and see the weird mural by Derek M. Besant that adorns the famous and highly photogenic:

7 Flatiron or Gooderham Building

This building was the headquarters of George Gooderham, who expanded his distilling business into railroads, insurance, and philanthropy; the original factories are now the Distillery District. At one time, his liquor business was the biggest in the British Empire. The very attractive five-story building occupies a triangular site, with the windows at the western edge beautifully curved and topped with a semicircular tower. The design is by David Roberts.

At the SW corner of Yonge and Front sts., you can stop in at:

8 The Sony Centre

The Sony Centre for the Performing Arts sits across Scott Street from the **St. Lawrence Centre.** In 1974, when the Sony was called the O'Keefe Centre, Mikhail Baryshnikov defected from the Soviet Union after performing here. The ballet has moved to another building, but this remains a busy theater with musicals and such.

Continue E along Front St. to the:

9 Beardmore Building

At 35–39 Front St. E., this and the many other cast-iron buildings lining the street were the heart of the late-19th-century warehouse district, close to the lakefront and railheads.

Continue E along Front St., crossing Church St. and then Market St., to the:

10 St. Lawrence Market

The old market building on the right holds this great market hall, which was constructed around the city's second city hall (1844–45). The pedimented facade that you see as you stand in the center of the hall was originally the center block of the city hall. Today, the market is packed with vendors selling fresh eggs, Mennonite sausage, seafood, meats, cheeses, and baked goods. Upstairs is a small gallery of city archival photographs.

11 St. Lawrence Hall

The focal point of the community in the mid–19th century, this hall, once the site of grand city occasions, political rallies, balls, and entertainment, was where Frederick Douglass delivered an antislavery lecture; Jenny Lind and Adelina Patti sang in 1851 and 1860, respectively; Gen. Tom Thumb appeared in 1862; and George Brown campaigned for Confederation.

William Thomas designed the elegant Palladian-style building, which boasts a domed cupola.

Cross King Street and enter the 19th-century garden. It has a cast-iron drinking fountain for people, horses, and dogs, and flowerbeds filled with seasonal blooms.

If you like, rest on a bench while you admire the handsome proportions of St. Lawrence Hall and listen to the chimes of:

12 St. James Cathedral

Adjacent to the garden on the north side of King Street, this is a beautiful Gothic church that is open to the public. The graceful building and its surrounding park make a serene setting to rest and gather one's thoughts, or to listen to one of the free summer concerts that take place here on warm evenings.

13 King Street East ☕

From St. James,' the venerable **Le Omni King Edward Hotel** (37 King St. E.; 📞 **416/863-9700**) is only a block away. You can stop for afternoon tea in the lobby lounge, or light fare or lunch at **Victoria** restaurant (📞 **416/863-4125**).

From St. James Cathedral, go S on Church St. for 1 block and turn right into Colborne St. From Colborne St., turn left down Leader Lane to Wellington St., where you can enjoy a fine view of the mural on the Flatiron Building and the rhythmic flow of mansard rooflines along the S side of Front St. Turn right and proceed to Yonge St.; then turn right and walk to King St. to catch the subway to your next destination.

WALKING TOUR 4: **CABBAGETOWN**

START:	**Allan Gardens.**
FINISH:	**Sumach and Gerrard streets (for streetcar to College Station).**
TIME:	**2 to 3 hours.**
BEST TIME:	**Tuesdays from May through October, when the Farmers' Market is open in Riverdale Park West.**
WORST TIME:	**There is no worst time; all of the other attractions on this tour can be seen on weekdays and weekends.**

Cabbagetown, one of the city's oldest neighborhoods, has gone from rags to riches more times than most can count. Built up in the 1840s by Irish immigrants fleeing the Great Famine, the district acquired its name from the cabbage plants they grew in their front yards. It has been both a wealthy enclave and a slum, but today, the residential streets have been gentrified, and the surrounding commercial streets are on an upswing.

1 Allan Gardens

This was Toronto's first civic park. For many years, it ran to the seedy side, but since the University of Toronto took over the care of the greenhouses in 2004, it has become a charming place to visit again. The

Children's Conservatory is well worth a look, but the crown jewel of the garden is the **Edwardian Palm House**.

At the corner of Carlton and Sherbourne sts., you'll see:

2 St. Luke's United Church

Known as Sherbourne Street Methodist when the first sermon was preached here in 1887, this is one of Toronto's most beautiful examples of religious architecture. From the outside, the imposing stonework and turrets make it look like a castle. Inside, the sanctuary has been completely refurbished in the past few years. The glorious stained-glass windows are the pièce de résistance (the church once had a wealthy congregation, and you'll see that the windows were all "dedicated" by businessmen trying to outdo one another).

On the N side of Carlton St. is:

3 St. Peter's Anglican Church

This parish was originally based in a cemetery chapel. In 1866, John Strachan, the Aberdeen-born Bishop of Toronto, opened this church. It's a pretty example of High Victorian Gothic, and later additions are in keeping with its original style.

Walk E along Carlton St. to:

4 Snack Attack ☕

Daniel et Daniel, a darling food shop at 248 Carlton St. (☎ **416/968-9275**), is a good place for simple but tasty fare, like meat pies and generous sandwiches. There are freshly baked pastries, pâtés, tarts, cakes, and other treats made in-house.

You're now at the intersection with:

5 Parliament Street

Parliament Street got its name because the first Upper Canada government buildings in "muddy little York" (as Toronto was then known) were built at its southern end in 1793. Today, it's the main commercial artery of Cabbagetown. This isn't exactly trendy, but you can make some great finds. **Green's Antiques,** at 529 Parliament St., is a true gem, with plenty of great chairs, ottomans, and sofas, many of which have been newly upholstered by the talented staff. **Tasso,** at 540 Parliament St., makes amazing croissants. They're so good that Tasso had to put a limit on the number of pastries per customer (it's eight). Tasso is only open Friday through Sunday, from 9am until it sells out, which is usually before noon. It's a crazy business model, but it seems to be working.

6 Kanpai or Jet Fuel ☕

One reliable place to grab a bite is **Kanpai** **6A** (252 Carlton St.; ☎ **416/968-6888**), which serves Taiwanese street-food-inspired small plates. Another great spot is **Jet Fuel** **6B** (519 Parliament St.; ☎ **416/968-9982**), a coffee shop that has become a local landmark (bike couriers love this place). Everything here is made with espresso, so be prepared for a good jolt.

Walking Tour: Cabbagetown

Legend:

1. Allan Gardens
2. St. Luke's United Church
3. St. Peter's Anglican Church
4. Daniel et Daniel
5. Parliament Street
6a. Kanpai
6b. Jet Fuel
7. 94 Winchester Street
8. Sackville Street
9. Riverdale Park West
10. Necropolis
11. Necropolis Chapel
12. Park Snacks
13. Riverdale Farm
14. The Don Valley

0.25 km
1/4 mi

start here — Granby St. / Carlton St. / Jarvis St.

finish here — Riverdale Park West

Turn onto Winchester St. and follow E to:

7 94 Winchester St.

This was once the home of magician Doug Henning. You can't go inside (it's someone else's home now), but a plaque at the front commemorates his life (1947–2000) and immortalizes him as "magician, teacher, politician." The first two are easy to get, but the last requires some explanation. In 1994, Henning stood for election to Parliament as a member of the Natural Law Party, an organization memorable mainly for its belief in levitation.

Continue walking E on Winchester St. and turn S onto:

8 Sackville Street

This quiet street had some of the loveliest homes in Cabbagetown. While the architecture is an eclectic mix, you'll mostly see variations on Victorian and Queen Anne styles. Walk down to Sackville Place (the street will be only on your left side). Across from it is Pine Terrace, a series of Victorian redbrick town houses built in 1886.

Walk N back to Winchester Ave. and follow it E to Sumach St., where you'll find:

9 Riverdale Park West

This is a lovely park that's a favorite with neighboring families. While you stop to enjoy the scenery, you can learn more about Cabbagetown's history. Look for the large maps and plaques in the park's northwestern corner, and you can read all about many of the fascinating people who once called the neighborhood theirs. (**Hint:** Doug Henning fit in very well.) Depending on when you visit, you may find a farmer's market operating in the park, too.

Across from the park, on the N side of Winchester Ave., is the:

10 Necropolis

Walk under the Gothic-inspired porte-cochère to enter Toronto's city of the dead. This is the prettiest cemetery you could hope to find, and if you stop at the office (on the right side as you step under the archway), you can pick up a free map that will guide you to the final resting places of some of Toronto's famous inhabitants. Check out the imposing stone Celtic cross that marks the grave of William Lyon Mackenzie, the leader of the Upper Canada rebellion who later became the mayor of Toronto.

When you finish here, exit through the porte-cochére; on your right is the:

11 Necropolis Chapel

This small chapel is a lovely example of High Victorian Gothic style. Architect Henry Langley built it in 1872 (he's the same person who designed the St. James Cathedral towers, p. 125). The chapel and the adjoining porte-cochère are widely considered to be two of the finest pieces of Gothic Revival architecture in Canada. (Langley is buried in the Necropolis, and his grave is on the map mentioned above at stop 10.)

12 Park Snacks or Riverdale Farm 🍴

You won't find many places to grab a snack within the residential heart of Cabbagetown. The exception is **Park Snacks** (161 Winchester St.; ✆ **647/668-6787**), a takeout-only spot. In summer, you can buy drinks, ice cream, or sandwiches here. Riverdale Park West provides many benches that are well shaded by trees. Year-round, you can buy snacks at **Riverdale Farm** (see stop 13, below).

On the eastern edge of the park, you'll see the entrance to:

13 Riverdale Farm

It's a rarity: a working farm in the heart of downtown. The grounds are clean and the animals very well cared for. It's a charming place to visit, particularly if you have children in tow, but even if you don't, you can appreciate the chicks, bunnies, cows, horses, rare-breed pigs, goats, and other animals. Watch out for baby animals, too.

When you leave the farm, turn to the left and follow its perimeter; this will give you a good view of:

14 The Don Valley

There's been a big movement to "Bring Back the Don" in Toronto, and the valley has been revitalized by it. The Don River is no longer a mighty force, but at least its valley is green. Across the valley, you can see the controversial renovation of the notorious Don Jail, which is becoming a health center. Also, consider leaving the area and winding your way north up the Bayview Extension to the revitalized **Evergreen Brick Works** (about a 15-minute hike), a unique heritage site that was once the city's brick factories. Today, it's an environmental project that offers a view into the past alongside beautiful parklands, a cafe, and on Saturday mornings, a bustling farmer's market.

Walk S along Spruce St. to Gerrard St.; from here, you can catch any westbound streetcar, which will take you to College Station.

DAY TRIPS FROM TORONTO

Toronto has plenty to offer visitors, but if you can take the time to add a side trip, some pleasant excursions are definitely worth considering. Within just a 2-hour drive beyond the sprawling suburbs, you'll find pretty scenery, quaint towns, superb theater, pastoral scenes, provincial parks, epic Bavarian festivals, and tempting culinary destinations. Here is a sampling of our favorite day trips from Toronto.

STRATFORD

145km (90 miles) SW of Toronto

For those who care: This is the hometown of Justin Bieber. But its real claim to fame is the great **Stratford Festival,** which has grown to become one of the most famous theater festivals in North America. Stratford's four theaters have put this scenic town on the cultural map. The festival has also triggered the development of fine restaurants, good hotels, and tours for everyone from theater-loving cyclists to history buffs. Additionally, Stratford itself is a charming and pretty place to amble before and after taking in a show.

Essentials

VISITOR INFORMATION   For first-rate visitor information, go to the **Stratford Tourism Alliance Visitors Centre** (47 Downie St.; www.visitstratford.ca; © **800/567-7926** or 519/271-5140), across from City Hall. There you can find maps, advice, as well as information for events. It's open April through December Monday to Saturday 10am to 6pm and Sunday 11am to 3pm; January to April Monday to Saturday 9am to 5pm and Sunday 11am to 3pm.

GETTING THERE   Driving from Toronto, take Hwy. 401 W to I-278 at Kitchener. Follow Hwy. 8 W onto Hwy. 7/8 to Stratford. (Hwy. 7/8 turns into Ontario St., Stratford's main drag, once you enter city limits.)

For me, nothing beats the train, and Stratford is a small and very walkable town and easily done without a car. So unless you're planning to tour the surrounding area, book a ticket with **VIA Rail** (www.viarail.ca; © **800/VIA-RAIL** [800/842-7245] or 416/366-8411). Canada's national rail company operates two trains to Stratford daily. You can book your rail travel in advance by phone,

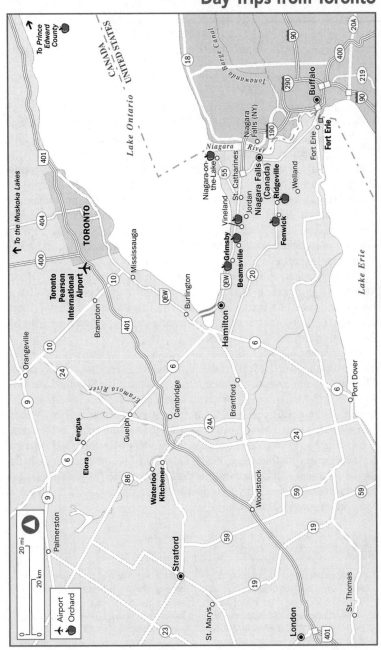

although it's easiest to book using the website. The train ride takes about 2 hours each way.

The festival also runs a direct $29 Toronto-return (round-trip) bus to Stratford from the **InterContinental Toronto Centre** (225 Front St. W.). The bus runs twice daily, at 10am and 3pm. Book through the Stratford Festival website at www.stratfordfestival.ca/whatson/busbooking.

Exploring Stratford

Stratford was settled in 1832, and much of its historic heart has been preserved. Wandering down its pristine residential street—lined with historic homes decorated with turrets, wraparound verandas, and stained-glass windows—is a little like stepping back in time.

Paddleboat, kayak, rowboat, and canoe rentals are available at **Avon Boat Rentals** (30 York St.; www.avonboatrentals.ca; ✆ **519/271-7739**). Despite the name, Avon does more than let boats, it also rent bicycles and runs a charming little restaurant called **Riverside Patio** that serves burgers, sandwiches, wraps, and fruit bowls. They also offer scenic half-hour tours on *Juliet III,* a pontoon boat ($8.50 adults; $7.50 seniors; $5.50 youth 13–18; and $3.50 children 12 and under).

The **Shakespearean Gardens**—a pretty, formal English garden at 5 Huron Street—is a great place to relax, contemplate the flowerbeds and tranquil river lagoon, and muse on a bust of Shakespeare by Toronto sculptor Cleeve Horne. It's open 24 hours daily. For a picnic-friendly patch of green, visit **Queen's Park,** a stone's throw from the Festival Theatre.

And speaking of picnics, Stratford is in the heart of an agricultural belt, and the abundant food options reflect the city's pride in its regional culinary riches. There are loads of restaurants and farm and dairy tours. The **Stratford Farmers Market,** 353 McCarthy Rd. (www.stratfordagriculturalsociety.com/farmers-market), is an indoor year-round market open every Saturday 7am to noon, selling baked goods, cheeses, meats, vegetables and fruit, crafts, and flowers.

Stratford also has a good art museum, the **Gallery Stratford** (54 Romeo St. S.; www.gallerystratford.on.ca; ✆ **519/271-5271**). Located in a historic building on the fringes of **Confederation Park,** the museum exhibits contemporary and historical works by Canadian artists. It's open daily from 10am to 5pm; admission is by donation.

Plein Air Art Gallery

Museums are grand, but who wants to spend a glorious summer day indoors? Thanks to Stratford's **Art in the Park** (www.artintheparkstratford.com), you can have both. On Wednesdays, Saturdays, and Sundays from late May to October, regional artists gather at Lakeside Drive and Front Street, and put on a show from 10am to 5pm, weather permitting. The artists and artisans work in various media, so you'll find paintings, sculptures, ceramics, jewelry, and glass, among other things. While many of the works are for sale, this isn't just a market: The artists are selected through a juried process.

The Stratford Festival

The Festival has humble roots. The idea of a theater was launched in 1953, when director Tyrone Guthrie lured the great Sir Alec Guinness to the stage. Whether Sir Alec knew the "stage" was set up in a makeshift tent is another question, but his acclaimed performance gave the festival the push—and press—it needed to become an annual tradition.

Stratford has four theaters. The **Festival Theatre** (55 Queen St.) has a dynamic thrust stage (a modern re-creation of an Elizabethan stage). The **Avon Theatre** (99 Downie St.) has a classic proscenium. The **Studio Theatre** (34 George St. E.) is a 278-seat space used for new and experimental works. In 2020, a new **Tom Patterson Theatre** will replace the old theater (a curling rink retrofit that was falling apart). The glorious new building takes its architectural inspiration from the meandering Avon River, undulating glass walls hung with bronze mullions in the spirit of a curving riverbank. When completed, the new space will seat 600 people.

World-famous for its Shakespearean productions, the festival also offers classic and modern theatrical masterpieces. Recent productions have included *The Music Man, The Rocky Horror Show,* and *To Kill a Mockingbird;* from the Bard, there's an encyclopedia of productions, including *Macbeth* and *A Midsummer Night's Dream.* The bill always presents an impressive lineup designed to suit a range of tastes from the contemporary to the historic, the comedic to the tragic.

The season usually begins in late April and continues through mid-November, with performances Tuesday through Sunday. Ticket prices range from $29 to $135, with special deals for students and seniors. For tickets, call Ⓒ **800/567-1600** or 519/273-1600, fax 519/273-3731, or visit www.stratford festival.ca.

A PEEK BEHIND THE FESTIVAL CURTAIN

The Stratford Festival offers several behind-the-scenes tours that are sure to thrill theater buffs. You can take a **backstage tour of the Festival Theatre,** which takes about an hour, or a **tour of the costume and props warehouse** at 350 Douro Street, which run roughly 45 minutes. Tours cost $8.85 adults ($7.08 seniors and students) and should be scheduled in advance by calling the box office at Ⓒ **800/567-1600** or 519/273-1600.

Some performances have **preshow lectures** or **post-performance discussions.** These are free of charge but need to be reserved in advance via the box office. There are also free "Meet the Festival" events with members of the acting company and a series of special lectures about the major plays of the season. For details, dates, and times, check out **www.stratfordfestival.ca.**

Where to Eat

EXPENSIVE

Bijou ★★★ FRENCH/TAPAS   Bijou is a true labor of love. Owners Aaron and Bronwyn Linley met while both studying at Stratford Chefs School back in the '90s. Before tying the knot, and returning to Stratford to start a family,

shopping IN STRATFORD

I know, we're all here for the theater scene, but you shouldn't miss out on Stratford's excellent shopping options. If you were expecting touristy, overpriced, and kitschy, you're in for a pleasant surprise. Many of the stores downtown sell clothing and housewares that rival what you'll see in the best boutiques in Toronto. Prices tend to be quite reasonable. Here are some of my favorite spots.

○ **Art: Gallery Indigena** (69 Ontario St.; www.galleryindigena.com; ✆ 519/271-7881) is filled with wonderful finds. It specializes in works by artists from Indigenous communities across Canada, including Inuit, Haudenosaunee, Plains Cree, Woodland Cree, and Northwest Coast communities. In business for more than 3 decades, the gallery hosts several "Meet the Artist" events throughout the summer, and ships artwork all over the world.

○ **Books:** If seeing the Bard on stage stirs in you the urge to pick up a printed play, pop into **Fanfare Books** (92 Ontario St.; www.fanfarebooks.ca; ✆ 519/273-1010). The well-curated selection also includes great kids' books, bestsellers, and new releases.

○ **Clothing:** The extensive collection at **Grace Boutique** (76 Ontario St.;

www.gracetheboutique.com; ✆ 519/273-0005) includes everything from fancy frocks and comfy jeans to the perfect undies to wear underneath that new outfit. For dapper men, head to **Gadsby** (56 Ontario St.; www.gadsbys.ca; ✆ 519/305-3555) for stylish menswear you'd expect to see for sale on West Queen West in Toronto, not in a town of 30,000 people.

○ **Gift Items:** You'll find both locally made cranberry glass and objects from Indonesia and Uzbekistan at **Watson's Chelsea Bazaar** (84 Ontario St.; www.watsonsofstratford.com; ✆ 519/273-1790). **Rheo Thompson Candies** (55 Albert St.; www.rheothompson.com; ✆ 519/271-6910) is a local institution that makes lovely chocolates, mints, jellies, and other candies.

○ **Housewares:** The venerable **Bradshaws** (129 Ontario St.; www.bradshawscanada.com; ✆ 519/271-6283) has been in business since 1895 selling fine crystal and china; cookware, bakeware, kitchen electronics, and gadgets; tableware, flatware, and barware; and gifts of all kinds.

the young cooking couple set off to work and travel throughout Europe, where both became enamored with France's neighborhood bistros. The kitchen at Bijou creates exquisite plates that change depending on what local farmers are pulling from their fields that week. The blackboard pre-theater dinner menu is a prix-fixe that runs until 7:30pm, after which the kitchen begins serving a menu of globally inspired tapas (grilled octopus with chorizo, foie gras parfait, mushroom risotto).

105 Erie St., Stratford. www.bijourestaurant.com. ✆ **519/273-5000.** Prix-fixe menus $55–$63; tapas $14–$18. Tues–Sat 4:45–10pm.

MODERATE

Keystone Alley Cafe ★ ASIAN/CONTINENTAL   The food here is better than at some pricier competitors. Lunch options may include a quiche

Lorraine, fried Lake Huron smelts, or steak frites. At dinner, entrées include mussel linguine with chorizo, fennel in a white-wine cream sauce, and Perth pork tenderloin served with cranberry-studded barley risotto. The short, international wine list is reasonably priced.

34 Brunswick St. www.keystonealley.com. © **519/271-5645.** Main courses $13–$29 lunch, $17–$31 dinner. Tues–Thurs 11:30am–2:30pm & 5–8pm; Fri–Sat 11:30am–2:30pm & 5–9pm; Sun 11:30am–2:30pm & 5–7:30pm.

Red Rabbit ★★★ CANADIAN   The hottest seats in town aren't front row at the steamy new *Tempest* production but at Red Rabbit, a farm-to-table joint serving elevated small plates. It's no surprise the kitchen's been winning fans by the dozen; chef Sean Collins, previously head instructor at the Stratford Chefs School, is running the show. He's divided the menu into two sections: carnivore and herbivore, and is sourcing from only the crème de la crème of Southern Ontario producers. Pork comes from Perth Farms, cheese from Mountainoak, and gorgeously marbled beef from Church Hill Farm. Desserts, like Cheddar ice cream served with caramel sauce and popcorn, are particularly creative. *Note:* From 5 to 7pm, Tuesday through Saturday, the restaurant observes a pre-theater dinner prix-fixe menu.

64 Wellington St. www.redrabbitresto.com. © **519/305-6464.** Main courses lunch $13–$20, dinner $13–$23. Sun–Mon 11:30am–2:30pm; Tues–Wed 11:30am–2:30pm & 5–7pm; Thurs–Sat 11:30am–2:30pm & 5–9pm.

INEXPENSIVE

York Street Kitchen SANDWICHES   This small restaurant is a fun, funky spot that serves reasonably priced, high-quality food. It's a favorite with locals, especially the arts and media set. Head here for great sandwiches (smoked meat, Reubens, turkey clubs) and tasty salads (cobb, Thai, Caesar).

51 York St. www.yorkstreetkitchen.com. © **519/273-7041.** Reservations not accepted. Main courses $9–$13. Sun–Thurs 11am–4pm; Fri–Sat 11am–7pm.

KITCHENER–WATERLOO

115km (71 miles) W of Toronto

The twin cities of **Kitchener** and **Waterloo** have established themselves as Canada's answer to Silicon Valley. Large-scale tech employers in the region include OpenText, Google, D2L, and the University of Waterloo, which promotes incubator hubs such as Communitech, where scrappy start-ups are encouraged to disrupt established industries through techno-innovation.

Although BlackBerry is no longer ubiquitous, the pioneering smartphone firm was born and based here, and was largely responsible for kick-starting Kitchener–Waterloo's techno-cultural revolution.

The twin cities, 3km (1 mile) apart, are a tale of contrasts. While AI breakthroughs are happening in ultra-modern coworking facilities, outside of the town you'll also see Old Order Mennonites—similar to the Amish in their beliefs and way of life—in their horse-drawn carriages clip-clopping down the roads.

Essentials

VISITOR INFORMATION For maps and advice, contact **Explore Waterloo Region** (151 Charles St. W. Kitchener; www.explorewaterlooregion.com; © **519/585-7517**).

In Kitchener, the **Kitchener Welcome Center** (www.kitchener.ca; © **519/741-2345**) is at 200 King St. West.

In Waterloo, the **City of Waterloo Visitor & Heritage Information Centre** (www.waterloo.ca; © **519/885-2297**) is located at 10 Father David Bauer Drive.

GETTING THERE It's best to visit with a car. The area is sprawling, and the local transit can be tricky to navigate for a short visit. Driving from Toronto, take Hwy. 401 W to ON-85 N. Take the Bridgeport Road W exit, which will bring you to downtown Kitchener.

VIA Rail (www.viarail.ca; © **800/VIA-RAIL** [800/842-7245] or 416/366-8411) is a luxurious way to travel, and boasts frequent service to Kitchener.

Exploring Kitchener–Waterloo

Although cutting-edge companies are taking over once-abandoned factories and turning them into swanky open-concept loft offices, the twin cities still are far from beautiful. These are industrial towns that are undergoing a metamorphosis, which means cool cafes and restaurants are coming online. But I wouldn't recommend visiting Kitchener–Waterloo without an itinerary, be it antiquing, farmer's markets, or donning lederhosen for the annual Bavarian harvest festival. The main draws are **Oktoberfest** (the world's second-largest) and the **St. Jacobs Farmers Market** (Canada's largest); see below. If pretty rural Ontario is what you're after, see Elora below.

In St. Jacobs, the **Mennonite Story** (1406 King St. N.; © **519/664-3518**) runs a short multi-media film, *The Old Order,* about the Mennonite way of life (Apr–Dec Mon–Sat 11am–5pm, Sun 1:30–5pm; Jan–March Sat 11am–4:30pm, Sun 2–4:30pm; $5 per person suggested donation).

OKTOBERFEST If the names Kitchener and Waterloo don't sound particularly Bavarian, that's on purpose. Originally, Kitchener was called Berlin, but during WWI the town voted to change its name in an effort to ease tensions between the German and British people living in the area. Today, a large population of Kitchener locals can still trace their lineage back to German settlers. Outside of the city, you might hear people in bonnets and broad-brimmed hats speaking a language that sounds like German, but it's actually Plautdietsch, a low German dialect spoken by the Mennonites who live in the area.

Every year, Kitchener welcomes some 700,000 visitors to help celebrate its German heritage during **Oktoberfest** (www.oktoberfest.ca; © **888/294-HANS** [888/294-4267] or 519/570-HANS [519/570-4267]). The 9-day Bavarian festival attracts lederhosen-sporting revelers who come mostly for the beer-based portion of the celebrations. But the festivities also include beauty pageants, live concerts, a parade, beer tastings, a golf experience, barrel and leg races, and more.

ST. JACOBS FARMERS MARKET Eight kilometers (5 miles) north of Kitchener is the town of **St. Jacobs.** The year-round Farmers Market, at 878 Weber St., is a whopper, Canada's biggest farm market, with some 300 vendors. Three indoor buildings serve the market in the colder months, and in seasonal weather, the market overflows outside. The Waterloo Region is home to the largest population of Old Order Mennonites in Canada, and many of the vendors at the farmers market are Mennonites. Make sure to try some of their homemade regional specialties like shoofly pie, apple butter, birch beer, and summer sausage. The St. Jacobs Farmers Market is open Thursdays and Saturdays from 7am to 3:30pm year-round (and Tues during summer months) (http://stjacobsmarket.com; ✆ **510/747-1830**).

Where to Eat

EXPENSIVE

Langdon Hall CANADIAN On the way home, it's worth the short diversion to Langdon Hall, the Relais & Châteaux property that was Ontario's first restaurant to earn the much-vaunted Relais Gourmands status (a title held by the French Laundry and Fat Duck, among others). The inn is spectacular, but if the weather's agreeable, work up an appetite by exploring its expansive grounds: a pleasing mix of manicured lawns, English gardens, and rustic woodlands. Even those not staying overnight can enjoy the inn's glamorous public rooms, with wood-burning fires in winter and lush garden views in summer. While the scenery is unparalleled, the kitchen aims to match, and it succeeds. Seasonal

shopping KITCHENER–WATERLOO

- **Antiques:** This region has some of the best antiquing in Southern Ontario. If you only have time for one stop, head to the **St. Jacobs Antiques Market** (805 King St. N.; www.stjacobs.com; ✆ **519/880-1944**), where 110 different vendors share a roof. Each booth has its own specialty, from offbeat LPs to rare coins, furniture, jewelry, and more.

- **Books:** Stuffed to the gills with great books, **Old Goat Books** (99 King St. N., Waterloo; www.oldgoatbooks.com; ✆ **519/880-9595**) sets itself apart from other used bookstores by keeping an impressive, easily accessible online catalog. Through their website, you can reserve your desired book in advance of your visit.

- **Clothing:** Deal hunters should check out the sales at the **St. Jacobs Outlet Mall** (25 Benjamin Rd. E., Waterloo; www.stjacobs outlets.com; ✆ **519/888-0138**); its offerings include Levi's, Lego, Paderno, and Royal Doulton.

- **Gift Items:** If actress Zooey Deschanel manifested into a store, she would be the cutesy knick-knack shop **Gifted** (181 Park St., Waterloo; www.giftedwaterloo.com; ✆ **519/208-4438**), where kawaii cat mugs, bibliophile-pandering tote bags printed with ISBN puns, whimsical cards, and adorable printed tea towels are just a few of the items on offer.

ingredients are turned into exquisite fare under the direction of chef Jonathan Gushue, and the wine list is extensive. Tea is served on the canopied veranda.

1 Langdon Dr., Cambridge. www.langdonhall.ca. ℂ **800/268-1898** or 519/740-2100. Breakfast $28 per person; main courses $26–$32 lunch, $40–$54 dinner. Free parking. From Kitchener–Waterloo, take ON-8 E to Shantz Hill Rd. in Cambridge, then take Fountain St. S and Blair Rd., follow signs to Langdon Hall.

MODERATE

Belmont Bistro CONTINENTAL The peripatetic menu travels the world, bouncing from traditional French (a slow-stewed beef bourguignon) to a South Asian–inspired plate of seared salmon in a red coconut curry sauce served with eggplant and bok choy. There are even German (chicken schnitzel) and Mexican (quesadillas) options. The uniting factor: Chef Brandon Gries' emphasis on making everything—including the sauces and herb blends—from scratch. Because the kitchen has full control over every element of a dish, this is a great choice for a group with allergies or vegan requirements.

703 Belmont Ave. W., Kitchener. www.facebook.com/belmontbistro. ℂ **519/576-5796.** Brunch $15–$18; main courses $23–$27. Wed–Fri 11:30am–2pm and 5–9pm; Sat 5–10pm.

Public Kitchen & Bar SPANISH The decor at this sliver of a tapas bar is wanting: white walls, a blackboard with the specials, and an L-shaped DIY pine bar that takes up half the width of the room. But people don't come here for the ambience. All focus is on the delights being sent out from the kitchen. The menu is in constant flux, save for one dish: potato rosti topped with cold smoked salmon. Locals would rebel if those two-bite morsels were ever nixed. The savory nosh is complemented by an excellent (and refreshing) drink list: new- and old-world wines, craft cocktails, and obscure Ontario craft beers, all at reasonable prices.

300 Victoria St. N., Kitchener. www.kwpublic.com. ℂ **519/954-8111.** Small plates $5–$19. Tues–Thurs 5–11pm; Fri–Sat 5pm–midnight.

INEXPENSIVE

Bread Heads ITALIAN This place is devoted to thin-crust wood-fired pies. The bubbly crust is perfectly floppy, in true Neapolitan style. The organic dough, San Marzano tomato sauce, and top-tier mozzarella get the Italian seal of approval, but this pie shop doesn't cater only to pizza purists (though their Margherita is on point). Some of the pies get pretty playful—one even comes topped with a sunny-side-up egg. Although the pizza is the star, the kitchen makes mighty tasty paninis, soups, and scones, too.

16 Duke St. E., Kitchener. www.breadheads.ca. No phone. Pizzas and sandwiches $8–$10. Mon–Fri 9am–3pm and 5–7pm.

ELORA & FERGUS

115km (71 miles) W of Toronto

Scotsman William Gilkinson put Elora on the map in 1832 when he purchased 5,591 hectares (13,816 acres) on both sides of the Grand River and built a mill and a general store. He named the community **Elora,** after his brother's ship, which was inspired by the Ellora Caves in India. Most of the houses that the settlers built in the 1850s stand today. You'll want to browse the stores along picturesque Mill Street.

Fergus was founded by Scottish immigrant Adam Ferguson and has a population of only 7,500 people. The towns of Elora and Fergus are 6km (4 miles) apart, about an 8-minute drive.

Essentials

VISITOR INFORMATION   For real insight into the town's history, pick up a walking-tour brochure from the **Elora & Fergus Tourism Information Centre**, located at 10 E. Mill St. (https://elorafergus.ca; © **877/242-6353** or 519/846-9691 ext. 382). It's open daily 10am to 5pm.

GETTING THERE   If you're driving from Toronto, take Hwy. 401 W to Hwy. 6, drive north to Hwy. 7 E, then get back on Hwy. 6 N and take it into Fergus. From Fergus, take Hwy. 18 W to Elora. **Greyhound** (© **877/463-6446.** www.greyhound.ca) buses do run to Elora, though infrequently, and the trip is not direct (often there is a multi-hour stop in Guelph). It's best to rent a car.

Exploring Elora & Fergus

The Elora Gorge is a 140-hectare (346-acre) park on both sides of the 20m (66-ft.) limestone gorge. Nature trails wind through it. Overhanging rock ledges, small caves, a waterfall, and the evergreen forest on its rim are some of the gorge's scenic delights. The park (© **519/846-9742**) has camping and swimming facilities, plus picnic areas and playing fields. It's a favorite with rock climbers. Located just west of Elora at the junction of the Grand and Irvine rivers, it is open from May 1 to October 15 from dawn to dusk. For information, contact the **Grand River Conservation Authority** (www.grandriver.ca; © **866/900-4722** or 519/621-2761).

Fergus may be small, but it has more than 250 well-preserved 1850s buildings to see—examples of Scottish limestone architecture—including the foundry, which now houses the Fergus market.

The most noteworthy Fergus event is the **Fergus Scottish Festival,** which includes Highland Games, featuring pipe band competitions, caber tossing, tug-of-war contests, Highland dancing, and the North American Scottish Heavy Events. The festival is held usually on the second weekend in August. For more information on the games, contact the Fergus Scottish Festival and Highland Games (www.fergusscottishfestival.com; © **866/871-9442** or 519/787-0099).

Where to Eat
EXPENSIVE
Elora Mill Inn ★★ CANADIAN   This inn is located in a former gristmill that was built in 1870 and operated until 1974. This explains both its rustic charm and its idyllic view of the Grand River and the Elora Gorge itself. The

SHOPPING ELORA AND FERGUS

The shopping around here is far from fabulous, but if you're hankering for a wee browse, there are a handful of shops worth popping into.

○ **Antiques:** For nostalgia, vinyl, and collectibles, **Iron Bucket Antiques** (380 St. Andrew St. W., Fergus; www.ironbucketantiques.com; ℂ 519/787-8287) is the best one-stop shop in this neck of the woods. Don't be intimidated by knowledgeable collector Ron Dodge's dry wit; he's game for a good back-and-forth banter 'n' barter.

○ **Books:** Cozy used bookshop **Twice Loved Books** (62 Metcalfe St., Elora; www.twicelovedbooks.ca; ℂ 226/369-0189) is jam-packed with more than 20,000 titles. To help browsers cull their choices, notes are scattered about the shelves effusing praise for particularly great novels, picture books, and poetry collections.

○ **Gourmet:** Run by the Bzikot family, the **Best Baa Dairy** (820 Gartshore St., Fergus; www.bestbaa.com; ℂ 519/787-0707) is a small operation that sources sheep's milk from 10 Amish farms that raise happy sheep, free to roam the countryside and graze where they please. Their product line includes cheeses, yogurts, and milk. Everything on offer is delectably creamy.

○ **Unique Gifts:** Sarah Barber has coined the term "chateau chic" to describe the wares she sells at **Honeychurch Lane** (65 Metcalfe St., Elora; www.honeychurchlane.com; ℂ 226/384-4058). Pinterest-inspired decorators come here for velvet upholstery and crystal-decked chandeliers, but between the larger items, there's also Dash & Albert rugs, vintage glass and silverware, as well as sparking jewelry to be found.

○ **Home Decor:** You've heard about statement jewelry, maybe a statement watch, but how about a statement clock to add zip (and punctuality) to a wall? **Chanticleer** (In the Elora Mews, 45 Mill St. W., Elora; www.chanticleershop.ca; ℂ 519/846-8796) is a whimsical shop that carries quirky art, attention-grabbing clocks, as well as tchotchkes—the collection of decorative roosters is particularly impressive.

dining room is a treat: While the seasonally driven menu is relatively short, it features tasty entrées like wild mushroom cavatelli and venison pot pie.

77 Mill St. W., Elora. www.eloramill.com. ℂ **866/713-5672** or 519/846-9118. Breakfast $12–$23; main courses $17–$28 lunch, $21–$47 dinner. Daily 8–10:30am, 11:30am–3pm, and 5:30–9:30pm.

MODERATE

Fergusson Room PUB FARE   Located in the heart of Fergus, the inn's main house is an excellent example of 1860s architecture. The stone imported from Scotland is complemented by intricate ironwork, walnut banisters, and newel posts. It was built by the Honorable Admiral Ferguson as a residence, but also served as a nursing home and rooming house before it was converted into a charming country hotel, which houses two restaurants; the better of the two is the Fergusson Room, which serves fancy comfort food like bocconcini-stuffed garlic bread and deep-fried cauliflower, alongside traditional Scottish pub grub (cottage pie, bangers and mash, and fish 'n' chips). The steaks, which come from Wellington County Black Angus, are particularly good value.

487 St. Andrew St. W. Fergus. www.fergussonroompub1.mylocalapp.ca. © **519/843-4770.** Main courses $15–$40. Sun–Tues 11:30am–11pm; Wed–Thurs 11:30am–midnight; Fri–Sat 11:30am–1am.

INEXPENSIVE

Lost and Found Café ★ CAFÉ/CANADIAN   This cozy, two-story cafe can be a challenge to squeeze into during a summer weekend, when the half-dozen tables are perennially bogarted, mostly by locals, who love to settle in for the long haul with a book and a chai latte. There's a reason snagging a seat here can be a bear: The service is infectiously cheerful, and the food is fresh, filling, and great value. Paninis are the main draw. The aged Cheddar with caramelized onions and aioli is a vegetarian sandwich so good, even the most die-hard meat eater will be sated. (Although the steak panini is good, too.)

45 W Mill St., Elora. www.thelostandfoundcafe.com. © **226/384-5400.** Sandwiches $9–$10. Daily 8am–6pm.

Somethin' Fishee ★ FISH & CHIPS   It's a pocket-sized grab-and-go joint that does one thing, and one thing only, but they do it so well that people have been known to expend a quarter tank of gas just to pop by and grab a few orders of the amazing fish and chips. The skin-on fries are fresh-cut, never frozen, and are crispy, soft-centered delights. The fish, too, holds up to scrutiny. Wild-caught cod comes in from Newfoundland, while the halibut is flown in from the Arctic. The batter is light with an excellent crunch, sating your deep-fried desires without masking the flakey fish underneath. There's no seating, but Bissell Park is a short stroll away and has picnic tables.

16 E Mill St., Elora. © **519/846-1088.** Combos $12–$15. Mon–Tues 4–7:30pm; Wed–Thurs 11:30am–7:30pm; Fri 11:30am–8pm; Sat–Sun 11:30am–7:30pm.

NIAGARA & THE WINE COUNTRY

Toronto is bookended by wine regions: Niagara to the southwest and Prince Edward County to the east. The former is closer (a 90-minute drive from Toronto), more established, and has the benefit of being a short drive from one of the seven natural wonders of the world, the famous falls. Prince Edward County, or the County as locals call it, is the new kid on the wine-swilling block. The drive is about an hour longer, but PEC packs quaint country charm—plus two provincial parks that offer great camping and beaches. If you're debating which wine region to commit to, I'd recommend Niagara for families, and PEC for outdoorsy epicureans.

NIAGARA

Outside of Canada, Niagara is best known for its eponymous waterfall; however, there's far more to this region than the Horseshoe Falls and the kitschy tourist traps that surround them. Since 1811, winemakers have been growing grapes along this fertile stretch, which benefits from mild winters (thanks to Lake Ontario's moderating effect) and the southern latitude. There are 99 wineries in the comparatively young wine region, the oldest of which were founded in the 1970s—for a swath of that century, prohibition stymied vinicultural development. Niagara isn't just about fast-moving water and award-winning wine, though. The historically important area was the site of numerous battles during the War of 1812. Two historical forts and the quaint Victorian village Niagara-on-the-Lake remind visitors that this wee berg was once a pivotally important place in Canada's history.

Essentials

VISITOR INFORMATION   The **Niagara-on-the-Lake Chamber of Commerce** (26 Queen St., Niagara-on-the-Lake; www.niagaraonthelake.com; ✆ **905/468-1950**) provides information and can help you find accommodations. It's open May through October daily 10am to 6pm, and from 10am to 5pm the rest of the year.

For Niagara Falls travel information, contact **Niagara Falls Tourism** (6815 Stanley Ave., Niagara Falls; www.niagarafallstourism.com; ✆ **905/356-6061**) or the **Niagara Parks Commission** (www.niagaraparks.com; ✆ **877/642-7275**).

GETTING THERE   Niagara-on-the-Lake is best seen by car. From Toronto, take the Queen Elizabeth Way (signs read QEW) to Niagara via the cities of Hamilton and St. Catharines, and exit at Hwy. 55. The trip takes about 90 minutes, but can take over 2 hours if you're traveling at peak periods (if possible, try to avoid making the trek weekday mornings before 9am or weekday afternoons from 3 to 7:30pm).

VIA (www.viarail.ca; © from Canada **888/842-7245** or 514/871-6000) operates a daily train to Niagara Falls, but not to Niagara-on-the-Lake. The train ride is from 2 to 3 hours long (depending on the train and how many stops it makes), and fares start at around $48 round-trip. A cheaper option is to take the regional **GO Train** (www.gotransit.com; © **416-869-3200**) to Niagara Falls, which runs a WEGO bus service to Niagara-on-the-Lake. Alternatively, take the GO Train to St. Catharines and rent a car there. Car-rental outlets in St. Catharines include **Hertz** (414 Ontario St.; © **905/934-0163**) and **Enterprise Rent-A-Car** (404 Ontario St.; © **905/685-1500**). In Niagara Falls, **Avis** is at 5127 Victoria Ave. (© **905/357-2847**).

Niagara-on-the-Lake

Never mind that Oscar Wilde called it "a bride's second great disappointment," the honeymoon capital of Niagara Falls is worth the 2-hour drive from Toronto just to witness the majesty of the falls themselves. The tacky shops, motels, attractions—it's an unabashed tourist trap—can either be ignored or enjoyed, depending on your sensibility. Then take a scenic drive about a half-hour back toward Toronto, along the **Niagara Parkway** (p. 226), to Niagara-on-the-Lake, a quiet and pretty 19th-century village that offers a welcome retreat after the carnival atmosphere of Niagara Falls. Many travelers prefer to stay at NOTL, where the food and wine offerings go well beyond the fast-food chains of the Falls and can be quite sophisticated for a tourist region. (You're now in the heart of Niagara wine country.) This is also home to the **Shaw Festival,** a theater event on par with Stratford's festival (p. 203).

THE SHAW FESTIVAL   Founded in 1962, the Shaw was known for many years for presenting the dramatic and comedic works of George Bernard Shaw and his contemporaries. In 2002, Jackie Maxwell became artistic director, and changed the mandate to feature forgotten plays from Shaw's era, as well as classics and new works by Canadian playwrights. In 2017, Tim Carroll took the reins, and expanded the mandate further. Now, the Shaw is putting on plays "inspired by the spirit of George Bernard Shaw" and creating "unforgettable theatrical encounters in any way we want." The lineup has become eclectic. One summer it included a solo show written and performed by Stephen Fry; a family-oriented adaptation of C.S. Lewis's *The Magician's Nephew*; and the romantic comedy *Stage Kiss,* a 2-hour romp about two bitter exes forced to play lovers on stage. Of course, the lineup included two Shaw plays, too, but they're no longer the big draws. The 2019 festival is a smorgasbord of the familiar and the new—and mash-ups of both. The docket includes *The Glass Menagerie, Brigadoon,* Shaw's *Man and Superman,* and the world premiere of C.S. Lewis's *The Horse and His Boy,* further adventures in the land of Narnia.

ATTRACTIONS & SHOPPING ●
Court House Theatre **12**
Fort George National
   Historic Site **23**
Greaves Jam **9**
Hatley Boutique **13**
Irish Design **7**
Maple Leaf Fudge **17**
Niagara Apothecary **18**
Niagara Historical
   Society Museum **16**
Royal George Theatre **4**
Scottish Loft **14**
Shaw Festival Theatre **22**
The Shawp **6**
Studio Theatre **22**

RESTAURANTS ◆
Epicurean **5**
Masaki Sushi **21**
Niagara Home Bakery **8**
Olde Angel Inn **11**
Shaw Café and Wine Bar **3**
Stagecoach Family Restaurant **10**

HOTELS ■
Harbour House **15**
Moffat Inn **20**
Oban Inn **1**
The Old Bank House **2**
Prince of Wales **19**
Staybridge Suites **24**
Woodbourne Inn **25**

As impressive a destination for theater-goers as Stratford, the Shaw runs from April until the third weekend of December and plays in the exquisite **Shaw Festival Theatre,** the **Royal George Theatre,** and the intimate **Jackie Maxwell Studio Theatre.**

Daily Toronto-Niagara **Shaw Express buses** run between downtown Toronto and Niagara-on-the-Lake from April to October. The luxury buses run from Wednesday to Sunday, departing at 10am from the Royal York Hotel at 100 Front Street and returning at 5pm. cost. Book online at www.shawfest.com or all the box office at ℂ **800/511-7429.** *Note:* If you book before January 31, you can snag tickets for $10 round-trip.

Festival prices range from $35 to $132; some "special matinees" offer tickets for $48 seniors and $25 students. For more information, contact the Shaw Festival (www.shawfest.com; ℂ **800/511-7429** or 905/468-2172).

EXPLORING NIAGARA-ON-THE-LAKE

Niagara-on-the Lake is small, and most of its attractions are along one main street, making it easy to explore on foot. In 1792, it briefly served as the capital of Upper Canada (though the town was then called Newark). The town was burned down during the War of 1812 but quickly rebuilt afterwards.

Fort George National Historic Site ★ FORT   The fort played a central role in the War of 1812: It was headquarters for the British Army's Centre Division. The division comprised British regulars, local militia, Runchey's corps of former slaves, and Indigenous forces. The fort was destroyed by American artillery fire in May 1813. After the war, it was partially rebuilt, but it was eventually abandoned in the 1820s, and not reconstructed until the 1930s. You can view the guardroom (with its hard plank beds), the officers' quarters, the enlisted men's quarters, and the sentry posts. Programming shifts depending on the time of year, from May through Labor Day, self-guided tours are animated by costumed interpreters. During the low season, Fort George runs hourly guided tours that end with a bang in the form of a musket demonstration.

51 Queen St., Niagara Pkwy. www.parkscanada.ca or www.friendsoffortgeorge.ca. ℂ **905/468-6614.** $11.70 adults; $10.05 seniors; free for youth 17 & under. May–Oct daily 10am–5pm; Apr & Nov weekends 10am–5pm; Dec–Mar 10am–4pm.

Niagara Apothecary ★ MUSEUM/HISTORIC SITE   This Victorian pharmacy has been dolling out cures since 1866. The gold-leaf and black-walnut counters are original, as are the glass and ceramic apothecary ware. Those hankering for a bloodletting can no longer buy leeches here; it's been turned into a museum dedicated to the somewhat terrifying medical practices of yesteryear.

5 Queen St., Niagara-on-the-Lake. www.niagaraapothecary.ca. ℂ **905/468-3845.** Free admission. May–Sept daily noon–6pm.; Sept 4–Oct 28 Sat–Sun noon–6pm. Closed for the winter season.

Niagara Historical Society Museum ★ MUSEUM   For history buffs, this museum has more than 8,000 artifacts pertaining to local history. The collection includes possessions of United Empire Loyalists who first settled the

For those who believe in ghosts, Fort George is one of Ontario's favorite haunted sites. Reported sightings include a soldier patrolling its perimeter and a young damsel who appears in an 18th-century mirror. Whether you're a believer or a skeptic, the **Ghost Tours** are fun for the whole family. They run Sunday evenings from May through June; during July and August, tours take place on Sundays, Tuesdays, and Thursdays, with bonus dates around Halloween. The cost is $20 adults and children 12 and up, and $10 children 11 and under; October tours cost $25 per person. Contact the **Friends of Fort George** at ✆ **905/468-6621,** or visit www.friendsoffortgeorge.ca for a schedule and for more details.

area at the end of the American Revolution. So, if branding-irons, portraits, maps, and early Canadian artifacts are your thing, take some time to peruse the museum. Two of the Society's three buildings are historical relics themselves: The High School building is from 1875, and the Memorial Hall building is circa-1906.

43 Castlereagh St., Niagara-on-the-Lake. www.niagarahistorical.museum. ✆ **905/468-3912.** Admission $5 adults; $3 seniors; $2 students (w/ID); $1 children 12 & under. May–Oct daily 10am–5pm; Nov–Apr daily 1–5pm.

Niagara's Wine Country

Visiting a local winery is a must while in Niagara. Even if you're not into vino, the wineries are a delight to stroll around. Many have excellent on-site restaurants and fun summer programming (movies in the vineyard, pig roasts, and dance-into-the-night concerts are but a few warm-weather offerings). In Niagara, you'll see some of the best in new and innovative wine design, architecture, and viticulture.

As with any major wine region, there are the big, commercial enterprises and small, artisan ones. Lately, celebrities have joined the club (here, as elsewhere), so you can try wines with names such as Wayne Gretzky and Dan Aykroyd; mostly for the novelty, not the nose.

For maps of the area and information about vintners, **Wine Country of Ontario** promotes wines with the **VQA (Vintners Quality Alliance)** label—wines made from 100% Ontario-grown grapes. It's an excellent resource (www.winecountryontario.ca; ✆ **905/562-8070,** ext. 221). Here are our recommended wineries.

13th Street Winery ★★ For the past 2 decades, Toronto restaurants that know good local wine have been pouring 13th Street. The boutique winery produces excellent delicate reds (Pinot and Gamay noirs), as well as top bubbly, and commendable Chardonnays. No visit is complete without a meander through the sculpture garden followed by a pit stop at the farmhouse, which houses a petite **bakery;** in July the cherry tarts—made with fresh, local fruit—are simply divine. For a truly Canadian snack, try the butter tarts: pure perfection.

It's a pleasant pastime to stroll along the Niagara-on-the-Lake's main artery, **Queen Street,** and check out some entertaining, albeit touristy, shops. The following are the best of the bunch. Serious shoppers also make a pit stop at the **Outlet Collection at Niagara** (see below) en route back to Toronto.

o **Greaves Jam ★★** Skip the labor of heading to the orchard to pick fruit, and grab some already preserved local goodness at Greaves Jam. This preserves emporium is run by fourth-generation jam makers. The jellies, jams, chutneys, and marmalades are truly good stuff. Specialty flavors include gooseberry, boysenberry, and rhubarb ginger (55 Queen St., Niagara-on-the-Lake; www.greavesjams.com; ℰ **905/468-7331;** Mon–Wed 9:30am–6pm, Thurs–Fri 9:30am–6:30pm, Sat–Sun 9:30am–7pm).

o **Hatley Boutique ★★** Painter Alice Oldland ran a quaint gift shop in North Hatley, Quebec, and painted for pleasure more than profit. When a series of pastoral landscapes she did started flying off the shelves of the gallery she opened above the gift shop, her husband thought it would be a great idea to create a line of aprons based on Alice's art. Cow and pig aprons soon gave way to moose and bear motifs, which are now printed on everything from pajamas and onesies to fetching raincoats (8 Queen St., Niagara-on-the-Lake; www.hatley.com; ℰ **905/468-2349;** daily 10am–6pm).

o **Irish Design ★** Irish expats Paul and Maureen Dickson head back to Emerald Isle every year seeking out only the best hand-knit sweaters, and traditional gold and silver jewelry. The quaint store also carries teas, Guinness memorabilia, and leather goods (75 Queen St., Niagara-on-the-Lake; www.irishdesign.com; ℰ **905/468-7233;** Sun–Fri 9:30am–6pm, Sat 9:30am–8pm).

o **Maple Leaf Fudge ★** Since 1967, this sweets stop has been fueling sugar crashes thanks to their small-batch fudge and nut brittles. Patrons watch as the aproned staff fashions fudge in 20-plus flavors, first cooked down in copper kettles, then shaped on marble slabs (114 Queen St., Niagara-on-the-Lake; www.mapleleaffudge.com; ℰ **905/468-2211;** Mon–Thurs 9:30am–6pm, Fri–Sat 9:30am–6:30pm, Sun 9:30am–7:30pm).

o **Outlet Collection at Niagara ★** This open-air shopping mall has more than 100 different stores to browse. Jocks flock to Bench, Adidas, and New Balance, while outdoorsmen prefer Columbia and the Bass Pro Shop. For deals, Marshall's, the Nike Factory Store, and the Banana Republic Factory Store are your best bets. High-end options include Brooks Brothers and Escada (300 Taylor Rd., Niagara-on-the-Lake; www.outletcollectionat niagara.com; ℰ **905/687-6777;** Mon–Sat 10am–9pm, Sun 10am–6pm).

o **Scottish Loft ★** Catering to William Wallace wannabes, this wee shop is filled with tartans, Celtic memorabilia, candy, books, and other assorted Scottish-themed notions (13 Queen St., Niagara-on-the-Lake; www.scottishloft.com; ℰ **905/468-0965;** daily 10am–5pm).

o **The Shawp ★** The Shaw Festival gift shop carries George Bernard Shaw memorabilia, books, and more (10 Queen's Parade, Niagara-on-the-Lake; www.shawfest.com; ℰ **905/468-2153 ext. 2276;** daily 9am–8pm).

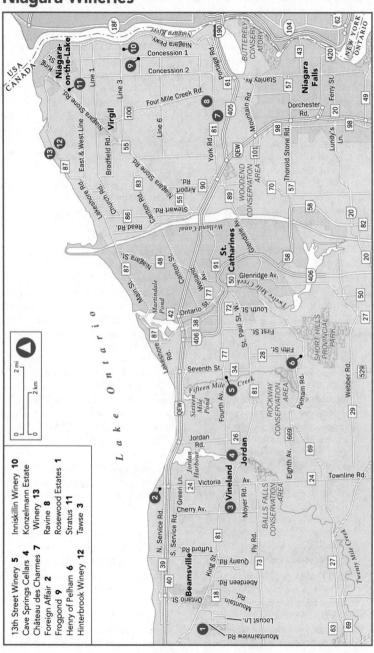

13th Street Winery **5**
Cave Springs Cellars **4**
Château des Charmes **7**
Foreign Affair **2**
Frogpond **9**
Henry of Pelham **6**
Hinterbrook Winery **12**

Inniskillin Winery **10**
Konzelmann Estate Winery **13**
Ravine **8**
Rosewood Estates **1**
Stratus **11**
Tawse **3**

yield award-winning wines. Fans of excellent Riesling, Chardonnay, Pinot Noir, and Cabernet Franc will not be disappointed.

3836 Main St., Jordan. www.cavespring.ca. ✆ **905/562-3581.** Wine tasting flights from $8. Tour plus four tasting samples paired with cheese $25. June–Sept Mon–Sun 10am–6pm; Oct–May Sun–Thurs 10am–5pm and Fri–Sat 10am–6pm.

Château des Charmes ★
The winery was built to resemble a French manor house, and its architecture is unique in the region. The winery was founded in 1978 by fifth-generation winemaker Paul Bosc, who had decided to relocate his then-young family to Niagara. He was the first in the region to plant European *vitis vinifera* (the vines that give us Pinot Noir and Cabernet Sauvignon). To this day, Bosc continues to only make wine from grapes he grows on the estate.

1025 York Rd., Niagara-on-the-Lake. www.fromtheboscfamily.com. ✆ **905/262-4219.** Tours from $15; tasting flights from $10. Daily 10am–6pm.

Foreign Affair ★★★
One of my favorite wineries in the region doesn't have a fancy kitchen, nor is it located in a faux château (it's in a retrofitted stone-fruit research facility tucked behind some Ministry of Agriculture greenhouses). The wine, however, has deep umami depth you'd expect in Tuscany, not Ontario. Foreign Affair's charismatic owners Len and Marisa Crispino—who fell in love with Amarones while working for the Canadian government in Italy—are brimming with unabashed enthusiasm, keen to teach visitors about the *appassimento* process that imbues their wine with its complexity. This was the first winery in Ontario to begin using *appassimento:* Grapes are left to dry on straw mats, until the fruit becomes concentrated, bursting with sugar and tannins. Stop by the tasting room, which has been decorated to look like a Florentine villa, and try some of my favorite reds being produced in Niagara.

4890 Victoria Ave. N. www.foreignaffairwinery.com. ✆ **905/562-9898.** Tasting flights from $5, fees waived with purchase. Daily 11am–5pm.

Frogpond ★
Best visited in summer, Frogpond was Ontario's first certified organic winery. True to its granola roots, the unfussy tasting room fits three comfortably. In summer, tastings are done behind the old farmhouse, while chickens cluck in the background and sheep graze in the fields. Walk the property to see the namesake pond, populated with leopard frogs.

1385 Larkin Rd., Niagara-on-the-Lake. www.frogpondfarm.ca. ✆ **905/468-1079.** Tastings $1–$3 per sample. May–Oct daily 11am–6pm; Nov–Apr daily 11am–5pm.

Henry of Pelham ★★★
Almost a century before Canadian confederation, Great-great-great-grandpa Nicholas Smith's military service was rewarded with the deed to the land that would one day become the Henry of Pelham winery. His son would later inherit the property and build an inn and a tavern called Henry of Pelham, but it wasn't until 1982, when Smith's descendants Paul and Bobby Speck planted Riesling and Chardonnay vines, that these acres would finally become a splendid winery. Winemaker

Lawrence Buhler's wine is excellent, but it's his rosé bubbly, the Cuvée Catharine (made from long-fermented, hand-picked grapes) that is some of the best sparkling made in Ontario. In summer, make sure to stop by the **Coach House Café** where chef Erik Peacock creates wine-friendly sharing plates made from locally sourced ingredients.

1469 Pelham Rd., R.R. #1, St. Catharines. https://henryofpelham.com. © **905/684-8423.** Tours from $10, includes four tastings. May–Oct daily 10am–6pm; the rest of the year daily 10am–5pm.

Hinterbrook Winery ★★   Drive down the winding gravel path, through the vineyards, and you'll spy the tasting room tucked behind a stately Victorian home. If you feel as if you've stepped into a sleek art gallery, you'd be spot-on. Proprietor George Lau is an artist (he sketched the fox and owl on the LCBO-sold bottles). Most of the Nomad wines feature blank white labels. The concept: Those drinking the wine should scrawl something artistic of their own on the bottles. If you're lucky, they may still have some Franc Blanc in stock—a white wine made from red Cabernet Franc grapes—in stock; it usually sells out within a few months of its release.

1181 Lakeshore Road, Niagara-on-the-Lake. www.hinterbrook.com. © **905/646-5133.** Tasting flights from $10, credited towards any purchases. May–Oct 10am–6pm; Nov–Apr 11am–5pm.

Inniskillin Winery ★   The pioneering winery behind Canada's famous **ice wine**—made from grapes frozen on the vine—Inniskillin was the first winery to resurrect Ontario's wine industry in the post-Prohibition era. Because Inniskillin is one of the most internationally recognizable Ontario wine brands, the place becomes a zoo during peak season (June–Aug). Make sure to call ahead to book a tour.

1499 Line #3, Niagara-on-the-Lake. www.inniskillin.com. © **905/468-2187** ext. 5400. Tours from $20; tastings $3–$5 per sample. May–Oct 10am–6pm; Nov–Apr 10am–5pm.

ice, ICE BABY

Bordeaux, Napa, Chianti, Rioja, Champagne, Sonoma: These names are synonymous with wine. Good wine. Niagara? Not so much. But that's changing. These days Niagara is growing excellent Pinot Noir, Chardonnay, Riesling, and Cabernet Franc, and vintners are experimenting with Gamay and Sauvignon Blanc with great results. Which means that the region is becoming known for more than just its celebrated ice wine. In the '80s Niagara ice wine became world-famous. Made from frozen-on-the-vine fruit, ice wine is thick and sweet, balanced with a zing of acidity. The dessert wine has become so popular in China that people have served jail sentences for smuggling the sweet nectar into the People's Republic. Personally, I find ice wine a bit too syrupy. I prefer to sip a dry sparkling wine from Henry of Pelham or 13th Street Winery. But the demand for ice wine remains strong. Be sure to try some while you're in Niagara, and make sure you do so at **Inniskillin,** which has been producing the stuff since 1977.

Konzelmann Estate Winery ★ When fourth-generation German wine-maker Herbert Konzelmann was looking to buy property in Niagara (his family has a well-established winery near the small German town of Uhlbach), he knew he wanted a waterfront winery. Lake Ontario creates a microclimate that extends the growing period well into autumn, allowing Konzelmann to grow a diverse selection of grapes (it has over 30 wines on offer at any one time, but the German-inspired bottles are the best). The wines produced at Niagara's only lakeshore winery have received dozens of international accolades. The winery's Vidal Icewine was the first Canadian wine to earn a prestigious spot on *Wine Spectator*'s Top 100 list. Don't try the peach wine, though; it tastes of gimmicks and penicillin.

1096 Lakeshore Rd., Niagara-on-the-Lake. www.konzelmann.ca. ✆ **905/935-2866.** Tours from $10; tasting flights from $5. May–Oct 10am–6pm; Nov–Apr 11am–5pm.

Ravine ★★★ The century-old farmhouse with its many brick fireplaces and creaky floors is a pleasant spot to sip acclaimed organic Chardonnays. It's a winning ambience, but just beyond the walls lie even more delights. Pop over to the winery's **bistro,** which backs onto 13.8 hectares (34 acres) of rolling vineyards, to take in the stunning vista. The food is truly excellent. In warmer months, enjoy a fresh pizza from the wood oven—best consumed on the patio.

1366 York Rd., St. Davids. www.ravinevineyard.com. ✆ **905/262-8463.** Tours from $15; tastings flights from $8. Sun–Thurs 11am–6pm; Fri–Sat 11am–8pm.

Rosewood Estates ★★ Another winery on my shortlist for best in Niagara is Rosewood, not only because its affordable rosé rivals the stuff coming out of Provence, but because of its dedication to low-intervention wine-making. Founded by a Ukrainian beekeeper, Rosewood has its own beehives, from which it produces delectable honey and very good mead. From May through October, Rosewood offers one of the most interesting tours in the region: Don a bee suit and get up close and personal with the bees.

4352 Mountainview Rd., Beamsville. www.rosewoodwine.com. ✆ **905/563-4383.** Tours from $20; tastings flights from $10. Nov–Apr Thurs–Mon 11am–5pm; May–Oct daily 11am–5pm.

Stratus ★★ This is one of the region's more cutting-edge wineries, with a focus on sustainable practices and eco-design. Take a look through the glass windows into the impressive French-oak-barrel aging room, which is kept at a cool 14 [°C] (57 [°F]) with geothermal heating. Status is famous for its award-winning blends (or "assemblages," as they call them). Guided tastings delve into the science of winemaking and look at how salt, sugar, acid, fat and protein affect the palate while sipping wine.

2059 Niagara Stone Rd. www.straTuswines.com. ✆ **905/468-1806.** Tours from $25; tasting flights from $10. Daily 11am–5pm.

Tawse ★★ Cutting corners is akin to blasphemy at Tawse. The grapes are harvested by hand from low-yield vines and hand-sorted before they're crushed and fermented. The stunning winery (it boasts some of the best landscaping in Niagara) implements gravity-flow design and geothermal systems to create its biodynamic wines. In the summer, the garden is a fabulous place to tuck into a charcuterie board while swilling Pinot Noir.

3955 Cherry Ave. www.tawsewinery.ca. ⓒ **905/562-9500.** Tours $15; flights from $8. Nov–Apr Mon–Fri 10am–5pm and Sat–Sun 10am–6pm; May–Oct daily 10am–6pm

Where to Stay

In summer, hotel space is in high demand. If you're having trouble nailing down a room, contact the **Niagara-on-the-Lake Chamber of Commerce** (www.niagaraonthelake.com; ⓒ **905/468-1950**), which provides information about accommodations, from luxurious hotels to charming bed-and-breakfasts. B&Bs can also be located and booked via **www.bbcanada.com**.

IN NIAGARA-ON-THE-LAKE

Harbour House ★★★   Tucked away on a quiet street that's close to the marina, this hotel offers serenity and tranquility from the moment you step through the front door. The focus is on comfort via understated luxury, from Frette robes to flickering fireplaces. The beds are particularly cozy, with king-sized mattresses topped by a layer of hypoallergenic duck feathers. (For those with allergies, alternative bedding is available.) Service is thoughtful and efficient, and guests are treated to lavish breakfasts and late afternoon wine-and-cheese receptions.

85 Melville St., Niagara-on-the-Lake. www.niagarasfinest.com ⓒ **866/277-6677** or 905/468-4683. 31 units. $195–$350 double. Rates include breakfast. Free parking. Pets permitted. **Amenities:** Concierge; limited room service; free Wi-Fi.

Moffat Inn ★   This is a fine budget-conscious choice in a convenient location. The inn bills itself as being "cottage chic," so imagine cozy rooms decorated by a grandma with a penchant for patterned accents. Some rooms have brass-framed beds, eight have fireplaces, and a few even have private terraces. If you have trouble climbing stairs, this hotel may not be a good choice—most of the guest rooms are on the second floor and there's no elevator and no porter to handle luggage.

60 Picton St., Niagara-on-the-Lake. www.moffatinn.com. ⓒ **905/468-4116.** 24 units. $150–$240 double. Free parking. **Amenities:** Restaurant; free Wi-Fi.

Oban Inn ★★   In a prime location overlooking the lake, the Oban Inn is a lovely place to stay. The town's first real country inn, it's in a charming, sizeable white Victorian house with a large veranda. The gorgeous gardens provide the fragrant bouquets throughout the house. A complete renovation updated the pretty rooms with modern amenities, including plasma televisions, Bose sound systems, and individual temperature controls in all rooms. The **spa** is also a popular attraction.

160 Front St., Niagara-on-the-Lake. www.obaninn.ca. ⓒ **866/359-6226** or 905/468-2165. 26 units. $165–$264 double. Rates include breakfast. Free parking. Some pet-friendly rooms available. **Amenities:** Restaurant; lounge; bike rental; concierge; outdoor pool and hot tub (open June–Sept); room service; spa; steam room, free Wi-Fi.

The Old Bank House ★   Beautifully situated down by the river, this two-story Georgian was built in 1817 as the first branch of the Bank of Canada. In 1902, it hosted the Prince and Princess of Wales, and today, it's a charming bed-and-breakfast inn. Suites are tastefully done, each with its own en suite, and some have access to decks overlooking the water below. If you're planning a romantic weekend away, you'll love the Gallery Suite, with its cathedral ceiling, or the Pine Suite with its Jacuzzi tub. Breakfast is truly excellent: a multi-course affair with homemade cinnamon granola, freshly baked muffins, quiches, poached eggs, and more.

10 Front St., Niagara-on-the-Lake. www.oldbankhouse.com. (⌀ **877/468-7136** or 905/468-7136. 9 units. $170–$260 suite. Rates include breakfast. Free parking. **Amenities:** Lounge; free Wi-Fi.

Prince of Wales ★★   This is one of Niagara-on-the-Lake's most luxurious hotels, and you could say it has it all: a central location across from the lovely gardens of Simcoe Park; recreational facilities, including an indoor pool; a full-service spa; lounges, bars, and restaurants; and conference facilities. If you're adverse to floral fabrics and overstuffed furniture, this is not the place for you. However, if you're looking to be seriously pampered in a faux-Victorian setting, it's a good bet. Also, it's one of the few hotels in town with a wheelchair-accessible room.

6 Picton St., Niagara-on-the-Lake. www.vintage-hotels.com/princeofwales. (⌀ **888/669-5566** or 905/468-3246. 110 units. $200–$380 double. Free parking. Pets permitted. **Amenities:** Dining room; lounge; bar; concierge; health club; hot tub; indoor pool; room service; spa; free Wi-Fi.

Staybridge Suites ★   This newly built, all-suites hotel is a perfect option for those who want to see the sights, buy some of the local produce, and cook a meal using Niagara's bounty. Suites come in a range of layouts, from studios to two-bedrooms, each with its own fully equipped kitchen outfitted with granite countertops, and everything you need to throw a dinner party, including the dining table. There's also a phenomenal outdoor entertaining area where guests can barbecue or relax by the bonfire. Family-friendly amenities include a putting green and a sun-drenched, heated indoor pool. Niagara can be pricey, so for those seeking a budget-friendly way to stay and tour the region, Staybridge is a great option.

524 York Rd., Niagara-On-The-Lake. www.ihg.com/staybridge. (⌀ **877/660-8550.** 70 units. $120–$160 suite. Rates include breakfast. Free parking. Pets permitted. **Amenities:** Concierge; laundry facilities; indoor pool; putting green; free Wi-Fi.

Woodbourne Inn ★★★   This stunning country inn was built in 1839, but a recent facelift has left Victorian details intact (Rumford fireplaces, restored heart-of-pine floors), while updating the rooms with Westin-Heavenly beds, deliciously deep soaker tubs, and rainfall showers. Despite the inn's vintage, there's nary a creak nor a floorboard squeak to be heard. Rooms and floors have been thoroughly soundproofed, so when you finish indulging in that bubble bath, and wrap yourself in the plush robe, it's almost too easy to doze off in the Egyptian cotton–swaddled bed. For breakfast, the hospitable inn staff delivers a tray to your room (at a preselected time), which comes with coffee, oatmeal, fruit muffins, and juice.

214 Four Mile Creek Rd, Niagara-on-the-Lake. ✆ **289/296-963.** www.woodbourneinn. com. 8 units. $150–$280 double. Rates include breakfast. Free parking. No pets allowed. **Amenities:** Library; free Wi-Fi.

IN WINE COUNTRY

Inn on the Twenty & the Vintage House ★★★   Cave Spring Cellars, one of Niagara's best-known wineries, offers modern, well-equipped, and generous suites. Each one has an elegantly furnished living room with a fireplace and a Jacuzzi tub in the bathroom. Five are loft suites with king beds on the second level. The inn's eatery, **Inn On the Twenty Restaurant,** across the street, is a great place to dine. The inn's spa offers a full range of services, and has special packages for couples. Next door is the Vintage House, an 1840 Georgian mansion with two suites, both with private entrances.

3845 Main St., Jordan. www.innonthetwenty.com. ✆ **800/701-8074** or 905/562-5336. 30 units. $190–$360 double. Free parking. Pets permitted. **Amenities:** Restaurant; concierge; spa; free Wi-Fi.

Where to Eat

IN NIAGARA-ON-THE LAKE

The stylish **Shaw Cafe and Wine Bar** (92 Queen St.; http://shawcafe.ca; ✆ 905/468-4772) serves lunch and light meals, and has a patio. The **Epicurean** (84 Queen St.; ✆ 905/468-3408) offers hearty soups, quiches, sandwiches, and other fine dishes in a sunny, Provence-inspired dining room. Service is cafeteria-style during the day; table service begins at 5pm. Half a block off Queen Street, the **Olde Angel Inn** (224 Regent St.; http://angel-inn. com/home.php; ✆ 905/468-3411) is a delightfully authentic English pub with the grub to match: bangers and mash, shepherd's pie, fish and chips.

For an inexpensive down-home breakfast, head to the **Stagecoach Family Restaurant** (45 Queen St.; www.stagecoachfamilyrestaurant.com; ✆ 905/468-3133). It also serves basic family fare, such as burgers, soups, and meatloaf. **Masaki Sushi** (60 Picton St.; https://masakisushi.ca; ✆ 905/468-1999) serves city-quality maki, aburi, and nigiri (although the omakase is overpriced for what it is); this place is best for a light lunch. In business for more than 75 years, **Niagara Home Bakery** (66 Queen St.; ✆ 905/468-3431) is the place to stop for sweet treats like chocolate-date squares and butter tarts, and savories such as individual quiches.

ALONG THE WINE ROAD
Expensive
Inn On The Twenty Restaurant ★ CANADIAN   This warm and friendly restaurant is a favorite among foodies for good service and a small but well-chosen selection of Ontario wines (with a few international additions)— but mostly for the cuisine. In addition to using ingredients from many local

producers, the kitchen creates food with wine pairings in mind; especially rich desserts are made to enjoy with ice wines and late-harvest wines.

3836 Main St., Jordan. www.innonthetwenty.com. © **905/562-7313.** Breakfast $8–$18; main courses $14–$28 lunch, $26–$44 dinner. Daily 8–10am, 11:30am–2:30pm and 5–10pm. Reservations recommended.

Pearl Morissette ★★★ CANADIAN   The region's most enigmatic and exciting winery is helmed by François Morissette, a man who doesn't like to be called a winemaker. No, he is a *vigneron,* a French term for someone who grows the grapes that will one day become wine; basically, he's a grape guru. The mandate is to only hand-pick fruit that is skin-ripe, which means each bottle, from one to the next, is different. At a place that puts so much emphasis on the right process behind the wine, it's no surprise that Pearl Morissette's recent foray into food-making has been equally well-received by epicureans. Much of the prix-fixe menu is grown or foraged from the surrounding land. There's a Noma-like quality to the food, which is why it topped *En Route* magazine's top-10 Best New Restaurants in Canada list.

3953 Jordan Rd. www.pearlmorissette.com. © **905/562-7709.** Five-course tasting menu $88. Thurs–Fri 6–9:30pm; Sat–Sun noon–1:30pm and 6–9:30pm. Reservations imperative.

The Restaurant at Vineland Estates ★★ CANADIAN   Situated in a renovated 1845 farmhouse with a sprawling patio that offers beautiful views, this restaurant serves some of the most innovative food along the wine trail. Start with a plate of mussels in a pickled–fennel Riesling broth. Follow with seared scallops and smoked sweetbreads served with Jerusalem artichoke and compressed apple; or an enticingly tender 16-hour braised short rib. For dessert, try the tasting plate of Canadian farm cheeses, including Abbey St. Benoit blue Ermite; those with sweet tooths can indulge in dark chocolate stout torte accompanied by a boule of sourdough gelato.

3620 Moyer Rd., Vineland. www.vineland.com. © **888/846-3526** or 905/562-7088. Prix-fixe lunch $40; dinner main courses $35–$40. Daily noon–3pm and 5–9pm. Reservations strongly recommended.

Trius Winery Restaurant ★ CANADIAN   The seasonal menus here feature such dishes as Lake Huron pickerel with bacon-studded lentils du Puy and crisp pork belly served with blood sausage croquettes and Parmesan gnocchi. The starters are equally luxurious. In case the food isn't enticing enough (and it should be), the winery also hosts special events throughout the year, including blues and rock concerts.

1249 Niagara Stone Rd. www.triuswines.com. © **905/468-7123.** Main courses $30–$34 lunch, $34–$60 dinner. Sun–Thurs 10am–7pm; Fri–Sat 10am–9pm.

Moderate

Caroline Cellars ★★ CANADIAN   The vino might be more Wednesday table wine than it is something to be coveted, but this attached-to-the-tasting-room restaurant serves up one of the best-value lunches in Niagara. Servings are generous: A filet of rainbow trout on top of a cranberry-quinoa salad for

BOUNTY OF THE orchard

Outside of Canada, Niagara is best known for its ice wine, and perhaps because of that, its grapes. But this fertile corner of Ontario also produces the province's **best fruit**. The season begins in June when strawberries ripen, followed by cherries, blackberries, and raspberries in July. Then come stone fruit and concord grapes, followed by pears and apples, which stay on the trees well into October. If you're keen to snack on the freshest of fruit, stop by one of Niagara's many **orchard stands** and **pick-your-own farms**. These stands and farms usually have an additional array of toothsome goodies, from fruit pies to preserves to ciders and more. In Niagara-on-the-Lake, you can celebrate summer's bounty at one of several fruit festivals: the **Strawberry Festival** (June); the **Cherry Festival** (early July); and the **Peach Festival** (Aug).

o **Bry-Anne Farms.** 471 Foss Rd., Fenwick; www.bry-annefarms.ca; *C* **905/892-8999**): Bry-Anne Farms' raspberries are absolutely amazing. A varietal called Nova, they're plump, juicy and big to boot. Throughout the summer, the farm also sells fresh-picked potatoes, peas, corn, strawberries, tomatoes, and peppers. The baked goods and pickles are, excellent, too. In the October, the farm transforms into a festive pumpkin patch.

o **Cherry Avenue Farms** (4303 Cherry Ave., Vineland Station; (www.cherry avenuefarms.org; *C* **905/562-5481**): Since 1799, the Moyer Family has been growing stone fruit on this acreage. The season opens with cherries, which are followed by apricots, nectarines, peaches, and a rainbow of different plum varietals that come in yellow, red, and blue.

o **Kurtz Orchards** (16006 Niagara Pkwy., Niagara-on-the-Lake; www. kurtzorchards.com; *C* **905/468-2937**): It's impossible to miss this 32-hectare (79-acre) farm on your way into NOTL from the wine trail. Although visitors are no longer free to pluck from the trees, you'll find a spread of fresh-picked fruit in the

$15 is fresh and filling, while the titanic poutine portions pack enough calories to fuel an entire weekend's worth of wine tasting. The barn setting is appropriately country, though far from fashionable. Best of all: Tastings are free and a great way to kill some time while waiting for your table.

1010 Line 2 Rd., Niagara-on-the-Lake. www.carolinecellars.com. *C* **905/468-8814.** Main courses $14–$16. Mon–Fri 11:30am–4pm; Sat–Sun 11:30am–5pm. Reservations recommended.

Along the Niagara Parkway

The Niagara Parkway, on the Canadian side of the falls, is a lovely, scenic drive. Unlike the American side, it offers plenty of natural beauty, including vast tracks of parkland. You can drive along the 56km (35-mile) parkway all the way from Niagara-on-the-Lake to Niagara Falls, taking in attractions en route. All are managed by Niagara Parks. Here are the major ones, listed in the order in which you'll encounter them:

The White Water Walk ★★ VIEWPOINT   A boardwalk runs beside the raging white waters of the Great Gorge Rapids. Take a self-guided stroll marketplace, where you can also find preserves, honey, and myriad other goodies. Activities such as the tractor-pulled tram make this a favorite family pit stop.

o **Mathias Farms** (1909 Effingham St., Ridgeville; mathiasfarmsniagara.com; ✆ **905/892-6166**). This family-run farm grows raspberries, blackberries, and cherries. They're a granola operation that prides themselves on their chemical-free fruit. Should what you're craving be out of season, ask about their jams, which make for a tasty curio, and their fresh-frozen berries.

o **Parkway Orchards** (15000 Niagara Pkwy., Niagara-on-the-Lake; www. parkwayorchards.com; ✆ **905/262-5097**): This no-frills farm sells fresh-cut flowers, plums, apricots, nectarines, peaches, apples, and grapes. You can buy them already picked or pick your own. Visitors must pay a minimum pick-your-own entry fee of $5 per adult, but that cost will be applied to the total picked. (The farm has had problems with visitors eating without paying, and because it's a small family affair, the precautions are reasonable.)

o **Two Century Farm** (400 Main St W, Grimsby; www.twocenturyfarm.com; no phone). Located between the lake and the Niagara Escarpment, this farm grows some of the sweetest peaches and cherries in the region thanks to its sandy, nutrient-rich soil—as well as the heaps of know-how behind the scenes, seven generations of it, in fact. The Smith family has been harvesting fruit here since 1787, and their trees are some of the most well-kept around.

o **Windwood Farms** (4198 King St., Beamsville; www.windwoodfarms.ca; ✆ **905/401-0515**): Looking to keep the doctor away? Then a stop at Windwood Farms is a must. They grow over 16 different types of apples. The Beamsville Bench farm also makes some really tasty apple cider.

on the viewing platforms along the river's edge and wonder at your leisure how it must feel to challenge this mighty torrent, where the river rushes through the narrow channel at an average speed of 35kmph (22 mph).

4330 River Rd., Niagara Parks. www.niagaraparks.com. ✆ **877-642-7275**, ext. 0. Admission $14 adults; $9 children 6–12; free for children 5 and under. Open (weather permitting) mid-Apr daily 10am–5pm; May–June weekdays 9:30am–5pm and weekends 9am–7pm; July–Aug daily 9am–9pm; Sept–Oct weekdays 9:30am–5pm and weekends 9am–6pm.

The Whirlpool Aero Car ★★ CABLE CAR   This red-and-yellow cable-car contraption is the only one of its kind. Spanish civil engineer Leonardo Torres Quevedo, who invented the world's first computer, also designed this acrophobia-inducing apparatus, which whisks you on a 1,097m (3,600-ft.) jaunt between two points on the Canadian side of the falls. High above the Niagara Whirlpool, you'll enjoy excellent views of the surrounding landscape.

Niagara Parks. www.niagaraparks.com. ✆ **877-642-7275,** ext. 0. Admission $16 adults; $10.25 children 6–12; free for kids 5 and under. Open daily mid-Apr (weather permitting) to early Nov: 10am–5pm until last week of June, 9am–8pm until Labor Day, 10am–5pm until early Nov.

Niagara Parks Botanical Gardens and Butterfly Conservatory ★★
GARDENS   Stop here and explore the vast gardens and the Butterfly Conservatory, where more than 2,000 butterflies (45 international species) float and flutter among the brightly colored tropical flowers. The large, electric-blue Morpho butterflies from Central and South America are particularly gorgeous. Interpretive programs and other presentations take place in the auditorium and two smaller theaters. The native butterfly garden outside attracts the more common swallowtails, fritillaries, and painted ladies. Visitors are encouraged to wear brightly colored clothing to attract the butterflies.

Niagara Parks. www.niagaraparks.com. ⓒ **877/642-7275,** ext. 0. Admission $16 adults; $10.25 children 6–12; free for children 5 and under. Open daily Sept–June 10am–5pm; July–Aug 10am–7pm.

Queenston Heights Park ★ HISTORIC SITE   This is the site of a famous War of 1812 battle, and you can take a walking tour of the battlefield. Picnic or play tennis in the shaded arbor before moving to the **Laura Secord Homestead.** This heroic woman threaded enemy lines to alert British authorities to a surprise attack by American soldiers during the War of 1812. Her home contains a fine collection of period furniture, plus artifacts recovered from an archaeological dig. History lessons come alive with the help of the costumed tour guides. Stop at the **candy shop** and **ice-cream parlor** for sweet treats.

29 Queenston St. www.niagaraparks.com. ⓒ **877/642-7275,** ext. 0. Admission for climbing and guided tours $4.50 adults; $3.50 children 6–12. Open daily mid-May until Labor Day 10am–5pm; Labor Day to Oct 31 10am–4pm. Closed Nov through mid-May.

Old Fort Erie ★ FORT   This is a reconstruction of the fort that was seized by the Americans in July 1814, besieged later by the British, and finally blown up as the Americans retreated across the river to Buffalo. Guards in period costume stand sentry duty, fire the cannons, and demonstrate drill and musket practice.

350 Lakeshore Rd., Fort Erie. www.niagaraparks.com. ⓒ **905/871-0540**. Admission $13.25 adults; $8.40 children 6–12; free for children 5 and under. Open daily mid-May to Oct 31 10am–5pm.

Seeing Niagara Falls

You simply cannot come this far and not see the Falls, one of the seven natural wonders of the world. When you arrive, step up to the low railing that runs along the road and take in the spectacular view over Horseshoe Falls. The Falls are equally dramatic in winter, when ice formations add a certain beauty to it all and the crowds of high summer are wonderfully absent.

The attractions and restaurants along the Niagara River Corridor, which includes Niagara Falls, are run by **Niagara Parks** (www.niagaraparks.com; **877/642-7275**), the park's official government agency. (A number of independent tour operators, including Hornblower Cruises [see below], also run concessions near the Falls.) Admission to the park itself is free, but most parking is in paid lots, where daily parking passes cost $26.55, plus HST tax.

The hop-on, hop-off visitor transportation buses **WEGO** (www.niagaraparks.com) connect all Niagara Parks destinations with nearby hotels. It also

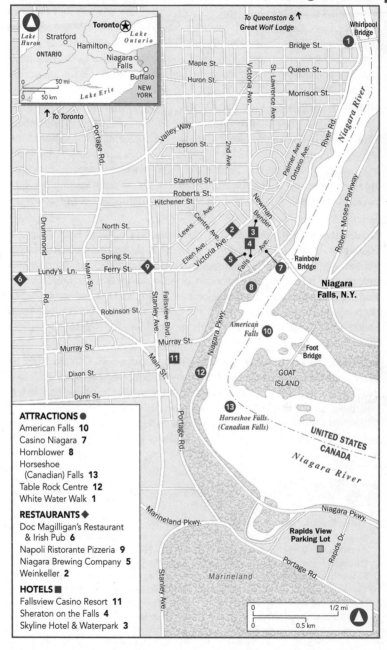

ATTRACTIONS ●
American Falls **10**
Casino Niagara **7**
Hornblower **8**
Horseshoe
(Canadian) Falls **13**
Table Rock Centre **12**
White Water Walk **1**

RESTAURANTS ◆
Doc Magilligan's Restaurant
& Irish Pub **6**
Napoli Ristorante Pizzeria **9**
Niagara Brewing Company **5**
Weinkeller **2**

HOTELS ■
Fallsview Casino Resort **11**
Sheraton on the Falls **4**
Skyline Hotel & Waterpark **3**

runs lines to Niagara-on-the-Lake. WEGO 24-hour fares are $8 adults, $5 children 6 to 12, and free for children 5 and under.

Note that if you plan on visiting several attractions, Niagara Parks offers a **Wonder Pass** package, which includes one-time admission to both Journey Behind the Falls and Niagara's Fury (see below), plus the Butterfly Conservatory (see "Along the Niagara Parkway," above) and the Floral Showhouse, as well as 2 consecutive days of WEGO + Falls Incline access. Online prices are $25 adults and $17 children 6 to 12.

JOURNEY BEHIND THE FALLS ★★ Of Niagara Parks' four Welcome Centers, **Table Rock Centre** is the site of the two of the most popular park attractions. Go down under the falls using the elevator at the Table Rock Centre, which drops you 38m (125 ft.) through solid rock to the tunnels and viewing portals of the Journey Behind the Falls (www.niagaraparks.com/visit/attractions/journey-behind-the-falls), which offers stunning views of the falls below and behind. Admission to this year-round attraction is $14 adults, $9 children 6 to 12, free for children 5 and under.

NIAGARA'S FURY ★ Another park attraction at Table Rock Centre is **Niagara's Fury** (www.niagaraparks.com/visit/attractions/niagaras-fury/). Visitors "experience" the creation of the falls in a chamber that swirls visual images over a 360-degree screen. It's a sense-surround ride, complete with shaking ground underfoot, an enveloping blizzard, and a temperature drop in the room that begets shivers even in midsummer. Fares are $16 adults, $10.25 children 6 to 12, free for children 5 and under (Mon–Fri 10:30am–5pm; Sat–Sun 10:30am–6pm).

HORNBLOWER CRUISES ★★★ Take a cruise right into the basin on the *Hornblower* (5920 River Rd.; www.niagaracruises.com; © **855/264-2427**). This sturdy boat takes you through the turbulent waters, past Bridal Veil Falls, and to the foot of the Horseshoe Falls, where 34 million liters (9 million gallons) of water tumble over the 54m-high (177-ft.) cataract each minute. Yes, you will get wet, and your glasses will mist—but that just adds to the thrill. Boats leave from the dock on the parkway just down from the

---

The Honeymoon Capital of the World

Seeing Niagara Falls as it is today—in all of its loud, neon, tacky glory—you might wonder how anyone would have thought it a romantic destination for a honeymoon. But back in 1801, when the Falls was simply a natural wonder of the highest order, Aaron Burr's daughter, Theodosia, chose it as the perfect place for her honeymoon. Napoleon's brother Jerome Bonaparte followed in her footsteps with his bride a few years later, and then suddenly everybody thought Niagara Falls was *the* place for newlyweds. Well, not *everybody*. Oscar Wilde visited Niagara Falls in 1881 and quipped: "Every American bride is taken there, and the sight of the stupendous waterfall must be one of the earliest if not the keenest disappointments in American married life."

Canada's first **Great Wolf Lodge** ★ (3950 Victoria Ave.; www.greatwolf. com/niagara; ✆ 905/354-4888 or 800/605-9653) brings the popular American chain and its massive indoor water park to Niagara Falls. But this a water park and more: It includes an interactive tree house water fort, a four-story Canada Vortex slide, a Niagara Rapids Run—like a watery roller coaster—falls, wave pools, and whirlpool hot spas. Add to that seven family-friendly dining options and a range of suites.

Rainbow Bridge. Trips operate daily from April through November. Fares are $26 adults, $16 children 5 to 12, and free for children 4 and under.

JET-BOATING THRILLS ★★ Don a rain suit, poncho, and life jacket, and climb aboard a **Whirlpool Jet Boat** (www.whirlpooljet.com; ✆ **888/438-4444** or 905/468-4800). The boat takes you out onto the Niagara River for a trip along the stonewalled canyon to the whirlpool downriver. The ride starts slow but gets into turbulent water. Trips, which operate from May to October, last an hour and cost $67 for adults and $45 for children 12 and under; reservations are required. There are pickup options; when booking, choose either NOTL or Niagara Falls.

WHERE TO STAY NEAR THE FALLS

Niagara Falls isn't Vegas—a good thing, for the most part—but it is showing signs of appreciating the demand for high-end hospitality. If you enjoy the bright lights and the casino scene of Niagara Falls after dark, one luxe hotel choice is the 374-room **Fallsview Casino Resort** (6380 Fallsview Blvd.; www.fallsviewcasinoresort.com; ✆ **888/325-5788**), which opened in 2004. It has its own 18,580-sq m (200,000–sq. ft.) casino, a performing-arts theater, a spa, and a whopping 20 dining options. Another good bet is the 669-room **Sheraton on the Falls Hotel** (5875 Falls Ave.; www.sheratononthefalls.com; ✆ **905/374-4445**), which offers rooms with truly gorgeous views of the Falls; many have balconies. The family-friendly **Skyline Hotel & Waterpark** (4800 Bender St.; https://skylinehotelniagarafalls.com; ✆ **800/263-7135** or 905/374-4444) has waterpark packages and family movie nights—and kids eat for free at the on-site Perkins Restaurant & Bakery.

WHERE TO EAT NEAR THE FALLS

Restaurants here grill-top steaks, steam expensive lobster, and plate overpriced pasta—much like other tourist destinations. **Weinkeller** (5633 Victoria Ave.; www.weinkeller.ca/entrees; ✆ **289/296-8000**) keeps the service fast and the food fresh by offering a short selection of proteins (salmon, chicken, steak), each done up in a handful of different ways. As the name suggests, Weinkeller (German for wine cellar) also ages and bottles its own wine—it's buvable, but there's better coming out of the region.

The *pizzaiolos* at **Napoli Ristorante Pizzeria** (5485 Ferry St.; www. napoliristorante.ca/location.html; ✆ **905/356-3345**) pull excellent blistered pies from the ovens at this trattoria, which offers great bang for your buck on pastas, *secondi* like roast chicken or pan-seared veal chop with mushrooms, and pizza.

For local craft beer and belt-busting bar food, head to **Niagara Brewing Company** (4915-A Clifton Hill; https://niagarabrewingcompany.com; $\textcircled{c}$ **905/374-4444**). Its beer list includes pale ales, chocolate porters, and even an ice-wine beer. Another no-fuss spot to grab a bite is **Doc Magilligan's Restaurant & Irish Pub** (6400 Lundy's Lane; www.docmagilligans.com; $\textcircled{c}$ **905/374-0021**); the prices are reasonable, the food is well-made, and the Victorian decor is well-done.

PRINCE EDWARD COUNTY

Culinary tourism is on the rise everywhere, and Ontario is definitely in on the game. Traveling to eat has turned **Prince Edward County (PEC,** or **the County**) into a favored escape for Torontonians seeking great wine, top food, and rustic country charms.

The County has long been a bastion of good drink. In the late 18th century, Prince Edward Island became a wealthy region rich in barley. As demand for beer grew across North America, so did the County's barley-baron mansions. Today, a handful of these beauties have been transformed into luxury inns. For most of the past century, however, PEC was a quiet, sometimes poor, agricultural area with just one small town, the struggling Picton. It still has one main town, but Picton is now thriving. And a number of smaller towns and villages, such as Bloomfield, Wellington, Milford, and Waupoos, have distinguished themselves with food-related attractions such as a craft brewery, a stellar ice-cream shop, and a unique cheese dairy.

A couple of decades ago, a back-to-the-land movement started attracting painters, artisans, glass blowers, and organic-minded farmers. Aspiring vintners came next, then chefs, bakers, even gourmet-hot-dog makers. Now, the place is a hot culinary spot, especially for Torontonians. Given the pristine sand dunes, inland lakes, Sandbanks Provincial Park, and a mysterious lake that sits perched 62m (203 ft.) above Lake Ontario, the County is worth a day trip or two to take in the sights and treat the other senses.

Keep in mind that this area is best explored in the warm months, from spring through fall. A number of shops, galleries, and restaurants close, or seriously cut back hours, during the winter months.

Essentials

VISITOR INFORMATION **Prince Edward County Chamber of Tourism & Commerce** is at 116 Main St., Picton (www.pecchamber.com; $\textcircled{c}$ 613/476-2421). It has a wealth of information about what to see and do, as well as where to dine and sleep. Hours change with the seasons, but it's generally open 9am to 4:30pm, with some added hours in summer and through autumn. Closed weekends in winter.

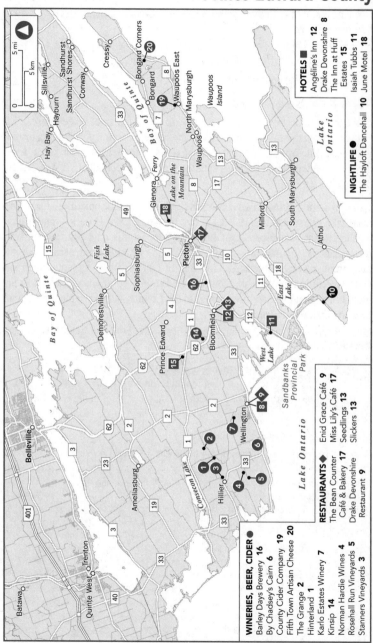

HOTELS ■
Angéline's Inn **12**
Drake Devonshire **8**
The Inn at Huff Estates **15**
Isaiah Tubbs **11**
June Motel **18**

NIGHTLIFE ●
The Hayloft Dancehall **10**

RESTAURANTS ◆
The Bean Counter Café & Bakery **17**
Drake Devonshire Restaurant **9**
Enid Grace Café **9**
Miss Lily's Café **17**
Seedlings **13**
Slickers **13**

WINERIES, BEER, CIDER ●
Barley Days Brewery **16**
By Chadsey's Cairn **6**
County Cider Company **19**
Fifth Town Artisan Cheese **20**
The Grange **2**
Hinterland **1**
Karlo Estates Winery **7**
Kinsip **14**
Norman Hardie Wines **4**
Rosehall Run Vineyards **5**
Stanners Vineyards **3**

The County (www.visitpec.ca; ℰ **613/476-2148**, ext. 2506) is the official tourism site, with info on lodging, dining, and attractions. To help you choose from the range of culinary vacations, visit the **Savour Ontario** website (www.savourontario.ca).

GETTING THERE   Prince Edward County is easy to reach by car. From Toronto, take Hwy. 401 east to exit 525 (before Trenton), then take Hwy. 33 to Picton. The drive takes about 2½ hours.

What to See & Do

The County is best explored by car, though it's also a great place to bike once you've arrived. You can visit wineries and restaurants on cycling tours or map your own itinerary. In fact, most of the tours in the region, from art to wine, are self-directed. It's in keeping with the region's independent, off-the-beaten-path character.

Lake on the Mountain ★ LAKE   It's a small, sometimes turquoise-hued lake perched 60m (197 ft.) above the great Lake Ontario—and a local legend because its source remains a mystery to this day. Surrounded by a pretty park, a popular pub, some lovely country homes, and a small inn, the lake offers a grand view across the Bay of Quinte. Bring a picnic lunch and watch the ferries below as they cross the 1km (½-mile) channel to the mainland. It's a great place to bid farewell to the County before hopping aboard the car ferry below at Glenora.

C.R. 7 (off Hwy. 33, near Glenora). www.ontarioparks.com/park/lakeonthemountain. ℰ **613/393-3319.**

Sandbanks Provincial Park ★★★ BEACH PARK   It's a short drive to this spectacular provincial park that includes the West Lake formation, claimed to be the largest freshwater bay-mouth sand-dune system in the world. In other words: It's an amazing beach (some say the best in Canada). The water is

---

ON THE TRAIL FOR art (AND tastings)

In addition to food and wine pros, the County is a busy community of artists. The **Arts Trail** ★★ (www.artstastetrail.com) initiative equips visitors with the routes they need to discover the County's artsy side in leisurely, self-guided treks into the PEC countryside. Follow the Arts Trail and visit art studios and galleries to see beautiful paintings, sculpture, contemporary photography, pottery, blown glass, handcrafted jewelry, and more, all made by local artisans. Eight galleries in the area represent multiple artists, as well; the **Oeno** (https://oenogallery.com)

is particularly cutting-edge. In addition to the Arts Trail, the County has a **Taste Trail** ★★ of wineries, breweries, restaurants, and farm markets that thread along the same roads as the Arts Trail—making for a delightful day of art and food appreciation. Go to www.artstastetrail.com for the latest route maps and brief listings on each destination. Once on the road, you'll find signs identifying both the Arts and the Taste trails. Take your time; this is slow grazing and gazing.

shallow, the sand clean, and the dunes—many between 12m (39 ft.) and 25m (82 ft.) high—provide a bit of topography that's good for hiking and also for sheltered picnic areas on blistering days. In fact, this natural water park features plenty of picnic areas and day-use programs like campfires and other activities.

If you have the time, Sandbanks Provincial Park is a splendid spot to camp for a night. Although the park has more than 500 campsites, they fill up quickly—holiday weekends are near impossible to snag. Reserving a campsite has been made simple by Ontario Parks, however. Visit **www.reservations.ontarioparks.com/sandbanks** and search the available sites that fit your needs. Some sites are barrier-free, others allow pets, and some are even have power outlets . . . although some would argue that's cheating, even for car camping.

3004 County Rd. 12 RR#1, Picton. www.ontarioparks.com/park/sandbanks. ✆ **613/393-3319.** Daily vehicle permit $11.25–$20. Daily 10am–8pm.

PRINCE EDWARD COUNTY WINERIES

By Chadsey's Cairn ★★   Run by self-described viticultural cowboys, By Chadsey's Cairn was one of the first wineries to pop up in PEC. Back in 1999, they planted 3,000 Riesling vines in an area that can be so abused by Ontario's cold season, even the hardiest grapes can barely survive the harsh winters. To help the grapes thrive, they began burying the vines before the frost. It's a laborious process, and one that has become standard County practice. Today, winemaker Vida Zalnieriunas oversees the wine program, creating low-intervention bottles. The Pinot Noirs and Gamays are particularly good here.

17432 Loyalist Pkwy., Wellington. www.bychadseyscairns.com. ✆ **613/399-2992.** Tastings $1. Jan–Feb Thurs–Mon 11am–5pm; Mar–April and Nov–Dec daily 11am–5pm; May–Oct daily 11am–6pm.

Karlo Estates Winery ★★   Even if you aren't a fan of oaked wines, tastings in this circa-1805 barn will have you falling for the charms of timber. The entire place is a carpenter's delight, from the vaulted ceiling to the live-edge bar propped up by wine barrels. Better yet, for those who do like a bit of a buttery white, Karlo's 2016 Chardonnay, aged for 10 months in French oak, medaled at the National Canadian Wine Awards. The resulting quaff is succulent, with hints of passion fruit and a caramel finish. On a summer day, exploring the gorgeously manicured 93-acre property is a delight. The owners of the winery encourage visitors to come with a picnic basket, and set up camp along the property. The biggest draw is the dry stone bridge, the largest in North America. When the skies are disagreeable, a glass on the back covered patio will do.

561 Danforth Rd., Wellington. www.karloestates.com. ✆ **613/399-3000.** Tasting flights $4–$15. Open Dec–Apr Sun–Thurs 11am–5pm, Fri–Sat 11am–11pm; May–Nov Sun–Thurs 11am–6pm, Fri–Sat 11am–11pm.

Hinterland ★★   The staff aren't as effervescent as the scrumptious bubbly, but they're forgiven after a flute (or two) of sparkling. The repurposed dairy barn is a charming spot to sip and learn the ins and outs of the charmant method of winemaking. But if the sun is shining, it's best to sit out back and take in the rolling countryside. This winery is dog- and kid-friendly; tykes can exhaust themselves playing ball hockey in the meadow while parental units snack on oysters and charcuterie from the outdoor kitchen.

1258 Closson Rd., Hillier. www.hinterlandwine.com. ☎ **613/399-2903.** Tasting flights from $6. Open daily 11am–6pm.

Norman Hardie Wines ★★ A popular spot to stop for still-bubbling pizzas fresh from the wood oven (which rival some of Toronto's best pies) and salad made from tomatoes grown a stone's throw from the Gamay grapes. This modern winery doesn't lean into any of the artifice of a faux-fancy tasting room—it's a pragmatic mezzanine that looks down on the winemaking operation below. The sizzle is in the wines, some of the most exciting being produced in Canada. It's a little taste of Burgundy in Ontario. In October, the public is invited to join in for the communal harvest, which is always a rompin', stompin' good time.

1152 Greer Rd., Wellington. www.normanhardie.com. ☎ **613/399-5297.** Tasting flights from $5. Nov–Mar daily 11am–5pm; April–Oct 10am–6pm.

Rosehall Run Vineyards ★★ The rich clay fields that feed the vines at this 150-acre estate winery sustain the standards cold-friendly grape varietals (Pinot Noir and Chardonnay) as well as some surprises, like Tempranillo. The wines of owner and winemaker Dan Sullivan wines are some of the most refined being produced in The County. Inside the sun-drenched tasting room, make sure to give the three-tiered chandelier a look: It's made by a local artist out of the winery's very own grapevines. Those of a peckish persuasion can hit up the wee on-site grocer (all local products) for cheese and charcuterie—best consumed immediately while reclining in a Muskoka chair overlooking the gorgeously groomed grapes.

1243 Greer Rd., Wellington. www.rosehallrun.com. ☎ **613/399-1183.** Tasting flights $5. May–Oct daily 10am–6pm; Mar–Dec Mon–Sat 10am–5pm.

Stanners Vineyard ★★ This petite winery doesn't kowtow to the touristy side of wine tasting. The no-frills tasting room is housed in a contemporary barn that doubles as a barrel room. The Stanners family isn't there to upsell you with wine gadgets or appeal to every Tom, Dick, and Tracy with boring-yet-accessible blends. Owners Cliff and Dorothy Stanners (along with their son Colin) are salt-of-the-earth folks who just want to make and share their really, really good wine, with a focus on Pinot Noir. Share your passion for vino with Dorothy, and she'll grab some still-fermenting juice straight from the barrel for you to sample. Cliff and Colin were both research scientists (molecular biology and chemistry, respectively) before ditching the laboratory for the fields. They've brought their science know-how to winemaking, and the results are delicious. Their whole-berry fermentation method retains the punchy fruit flavors you don't expect from cool-climate–grown grapes. Stanners' reds get further complexity from being left on the skin for up to 3

DRINKING THE COUNTY dry

Wine isn't the only drink percolating in these parts. The County was built on beer and barley, but they're fermenting all types of deliciousness nowadays. From cider to whisky and ales, there's plenty to swill, sip, and even sup—throughout the summer many places run very respectable food programs.

○ **Barley Days Brewery** ★ With a nod to the County's barley-rich past, this craft brewery is an entirely modern enterprise. Of the many ales, kolschs, and lagers on offer, the fig-redolent Saison-Brett is my go-to. (13730 Loyalist Pkwy., Picton. www.barleydaysbrewery.com. ✆ **613/476-7468.** Daily 11am–5pm.)

○ **County Cider Company** ★ The cider here isn't the best in the County (Hinterland and the Grange do more justice to apples than this cidery does). However, the grounds are splendid. Atop the hillside, the lake fans out below and the orchard and vineyard are a marvel to stroll through. If enjoying a pizza and some snacks at the alfresco eatery, try a glass of the County Feral—it's made from wild apples, a perfect balance of tart and sweet with a crisp finish. (657 Bongards Crossroad, Waupoos. www.countycider. com. ✆ **613/476-1022.** Tastings $1–$2 a sample. Fri–Tues 11am–6pm.)

○ **The Grange** ★★ Yes, the Grange is a winery, but it also makes some fab farmhouse cider. This family-run farm tends to 60 acres of vines that yield over 120 tons of grapes, which is then turned into the winery's 100%-estate-grown wines. The farmhouse tasting room is brimming with country cheer. Board games and antique couches invite visitors to decompress while savoring Sauvignon Blanc and the excellent ciders (the flat farmhouse-style cider drinks like a wine). In summer, order a picnic basket and enjoy some of the property's wine or cider while tucking into wood-fired bread, local pickles, and cheeses. (990 Closson Rd., Hillier. www.grangewinery.com. ✆ **613/399-1048.** Tastings $5 for 3 samples. Nov–Apr Wed–Sun 11am–5pm; May–Oct daily 11am–5pm.)

○ **Kinsip** ★★★ You'll be immediately charmed by the roving white chickens, the inviting swing hanging from the old maple tree, the firepit that invites strangers to become friends, and the tasting room, which occupies a Canadian confederation–era house. The grounds offer an appealing spot to while away an afternoon, sipping on locally made spirits. The vodka made from local wheat and pine is splendid, as is the County Cassis made from Bay of Quinte black currants. The whisky-barrel-aged maple syrup is some of the best sap on sale in Ontario. (66 Gilead Rd., Bloomfield. www.kinsip.ca. ✆ **613/393-1890.** Tastings $2–$3 a sample. Tours $10–$25. Open spring through fall 10am–5pm.)

weeks. It's a labor of love, but the resulting bottles are truly excellent. If you don't believe me, believe the critics, who continuously bestow praise on the Stanners products.

76 Station Rd., Hillier. www.stannersvineyard.ca. ✆ **613/661-3361.** Tastings from $3. Jan–Apr Sat and Sun 11am–5pm; May–Nov daily 11am–6pm; Nov–Dec 15 daily 11am–5pm. Closed Dec 15–Jan 1.

Fifth Town Artisan Cheese ★★ (4309 Prince Edward County Rd. 8, Prince Edward; www.fifthtown.ca; ℂ **613/476-5755**) is the world's first LEED-certified dairy, meaning it has outstanding eco-practices. It's worth a visit and tour just to see the process in action. Making cheese creates a lot of water waste. Rather than dumping it down the drain, Fifth Town has built a filtering system out of ponds, which has created a wetland that is now home to many birds and butterflies. While the property is a pastoral paradise, it's also worth checking out the ultramodern building. More important, the cheeses are works of art. During the summer, Fifth Town also offers cheese and charcuterie boards, which can be enjoyed in the garden. Call ahead to check on hours and tours.

Where to Stay

The County has many good options for staying a night or two, from homey B&Bs to lakeside self-catering cottages to very pretty inns. The County's inns are some of the best choices if you're looking for good dining and lodging all in one locale.

Angéline's Inn ★★ This family-run inn offers various types of lodging to suit a variety of travelers. Those looking for a luxurious experience will be wooed by the property's crown jewel: a grand old Victorian home that has been carved into elegant suites. From the outside, the building maintains its 1869 architectural allure, but inside, it's entirely modern (save for a few era-appropriate furnishings). Each of the five rooms is outfitted with rainfall showers and down pillow–topped beds that promise luxurious sleep-ins. Travelers on a budget will appreciate the Walter Economy rooms, an adorably retrofit motel that was built in 1953 and freshly updated to suit millennials' twee sensibilities. The frill-free rooms are quaint and compact. The property also has four fully furnished homes, providing ultimate privacy.

433 Main St., Bloomfield. www.angelines.ca. ℂ **877/391-3301** or 613/393-3301. 17 units. $139–$449 double. Free parking. Pets permitted in some rooms. **Amenities:** Restaurant; free Wi-Fi. Certain accommodations only available seasonally.

Drake Devonshire ★★★ A favorite retreat for Toronto's literati seeking an escape from the bustle of the city, but who refuse to forgo their daily dose of arts and culture. Hotelier Jeff Stober—the visionary behind Toronto's Drake Hotel and its associated clutch of restaurants—has retrofit an 1897-built Wellington Iron foundry into a boutique hotel that appeals to the most worldly of travelers. The space marries country charm (carefully selected antiques, pastoral vistas, a private pebble beach animated at night by a bonfire) with artsy panache. Each room is distinct, not only in terms of furnishings and layout, but in the original artwork by artists such as Team Macho and Rick Leong. The Owner's Suite is the most coveted hotel room in the County: a chic cottage-reminiscent A-frame room with an unbelievable south-facing view of Lake Ontario, a fireplace, a private patio, and a palatial marble bathroom. All rooms have only either a king or queen bed.

24 Wharf St., Wellington. www.drakedevonshire.ca. © **613/399-3338.** 13 units. $329–$577 double. Free parking. Pets not permitted. **Amenities:** Restaurant/bar; concierge; bike rentals; permanent art collection and rotating exhibits; games room; lakeside massage hut; room service; spa services; yoga and Pilates classes; free Wi-Fi.

The Inn at Huff Estates ★   There might not be a gym or a pool, but the location—sandwiched between the Huff Estates Winery, Oeno Gallery, and a sculpture garden—can't be beat. Fireplaces and private gardens come standard at this inn. Of all 21 rooms, the Winemaker's Suite is the most elegant. The private, wraparound terrace that looks over the vineyard below is a summer splendor. In cooler months, the floor-to-ceiling limestone fireplace is the pièce de résistance.

2274 County Rd 1 Bloomfield. www.huffestates.com. © **866/484-4667** or 613/393-1414. 21 units. $179–$229 double. Rates include breakfast. Free parking. Pets under 40 pounds permitted. **Amenities:** Electric-car charging stations; free Wi-Fi.

Isaiah Tubbs ★   This is the biggest resort around these parts, with acres of gardens and woodlands very close to Sandbanks Provincial Park. The rooms range from simple ones in the restored 1820s home to more spacious suites in outlying lodges; best of all are the Beach House Suites, which give you a taste of the exceptional location. The food is pretty standard but better than that at many family-style resorts.

1642 County Rd. 12, Picton. www.isaiahtubbs.com. © **800/724-2393** or 613/393-2090. 88 units. $169 and up double. No pets permitted. **Amenities:** 2 restaurants; bar; fitness center; heated pool (seasonal); sauna; tennis courts; water recreation facility with kayaks and canoes; complimentary access to Sandbanks Provincial Park; free Wi-Fi. Certain accommodations only available seasonally.

June Motel ★★   Apart from the bricks and mortar, all that's left of this midcentury fishermen's motel are the 60-year-old signs (now decorative) that read "DO NOT GUT FISH." Motelier gal-pal co-owners April Brown and Sarah Sklash have transformed this 16-room motel in a rosé-swilling, Pinterest-loving yuppie sanctuary complete with palm-printed wallpaper, cutesy neon signs, and decorative plastic flamingos. It's unapologetically fun, feminine, and fabulous. Details like plant-based toiletries from Northumberland County's Sunday Company are a nice touch.

12351 Loyalist Pkwy, Picton. www.thejunemotel.com. © **613/476-2424.** $205–$370 double. Free parking (1 vehicle per room). **Amenities:** Bar; bike rentals; concierge; limited room service (wine and charcuterie); free Wi-Fi. Closed Dec–Apr.

Where to Eat

Food is a major attraction here, with plenty of places to feast, graze, sip, and sample. Road trips around the region will lead you to discoveries like a beautiful little winery, or you can opt for staying in Picton and enjoying its many cafes, restaurants, pubs, and specialty shops. For a more complete list of what's on offer, visit **www.visitpec.ca** or **www.prince-edward-county.com**.

The Bean Counter Café & Bakery ★ CAFE   One of the many good choices on Picton's main street, this open and airy cafe serves fair-trade coffee, homemade cakes, light lunch fare, and more than 20 flavors of gelato made in-house. This is a perfect spot for refueling after a day on the dunes.

172 Main St., Unit 101, Picton. www.beancountercafe.com. © **613/476-1718.** Sandwiches, salads, quiches, and combos $8–$14. Daily 7am–5pm.

Drake Devonshire Restaurant ★★ CANADIAN   Talented Toronto chef Alexandra Feswick has moved to the County to take over one of the PEC's most elegant dinner destinations. The glass-encased dining room looks out over Lake Ontario and is often backlit by romantic mauve sunsets. Start your meal with one of the amazing cocktails. The craft quaffs have creative names like Rust + Bone, which sounds like a lo-fi punk band but is actually a cedar-infused bourbon sipper. The seasonal dinner options include plates like lime and chili–redolent Ontario perch served with fried lotus root, sweet potato, and edamame. Everything is made from scratch, even the bread.

24 Wharf St, Wellington. www.thedrake.ca/drakedevonshire. © **613/399-3338.** Breakfast $12–$17; brunch $12–$23; main courses lunch $17–$29, dinner $26–$35. Sun–Thurs 8am–9pm; Fri–Sat 8am–10pm.

Enid Grace Café ★★★ CAFE   Quaint and wholesome best describe this squeeze of a brunch gem. The cafe makes only enough food for a single daily service, the last French toast and sandwiches of the day are ordered by 1:45pm, or until the food runs out. According to owner Enid Grace, "This model eliminates food waste, keeps costs low, and promotes efficiency in our back of house." The bread and pastries are all house-made, and the food is perfection: Expect a simple menu of quiche, soup, and sandwiches. Not good for groups.

303 Wellington Main St, Wellington. www.enidgrace.com. © **613/399-3488.** Brunch $9–$10. Daily 7:30am–2pm, closed Tues.

Miss Lily's Café ★ CAFE   Situated in Books & Company, the charming Picton bookstore on the town's main strip, this is a local hangout and a great place to relax over a cup of coffee, light breakfast, or lunch.

289 Main St., Picton. © **613/476-9289.** Light fare from $12. Mon–Fri 7am–6pm; Sat 8am–6pm; Sun 8am–5pm.

Apple Pie Ice Cream, Anyone?

The County is known for a healthy sense of pride in local foods, and even the ice-cream shops are in on the trend. **Slickers** ★★, 271 Main St., Bloomfield (www.slickersicecream.com), a small spot with a pretty patio, serves up an eclectic collection of flavors, each one inspired by what's in season. Flavors include rhubarb ginger, local cantaloupe, apple pie, and even a maple walnut made with local syrup. They're all delicious. A single scoop runs from $3.65. It's open in summer only, Sunday to Wednesday 11am to 5pm and Thursday to Saturday 11am to 6pm.

Seedlings ★★★ CANADIAN   Chef Michael Portigal first moved to the County in 2015, when the Drake Devonshire wooed him from Ottawa to helm the hotel kitchen. After 2 years at the Drake, Portigal was ready to stretch his wings and open his own eatery with wife and business partner, Ashley O'Neil. The duo were keen to stay rooted in PEC, their newfound home, and they happened to find the perfect spot to nest: a quaint, 35-seat dining room in a historic Victorian inn (Angéline's Inn, see p.238). The exquisite food coming out of this highly competent kitchen echoes the couple's love of the landscape: 80% of the menu is sourced from local producers, which means the options change weekly, reflecting what's in season. Beef comes from Walt's Sugar Shack; lamb is sourced from Tamarack Farms in Roseneath, Ontario; the Lake Ontario–plucked pickerel and perch is from Dewey Fisheries; and the veg comes from the many farms that surround Bloomfield. During one visit, a rabbit schnitzel with late summer succotash was delectably tender—the fact that it may never appear on the menu again made it doubly delicious. *Note:* At press time, the restaurant was up for sale; call ahead for the latest details.

433 Bloomfield Main St., Bloomfield. www.seedlings-pec.ca. ℭ **613/393-3301.** Breakfast $10–$17; main courses $10–18 lunch, $22–$32 dinner.

Nightlife

The Hayloft Dancehall ★   This charming, weather-beaten barn, illuminated by the orange glow of string lights, is the County's go-to seasonal destination to dance the night away. The barn is located smack-dab in the middle of the touring route between Montreal and Toronto, and because of its honky-tonk appeal, it's has attracted a who's-who roster from the Canadian indie scene. The Rheostatics, the Sadies, Hey Rosetta!, and the Kiefer Sutherland Band are just a few of the celebrated groups who have stopped by to serenade this 200-person venue. If you're hungry, the venue hosts a different food truck each night. On nights the DJs come in: Expect a full-blown barn burner. Check the website for info on the **pickup/drop-off shuttle** to and from the Hayloft.

344 Salmon Pt., Picton. http://thehayloftdancehall.com. ℭ **613/476-0200.** Tickets $10–$40. Open weekends only May long weekend through Halloween weekend. Doors open at 7:30pm for 8:45pm showtimes.

PLANNING YOUR TRIP TO TORONTO

Toronto is an easy place to go for a spur-of-the-moment visit. Still, whether you're traveling on a whim or charting your course months in advance, some planning will help you make the most of your trip. This chapter will help you prepare.

GETTING THERE

By Plane

Toronto Pearson International Airport (YYZ) (https://toronto pearson.com) is the busiest airport in Canada, and its terminals are massive (particularly Terminal 1). Almost all flights into Toronto arrive here. Expect a long walk to the Immigration and Customs area, which you will have to clear in Toronto, even if you're flying on to another Canadian destination. (Maps of both terminals can be found online at www.gtaa.com.) Both terminals have tourism information booths.

Canada's only national airline, **Air Canada** (www.aircanada.ca; ✆ 888/247-2262), operates direct flights to Toronto from most major American cities and many smaller ones. It also flies from major cities around the world and operates connecting flights from other U.S. cities. It is based in Pearson's Terminal 1. **WestJet** (www.westjet.com; ✆ 888/937-8538), based in Calgary, has become an increasingly popular choice for anyone coming to Toronto from the United States, as well as some locations in the Caribbean and Mexico.

Upstart **Porter Airlines** (www.flyporter.com; ✆ 416/619-8622) has gained a great reputation for service and flies to **Billy Bishop Toronto City Centre Airport** (www.billybishopairport.com) from seven U.S. locations, including New York, Chicago, Boston, and Myrtle Beach, as well as a rapidly increasing number of Canadian cities. Porter, along with a handful of commuter flight services, is the only airline that flies to the Toronto City Centre Airport, which is located on the western side of the Toronto Islands.

GETTING INTO TOWN FROM THE AIRPORT

To get from the airport to downtown, take Hwy. 427 south to the Gardiner Expressway East. A **taxi** costs about $60 if you're going downtown (it's higher if you're heading to north or east Toronto).

In operation since 2015, the **UP Express airport rail link** (www.up express.com) makes getting downtown a snap. Trains leave from Pearson's Terminal 1, with two stops en route to Union Station. The $13.25 price tag is worth every penny: You'll be downtown in 25 minutes, and you won't be wasting away in highway traffic.

The cheapest way to get into town is by **bus and subway,** which takes about an hour. During the day, take the 192 "Airport Rocket" bus to Kipling station. In the middle of the night, you can take the no. 300A bus to Yonge and Bloor streets. The fare of $3.25 includes free transfer to the subway (which is available until 1:30am).

By Car

Crossing the border between Canada and the U.S. by car gives you a lot of options. If you're driving from Michigan, you'll enter at Detroit-Windsor (I-75 and the Ambassador Bridge) or Port Huron–Sarnia (I-94 and the Bluewater Bridge). If you're coming from New York, you have more options. On I-190, you can enter at Buffalo–Fort Erie; Niagara Falls, New York–Niagara Falls, Ontario; or Niagara Falls, New York–Lewiston. On I-81, you'll cross the Canadian border at Hill Island; on Rte. 37, you'll enter at either Ogdensburg-Johnstown or Rooseveltown-Cornwall.

From the United States, you are most likely to enter Toronto from the west on Hwy. 401 or Hwy. 2 and the Queen Elizabeth Way. If you come from the east, via Montreal, you'll also use hwys. 401 and 2.

Be sure you have your driver's license and car registration if you plan to drive your own vehicle into Canada. It isn't a bad idea to carry proof of automobile liability insurance, too.

By Train

Amtrak's "Maple Leaf" service links New York City and Toronto via Niagara Falls, Syracuse, and Albany (www.amtrak.com; © **800/USA-RAIL** [800/872-7245]). It departs daily from New York's Penn Station. The journey takes 12½ hours. Note that the lengthy schedule allows for extended stops at Customs and Immigration checkpoints at the border.

VIA Rail Canada (www.viarail.ca; © **888/VIA-RAIL** [888/842-7245]) is the nation's top rail line and offers many routes and generally pleasant service. Trains arrive in Toronto at **Union Station** (https://torontounion.ca). The station has direct access to the subway.

By Bus

Greyhound (www.greyhound.ca; © **877/463-6446**) is the best-known bus company that crosses the U.S. border. You can travel from almost anywhere in the United States and Canada. You'll arrive at the **Toronto Coach**

Terminal downtown at 610 Bay St., near the corner of Dundas Street. Other options include **Coach Canada** (www.coachcanada.com), which travels from many places in the United States, as well as from Quebec, to Ontario, and **Megabus** (www.ca.megabus.com).

The bus may be faster and cheaper than the train, and its routes may be more flexible if you want to stop along the way. Bear in mind that it's more cramped, toilet facilities are meager, and meals are taken at fast-food rest stops.

GETTING AROUND
By Public Transportation

The **Toronto Transit Commission,** or TTC (www.ttc.ca; ✆ **416/393-4636** for 24-hr. information, recordings available in 18 languages), operates the subway, bus, and streetcars.

Fares, including transfers to buses or streetcars, are $3.25. Seniors and students ages 13 to 19 with valid ID pay $2.10, or five tickets for $10.25; children 12 and under are free. You can buy a special day pass for $12.50 that's good for unlimited travel for one adult on weekdays and for up to two adults and four children on weekends.

For surface transportation, you need a Presto Card, a token, a ticket (for seniors or kids), or exact change. You can buy tokens and tickets at subway entrances and at authorized stores that display the sign TTC TICKETS MAY BE PURCHASED HERE. Bus drivers do not sell tickets, nor will they make change. Always obtain a free transfer where you board the train or bus, in case you need it. In the subways, use the push-button machine just inside the entrance. On streetcars and buses, ask the driver for a transfer.

The TTC plans to phase out tokens by the end of 2019, replacing them with the Presto Card system. The cards cost $6 to purchase (they're sold online at www.prestocard.ca, or can be purchased from vending machines at subway entrances). Everything from loading the card with money to checking a balance, is done through the Presto website. Using the card has three advantages: first, users automatically get the discount fare rate ($3 for adults, $2.10 for seniors and students); second, users get a 2-hour transfer, an asset for sightseers looking to hop on and off the Rocket; finally, should you lose a registered Presto Card, the card can be blocked and the remaining balance can be transferred over to a new card.

THE SUBWAY Compared with snarled surface traffic, the subway is the best way to get around the city. It's clean and very simple to use. There are two major lines—**Bloor-Danforth** and **Yonge-University-Spadina**—and two smaller lines, **Sheppard,** in the northern part of the city, and **Scarborough,** in the northeastern part of the city. The Bloor Street east-west line runs from Kipling Avenue in the west to Kennedy Road in the east (where it connects with the Scarborough Line, which runs north-east for five stops to McCowan). The Yonge Street north-south line runs from Finch Avenue in the north to Union Station (Front St.) in the south. From there, it loops north along

A Streetcar Named the Red Rocket

Most North American cities did away with their streetcars decades ago, and there remains a fraternal bond between light-rail-loving metropolises in this land of the car. San Francisco even painted one of its trams red in honor of T.O.'s **Red Rockets**—the loving name Torontonians call the bright red streetcars. Since 1892, streetcars have been an everyday part of the Toronto commute. Today the city has 11 streetcar lines on 82km (50 miles) of track. The 501 streetcar is the longest surface transit route in North America. Every so often, you'll spy a vintage trolley careening down a route, but these old beauts are generally deployed only for special occasions. That doesn't mean that streetcars aren't great for visitors. A **Presto card** (www. ttc.ca) grants you 2 hours of unlimited travel. I suggest getting off at Osgoode and taking the 501 Queen car westward: Hop on and off and explore the vibrant neighborhoods of Queen West, Trinity Bellwoods, West Queen West, and Parkdale, and finish by walking up Roncesvalles, the city's Polish strip, where you'll find heaps of cute bars, cafes, and locally run shops. Plus, some really, really good pierogi.

University Avenue and connects with the Bloor line at the St. George station. A Spadina extension runs north from St. George to Vaughan Metropolitan Centre. The Sheppard line connects only with the Yonge line at Sheppard station and runs east through north Toronto for just 6km (3¾ miles).

The subway operates Monday to Saturday from 6am to 1:30am and Sunday from 8am to 1:30am. From 1am to 5am, the **Blue Night Network** operates on basic surface routes, running about every 30 minutes. For help planning a route, use the TTC's Trip Planer (www.ttc.ca/Trip_planner). Given two addresses and a departure time, it will tell you the best transit options.

BUSES & STREETCARS   Where the subway leaves off, buses and streetcars take over. They run east-west and north-south along the city's arteries. When you pay your fare (on bus, streetcar, or subway), always pick up a transfer (unless you are using a Presto Card) so that you won't have to pay again if you want to transfer to another mode of transportation.

TAXIS & RIDESHARING SERVICES   In many cities, taxis are an expensive mode of transportation, but this is especially true of Toronto. Rates are $3.25 the minute you step in and $0.25 for each additional 0.143km (469 ft.). Fares can quickly mount up.

You can hail a cab on the street, find one in line in front of a big hotel, or call one of the major companies—**Beck** (© **416/751-5555**), **Diamond** (© **416/ 366-6868**), or **Co-Op Cabs** (© **416/504-2667**). If you experience any problems with cab service, call the **Metro Licensing Commission** (© **416/ 392-3082**).

At the time of publication, both **Lyft** and **Uber** were legal and operating in Toronto. Check for surge pricing before ordering a lift using these apps. At peak hours hailing a ride using Lyft or Uber can be double (or more!) the normal rates. During these periods, a standard taxi is often the cheaper option.

FERRY SERVICE   Day trips by ferry to the Toronto Islands are popular excursions for outdoor activities and great views of the city. Ferries to **Toronto Island Park** are operated by the city's Toronto Parks, Forestry, and Recreation Division. Ferries leave from the **Jack Layton Ferry Terminal,** at the foot of Bay Street and Queens Quay. Round-trip fares are $7.90 adults, $5.15 seniors and youths 15–19 (with valid student ID), $3.80 children 2–14, and free for infants under 2. Go to www.toronto.ca or call ✆ **416/392-8193** for schedules and information.

By Car

Toronto is a rambling city, but that doesn't mean the best way to get around is by car. There are long traffic jams, especially during morning and afternoon rush hours. A reputation for "two seasons: winter and construction" means the warmer months are especially busy with roadwork. And to make matters worse, there is an escalating turf war between the numerous cyclists and motorists sharing the road.

Parking can be very expensive, too, and the city's meter maids are notoriously aggressive in issuing pricey parking tickets at any opportunity.

RENTAL CARS   If you decide to rent a car, try to make arrangements in advance. Companies with outlets at Toronto Pearson International Airport include **Thrifty, Budget, Avis, Hertz, National,** and **Enterprise.** The rental fee depends on the type of vehicle, but do keep in mind that the quoted price does not include an added sales tax. It also does not include insurance; if you pay with a particular credit card, you might get automatic coverage (check with your credit-card issuer before you go). *Note:* If you're under 25, check with the company—many will rent on a cash-only basis, some only with a credit card, and others will not rent to you at all. Also, keep in mind that you must be 21 or older to rent a car.

Car-rental insurance probably does not cover liability if you cause an accident. Check your own auto insurance policy, the rental company policy, and your credit card coverage for the extent of coverage: Is your destination covered? Are other drivers covered? How much liability is covered if a passenger is injured? (If you rely on your credit card for coverage, you may want to bring a second credit card with you, as damages may be charged to your card and you may find yourself stranded with no money.)

PARKING   It can be a hassle to find parking in downtown Toronto, and parking lots have a wide range of fees. Generally speaking, the city-owned lots, marked with a big green "P," are the most affordable. They charge about $2 per half-hour. After 6pm and on Sunday, there is usually a maximum rate of $12. Observe the parking restrictions—otherwise, the city will tow your car away, and it'll cost more than $100 to get it back.

DRIVING RULES   A right turn at a red light is legal after coming to a full stop, unless posted otherwise. Passengers must wear seat belts; if you're caught not wearing one, the fine is substantial. The speed limit in the city is 50kmph (31 mph). You must stop at pedestrian crosswalks if someone is trying to cross (flashing lights indicate this, but not always—be vigilant and give pedestrians the right of way at all crosswalks). If you are following a streetcar and it stops, you must stop well back from the rear doors so passengers can exit easily and safely. (Where there are concrete safety islands in the middle of the street for streetcar stops, this rule does not apply, but exercise care, nonetheless.) Radar detectors are illegal.

In 2019, Ontario began enforcing a tough new **distracted driving law,** cracking down on drivers using handheld electronic devices (cellphones, iPods, game devices), with hefty fines and a possible driver's license suspension.

By Bike

Toronto is fairly flat and not known for its stunning vistas, making it an easy place to explore by bike. Like many cities in North America, however, the tensions between bikes and cars have been exacerbated in recent years as traffic congestion worsens. Still, the city has begun to embracing cycling culture, with separated bike lanes along key arteries such as Bloor, Richmond, and Adelaide Streets. There are even mixed-use trails that can take you across the city, away from the cars, including the **Martin Goodman Trail** (a 56km/34-mile waterfront trail that traverses the city, hugging the lake) and the soon-to-be-expanded **West Toronto Railpath,** which straddles the rail lines, connecting the Junction to Little Portugal. For those who want to escape the motor madness completely: Head to the **Toronto Islands,** where bikes rule and cars are forbidden.

Cycling is the most effective way to see Toronto, so long as you stick, primarily, to the bike paths. Bike lanes, which are clearly marked, include routes along Davenport Road, Bloor, College/Carlton, Harbord, Richmond, Adelaide, St. George/Beverly, and Sherbourne streets. For cycling maps, and more information, visit **www.toronto/ca/cycling**. Google Maps has an excellent function that will plot out the most bike-friendly routes.

Renting a bike in Toronto is as easy as downloading an app. Toronto's bike-share program, **Bike Share Toronto** has over 3,750 bikes, spread across 75 sq. km (29 sq. miles) of the city. Simply download the CycleFinder app, which will tell you where all 360 bike stations are and allow you to pay for, and have access to, Bike Share rentals. A single trip costs $3.25, a day pass $7, and a 3-day pass is the best value at $15.

Three-day and single-day passes permit unlimited trips; however, each trip is limited to 30 minutes, with penalties of $4 per half-hour of overage time. To circumvent the penalty, simply stop at a station en route and swap bikes. Bikes can be returned to any docking station, so there's no need to plan a return trip; simply grab a bike and go. The CycleFinder app is a key tool for locating docking stations that have space, and has functions to help with route planning.

In Toronto bikes are expected to follow the same rules of the road that cars do, which means follow all street signs, including stop signs (even on small side streets), never bike on the sidewalk, and always stop behind a streetcar when people are dismounting. You could face a hefty fine for blowing past open streetcar doors.

As a cyclist myself, the best advice I can give you on seeing Toronto by bike is: Be wary of the streetcar tracks, which are the prefect size for catching bike tires—a truly traumatic way to be thrown from your steed. Make sure to cross streetcar tracks at a perpendicular angle.

RESPONSIBLE TOURISM

By North American standards, Toronto is an exceptionally green city. It boasts good eco-initiatives such as composting and recycling programs, a powerful local-foods movement, and more. The city's wealth of parkland, even in the downtown core, is a standout. And although there is nothing on the scale of, say, Central Park, green spaces are scattered throughout, from tiny plots in the Financial District to neighborhood gems like **Riverdale, Allan Gardens, Trinity Bellwoods, Dufferin Grove,** and **High Park.** (The green spaces are well maintained, but you may notice a fair number of weeds—cosmetic use of pesticides is banned in the city.)

For the eco-conscious visitor looking to conserve fuel and energy when they travel, here are a few simple ways you can help reduce your environmental impact when visiting Toronto:

To help keep the city green, I recommend **renting a bike** (see "Getting Around," above, for details on Bike Share Toronto), rather than a car. Between the traffic jams, streetcars, and rule-flouting pedestrians, driving in Toronto is a bear anyway, and best avoided. If biking doesn't appeal, Toronto is an extremely walkable city, with a fabulous transit system that is sure to help you get to where you're going without an ounce of carbon-footprint guilt.

Each time you take a flight or drive a car, greenhouse gases release into the atmosphere. You can help neutralize this danger to the planet through **"carbon offsetting"**—paying someone to invest your money in programs that reduce greenhouse gas emissions by the same amount you've added. Before buying carbon offset credits, just make sure that you're using a reputable company such as **Carbonfund** (www.carbonfund.org).

Where you stay during your travels can have a major environmental impact. To determine the **green credentials of a property,** ask about trash disposal and recycling, water conservation, and energy use; also ask whether sustainable materials were used in the construction of the property. The **Drake,** the **Gladstone,** and the **Fairmont Royal York** are three particularly green hotels that go above and beyond the typical eco norm. No matter where you lay your head (be it a five-star hotel or a B&B), you can help minimize your environmental impact by requesting that your sheets and towels not be changed daily. (Many hotels already do this.) Also, remember to turn off the lights and air-conditioner when you leave your room.

Last, but definitely not least, eat at **locally owned and operated restaurants that use local, seasonal produce.** Ditto for meats: Look for pasture-raised and non-industrial suppliers. Not only do these choices contribute to the local economy, they cut down on greenhouse gas emissions. Toronto has too many restaurants that support the local foods movement to list here, but some suggestions include **Edulis, Chantecler, Montecito, Richmond Station,** and **Actinolite.**

[Fast FACTS] TORONTO

Area Codes Toronto's area codes are **416**, **647, and 437;** outside the city, the code is **905** or **289.** You must dial all 10 digits for all local phone numbers.

Business Hours Banks are generally open Monday through Thursday from 10am to 5pm, Friday 10am to 6pm. Most stores are open Monday through Wednesday from 10am to 6pm, and Saturday and Sunday from 10am to 5pm, with extended hours (until 8 or 9pm) on Thursday and often on Friday.

Customs
What You Can Bring into Canada
Generally speaking, Canadian Customs regulations are generous, but they get complicated when it comes to firearms, plants, meat, and pets. Visitors can bring rifles into Canada during hunting season; handguns and automatic rifles are not permitted. You can bring in, free of duty, up to 50 cigars, 200 cigarettes, and 200g (7 oz.) of tobacco. You are also allowed 1.14L (38 oz.) of liquor, 1.5L (51 oz.) of wine, or 24 cans or bottles of beer. To bring in either alcohol or tobacco, you must be of legal age in the province you're visiting (19 in Ontario). There are no restrictions on what you can

take out. In terms of pets, dogs and cats from rabies-free countries can enter without being quarantined so long as they are up-to-date on their vaccinations with proper veterinarian-provided documentation in hand. For more information (and for updates on these policies), check with the **Canada Border Services Agency** (✆ **800/461-9999** or 506/636-5064; www.cbsa. gc.ca).

Disabled Travelers
Toronto is a very accessible city. Curb cuts are well-made and common throughout the downtown area; special parking privileges are extended to people with disabilities who have special plates or a pass that allows parking in no-parking zones. The old-generation streetcars are not accessible, though the new generation of streetcars are wheelchair accessible. A growing number of Toronto's subway stations are wheelchair accessible. Upgrade plans call for all stations to be barrier-free and have elevator access by 2025. The city operates **Wheel-Trans,** a special service for those with disabilities. Visitors can register for this service. For information, call ✆ **416/ 393-4111** or visit **www. mywheel-trans.ttc.ca**.

Doctors The staff or concierge at your hotel should be able to help you locate a doctor. You can also call the **College of Physicians and Surgeons of Ontario** (80 College St.; ✆ **800/268-7096**) for a referral from 8am to 5pm, Monday through Friday.

Drinking Laws The legal age for purchase and consumption of alcoholic beverages is 19 throughout Ontario; proof of age is required and often requested at bars, nightclubs, and restaurants, so it's always a good idea to bring ID when you go out.

Bars are usually open until 2am in Toronto, except during special events like the Toronto International Film Festival, when many venues are open later. A government monopoly runs liquor sales: **Liquor Control Board of Ontario (LCBO)** stores sell liquor, wine, and some beers. Most are open daily from 10am to 6pm (some have extended evening hours). The nicest shop is the **LCBO Summerhill** (10 Scrivener Sq.; ✆ **416/922-0403;** subway: Summerhill). Built in a former train station, this outpost hosts cooking classes, wine and spirit tastings, and party-planning seminars. Many large grocery chains now also carry wine, beer, and cider, though the harder stuff is only available through the LCBO.

Do not carry open containers of alcohol in your car or any public area that isn't zoned for alcohol consumption. The police can fine you on the spot.

Electricity Like the United States, Canada uses 110 to 120 volts AC (60 cycles), compared to 220 to 240 volts AC (50 cycles) in most of Europe, Australia, and New Zealand. Downward converters that change 220 to 240 volts to 110 to 120 volts are difficult to find in Canada, so bring one with you if you need it.

Embassies & Consulates All embassies are in Ottawa, the national capital. Consulates in Toronto include the **Australian Consulate-General** (175 Bloor St. E., Ste. 314, at Church St.; ✆ **416/323-1155**), the **British Consulate-General** (777 Bay St., Ste. 2800, at College St.; ✆ **416/593-1290**), and the **U.S. Consulate** (360 University Ave.; ✆ **416/595-1700**).

Emergencies Call ✆ **911** for fire, police, or ambulance.

For emergency dental services from 8am till midnight, call the **Dental Emergency Service** (✆ **416/485-7121**). After midnight, your best bet is to call, **Telehealth** (✆ **866/797-0000**), where a registered nurse can advise you on what to do, and which hospitals are optimal for your situation.

Family Travel Toronto is a kid-friendly town. There

are plenty of great attractions, such as the idiosyncratic Ontario Science Centre; Paramount Canada's Wonderland, a conventional theme park on the outskirts of town noted for its super roller coasters; the artsy Harbourfront Centre; and the Toronto Zoo, which rivals the great zoos of the world. For more suggestions on family and kid-oriented entertainment in Toronto, see "Especially for Kids," in chapter 6.

Gasoline (Petrol) Gasoline is sold by the liter, and taxes are already included in the printed price (unlike most products in Canada). Fill-up locations are known as gas stations or service stations.

Hospitals In the downtown core, the **University Health Network** (UHN) manages three hospitals: **Toronto General,** at 200 Elizabeth St.; **Princess Margaret,** at 610 University Ave.; and **Toronto Western,** at 399 Bathurst St. The UHN has a central switchboard for all three (✆ **416/340-3111**). Other hospitals include **St. Michael's** (30 Bond St.; ✆ **416/360-4000**) and **Mount Sinai** (600 University Ave.; ✆ **416/596-4200**). Also downtown is the **Hospital for Sick Children** (555 University Ave.; ✆ **416/813-1500**). Uptown, there's **Sunnybrook Hospital** (2075 Bayview Ave., north of Eglinton Ave. E.; ✆ **416/480-6100**). In the eastern part of the city, go to **Toronto East General Hospital** (825 Coxwell Ave.; ✆ **416/461-8272**).

Health Toronto has excellent hospitals and doctors—though hopefully you won't have any occasion to need these services. Bring any prescriptions you might require with you. Decongestants, cough and cold remedies, and allergy medications are available without prescription in pharmacies. **Shopper's Drug Mart** is ubiquitous; there you can buy over-the-counter drugs, have prescriptions filled, and pick up any toiletries you might need. The only 24-hour drugstore near downtown is the **Shopper's Drug Mart,** 700 Bay St., at Gerrard Street West (✆ **416/979-2424**).

Insurance Even though Canada is just a short drive or flight away for many Americans, U.S. health plans (including Medicare and Medicaid) do not provide coverage here, and the ones that do often require you to pay for services up front and reimburse you only after you return home. Similarly, for Europeans, EHIC is not accepted in Canada. As a safety net, you may want to buy travel medical insurance. For repatriation costs, lost money, baggage, or cancellation, it is also recommended to purchase travel insurance from a reputable company.

For information on traveler's insurance, trip cancellation insurance, and medical insurance while traveling, please visit **www.frommers. com/planning**.

Internet & Wi-Fi Even budget hotels in Toronto now provide Wi-Fi access.

Most cafes and restaurants are happy to share Wi-Fi passwords with their customers; just ask.

Legal Aid If you are pulled over for a minor infraction (such as speeding), you'll be given a ticket that you pay at a later date. Pay fines online, by mail or directly into the hands of the clerk of the court. If accused of a more serious offense, say and do nothing before consulting a lawyer. Here, the burden is on the state to prove a person's guilt beyond a reasonable doubt, and everyone has the right to remain silent, whether he or she is suspected of a crime or actually arrested. Once arrested, a person can make one telephone call to a party of his or her choice. International visitors should call their embassy or consulate. If you need to get a lawyer while in Toronto, contact the **Law Society of Upper Canada** (℃ **800/668-7380** or 416/947-3300; www.lsuc.on.ca).

LGBT Travelers After same-sex marriage became legal in Ontario in 2003, gay and lesbian couples flocked to Toronto to marry. Although in July 2006, the Civil Marriage Act legalized same-sex marriage across Canada, pioneer Toronto remains one of the most in-demand wedding destinations for same-sex couples.

If you want to get married in Toronto, it's pretty simple: download the marriage license from the **Toronto City website** (www.toronto.ca) and bring the completed form and ID (including your passport and birth certificate) to the City Clerk's Office (100 Queen St.), where you'll be asked to pay a small fee; there's no residency requirement.

Mail Postage for letter mail (up to 30g/1 oz.) to the United States costs $1.20; overseas, it's $2.50. Mailing letters within Canada costs $1. Note that there is no discounted rate for mailing postcards. For more

information, go to **www. canadapost.ca**.

Postal services are available at some drugstores. Almost all drugstores sell stamps, and many have a separate counter where you can ship packages from 8:30am to 5pm Look for a sign in the window indicating such services. There are also post-office windows in **Atrium on Bay** (℃ **416/ 506-0911**), in **Commerce Court** (℃ **416/956-7452**), and at the **TD Centre** (℃ **416/360-7105**).

Mobile Phones Most U.S. cellphone carriers have roaming agreements with Canadian cellphone carriers. Before leaving home, check with your carrier for rates and availability. If your phone is unlocked, buying a prepaid local SIM card is probably your cheapest option. Local telecom companies (Fido, Rogers, Telus, Bell, and Freedom Mobile) have stores scattered around the city, as well as booths in most malls.

THE VALUE OF THE CANADIAN DOLLAR VS. OTHER POPULAR CURRENCIES

Can$	US$	UK£	Euro (€)	Aus$	NZ$
C$1	US$0.75	65p	0.74€	A$1	NZ$1.20

Money & Costs Frommer's lists exact prices in the local currency. The currency conversions quoted above were correct at press time. However, rates fluctuate, so before departing, consult a currency exchange website for up-to-the-minute rates.

Currency
Canadians use **dollars** and **cents:** Paper currency comes in $5, $10, $20, $50, and $100 denominations. Coins come in 1-, 5-, 10-, and 25-cent, and 1- and 2-dollar denominations. The gold-colored $1 coin is a

"loonie"—it sports a loon on its "tails" side—and the large gold-and-silver-colored $2 coin is a "toonie." If you find these names somewhat...ah, colorful, just remember that there's no swifter way to reveal that you're a tourist than to say "one-dollar coin."

Ideally, you should exchange enough petty cash to cover airport incidentals, tipping, and transportation to your hotel before you leave home; however, it's very easy to withdraw money upon arrival at an ATM at Pearson airport.

It's best to exchange currency at a bank, not a currency exchange, hotel, or shop. Get up-to-the-minute exchange rates online before you go at **www.oanda. com/currency/converter** or **www.xe.com/ucc**.

ATMs

The easiest and best way to get cash away from home is from an ATM (automated teller machine), sometimes referred to as a "cash machine," or a "cashpoint." The **Cirrus** (© **800/424-7787;** www.mastercard.com) and **PLUS** (© **800/843-7587;** www.visa.com) networks span the globe. Go to your bank card's website to find ATM locations at your destination. Be sure you know your daily withdrawal limit before you depart. **Note:** Many banks impose a fee every time you use a card at another bank's ATM, and that fee can be higher for international transactions than for domestic ones. In addition, the bank from which you withdraw cash may charge its own fee. For international withdrawal fees, ask your bank.

Credit Cards

MasterCard and Visa are almost universally accepted in Toronto; American Express has become more

common, but many independent boutiques and small restaurants still don't accept it. Overall, credit cards are a smart way to "carry" money. They also provide a convenient record of all your expenses, and they generally offer relatively good exchange rates. You can withdraw cash advances from your credit cards at banks or ATMs, but high fees make credit card cash advances a pricey way to get cash. Keep in mind that you'll pay interest from the moment of your withdrawal, even if you pay your monthly bills on time. Also, note that many banks now assess a 1% to 3% "transaction fee" on *all* charges you incur abroad (whether you're using the local currency or your native currency).

Traveler's Checks

Traveler's checks are something of an anachronism in Toronto. Most banks no longer issue traveler's checks, nor do they cash them.

Medical Conditions If

you have a medical condition that requires **syringe-administered medications,** carry a valid signed prescription from your physician; syringes in carry-on baggage will be inspected. Insulin in any form should have the proper pharmaceutical documentation. If you have a disease that requires treatment with **narcotics,** you should also carry documented proof with you—smuggling narcotics aboard a plane carries severe penalties.

For **HIV-positive visitors,** Canada does not

require testing to enter the country on a tourist visa. However, travelers can be denied entry to Canada if they are assessed as requiring health services during their stay. (Canada does not cover medical costs incurred by travelers.)

Newspapers & Magazines The four daily newspapers are the *Globe and Mail,* the *National Post,* the *Toronto Star,* and the *Toronto Sun. Now* is the free arts-and-entertainment weekly. *Xtra!* is a free weekly targeted at the gay and lesbian community. In addition, many English-language ethnic newspapers serve Toronto's Portuguese, Hungarian, Italian, East Indian, Korean, Chinese, and Caribbean communities. *Toronto Life* is the major monthly city magazine.

Petrol Please see "Gasoline," earlier in this section.

Passports See **www. frommers.com/planning** for information on how to obtain a passport. For information specific to your country's passport application process, contact the appropriate agency:

For Residents of Australia Contact the **Australian Passport Information Service** at © **131-232** or visit the government website at www.passports.gov.au.

For Residents of Ireland Contact the **Passport Office** (© **1/671-1633;** www.foreignaffairs.gov.ie).

For Residents of New Zealand Contact the **Passports Office** at © **0800/ 225-050** in New Zealand or

4/463-9360, or log on to www.passports.govt.nz.

For Residents of the United Kingdom Visit your nearest passport office, major post office, or travel agency, or contact the **Identity and Passport Service (IPS)** at ✆ **300/222-0000** or search its website at www.ips.gov.uk.

For Residents of the United States To find your regional passport office, either check the U.S. Department of State website http://travel.state.gov or call the **National Passport Information Center** toll-free number (✆ **877/487-2778**) for automated information.

Police In a life-threatening emergency, call ✆ **911.** For all other matters, contact the **Toronto Police Service** (40 College St.; ✆ **416/808-2222**).

Safety Toronto enjoys an unusually safe reputation as far as big cities go, although a steady supply of guns coming across the border from the U.S. is damaging the now worn-out reputation of "Toronto the Good." But keep in mind that Toronto is a big city, with all of the difficulties that implies. During the day, keep your valuables close and your eyes peeled for pickpockets. This is important to keep in mind when you're at a major tourist attraction, on a crowded shopping strip such as Yonge Dundas Square, and on the subway or streetcar.

More about safety on Toronto's public transit system: If it's late and you're alone on an almost-empty platform, wait for the train by the big "DWA" sign (it stands for **"Designated Waiting Area,"** and it has an intercom and a closed-circuit TV camera trained on it). There is a DWA area at every TTC station. If there is an incident on a subway car, press the alarm—the yellow strip is very visible—and note that it is silent. If you are traveling by bus, there is a **"Request Stop"** program in effect between 9pm and 5am, in which vulnerable passengers can disembark at streets in between regular TTC bus stops. For information about these safety features, visit **www3.ttc.ca/Riding_the_TTC/Safety_and_Security/index.jsp**.

Senior Travel The term "seniors" is proving to be more elastic than most face-lifts. Boomers in the above-50 group should check out the local magazine *Zoomer*, which is connected to **CARP** (Canadian Association of Retired Persons; ✆ **416/363-8748;** www.carp.ca). Members of **CARP** or **AARP** (the American analog; ✆ **888/687-2277;** www.aarp.org) can get discounts on hotels, airfares, and car rentals. Otherwise, seniors can expect to receive discounts on the TTC (subway and bus), and on many (but not all) admissions to attractions. Keep in mind that it is usually necessary to show photo identification when purchasing discounted tickets or admissions.

Smoking The **Smoke-Free Ontario Act,** which came into effect in 2006, is one of the most stringent in North America. It bans smoking in all workplaces and in all public spaces. In Ontario, smoking is not permitted in restaurants, bars, or on patios. In 2014, the city council passed a city by-law also making parks, beaches, and sports fields smoke-free zones.

Taxes On July 1, 2010, the Ontario government implemented a "harmonized" tax system, with a 13% sales tax on virtually everything for sale. (Previously, the federal GST was 5% and the Ontario sales tax was 8%, but the Ontario sales tax was not applied to purchases such as fast-food meals.) Taxes are added when you purchase an item, rather than being included in the original price, as is common in much of Europe.

Within the city of Toronto, a bylaw was introduced in 2009 that obliges retailers to charge a minimum of 5¢ per plastic bag. There are no exceptions to this rule. (The funds collected are not really a tax, since they go into the store's coffers and not the city's, but some people consider this a tax on shoppers.)

Telephones To call **Toronto from the U.S.:** Canada and the U.S. use the same area-code system. Simply dial 1, the Toronto area code (416, 437, or 647), and the number.
To call Toronto from other countries:
1. Dial the international access code: 00 from the U.K., Ireland, or New Zealand; or 0011 from Australia.

2. Dial the country code 1.
3. Dial the city code 416 or 647, and then the number.

To make international calls
To make international calls from a Toronto landline, first dial 00, and then the country code (U.K. 44, Ireland 353, Australia 61, New Zealand 64). Next, dial the area code and number. However, if you are calling the U.S. from Toronto, you need only to dial 1 and then the area code and phone number.

For directory assistance Dial 🕿 **411** if you're looking for a phone number; online, visit **www.canada411.com**.

For operator assistance If you need operator assistance in making a call, dial 🕿 **0** (zero).

Toll-free numbers Numbers beginning with 800 or 866 are toll-free within Canada and the U.S. However, calling an 800 number from other countries isn't toll-free. In fact, it costs the same as an overseas call.

Many convenience stores and packaging services sell **prepaid calling cards** in denominations up to $50; for international visitors, these can be the least expensive way to call home. It's hard to find public pay phones; those at airports now accept American Express, MasterCard, and Visa credit cards. **Local calls** made from pay phones in most locales cost C50¢ (no pennies). Most long-distance and international calls can be dialed directly from any phone. **For calls within Canada and to the United**

States, dial 1 followed by the area code and the seven-digit number. **For other international calls,** dial 011 followed by the country code, city code, and the number you are calling.

Calls to area codes **800, 888, 877,** and **866** are toll-free. However, calls to area code **900** (chat lines, bulletin boards, "dating" services, and so on) can be very expensive—usually a charge of $1 to $3 or more per minute, and they sometimes have minimum charges that can run as high as $15 or more.

For **reversed-charge or collect calls,** and for person-to-person calls, dial the number 0, then the area code and number; an operator will come on the line, and you should specify whether you are calling collect, person-to-person, or both. If your operator-assisted call is international, ask for the overseas operator.

For **local directory assistance** ("information"), dial 🕿 **411;** for long-distance information, dial 1, then the appropriate area code, and 555-1212.

Time Toronto is on Eastern Standard Time. When it's noon in Toronto, it's 9am in Los Angeles (PST), it's 7am in Honolulu (HST), 10am in Denver (MST), 11am in Chicago (CST), noon in New York City (also on EST), 5pm in London (GMT), and 2am the next day in Sydney (UTC + 9).

Daylight Saving Time is in effect from 1am on the

second Sunday in March to 1am on the first Sunday in November. Daylight Saving Time moves the clock 1 hour ahead of standard time.

Tipping Tips are a very important part of certain workers' income, and gratuities are the standard way of showing appreciation for services provided. (Tipping is certainly not compulsory if the service is poor!) In hotels, tip **bellhops** at least $1 per bag ($2–$3 if you have a lot of luggage) and tip the **chamber staff** $1 to $2 per day (more if you've left a disaster area for him or her to clean up). Tip the **doorman** or **concierge** $2 or more only if he or she has provided you with some specific service (for example, calling a cab for you or obtaining difficult-to-get theater tickets). Tip the **valet-parking attendant** $1 or more every time you get your car.

In restaurants, bars, and nightclubs, tip **service staff** 15% to 20% of the check, tip **checkroom attendants** $1 per garment, and tip **valet-parking attendants** $1 per vehicle.

As for other service personnel, tip **cab drivers** 15% of the fare; tip **skycaps** at airports at least $1 per bag ($2–$3 if you have a lot of luggage); and tip **hairdressers** and **barbers** 15% to 20%.

Toilets You won't find public toilets or "restrooms" on the streets in Toronto, but they can be found in hotel lobbies, bars, restaurants, museums, department stores, railway and bus stations, and service stations. Public parks also offer restrooms, although they may be closed and/or not very clean. Large hotels and fast-food restaurants are often the best bet for clean facilities. Restaurants and bars in resorts or heavily visited areas may reserve their restrooms for patrons. You can also find restrooms throughout the underground PATH system near the various food courts. There are restrooms at major subway stations, such as Yonge-Bloor, which are best used in the daytime when the subways are busy.

VAT See "Taxes," above.

Visas For citizens of many countries, including the U.S., U.K., Ireland, Australia, and New Zealand, only a passport is required to visit Canada for up to 90 days; no visas or proof of vaccinations are necessary. For the most up-to-date list of visitor visa exemptions, visit **Citizenship and**

Immigration Canada at **www.cic.gc.ca**.

Visitor Information
The best source for Toronto-specific information is **Tourism Toronto** (www.see torontonow.com; ✆ **800/499-2514** from North America or 416/203-2600). The website includes sections on accommodations, sights, shopping, and dining, plus up-to-the-minute events information.

For information about traveling in the province of Ontario, contact **Tourism Ontario** (www.ontariotravel. net; ✆ **800/668-2746** from North America or 416/314-5899). While in Toronto, visit its information center at Union Station.

Toronto.com (www. toronto.com), operated by the *Toronto Star*, offers extensive restaurant reviews, events listings, and feature articles. A couple of other great sources for local goings-on and news: **Toronto Life** (www.toronto-life.com) and **blogTO** (www. blogto.com).

Water Toronto's tap water is safe to drink, and it is tested continuously to guarantee public safety. For details, visit the City of Toronto's water information page at **www.toronto.ca/water**. When it comes to swimming, only swim at one of the city's eight Blue Flag beaches, and make sure to check water-quality levels before wading into the lake. You can download the Swim Guide app, or check the website (www.theswimguide. org) to see the latest testing results. This is particularly important after heavy rains, when E. coli levels are often highest.

Wi-Fi See "Internet & Wi-Fi," earlier in this section.

Women Travelers
Toronto is an easy place to be for solo travelers, male or female. At night, take note of the TTC's "Request Stop" program for women traveling on buses (see "Safety," above). For general travel resources for women, go to Frommers.com.

AIRLINE WEBSITES

Canadian Airlines

Air Canada
www.aircanada.com

Porter Airlines
www.flyporter.com

WestJet
www.westjet.com

Major Airlines

Aeroméxico
www.aeromexico.com

Air Canada
www.aircanada.com

Air France
www.airfrance.com

Air India
www.airindia.com

Air Jamaica
www.airjamaica.com

Air New Zealand
www.airnewzealand.com

Alitalia
www.alitalia.com

American Airlines
www.aa.com

British Airways
www.british-airways.com

Caribbean Airlines (formerly BWIA)
www.caribbean-airlines.com

China Airlines
www.china-airlines.com

Continental Airlines
www.continental.com

Cubana
www.cubana.cu

Delta Air Lines
www.delta.com

El Al Airlines
www.elal.co.il

Emirates Airlines
www.emirates.com

globespan
www.flyglobespan.ca

Hawaiian Airlines
www.hawaiianair.com

Iberia Airlines
www.iberia.com

Lan Airlines
www.lan.com

Lufthansa
www.lufthansa.com

Qantas Airways
www.qantas.com

TACA
www.taca.com

United Airlines
www.united.com

US Airways
www.usairways.com

Virgin Atlantic Airways
www.virgin-atlantic.com

Index

See also Accommodations and Restaurant indexes, below.

General Index

Photo Credits

Map List

Frommer's EasyGuide to Toronto, Niagara Falls and Wine Country, 1st Edition

Published by
FROMMER MEDIA LLC

ISBN 978-1-62887-446-4 (paper), 978-1-62887-447-1 (e-book)

Editorial Director: Pauline Frommer
Editor: Alexis Lipsitz Flippin
Production Editor: Lindsay Conner
Photo Editor: Meghan Lamb
Assistant Photo Editor: Phil Vinke
Cartographer: Liz Puhl
Cover Design: Dave Riedy

Front cover photo: Tourists at the Horseshoe Fall, Niagara Falls © Igor Sh / Shutterstock.com

For information on our other products or services, see www.frommers.com.

Frommer Media LLC also publishes its books in a variety of electronic formats. Some content that appears in print may not be available in electronic formats.

Manufactured in the United States of America

5 4 3 2 1

ABOUT THE AUTHOR

Caroline Aksich is a writer and researcher living in Toronto, Canada. Caroline is an omnivorous writer, who has penned everything from first-person narratives about hunting octopus in the Adriatic to celebrity profiles and restaurant reviews. The two-time National Magazine Award nominee is passionate about food, chef culture, urban planning, and municipal politics. When not tethered to her laptop, Caroline enjoys running, kayaking, and biking around her ever-growing city.

ABOUT THE FROMMER TRAVEL GUIDES

For most of the past 50 years, Frommer's has been the leading series of travel guides in North America, accounting for as many as 24% of all guidebooks sold. I think I know why.

Though we hope our books are entertaining, we nevertheless deal with travel in a serious fashion. Our guidebooks have never looked on such journeys as a mere recreation, but as a far more important human function, a time of learning and introspection, an essential part of a civilized life. We stress the culture, lifestyle, history, and beliefs of the destinations we cover, and urge our readers to seek out people and new ideas as the chief rewards of travel.

We have never shied from controversy. We have, from the beginning, encouraged our authors to be intensely judgmental, critical—both pro and con—in their comments, and wholly independent. Our only clients are our readers, and we have triggered the ire of countless prominent sorts, from a tourist newspaper we called "practically worthless" (it unsuccessfully sued us) to the many rip-offs we've condemned.

And because we believe that travel should be available to everyone regardless of their incomes, we have always been cost-conscious at every level of expenditure. Though we have broadened our recommendations beyond the budget category, we insist that every lodging we include be sensibly priced. We use every form of media to assist our readers, and are particularly proud of our feisty daily website, the award-winning Frommers.com.

I have high hopes for the future of Frommer's. May these guidebooks, in all the years ahead, continue to reflect the joy of travel and the freedom that travel represents. May they always pursue a cost-conscious path, so that people of all incomes can enjoy the rewards of travel. And may they create, for both the traveler and the persons among whom we travel, a community of friends, where all human beings live in harmony and peace.

Arthur Frommer